RELAXATION & IMAGERY:

Tools for Therapeutic Communication and Intervention

Edited by:

ROTHLYN P. ZAHOUREK, M.S., R.N., C.S.

Coordinator, Counseling, Education and Liaison
for the Alcoholism Service
Department of Psychiatry, St. Vincent's Hospital
and Medical Center, New York, New York
Private Psychotherapy Practice, New York, New York

1988

W. B. SAUNDERS COMPANY
A division of Harcourt Brace Jovanovich, Inc.

Philadelphia, London, Toronto, Montreal, Sydney, Tokyo

W. B. SAUNDERS COMPANY
Harcourt Brace Jovanovich, Inc.

The Curtis Center
Independence Square West
Philadelphia, PA 19106

Library of Congress Cataloging-in-Publicaton Data

Relaxation & imagery.

1. Medicine, Psychosomatic.   2. Relaxation.
3. Imagery (Psychology)   4. Stress (Psychology)
I. Zahourek, Rothlyn P., 1943–   .   II. Title:
Relaxation and imagery.   [DNLM: 1. Imagination.
2. Relaxation Technics.   3. Stress, Psychological—
therapy.   WM 425 R3823]
RC49.R45   1988   616'.001'9   87-32307
ISBN 0-7216-2589-4

Editor: Thomas Eoyang

RELAXATION AND IMAGERY:
Tools for Therapeutic Communication and Intervention   ISBN   0-7216-2589-4

Last digit is the print number: 9   8   7   6   5   4   3   2

CONTRIBUTORS

SUSAN BERENSON, M.S., R.N.

Psychiatric Nurse Clinician, Memorial Sloan Kettering Cancer Center, New York, New York.
The Cancer Patient

EMILY M. BORNSTEIN, M.S.W., PSY. D.

Teaching Associate, School of Professional Psychology, University of Denver; Private Psychotherapy Practice, Denver, Colorado.
Therapeutic Storytelling

CAROLYN CHAMBERS CLARK, A.R.N.P., Ed. D., F.A.A.N.

Editor/Publisher, THE WELLNESS NEWSLETTER, Wellness Consultant, St. Petersberg, Florida.
Stress and Coping

MARCIA FISHMAN, M.A., R.N.

Nursing Practice Advocate, The Presbyterian Hospital at Columbia-Presbyterian Medical Center; Private Practice, Pain and Stress Management, New York, New York.
Imagery and Relaxation as a Therapeutic Intervention with the Dying

GLORIA KUTNER, B.A., R.N.C., CAC

Staff Nurse, Therapist, Brooklyn VA Medical Center, Brooklyn, New York.
Relaxation/Imagery with Alcoholics in Group Treatment

DOROTHY M. LARKIN, M.A., R.N.

Pain Management Consultant, Cabrini Hospice; Private Practice, Pain and Stress Management, New York, New York.
Therapeutic Suggestion

ESTHER SIEGEL, Ed.D., R.N., C.S.

Chairperson, Associate Professor, Department of Nursing, C.W. Post, Greenvale, New York; Private Practice in Psychotherapy, New York, New York.
Stress Management with Staff Groups

PAUL SLOAN, A.C.S.W., LSW II

Community College of Aurora; Private Practice, Denver, Colorado.
Stress Management, Relaxation Training, and Imagery
* with Prison Inmates*

HOPE TITLEBAUM, R.N., M.S., C.S.

Assistant Professor of Psychiatric Nursing, University of Rochester, Rochester, New York; Clinician II, Strong Memorial Hospital, Rochester, New York.
Relaxation

ROTHLYN P. ZAHOUREK, M.S., R.N., CS

Coordinator, Counseling, Education, and Liaison, Alcoholism Service, Department of Psychiatry, St. Vincent's Hospital and Medical Center; Private Psychotherapy Practice, New York, New York.
The Difficult Patient
Overview: Relaxation and Imagery: Tools for Therapeutic
* Communication and Intervention*
Relaxation/Weight Loss
Relaxation/Imagery with Alcoholics in Group Treatment
Imagery

ACKNOWLEDGMENTS

The task of writing and editing a book never occurs in isolation; family members, friends, pets, and even the house plants suffer in the process. I'm grateful to my son, Jonny, for his patience and skill in teaching me the computer, which was an invaluable tool in compiling and finishing this book. He also taught me how effective relaxation/imagery techniques can be with children; his imagination never ceases to amaze and instruct me.

I'm also grateful to Mayra Fernandez who typed much of my contributions, often at odd hours; she also struggled to learn how to use the computer.

Numerous colleagues throughout the years have supported my learning these techniques and I'm especially thankful to the patients who often have been my best teachers. Elizabeth Mudd, RN CAC, St. Vincent's Hospital, New York City, has been a stimulating colleague and contributed a challenging case example in the Difficult Patient chapter. Similarly, two other colleagues, Jenifer White, BSN, RN, Portland, Maine, and Lissa Armstrong, LPN Hartford, Connecticut, contributed case examples to Dorothy Larkin's chapter on Therapeutic Suggestion.

I wish to thank Jay Holtzman, MD, Amherst, Massachusetts, for his enthusiastic support and for his critical and insightful input. Thomas Eoyang, Senior Nursing Editor at Grune & Stratton, has provided valuable content and editing advice and counsel.

St. Vincent's Department of Psychiatry was also supportive of my efforts to utilize these techniques with recovering alcoholic patients in the Alcoholism Service.

Finally, I wish to dedicate this book to my parents, Lynne Orscher and Robert D. Pond. They read to me as a child and later bought me books; they sometimes wondered about my active imagination but they never squelched it.

Rothlyn P. Zahourek

FOREWORD

Since the dawn of civilization, indeed even in prehistoric times, the power of the mind has been the greatest healing resource. And for the millennia, those who chose the vocation of curing knew that it was inseparable from acts of caring. The mind's capacity to foster health and the will to nurture others are among the most distinctive of all human gifts. Yet, precisely these qualities were banished to the fringe of medicine as it began its love affair with technology and donned the garb of the reductionistic, dualistic scientific model.

But times are changing. First of all, we are a nation faced with a multifaceted health crisis wrought by economic exigency and by the chronic and catastrophic "diseases of civilization" for which there is no known cause nor cure. Still another crisis is being provoked by a growing body of consumers and practitioners who insist that modern medicine take another path—one that honors the whole person and his or her feelings, behaviors, thoughts, and lifestyles.

Secondly, it is no longer possible to ignore the voluminous and sound research that demonstrates that the mind, at all levels of consciousness, must be considered a primary factor in whether and how one gets sick, recovers, or stays well. We are rapidly approaching a time when any medical practice that avoids dealing with these issues will be considered unethical.

Crisis, consumer awareness, and new research supporting the inseparability of mind and body, all herald the development of new modalities and ideas that foster the best possible healing milieu. *Relaxation and Imagery: Tools for Therapeutic Communication and Intervention* addresses this new frontier for medicine. The wisdom that can come only from sensitive clinical observations shines through the words of the contributors. On the other hand, they present an overwhelming number of scientific investigations in a critical appraisal of the topics discussed. The balance between science and art is unusual, refreshing, and even mandatory at this stage of the evolution of health care.

The interventions of relaxation and imagery were well chosen. Indeed, they may represent the epiphenomena that embrace most other cognitive and behavioral strategies; as well as account for the dramatic changes associated with expectancy, hope, the placebo effect, and spontaneous remission.

The book is addressed primarily, although not exclusively, to nurses and those in allied health fields; and rightly so. The interventions will grow and flourish in their hands; in turn, it will empower them as professionals, giving them vigor and authority in patient care.

Jeanne Achterberg, Ph.D.

PREFACE

Lucy*, not yet woman nor even *Homo sapiens*, sat playing with a stick. The dawn had been warm and day's heat had her lazy and dreamy. Sheltering in the shadow of a termite mound, she scratched in the red earth. An even redder ant, scurrying across her drawing, oblivious to its beauty, brought her out of her reverie. Ants were tasty, and she was hungry!

For as long as she could remember, Lucy's family had snacked at ant and termite hills, delicately probing their entrances with twigs or grass stalks. Withdrawn from the mound covered with "beliger-ants," twigs were reliable dining tools. Loath to leave her shady spot to follow the ant, Lucy examined the termite fortress's dark side for a portal. Finding none, she sulkily prodded the tower wall with her stick. To her surprise, the mound crumbled a bit under the end of the stout stick. Only a little careful work opened a *new* passage into the heart of the termite world, and she lunched upon the whitest, fattest termites she'd ever seen, and without leaving her cool spot. Having done it once, it seemed so obvious. She resolved to remember this and tell the others.

The use of tools marked the increasing ability of people to live better. In time Lucy's stick would become a scraper, a hoe, and eventually an earth mover; big, yellow, and loud. Choosing the right tool for the task is important. In *turning* and planting the earth, sometimes a simple stick will do the trick, other times a stout spade or a pronged pitchfork. We now use heavy equipment and explosives to move the earth.

The process of finding appropriate tools to solve problems is what this book is all about. In working with people all aspects of this process have been necessary: the need, the vision, the accumulated knowledge and the experience, and willingness to experiment and finally the ability to objectively evaluate the results. Human care demands nothing less than this constant re-evaluation of problems and solutions.

Imagery and relaxation techniques fit nicely into this "Lucy" metaphor of learning from necessity. Every day, nurses and health care workers find novel and ingenious solutions to tough problems, often with the most outlandish approaches or equipment. These techniques help us discover and utilize more effectively the nature, thoughts, feelings, and behaviors of people. They can tap the best potential in all of us.

Imagery is part of our ability to think and to know about ourselves and our relationships; our imaginative capacity helps us to learn and to understand the more

---

* The hypothetical anthropological "missing link" in the evolution of mankind.

abstract concepts of love, forgiveness, and hope. The purposeful and creative use of the imagination is often lost in adulthood as we are encouraged to develop more cognitive skills. Rediscovering and redirecting this early skill can not only promote a healthy productive life but also augment daily problem-solving and decision-making abilities.

During the past 10 years imagery has also become an adjunctive treatment modality for numerous illnesses including infections, cancer, and cardiovascular disorders. Research has demonstrated that the imaginative process does in fact influence the physiology of an individual but the exact relationship to specific disease processes or their cure remains unclear.

Relaxation is a state in which both repair and growth can occur. For centuries, people from various cultures have practiced a goal directed state in which both mind and body were quiet. It was in this state that healing, spiritual growth, and the birth of new ideas took place.

This current book follows an earlier book by the editor, *Clinical Hypnosis and Therapeutic Suggestion in Nursing* (1985). Initially the plan with Grune & Stratton, Inc. was to do a book on relaxation, imagery, hypnosis, and related techniques in health care with an emphasis on nursing practice. The manuscript grew as more research was published in each field and as more contributors were found doing interesting interventions in often novel settings. As a result, it was decided to make two separate volumes, one with a primary focus on hypnosis and the other with an emphasis on relaxation and imagery. The approaches share much in common; the books can be used as separate volumes or together. Those devoted to these approaches in health care will find studying and applying techniques from all three areas of practice enriching and gratifying; both books as a result provide useful theoretical and clinical information.

This book is divided into two sections: 1. *Research and Theoretical Base*; 2. *Clinical Case Examples* The theory chapters on relaxation and imagery describe basic theoretical frameworks, research, and general applications of relaxation and imagery. Chapters on therapeutic communication and suggestion (adapted and expanded from *Clinical Hypnosis and Therapeutic Suggestion in Nursing*, 1985) and the use of fairy tales in treatment are included because relaxation/imagery techniques rely on a therapeutic relationship, and are most often verbal interventions. The chapter on fairy tales was included to demonstrate the variety of therapeutic interventions that have grown out of basic relaxation/imagery approaches.

The section of case examples has been compiled to address some common problems in practice. "Working with the Well Population" by Carolyn Chambers Clarke has been adapted and revised from its original publication in 1985 in *Clinical Hypnosis and Therapeutic Suggestion in Nursing*. This chapter provides a wealth of information on a variety of interventions that can be adapted to numerous clinical situations. The chapters on working with "difficult," cancer, and dying patients and with those who are trying to lose weight are directed toward individual work although the approaches described can be utilized in groups, and with families. Each chapter presents a different set of problems and approaches for modifying maladaptive perceptions and behaviors. Writing and presentation differ in style, focus, and methods of implementation and have purposefully been left as such to communicate the immense variety possible in using these techniques. Additional emphasis is placed on how to "make lemonade out of lemon juice," or reframing highly difficult situations into opportunities for growth.

The chapters on working with alcoholic patients in groups, prison inmates, and staff groups for stress management describe stress management techniques, behavioral rehearsal and ego building imagery-relaxation techniques in group settings. The editor realizes that many specific areas of practice have not been explored. The life span of patients from childhood to death has, however, been covered and it is hoped that readers can easily implement ideas into their own areas of practice.

This book is intended for nurses and health care workers in all clinical areas and at all levels of practice and education. The approaches presented here are but samples of information appearing in the rapidly growing literature of scientific research and descriptive case examples.

The case examples presented in this book show the diversity of: l. patients who can benefit; 2. clinical settings; and 3. interpretations of how these techniques might be best utilized. Some interventions are standard with new twists while others are unique and highly creative.

While these approaches may belong primarily to the "art" of nursing and health care, they have, of late, been studied by many disciplines. The growing evidence of neurophysiologic, psychologic, and nursing literature substantiate the scientific rationale for these practices although many research questions remain.

In summary, this book is dedicated to all those who have struggled with a seemingly impossible situation and discovered a solution. When thinking about the process later, the practitioner realized that the solution came from a new way to put old knowledge to use. Relaxation/imagery techniques fall into this creative category of intervention; knowledgeably experimenting with techniques is still the norm in clinical practice. More theory and guides for practice are being generated through both the intuitive and the research process.

This book should be an adventure into the land of realistic make-believe, into the land where patients live with uncontrolled anxiety, fear, stress, pain, and death and where miracles of rebirth and renewal happen. It should be a trip that finds comfort and hope when nothing else seems to work. This book should also be a basic tool for "fixing" malfunctions with patients and staff. That "fixing" may not be a cure in the traditional sense, but rather an improved sense of well being; a temporary respite or escape from a difficult situation.

CONTENTS

PART I   THEORETICAL AND CONCEPTUAL BASIS1

1. Overview: Relaxation and Imagery: Tools for Therapeutic
   Communication and Intervention 3
   Rothlyn P. Zahourek

2. Relaxation 28
   Hope Titlebaum

3. Imagery 53
   Rothlyn P. Zahourek

4. Therapeutic Suggestion 84
   Dorothy M. Larkin

5. Therapeutic Storytelling...................................... 101
   Emily M. Bornstein

PART II   CLINICAL APPLICATIONS

6. Stress and Coping 121
   Carolyn Chambers Clark

7. The Difficult Patient 139
   Rothlyn P. Zahourek

8. Imagery and Relaxation as a Therapeutic Intervention
   with the Dying 155
   Marcia Fishman

9. The Cancer Patient 168
   Susan Berenson

10. Relaxation/Weight Loss 192
    Rothlyn P. Zahourek

11. Relaxation/Imagery with Alcoholics in Group Treatment.............. 203
    Gloria Kutner and Rothlyn P. Zahourek

12. Stress Management, Relaxation Training, and Imagery
with Prison Inmates 216
Paul Sloan

13. Stress Management with Staff Groups 227
Esther Siegel

Appendices 239

Afterword 250

Index 251

PART I

THEORETICAL AND CONCEPTUAL BASIS

1

OVERVIEW:
RELAXATION AND IMAGERY: TOOLS FOR THERAPEUTIC COMMUNICATION AND INTERVENTION

ROTHLYN P. ZAHOUREK

INTRODUCTION

The world around us is tense and harried, and our bodies and minds respond in kind. We want to let go but physically we forget how. We remember that as children, imagination and fantasy provided relief, a chance to practice different roles and escape. Rediscovering and harnessing these abilities and utilizing them for therapeutic purposes constitute the focus of this book.

"Relax. This won't hurt"; "Think about something different and you'll feel better"; "Imagine all the possibilities before you make your decision": these are all common phrases told by helpers to people experiencing one difficulty or another. Seldom, however, does anyone explain *how* to relax, to imaginatively or creatively solve a problem, or to feel more comfortable.

We know that relaxation and imagery influence a person's physiology, mental state, and behavior. We know relaxation and imagery can counter stress, pain, and anxiety and promote more positive perceptions and a stronger sense of well-being. We also now accept that chronic distress can precipitate physiological damage and enhance the development of such problems as heart disease, ulcers, and destructive habit disorders. Chronic distress also becomes manifest in such emotional difficulties as depression, dysthymia, and chronic anxiety.

While sometimes controversial in traditional practice, relaxation/imagery (R/I) techniques are interventions now commonly taught and integrated into a variety of treatment modalities. R/I is believed to interrupt the disease process and to foster health by dramatically reducing stress and discomfort, enhancing positive feeling states, and enriching perceptions; all of these effects subsequently encourage healing.

These approaches creatively challenge caregivers to involve themselves in new and often novel interactions with patients (clients). Integrating these tools into practice, then, has at least two advantages: they help the patient *and* stimulate new thinking by expanding the therapeutic approaches available to the caregiver.

In the last few years, research efforts on relaxation and imagery have reflected the growing interest in demonstrating the mind-body connection. Since studies have often substantiated *both* emphatic positive *and* negative claims, many questions remain unanswered. Overall, the trend has been to accept the positive evidence that the mind and the body are interactive, interrelated, and interdependent.

This overview chapter provides the historical, conceptual, and clinical background for the rest of the book. A brief historical perspective and basic definitions are provided. The definitions will be amplified in the next two chapters, which discuss each concept in depth. Because these interventions occur within the therapeutic relationship, aspects of communication, particularly therapeutic suggestion, are first explored in this overview chapter and then developed more extensively in a later chapter. Closely related to other forms of intervention, particularly hypnosis, the similarities and differences between R/I and other interventions are reviewed. These specific comparisons have relevance not only for the conceptual understanding of the techniques and their relationship to nursing theory but also for clinical implementation.

MIND-BODY CONTROVERSY (DUALISM VERSUS HOLISM)

Through time people have tried to understand the nature of being human and have questioned how and if the body, mind, and spirit are related. The first practitioners of modern medicine and nursing were ancient healers who did not question that a human being was at least the sum of all of its parts (body, mind, and spirit). Their pre-Cartesian philosophy viewed mental processes, particularly the imagination, as highly influential on the body's physiology. McMahon (1976) described this era of medicine as strongly holistic and psychosomatic. Within the historical frame of nursing, Florence Nightingale was philosophically holistic and pre-Cartesian, eloquently describing how mind-body interactions affected the health and well-being of people in *Notes on Nursing* (1859).

During the Renaissance, Descartes popularized the theory of "dualism," which maintained that the mind and the body were split and noninfluential on each other. As a result, the body could be manipulated and invaded without damaging the soul. Ironically, because of the strong religious ideas of the time, Descartes' dualism enabled modern medicine to develop. Today we rarely hear fears of risking the soul by working on the body. However, dualism continues as a strong tradition in both medicine and nursing practice when caregivers are oriented primarily to fixing the body in a mechanistic manner.

Recent Historical Perspectives

Several trends have influenced health care's evolution away from Cartesian dualism. After years of analytic, often reductionistic thinking emphasizing simplistic physical causes for disease, a movement began to reintegrate mind-body-spirit and behavior. Health care scientists and practitioners came to believe that: (1) psychic problems were felt in bodily tension and were manifest in maladaptive behaviors; (2) physiology influenced thinking and feeling; (3) mental mechanisms altered physiological processes; (4) an individual's expectation of results could influence outcome; and (5) learning a new skill could influence perception, emotions, physiologic responses, and behavior. This movement, often termed *holistic* or *humanistic*, intrigued nurses as well as other health care givers.

These theorists and practitioners emphasized the individual's total experience; the imagination and altered states of consciousness were valued as mechanisms for promoting self growth and for enhancing total health. Meditation, yoga, and other means of utilizing altered states were rediscovered, practiced, and integrated into various treatment modalities. As many communicable and dread diseases came under control, attention turned to prevention, as well as the achievement of a "high level of wellness." This "high level wellness" (Dunn, 1960) emphasized not merely an absence of illness but a state of physical and emotional well-being characterized by high energy and vitality and an individual's movement toward self-actualization. Both health care givers and the general population began to strive for this. Practitioners experimented with less invasive methods of providing comfort and more creative methods of solving problems. Stress became a popular concern, and stress management approaches incorporated both relaxation and imagery techniques for executives and staff groups as well as for patients. The capacity for relaxation and imagination was valued as a powerful innate capacity that needed to be developed, nurtured, and directed.

In the past 10 years many articles, books, and research reports have described R/I techniques as part of an integrated mind and body approach. The consumer has become more knowledgeable and active in pursuit of such care. For example, the Lamaze method of prepared childbirth has become common in obstetrics; Norman Cousins' description of his antiestablishment approach to recovery from a severe illness became a best selling book; and the work of the Simmontons with cancer patients is widely known and discussed. Bernie Seigel's book (1986) has remained on the *New York Times* bestseller list for months. The popularity of these works reflects the growing consumer interest in noninvasive, self-directed health and illness care.

Interest has also grown among health care providers. Behavior therapists, cognitive therapists, hypnotherapists and biofeedback practitioners have demonstrated success using progressive relaxation and guided imagery for treating several maladies including phobias, migraine headaches, hypertension, chronic and acute pain, depression, anxiety disorders, and stress. Psychotherapists have integrated these techniques into dynamic psychotherapy as well as into specific approaches such as gestalt therapy, psychodrama, hypnotherapy, cognitive therapies, and desensitization procedures.

It is now generally believed that if relaxation responses are learned and incorporated into one's life as coping mechanisms, then anxiety, tension, and pain cannot exist at the same time (Benson, 1975; Selye, 1974). Similarly, the power of the imagination can be harnessed to promote wellness, happiness, and success as well as to counter disease processes (Achterberg, 1985; Achterberg & Lawlis, 1978; Lazarus, 1977; LeShan, 1975).

Summary of Mind-Body Controversy

Recently the mind-body connection controversy reached a peak, evidenced in editorials first in the *New England Journal of Medicine* (June 13, 1985) and a month later in *Lancet* (June 20, 1985). Both articles emphasized the influence of the mind on the immune system, the impact of stress on health, and the relationship between emotions and cancer. The *Journal* article criticized the popularity of alternative methods, expressing concern that patients should not feel responsible for the development of their disease or for its cure. The *Journal* article also criticized the lack of consistent research and concluded that believing disease is a reflection of mental state is largely based on "folklore." The *Lancet* editorial, on the other hand, reviewed many studies in psychoimmunology. It argued that since 1977, research has substantiated that a positive relationship exists between both stress and mental attitudes and the development and remission of several disease processes. Even though the literature is rich in positive data, the findings continue to be controversial and poorly accepted by the traditional medical community. For example, a 1982 textbook on immunology did not even mention the relationship of psychological stress and the immune system (Lachmann, 1982). The *Lancet* editor contends this must change and argues for the return of "whole person" medicine: "The answer is that counseling in the acute phase of disease and psychological support in the chronic phase may be as important to outcome as many other therapeutic measures now undertaken" (*Lancet*, p. 134).

Daniel Goleman, the science editor for the *New York Times*, reported on this debate, stating that the editorial in the *Journal* precipitated one of their largest onslaughts of negative mail (Goleman, 1985). Goleman, interviewing many experts in psychoimmunology, concluded that most agree that an important relationship exists between emotions and disease, but because of the complexity of the immune system the exact relationship remains unclear. His article also emphasized that simplistic approaches toward healing should be avoided but that continued exploration is vital to tease out the numerous complex variables.

During this controversy the Institute for the Advancement of Health sent its subscribers a copy of their letter to the editor of the *Journal*. M. Barry Flint, executive director of the Institute, reminded the editor of the *Journal* that the institute had published *Mind and Immunity*, an annotated bibliography edited by Steven Locke and Mary Hornig-Rohan; this publication summarized 1400 separate scientific reports. In addition, *Psychological and Behavioral Treatments for Disorders of the Heart and*

Blood Vessels reported on 916 research projects. A forthcoming volume will review over a thousand studies in all major disease categories. According to Flint, "The overwhelming majority of reports . . . show evidence for connections between mental processes and disease" (Flint, 1985).

This discussion is highly relevant for nurse researchers and clinicians. Nursing literature often states that little research on the efficacy of R/I techniques exists. While the research differs greatly in methodology and must be scrutinized carefully, it does exist and strongly supports both the mind-body connection and the positive impact of R/I techniques.

DEFINITIONS OF BASIC CONCEPTS

In appreciating the following definitions it must be remembered that each concept (1) entails a set of beliefs and theories, (2) describes a specific state of being, and (3) is a set of techniques and interventions. In addition to relaxation and imagery, definitions of an altered state of consciousness, hypnosis, trance, and suggestion are included since clinically and theoretically these concepts are sometimes confused.

Relaxation and *imagery* can be seen as two basic and generic terms (conceptual frameworks) and principles from which many clinical applications and approaches have sprung. Relaxation and imagery are psychophysiological concepts, the latter being more mental and the former more physical in emphasis. In application, relaxation and imagery may be implemented together to provide a restful, pleasant state of being. An altered state of consciousness may or may not be the result. With R/I techniques this altered state is not the goal. Practitioners, however, need to be knowledgeable about such states, since clients may spontaneously enter altered states when relaxed, highly stressed, or bored, or when their attention is focused and imagination is active during daydream-like activities.

Relaxation

Relaxation is usually defined by what it is not—the absence of tension. Both a state and a set of techniques, relaxation is defined by Jacobsen as a "muscular lengthening as it occurs within a common natural, physiological process requiring internal energy expenditure and giving off heat" (Jacobsen, 1929; 1967, p. 7). According to Sweeney, relaxation is a "positively perceived state or response in which a person feels relief of tension or strain. Relaxation . . . may be psychological or physiological in origin. It is psychological in control . . . an active and conscious process and can be influenced by both internal and external stimuli. It is manifested by both psychological and physiological responses" (Sweeney, 1978, p. 242). Furthermore, McCaffery stated that "relaxation can be present or absent throughout the body, affecting visceral functions, skeletal muscle activity, and cerebral activities such as thoughts, perceptions and emotional states" (1979, p. 137).

Although many exist, two techniques are primarily associated with relaxation: Benson's "relaxation response" and Jacobsen's "progressive relaxation." Imagery techniques are often employed to enhance the relaxation process, and relaxation subsequently promotes images.

Imagery

Imagery is a mental process. It draws on the senses and consists of mental representations of external reality. According to Horowitz, "Any thought representation that has a sensory quality we call an image" (1983, p. 3). Encompassing all the senses, images are not only visual pictures in the mind, but also the "mental sensations" of hearing, smell, touch, taste, and movement. By stimulating the autonomic nervous system and the production of adrenal and pituitary hormones and neurotransmitters in the brain, imagery affects such physiological processes as circulation, heart rate, salivation, the immune response, gastric motility, and stress reactions. *Imagery*, in this book may used synonymously with *imagination*, *visualization*, and *fantasy*; it is the internal experience of an event without the external stimuli.

Imagery provides communication between perception, emotion, and physiological change (Achterberg, 1985). Images occur spontaneously or are induced by one's self or another. Images have an important role in storing and processing mental information. Memory, learning, information retention, artistry, creativity, and invention all are influenced by one's ability to utilize imagery (Achterberg & Lawlis, 1980). Because it is not dependent on the retrieval of a stored memory, imagery may deviate significantly from anything based on perceived or previously experienced reality. As a result, imagery can be highly creative.

This definition describes the *imagic state*, but *imagery* is also a set of procedures. Some therapeutic approaches using imagery include: guided imagery, guided affective imagery, visualization, self talk, inner dialogue, and focusing, desensitization, cognitive therapy, and neurolinguistic programming.

Altered State of Consciousness—Trance, Hypnosis, Suggestion

Relaxation and imagery techniques are often used to induce an altered state of consciousness or a hypnotic trance state. An altered state of consciousness or awareness differs from the normal waking state and occurs normally throughout wakeful periods. Typically the individual is more focused on inner processes. Mental imagery may be active and vivid and the person appears less physically active and reactive, and generally more relaxed. The daydreaming student, the preoccupied subway traveler, and the patient in a waiting room are all good examples of individuals who are probably in an altered state of awareness. Clinically it is important to recognize this state, as the individual is typically more suggestible and this increased suggestibility can be used constructively if recognized.

A modified sensorium, altered psychological state, and minimal motor functioning characterize the "trance." A *wakeful dissociative* state of intense focal awareness, a hypnotic trance maximizes involvement with one sensory precept at a time (Spiegel & Spiegel, 1978, pp. 22–23). In this altered state the individual is more receptive to suggestion, the acceptance of new ideas, and initiation of new behaviors. According to Milton Erickson, the "limits of one's usual frame of reference and beliefs are temporarily altered so one can be receptive to other patterns of association and modes of mental functioning that are more conducive to problem solving" (1979, p. 3).

The word *hypnosis* "refers to an induction procedure performed by a hypnotist, to a state of consciousness called a 'trance,' and to several effects which can be achieved in this state" (Horowitz, 1983, p. 47). These "effects" include visual images, dreams, and even hallucinations. Hypnosis enhances image formation because of the purposeful use of suggestion and the regressed state of consciousness in hypnosis (Horowitz, 1983, p. 48).

Whether the hypnotic state is a specific one, however, is often debated by the experts (Barber, 1969). Many believe the hypnotic state is simply a high level of relaxation during which attention is focused, imagining is active, and responsiveness to suggestion is great. If this is in fact true, one might conceptualize relaxation, imagery, and the hypnotic trance state as existing on a continuum. Relaxation would be the first level and a deep trance would be the final level. Other experts, however, view hypnosis as a specific state rather than a place on a continuum of consciousness.

The capacity for vivid imagination has often been associated with hypnotizability. Over the years numerous researchers have demonstrated that the ability to image and fantasize increases an individual's capacity to enter an altered or hypnotic state (Hilgard, 1970, 1974; Spanos & Barber, 1974; Barber, 1985). Most recently Lynn and Rhue (1987) studied this relationship. In their test situations they found that imagery and the ability to enter a trance were positively related. They also learned that some highly imaginative individuals did not carry out *action oriented* hypnotic suggestions because they were so involved in the imagery it seemed like too much effort. They explained further that, "Vividly imagining suggestions facilitates responding when subjects are motivated to respond . . . and associate imagining with hypnotic responding. Responsiveness even in highly imaginative subjects will be resisted if the action does not match personal goals and objectives, when negative attitudes toward hypnosis exist, lack of motivation, poor rapport with the clinician or atypical interpretation of the suggestion occurs" (Lynn & Rhue, 1987, p.106). In addition, they found that people who are active imaginers and good hypnotic subjects responded to suggestion in nonhypnotic situations that "require a lessening of rational, 'reality bound' analytical thinking" (p. 109). Such individuals were cognitively more flexible and were, in addition to being motivated, capable of exceptional empathic responses to characters in novels, plays, etc.

Although often associated with hypnosis, *suggestive techniques* are important when providing R/I therapy. Therapeutic suggestion is vital to the development and maintenance of a therapeutic relationship and is the mechanism through which a problem or symptom is altered.

Four types of suggestion are relevant to implementing relaxation/imagery: (1) verbal suggestion, which includes words and sounds; (2) nonverbal suggestion, which applies to body language and gestures; (3) intraverbal suggestion, which is the intonation of words; and (4) extraverbal suggestion, which utilizes the implications of words and gestures to facilitate the acceptance of ideas (Kroger & Fezler, 1976, p. 12). Suggestions are also categorized as obvious and direct or indirect (metaphor, stories, double binds, and embedded commands).

Integrating and Contrasting Concepts

Clinically both relaxation and imagery have been purposefully used to promote an altered state of consciousness and to alter maladaptive behavior, negative feeling states, tension, and physical or psychological pain. Relaxation and imagery are often employed together in different patterns and with varying emphases. For example, biofeedback, meditation, hypnosis, cognitive therapy, and behavioral rehearsal all incorporate R/I techniques but in slightly different ways and with slightly different theoretical frameworks. Each approach has incorporated basic beliefs and approaches from R/I theory and practice. Understanding the principles behind these interventions then will provide a basic orientation and set of skills that can be applied to other more specific approaches (See Fig. 1-1).

Relaxation focuses on a physiologically progressive softening of muscles and a subsequent relaxed mental state; imagery is a mental representation of "reality," fabricated or "real." Imagery utilizes and depends on mental processes that may or may not potentiate relaxation or physiological responses. Each technique (R/I) may be utilized to promote the other. When imagery occurs spontaneously it may or may not be associated with physiological relaxation. But when imagery is used therapeutically it is most often preceded by some form of relaxation exercise, such as progressive relaxation. Imagery may also be used to enhance a relaxation experience. For example, progressive relaxation focuses on attending to muscle groups. Imagery can augment this process by encouraging a visualization of the muscles as soft or as "like bread dough" and easy to mold.

Hypnosis differs from relaxation and imagery in purposefully striving for evidence and use of a trance state and on emphasizing therapeutic suggestion. Suggestive communication can and should be integrated into all interventions.

The differences and similarities between relaxation, imagery, and other techniques are of interest conceptually but are most important in clinical application. Differences exist in approaches to the patient's and therapist's expressed goals. When using a technique such as guided imagery, hypnosis, desensitization, or the like, the clinician usually begins with a general relaxation procedure, then follows with an imagery experience that incorporates therapeutic suggestion. The clinician accepts that any R/I approach can evoke an altered state of consciousness and produce a suggestible trancelike state. Whether or not an altered state occurs, using suggestive, therapeutic communication potentiates the realization of a desired goal.

When implementing these techniques patients may ask how relaxation and imagery differ from hypnosis, which is of concern since hypnosis still connotes magic, a deep sleep, relinquishment of control to another, or the idea of being put "under a spell." Some respond positively to these "magical" misperceptions, feeling as if something powerful and special is being done to them. If suggestive techniques are mentioned, some may have a similar reaction or may interpret the word *suggestion* to mean that their symptoms are all of a psychogenic nature and are experienced on pur-

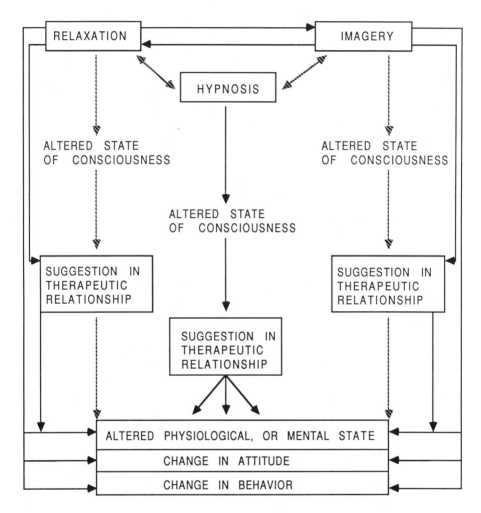

Figure 1-1. A separate process can exist for relaxation, imagery, hypnosis, or a related technique. The processes can also be combined, i.e., relaxation and imagery can be used together to promote a hypnotic state; and usually relaxation is used as a beginning step in the process. Broken line indicates that a result may or may not result in an altered state of consciousness, and suggestion may or may not be used to produce the end result of altered physiologic or mental state, change in attitude or behavior.

pose for secondary gain. Use of the word *imagination*, on the other hand, is usually acceptable and carries connotations of something fun and novel. To the general population, relaxation is now a well-known method of stress management. With both relaxation and imagery the question of who is doing what to whom and who has the ultimate control seems less an issue than when techniques are labeled *hypnosis*, *trance*, or *suggestion*. Regardless of what the technique is called the result may be the same—a relaxed, actively focused, pleasant, suggestible state that has the potential for altering mental attitudes, physiological states, and behaviors.

In summary, R/I theory and techniques are basic generic frameworks used in many therapeutic approaches (Table 1–1). As a result, some of the case examples presented in the second section of the book will seem to resemble hypnosis, biofeedback, or some other approach. The basic therapeutic process presented, however, will always originate from a theoretical framework of mind-body connection and incorporate a relaxation/imagery approach.

NURSING FRAMEWORKS

In the development of its own theoretical base, nursing has been highly influenced by cognitive, humanistic, behavioral, and holistic movements. Always aware of the mind-body connection, the profession accepts a philosophical belief of human beings as complex, diversified, dynamic, unified systems in which mind and body are intricately related and mutually dependent and interdependent. Martha Rogers, perhaps the most recent influential nursing theorist, describes the human being as a "synergistic dynamic, open system" characterized by continuous interaction within the self and with the environment. Individual inner psychic processes occur on a continuum in an open dynamic interaction as the individual relates to the environment. Human developmental processes become increasingly complex and diverse in pattern organization and relate to the individual's relationship to time and intra- and interpersonal space (Rogers, 1980). Rogers believes that abstraction and imagery, language and thought, and sensorium and emotion comprise human nature (Rogers, 1970). The dynamic qualities of this complex unified human being involve movement from: heaviness to lightness toward weightlessness; the pragmatic through the imagination to the visionary; sleeping through waking to altered states of consciousness. These concepts also describe the nature of imagery and relaxation.

Rogers' theories have stimulated nurses and other health care givers to deviate from classical medical, interpersonal, or sociocultural models of care to a more dynamic holistic approach. Therapeutic touch, or the "laying on of hands" for healing, has been one such diversion popular with many nurses (Krieger, 1979). R/I techniques as well as clinician self-awareness and a therapeutic relationship are emphasized components of this process. Cognizance of interpersonal dynamics is particularly important, according to Krieger, when introducing a novel approach such as relaxation, imagery, or therapeutic touch. In therapeutic touch the healer uses images of color for diagnostic as well as healing purposes. Using relaxation, "centering," and attending to rhythmic breathing, the healer engages in meditation that, according to Krieger (1979)

TABLE 1–1.   **Comparison of Relaxation, Imagery, and Hypnosis**

RELAXATION THERAPY	GUIDED IMAGERY	HYPNOSIS-TRANCE
Muscle and/or physiologically oriented	Mentally and/or imaginatively oriented	Muscles, mental, or both
Directive in approach	Direct or indirect	Direct or indirect
Involves the patient's trying	Usually involves the patient's trying	May or may not involve patient's trying
Expectation of specific physical results	May or may not be geared to specific expectations of mental process	May or may not involve specific results
Alters physiological processes	Usually alters physiological processes	Usually alters physiological processes
May alter mental processes	Usually alters mental processes	Usually alters mental processes
May stimulate imagery	May stimulate relaxation	May stimulate relaxation and/or imagery
Provides mental distraction	Provides mental distraction	Provides mental distraction
May promote creative thinking	Promotes creative thinking	Promotes creative thinking
May use direct suggestion of comfort and relaxation	Usually uses direct suggestion of comfort associated with a specific image	May use direct or indirect suggestions for comfort
May be used to promote healing	May be used to promote healing	May be used to promote healing

is a "focused, passive, act of inattention." Relaxation aids receptivity, and vivid imagery intensifies the healing state. The inherent suggestion in the therapeutic touch process becomes "this is a special and unusual process that will help you get or feel better; I am going to actively participate in that process with you." This approach replicates the inherent suggestion in many holistic interventions, including relaxation and imagery.

According to the premise of a recent book by Mariah Snyder (1985), these techniques are truly independent nursing interventions. She believes that much of what nurses call interventions fit more into the category of carrying out medical procedures and not providing nursing "intervention." Snyder includes relaxation and imagery as independent interventions and expresses concern that little attention has been paid to these in nursing textbooks, nursing education, and in practice procedure manuals. Often, she contends, nurses are reluctant to make nursing diagnoses, plan care, and assume responsibility for these actions. To nurse educators, these independent nursing interventions are nice to know but are frosting on the cake, to be practiced on the advanced level. They are seldom viewed as a set of skills to be learned and practiced at the basic level. This passivity, she believes, is reflected in the few nursing studies that have accepted the challenge of grappling with the complex variables in the clinical situation. Snyder throws down the gauntlet to nurse educators and practitioners to integrate such interventions as relaxation and imagery, stating, "Nurses must be convinced of the challenge and excitement associated with autonomous functioning. It is a characteristic of a true professional" (Snyder, 1985, p. 6).

Furthermore, the scope of nursing practice as described in *Nursing: A Social Policy Statement* (1980) relates more directly to the use of independent comfort-producing activities that alleviate identified problems and promote health (see Appendix I for list of areas defined as specific to nursing's purview).

INTERVENTION WITH RELAXATION/IMAGERY TECHNIQUES

Recently the numbers of articles and books reporting cases or research on R/I have increased in the nursing as well as general health care literature. Jean Achterberg and Frank Lawlis (1980, 1985), well-known in the field of imagery, consistently talk about the importance of nurses integrating these techniques into their practices.

Nursing literature has included work with specific patient populations, including the following: music and imagery to combat nausea and vomiting with cancer patients (Frank, 1985); relaxation for pain relief after open-heart surgery (Horowitz, Fitzpatric, & Flaherty, 1984); relaxation for cardiac catheterization (Rice, Caldwell, Butler, & Robinson, 1986); R/I techniques (sensory information) to increase postoperative comfort and coping (Johnson, 1978); relaxation with anxious patients (Trygstad, 1980); hypnosis for pain management (Zahourek, 1983); and pain management with the elderly (Hamm & King, 1984).

Working with obstetric and gynecologic patients, nurses have numerous opportunities to use these tools not only during labor and delivery but also with breast feeding mothers and during pelvic and other potentially uncomfortable examinations or procedures. Pediatric nurses similarly can help children relax or use distracting imagery during painful procedures and when sleep is difficult. Likewise, in community health and outpatient settings nurses have opportunities to apply these techniques with longer-term patients suffering from chronic illnesses and disabilities. Nurse educators have found R/I exercises valuable in teaching concepts through role playing and in supporting their students during stressful times. In preventing or combating burnout supervisors and consultants utilize these tools with other approaches.

Pain and Discomfort

Nurses are learning biofeedback, therapeutic touch, hypnosis, and cognitive behavioral techniques. These approaches incorporate R/I for patients experiencing acute and chronic pain to help modify patients' perceptions of illness, to enlist their active cooperation, and to reduce anticipated pain postoperatively.

Jean Johnson (1978) investigated sensory information as a method of patient preoperative teaching. In this method the coping strategy taught utilizes imagery and behavioral rehearsal of what might be felt during and after procedures such as cholecystectomy, lab-induced ischemic pain, cast removal, pelvic exam, and endoscopy. Patients experiencing sensory information and relaxation consistently responded with increased comfort *and* with a decrease in the number of postoperative hospital days (Johnson, Rice, Fuller, & Endress, 1978).

Jean Achterberg, Cornelia Kenner, and Frank Lawlis tested three methods of pain and anxiety control with burn patients: (1) relaxation alone, (2) relaxation and imagery, and (3) R/I and biofeedback. Relaxation and imagery was the most effective method of decreasing pain and anxiety. These patients suffered less muscle tension and required significantly less pain and sedative medications than patients in the other two groups (Achterberg & Lawlis, 1980). In interpreting their data they speculate that during acute pain individuals find a mental mechanism more helpful than one that relates only to the body, e.g., relaxation alone (Achterberg, 1985; Achterberg, Kenner, & Lawlis, 1982; Kenner & Achterberg, 1983).

Stress Management

A common goal of nurses has been to help both clients and themselves counter the negative effects of stress by coping more effectively and creatively. Much of the recent literature describes methods to prevent burnout and enhance staff's coping capacity by using R/I techniques (Brallier, 1982; Donovan, 1981; Hoover & Parnell, 1984; Jacobsen & McGrath, 1983; Lachman, 1983; Smythe, 1984).

Marilee Donovan investigated the impact of R/I on stress among cancer patients (1980) and oncology nurses (1981). In the study of nurses, she compared two groups (a training group and a wait-list control group) on six stress-related variables: anxiety, depression, physical complaints, pulse, blood pressure, and perceived level of tension. Subjects in the study group experienced three 15–20-minute training sessions and audio-taped instructions on R/I techniques. The trainees were enthusiastically positive. Surprisingly, those who benefited most had been classified as "ineffective copers." Donovan speculated that the "good copers" already had alternative methods for coping with stress and simply added this as another method. The ineffective copers, however, used the technique to produce more dramatic change.

Coburn and Manderino (1986) studied stress innoculation techniques on rehabilitation patients who were incapacitated with anxiety. Patients learned cognitive, behavioral skills including R/I to modify negative, anxiety-evoking self-statements and to control autonomic arousal.

Adequate problem-solving skills are also stress management skills. Yvonne Vissing (1984) investigated visualization techniques as a method of problem-solving. Of the 15 health care workers who comprised her sample, those who spent the most time practicing visualizations had the most success in finding solutions to the selected problems.

Smith (1982) taught imagery skills to college students in a workshop situation. Her goal was to help them combat hopelessness. On a scale measuring hopelessness, changes were not significant, but behavioral modifications were observed, suggesting that the students had improved communication skills and reduced stress. Since hopelessness is a profound affective state one might predict that learning imagery in a workshop situation might have less effect than in a therapeutic situation. In such, the total process would be directed toward engendering a sense of hopefulness, and imagery techniques would be one aspect of that process.

Chemotherapy-Induced Nausea and Vomiting

Janice Frank (1985) studied the effect of music therapy and guided imagery on chemotherapy-induced nausea and vomiting. She found a statistically significant decrease between pre- and post-state anxiety for the study group. The perception of the intensity of the vomiting also decreased significantly in the study group. The perceived degree of nausea, however, remained unchanged. The duration of both nausea and vomiting were decreased in the study group, but just short of statistical significance. Frank speculated that nausea and vomiting may need to be considered separate symptoms in future research.

In outlining limitations of the study she stated: (1) the testing may have suggested the symptoms; (2) perceptions of previous experiences of nausea and vomiting were based on recall; (3) the study was conducted over only one incident of chemotherapy; (4) data should be prospective; and (5) all participants had previous experiences with chemotherapy-associated nausea and vomiting. These research limitations can also be considered in other studies of R/I intervention.

A similar study (Scott, Donohue, Mastrovito, & Hakess, 1986) compared the antiemetic effects of (1) a program of patient education and relaxation with guided imagery versus (2) a combined regimen of antiemetic medications. Both programs were helpful, but the education/relaxation/imagery group had a 4-hour shorter emetic period.

Weight gain and nutritional status in cancer patients has also been studied in relation to R/I techniques (Dixon, 1984). The group receiving R/I treatment had the greatest weight gain when compared with four other interventions.

These studies are beginning research efforts by nurses in the R/I field. Evaluating the process as a clinical intervention continues to be difficult for all health care professionals wishing to study these phenomena. This research resembles the evaluation process of other multivariable, subtle, and highly personal behavioral and subjective effects of similar interventions, e.g., psychotherapy.

R/I techniques involve more than doing a procedure in isolation; they must be implemented within the context of a relationship. The remainder of this chapter discusses how R/I tools are incorporated into the therapeutic process.

R/I TECHNIQUES IN NURSING PROCESS

As an intervention, R/I techniques incorporate several aspects of the therapeutic process. This process is dependent on an adequate assessment and understanding of (1) the patient, (2) the illness or presenting problem, (3) the symptom and its potential meaning, and (4) the patient's strengths and liabilities. In addition, how the patient processes information and interprets reality influences how these tools are utilized.

Standard techniques of progressive relaxation and scripted guided imagery exercises may be used, but clinicians are encouraged to develop approaches that are more tailored to specific individual needs. As the clinician's skills develop, relaxation and guided fantasies become naturally more entwined with therapeutic communication skills and purposeful suggestions for mobilizing change. As the process develops it is actively evaluated with the patient. This collaboration encourages the patient's sense of participation in his or her recovery and growth. Similarly, family, friends, and coworkers can become involved, which will decrease the patient's sense of alienation and the family's sense of helplessness.

The following sections overview the integration of relaxation and imagery into the nursing process: (1) how to choose a patient, (2) the development of the relationship, (3) implementation, and (4) precautions. Success seems to be related to several factors that exist within the therapeutic relationship. Trust, expectation, belief, and rapport are those necessary ingredients that will be addressed.

Choosing a Patient (Client)

Many people can benefit from these techniques. Generally, the more intelligent, highly motivated patient who expects positive outcomes and is able to concentrate will do the best. An imaginative individual who is willing to trust and is cooperative is also a likely successful candidate. As described in Chapter 7, these characteristics are not fixed requirements. The severely retarded, severely organic, and senile patient will not do well (Kroger, 1977, p. 45). Similarly, psychotic patients and children under 6 years of age are less likely to do well with R/I because of their minimal ability to maintain focused attention. Furthermore, R/I techniques should be used carefully and only by experienced psychiatric clinicians with psychotic, prepsychotic, and severely depressed and suicidal patients. While some theorists and clinicians warn that R/I techniques should not be used at all with this population, other clinical reports substantiate their both safe and effective use by the experienced clinician. Those who fear that the techniques might be dangerous believe that when a client is relaxed or using visualization, the unconscious is more accessible and upsetting material may surface. "Out-of-body," or dissociated, feelings can also worsen the patient's symptoms or illness if not dealt with properly. A skilled clinician can watch for these occasional untoward signs and help the patient through them, in some cases building on already existing defenses while at other times helping the patient explore the various sensations and feelings.

At St. Vincent's Hospital in New York City, nurses in the Department of Psychiatry use a psychoeducational model in working with long-term, chronic psychiatric patients. R/I techniques are integrated into groups on stress management and assertiveness training with no unpleasant side effects and with reports of sizeable benefits from the patients.

For the beginning practitioner, R/I techniques are most likely to be successful with motivated, intelligent patients who have a specific symptom for which there is little secondary gain. These patients generally have rapid positive results.

Developing the Relationship

Trust and Rapport

Trust and rapport can be promoted quickly or be built slowly. Initially, the nurse enlists and maintains the patient's attention and establishes himself or herself as a helper. If the interaction occurs during a crisis, as in an emergency room, the nurse must consider that the patient's attention span and ability to concentrate and remember might be impaired. In a crisis, sensations are heightened and hearing becomes selective. Verbal communication must be simple and clear; patient comprehension should be frequently assessed. Even in longer-term relationships, patients are often stressed and anxious when they encounter the nurse. Suggestibility is high in both instances and the following steps can apply in both types of relationships.

Getting in tune with the patient by pacing his or her breathing and mirroring the same position whenever possible enhances the clinician's understanding. The patient also experiences a sense that the nurse is in rhythm with him or her, which is essential for rapport.

Ruth Dailey Knowles discusses several additional rapport-building techniques from neurolinguistic programming (NLP) (Knowles, 1983). In NLP verbal and nonverbal approaches utilize the person's predominant *representational system*, whether visual, auditory, or kinesthetic. People demonstrate their primary mode by such statements as "I *see* what you mean" (visual), "That doesn't *sound* good to me" (auditory), or "I have a *sense* that's a *touchy* issue for you" (kinesthetic). Other senses may also be implied, for example "That *stinks*" or "That leaves a *bad taste* in my mouth." Nonverbally, eye movements and body language also communicate these representational systems. Briefly, NLP theory states that eye movements up indicate visual processing and eye movements to the side, auditory processing. Looking down and to the left (as you face the person) is kinesthetic and looking down and to the right indicates an inner dialogue. If the nurse is sensitive to how the patient is utilizing information and making decisions and responds in the same system, communication occurs easily and rapport can develop rapidly. Bandler and Grinder (1979) emphasize that these are the subtle building blocks to all empathic and close relationships. While people vary systems during an interaction, most utilize one that is predominant. Because patients under stress regress to their predominant mode and use it almost exclusively, it is important to give information through that mode so it can be best utilized by the patient (Bandler & Grinder, 1979; Brokopp, 1983).

Rapport is also built through the nurse's constant feedback to the patient. This feedback includes how the patient is doing medically, what is happening in the environment, and what to expect in the next few moments; these communications provide reality testing and help the patient feel valued and more in control. Perceptions can also be validated and corrected, if inaccurate, and the patient feels the nurse is active and caring.

Motivation and Expectation

The impact of positive expectation has long been a controversial but recognized important component of care. Jerome Frank, well-known for his work on the importance of persuasion in healing and in psychotherapy, emphasizes that positive expectations are hopefulness and therefore have both a positive affective impact as well as a positive potential placebo effect (Frank, 1974, 1978).

In screening, motivation is assessed by evaluating the meaning of the symptoms and estimating the individual's level of emotional stability. Explaining the meaning of certain organic symptoms, dispelling any misconceptions and fears, and communicating expectations of positive results enhance motivation. Expectations are also built through positive direct and indirect suggestions. For motivation to work, the patient must believe in the suggestion, must believe in the integrity and well-meaning intentions of the nurse, and, most importantly, feel that the ideas given "echo in a profound way the patient's own deeper inner voice" (Crasilneck & Hall, 1975, p. 43).

Patients with similar experiences can sometimes help in building expectations. Helen, a patient who used R/I techniques successfully for dressing changes, skin grafts, and debridement, was often enlisted to tell other patients how helpful these techniques had been for her. Similarly, explaining to patients how well others have done (storytelling) enhances motivation.

According to Crasilneck and Hall, "motivation is more than persistence, greater than mere involvement of time in problem-solving. It is an emerging process, one whose momentum carries forward in spite of momentary reverses or discouragements" (Crasilneck & Hall, 1975, p. 43).

Assessment and Diagnosis of the Problem

Assessment and diagnosis encompass the following: (1) asking the questions "who?," "what?," "why?," and "when?" (defining the problem); (2) choosing an intervention based on the problem; (3) intervening; and (4) subsequently evaluating the results.

The following questions explore how the patients describe the symptom(s) both metaphorically and concretely:

1. Why have you come for treatment at this time?
2. How would you describe your problematic symptom(s)? Does it have a color, a shape, or is it like an animal or thing?
3. What will happen if you no longer have the symptom?
4. What does the symptom do to others?
5. How patient are you in frustrating situations?
6. How willing are you to find a new way to cope with the symptom?

This assessment process will vary if the patient's situation is acute or chronic. For example, a patient with pain due to an injury can usually describe the nature of the pain graphically. He or she has probably not experienced much secondary gain, is anxious and fearful, and is therefore motivated to try anything to feel more comfortable. If the wait in the emergency room has been long, frustration-tolerance may well be at an end. Is the patient worried about the cause of pain or does he or she suspect relatively benign problems? Has the patient tried methods of relaxation or found distraction useful when experiencing other incidents of pain or distress? What else has helped in similar situations?

When assessing chronic pain the process will differ, and the nurse will need to consider in more detail the individual's total family and social situation. For example, when ascertaining the history of a patient with chronic incapacitating low back pain, the clinician may learn that the spouse is fed up and has insisted that the patient seek treatment. Although wishing to be free of pain, the patient prefers workmen's compensation to working. Developing an intervention with chronic back pain will take longer and be a far more complex process than with acute emergency pain.

The Intervention

The following summarizes the process of intervention, which is then demonstrated in case examples throughout the book.

1. Explain the rationale and what you are going to do. Encourage the active participation and invite questions from the patient. Explain that further interventions will be based on his or her feedback of the experience. Phrase anticipated results as a positive suggestion. This builds expectations of a positive outcome.
2. Choose a procedure based on the assessment: progressive relaxation, guided imagery, inner dialogue, or a combination of techniques. Generally precede the technique with some sort of relaxation procedure (See Appendix II for guidelines for relaxation and imagery techniques).
3. Observe the patient's reaction during the process. Did the patient look more relaxed and comfortable? Observe breathing rate and depth, muscle tension and relaxation in the face and shoulders.
4. Evaluate the experience with the patient. Was it relaxing and pleasant; how

did the images chosen fit for providing relaxation and/or comfort?
5.   Alter the technique based on the patient's feedback.
6.   Plan for the subsequent process of intervention, i.e., make a tape of the process, involve other staff or family members, give instructions to the patient for practice, make plans to return.

Potential Problems

If problems develop they generally can be solved by further investigating the cause, modifying the approach, or altering the manner the exercise is performed with the patient. A frequent cause of poor success with R/I techniques is secondary gain for a symptom or a conscious or unconscious need for a symptom. Patients suffering with chronic pain often fit into this category. The pain has meaning and therefore is not easily given up; as a result, these patients often are unrelieved no matter what the intervention.

Some patients complain they cannot concentrate and their minds wander. Encouraging the patient to allow this to happen rather than struggling against it relieves performance anxiety and the feeling that "I have to do it just right." Other times suggesting the patient visualize a black velvet curtain helps sharpen attention. If the patient appears relaxed even though some wandering of attention occurs, the clinician might positively reinforce that part of the goal was achieved. Some people complain they cannot relax completely or that part of their body remains tense. Again, the clinician might inform the patient of how he or she appears (relaxed), and emphasizes that with increased practice the depth of relaxation increases. If a patient has difficulty relaxing one part of the body, he or she can be helped to focus on that part by first tensing then relaxing the muscles. For other patients, ignoring that unrelaxed part is helpful.

If, for example, pain is being treated, the determination of which intervention to use may be based on whether pain is present and trial-and-error determination of which works better. Breathing white light, a restful color, or "softness" into a tense part can relieve isolated areas of both pain and tension. During exhalation the tension or pain is breathed out and away and is encased in a bright helium-filled balloon. This kind of active visualization can counter persistent problematic tension.

On occasion patients will describe feeling jumpy or more tense during R/I exercises. Focusing on breathing often helps these physical reactions, and the clinician's active encouragement to continue focusing, breathing easily, and listening simply to the rhythm of the voice similarly helps. Allowing the restless patient to move and find a more comfortable position is a positive way to utilize the restlessness, again avoiding the tension resulting from fighting against it.

An overall rule of thumb is to interpret the patient's experience as positively as possible. This approach increases the sense of success and promotes motivation to continue.

Self Techniques and Teaching Others

The patient's independent control of symptoms is important to maintain a sense of self-reliance and because, realistically, the nurse is not always available. In teaching patients, the nurse should emphasize that R/I is not hard to learn and is a natural process, but like other skills needs to be practiced for proficiency to develop.

Self techniques are taught once the patient has had a positive experience. The guidelines (see Appendix III) can be given verbally, on tape, or in writing, to the patient or a significant other. The patient is encouraged to practice soon after the procedure because learning takes place more quickly when the experience is fresh. The patient should avoid any tests of depth or attempts to produce any unusual phenomena. Frequently patients report feeling more relaxed when helped by another; an individualized tape or the involvement of others is useful in such cases. Patients should also be told that instructions and tapes can be modified based on their individual needs.

Often a patient's significant others are grateful to have "something to do," particularly when chronic unrelieved pain or stress is the problem. To serve as a guide these individuals need the same instructions and cautions as those given to the patient. The clinician might demonstrate progressive relaxation, emphasizing that the body itself provides the framework. When imagery is used, the clinician can explain that a clearly painted picture helps the vividness of the imagination and promotes greater distraction. Emphasizing that the patient can develop his or her own images also builds the significant other's confidence. Similarly, instructing the new caregiver to use reinforcing key words and explaining that using positive suggestions, a repetitious monotone, and silence can enhance relaxation guides and reassures the helper. Significant others should also be cautioned to phrase their comments in a positive way and to avoid any new or physiological suggestions other than those specifically given. One would not want, for example, to remove all pain when pain was needed for diagnostic purposes, or when it provided valued secondary gain. In the same vein, these significant others should be told to report any unusual signs or symptoms before or after using the technique.

Enlisting the help of others provides relief for the busy nurse, increases the patient's involvement with others, and provides a sense of usefulness and purpose to significant others. Usually all involved experience a sense that something is being done, and isolation and frustration diminish markedly.

Precautions

These techniques are generally considered safe with few adverse reactions reported. Daydreaming is a common human experience that seldom causes trouble unless the daydreamer becomes pathologically obsessional or focuses on negative thoughts exclusively. If an altered state occurs, it is, in reality, self-induced. The nurse participating as a guide with the patient has a valuable role in helping the patient choose from alternative effects. The few potential dangers include:

1. Making an illness worse by indiscriminant symptom removal (pain that is a new and undiagnosed symptom).
2. Masking other illnesses.
3. Providing superficial relief, particularly with psychiatric difficulties.
4. Fantasizing seduction.
5. Experiencing panic with relief of superego controls.

6. Causing tension by using images that promote fear.
7. Causing a counterproductive physiological response.
8. Withholding other treatment modalities.

Additional and rather specific dangers have been listed in Snyder's book on nursing interventions (1985). Specific precautions related to progressive relaxation include:

1. An unwanted drug action is precipitated. For example, a hypoglycemic state might result from a usual amount of insulin causing a greater than usual reaction because of the patient's relaxed state.
2. Total relaxation can produce a hypotensive state. Remaining seated for a few moments and gradually resuming activity helps alleviate this.
3. Relaxation with people who have delusions or hallucinations should be used with caution as out-of-body or out-of-reality sensations can occur. Similarly, relaxation may promote withdrawal in depressed patients and on occasion has intensified anxiety. The symptoms of relaxation-induced anxiety include intense restlessness, profuse perspiration, shivering, trembling, and rapid breathing.
4. Some patients with chronic pain have found that relaxation intensifies pain because of the focus on the body.

Some few additional dangers to the clinician need to be considered:

1. Excessive grandiosity and unrealistic expectations about the potential outcome.
2. Narrowing one's practice to only using these techniques.

These dangers are similar to the dangers faced by clinicians using tools such as hypnosis or therapeutic touch. They accompany any psychotherapeutic relationship and are most often understood as tranference-counter-transference reactions.

Nurses do not want to use these tools indiscriminantly with all patients and should remember they are valuable interventions within a therapeutic relationship and process. They should be used with a clear understanding of the patient's problems, needs, and coping capacities.

Questions for Nursing Research

The nursing research ground in this field is fertile, has just begun to be broken, and is rocky. Questions relate to the numerous, often uncontrollable, variables found in all clinical studies. Some include:

1. Is one kind of patient more receptive than another?
2. Do specific techniques work better with specific illnesses, procedures, or personality types or styles?
3. How valuable are standardized versus individualized procedures?
4. What are the pros and cons of using tapes?
5. What is the impact of the therapeutic relationship?

6. What is the impact of relaxation or imagery techniques directed toward or away from the body or physiological processes?
7. What is the impact of the length of time spent in the procedure and with the patient on the outcome?
8. How do we reliably measure outcome?

SUMMARY

This chapter has presented an overview for the student, educator, and clinician who use relaxation and imagery in their practices. These techniques bridge both ancient and seemingly primitive methods of promoting comfort, healing, and health with future methods in health care. Being such a bridge, these techniques are not practiced exactly as the ancient healer would, or in ways that are always acceptable to those locked into the present. This body-mind-spirit bridge is one on which nurses have walked since the beginning of caring for the sick. If we can allow it, our patients will be our guides.

While our capacity to cure disease is often limited, we can profoundly influence that illness experience. We can be like the ancient healers and approach the illness process with a belief in the individual's innate power to make the end result better than the starting point, or we can be dualistic and simply treat the physical aspects of the disease. The R/I mode of conceptualizing and intervening in the process of illness utilizes this pre-Cartesian mind-body-spirit holistic philosophy.

The next dimension in health care must pull together science and intuition as well as keep the mind, body, and spirit together. We must use the best from our advanced technology but also must recapture the art of participating with and capturing both our own and our patient's creative potential. The holistic health care movement in the 1970s and 1980s enthusiastically adopted by many nurses has been a reaction to the high degree of dualistic and dehumanized mechanization occurring in health care. Noninvasive, nonchemical means to health and well-being keep the mind, body, and spirit together. Alternative treatments are encouraged for countering the often painful and excessively life-prolonging treatments prescribed. Holistic health care givers value comfortable quality time rather than a lengthy, miserable extended life.

R/I techniques tap that potential as broad concepts underlying various techniques and approaches to health and illness care. This book focuses on how the pre-Cartesian tradition of putting the mind, body, and spirit together as a dynamic, continuously interacting whole is realized through relaxation and imagery.

REFERENCES

Achterberg, J. (1985). *Imagery in healing: shamanism and modern medicine.* Boston: New Science Library.

Achterberg, J., Kenner, C., & Lawlis, G. F. (1982). *Biofeedback, imagery, and relaxation: Pain and stress intervention for severely burned patients.* Paper presented at the annual meeting of the Biofeedback Society of America, Chicago.

Achterberg, J., & Lawlis, F. (1978). *Imagery and disease.* Champaign, IL: Institute for Personality and Ability Testing, Inc.

Achterberg, J., & Lawlis, F. (1980). *Bridges of the body mind: Behavioral approaches to health care.* Champaign, IL: Institute for Personality and Ability Testing, Inc.

Achterberg, J., & Lawlis, F. (1982). Imagery and health care. *Topics in Clinical Nursing, 3,* 55–60.

American Nurses' Association (1980). *Nursing: A social policy statement.* Kansas City, MO: American Nurses' Association.

Bandler, R., & Grinder, J. (1979). *Frogs into princes.* Moab, UT: Real People Press.

Barber, T. X. (1969). *Hypnosis: A scientific approach.* New York: Van Nostrand-Reinhold.

Barber, T. X. (1984). Changing "unchangeable" bodily processes by (hypnotic) suggestions: A new look at hypnosis, cognitions, imagining and the mind-body problem. In A. A. Sheikh (Ed.), *Imagination and healing: Imagery and human development series* (69–127). Farmingdale, NY: Baywood.

Barber, T. X. (1985). Hypnosuggestive procedures as catalysts for psychotherapies. In S. J. Lynn and J. P. Garske (Eds.), *Contemporary psychotherapies: Models and methods* (pp. 333–375). Columbus: Charles E. Merrill.

Beck, A. T., & Emery, G. (1985). *Anxiety disorders and phobias: A cognitive perspective.* New York: Basic Books.

Beck, A. T., Rush, J., Shaw, B. F., & Emery, G. (1979). *Cognitive therapy of depression.* New York: Guilford.

Benson, H. (1975). *The relaxation response.* New York: William Morrow.

Billars, K. (1970). You have pain? I think this will help. *American Journal of Nursing, 70,* 21–23.

Brallier, L. (1982). *Transition and transformation: Successfully managing stress.* Palo Alto, CA: National Nursing Review.

Brokopp, D. Y. (1983). What is NLP? *American Journal of Nursing, 82,* l0, 12–14.

Clark, C. C. (1981). *Enhancing wellness: A guide of self care.* New York: Springer.

Coburn, J., & Manderino, M. A. (1986). Stress inoculation: An illustration of coping skills training. *Rehabilitation Nursing, 11,*14–17.

Crasilneck, H. B., & Hall, J. A. (1975). *Clinical hypnosis: Principles and applications.* New York: Grune & Stratton.

Daley, T. J., & Greenspan, E. L. (1979). Stress management through hypnosis. *Topics in Clinical Nursing, 1,* 59–65.

Dixon, J. (1984). Effect of nursing interventions on nutritional and performance status in cancer patients. *Nursing Research, 33,* 330–335.

Donovan, M. I. (1980). Relaxation with guided imagery: A useful technique. *Cancer Nursing, 3,* 27–32.

Donovan, M. (1981). Study of the impact of relaxation with guided imagery on stress among cancer nurses. *Cancer Nursing, 4,* 121–126.

Dunn, H. L. (1961). *High level wellness.* Arlington, VA: R. W. Beatty.

Editorial. (1985). *New England Journal of Medicine, 312,* 1770–1772.

Editorial. (1985, July 20). *Lancet.*

Erickson, M., & Rossi, E. L. (1979). *Hypnotherapy: An exploratory casebook.* New York: Irvington.

Flint, B. (1985, August 20). Letter to the editor. *New England Journal of Medicine.*

Flint, B. (1987, September 23). Special mailing to members by the executive director of the Institute for Advancement of Health. (New York)

Frank, J. D. (1974). *Persuasion and healing* (rev. ed.). New York: Schocken.

Frank, J. D. (1978). Psychotherapy and the healing arts. In J. Fosshage & P. Olsen (Eds.), *Healing: Implications for psychotherapy.* New York: Human Services.

Frank, J. M. (1985). The effects of music therapy and guided visual imagery on chemotherapy induced nausea and vomiting. *Oncology Nursing Forum, 12,* 47–52.

Goleman, D. (1985, October 29). Debate intensifies on attitude and health. *New York Times,* pp. Cl, C7.

Hamm, B., & King, V. (1984). A holistic approach to pain control with geriatric clients. *Journal of Holistic Nursing, 2,* 32–36.

Hilgard, J. R. (1970). Personality and hypnotizeability: Inferences from case studies. In E. R. Hilgard (Ed.), *Hypnotic Susceptibility.* New York: Harcourt, Brace and World.

Hilgard, J. R. (1974). Imaginative involvement: Some characteristics of highly hypnotizeable and non-hypnotizeable. *International Journal of Clinical and Experimental Hypnosis, 22,* 138–156.

Hoover, R. M., & Parnell, P. K. (1984). An inpatient educational group on stress and coping. *Journal of*

Psychosocial Nursing, 22, 17–22.

Horowitz, B. F., Fitzpatric, J. J., & Flaherty, G. G. (1984). Relaxation techniques for pain relief after open heart surgery. *Dimensions of Critical Care Nursing, 3,* 364–371.

Horowitz, M. (1983). Image formation. New York: Jason Aronson.

Jacobson, E. (1929). *Progressive relaxation: A physiological and clinical investigation of muscular states and their significance in psychology and medical practice.* Chicago: University of Chicago.

Jacobson, E. (1967). *Tension in medicine.* Springfield, IL: Thomas.

Jacobsen, S. F., & McGrath, M. (1983). *Nurses under stress.* New York: John Wiley and Sons.

Johnson, J. E., Rice, V. H., Fuller, S. S., & Endress, M. P. (1978). Sensory information, instruction in a coping strategy and recovery from surgery. *Research in Nursing and Health, 1,* 4–17.

Kenner, C., & Achterberg, J. (1983). *Non-pharmacologic pain relief for patients.* Paper presented at the annual meeting of the American Burn Association, New Orleans.

Knowles, R. D. (1983). Building rapport through neurolinguistic programming. *American Journal of Nursing, 82,* 1011–1014.

Krieger, D. (1979). *Therapeutic touch: How to use your hands to help or to heal.* Englewood Cliffs, NJ: Prentice-Hall.

Kroger, W. S. (1977). *Clinical and experimental hypnosis* (2nd ed.). Philadelphia: J. B. Lippincott.

Kroger, W. S., & Fezler, W. D. (1976). *Hypnosis and behavior modification: Imagery conditioning.* Philadelphia: J. B. Lippincott.

Lachman, V. (1983). *Stress management: A manual for nurses.* New York: Grune & Stratton.

Lachmann, P. J., & Peters, D. K. (Eds.) (1982). *Clinical aspects of immunology* (4th ed.). Oxford: Blackwell Scientific.

Larkin D. (1985). *Therapeutic suggestion in clinical hypnosis and therapeutic suggestion in nursing.* Orlando, FL: Grune & Stratton.

Lazarus, A. (1977). *In the mind's eye: The power of imagery therapy to give you control over your life.* New York: Rawson.

LeShan, L. I. (1975). Toward a general theory of healing. In S. R. Dean (Ed.), *Psychiatry and mysticism* (pp. 247–270). Chicago: Nelson-Hall.

Lynn, S. J., & Rhue, J. W. (1977). Hypnosis, imagination and fantasy. *Journal of Mental Imagery, 11,* 101–113.

Matje, Sr. D. (1984). Stress and cancer: A review of the literature. *Cancer Nursing, 7,* 399–403.

McCaffery, M. (1979). *Nursing management of the patient with pain* (2nd ed.). Philadelphia: J. B. Lippincott.

McMahon, C. E. (1976). The role of imagination in the disease process: Pre-Cartesian history. *Psychological Medicine, 6,* 179–184.

Miller, B. (1985). Teaching biofeedback techniques in critical care. *Dimensions of Critical Care Nursing, 4,* 314–318.

Nightingale, F. (1859). *Notes on nursing.* London: Harrison and Sons.

Rice, V. H., Caldwell, M., Butler, S., & Robinson, J. (1986). Relaxation training and response to cardiac catheterization: A pilot study. *Nursing Research, 35,* 39–43.

Rogers, M. E. (1970). *An introduction to the theoretical basis of nursing.* Philadelphia: F. A. Davis.

Rogers, M. E. (1970). *The theoretical basis of nursing* (pp. 4–10). Philadelphia: F. A. Davis.

Scott, D. W., Donohue, D. C., Mastrovito, R. C., & Hakess, T. B. (1986). Comparative trial of clinical relaxation and an antiemetic drug regimen in reducing chemotherapy related nausea and vomiting. *Cancer Nursing, 9,* 178–187.

Selye, H. (1974). *Stress without distress.* Philadelphia: J. B. Lippincott.

Siegel, B. (1986). *Love, medicine and miracles.* New York: Harper & Row.

Smith, D. M. Y. (1982). Guided imagination as an intervention in hopelessness. *Journal of Psychosocial Nursing and Mental Health Services, 20,* 29–32.

Smythe, E. E. M. (1984). *Surviving nursing.* Menlo Park, CA: Addison-Wesley.

Snyder, M. (1985). *Independent nursing interventions.* New York: John Wiley and Sons.

Spanos, N. P., & Barber, T. X. (1974). Toward a convergence in hypnosis research. *American Psychologist, 29,* 500–511.

Spiegel, H., & Rockey, E. (1985). Hypnosis in surgery: Exploding the myths. *The Surgical Team, 3,* 31–37.

Spiegel, H., & Spiegel, D. (1978). *Trance and treatment* (pp. 22–23). New York: Basic Books.

Sweeney, S. S. (1978). Relaxation. In C. Carlson & B. Blackwell (Eds.), *Behavioral concepts and nursing interventions* (2nd ed.). Philadelphia: J. B. Lippincott.

Trygstad, L. (1980). Simple new way to help anxious patients. *RN, 43*, 28–32.

Vissing, Y., & Burke, M. (1984). Visualization: Techniques for health care workers. *Journal of Psychosocial Nursing and Mental Health Services, 22*, 29–32.

Zahourek, R. P. (1983). Hypnosis in nursing practice: Emphasis on the patient who has pain (Parts I and II). *Journal of Psychosocial Nursing and Mental Health Services, 20*, 13–17, 21–24.

Zahourek, R. P. (Ed.) (1985). *Clinical hypnosis and therapeutic suggestion in nursing*. Orlando, FL: Grune & Stratton.

BIBLIOGRAPHY

Fosshage, J.L., & Olsen, P. (1978). *Healing inplications for Psychotherapy*. New York: Human Sciences.

Gordon, J.S., Jaffe, D/T., Bresler, D.E. (1984). *Mind, body and health: Toward an integral medicine*. New York: Human Sciences.

Larkin, D.L., & Zahourek, R. P. (1988) Issue editors for Alternative Approaches to Pain and Stress. *Holistic Nursing Practice Journal*.

Rossi, E.L. (1986). *The psychobiology of mind-body healing: New concepts of therapeutic hypnosis*. New York: W.W. Norton.

Zahourek, R.P. (1987). Clinical hypnosis in controversies in holistic nursing. 2:pages (in press).

2

RELAXATION

HOPE TITLEBAUM

OVERVIEW

Relaxation is a familiar, commonly used term, and yet the concept needs further development and an operational definition. Is relaxation a state of mind, a physiological condition that is measurable, or a behavior that can be learned? This chapter will explore the theoretical foundations of relaxation, review the research literature on relaxation therapy, and finally describe clinical applications and techniques that are relevant to nursing practice.

Relaxation is the mental and physical freedom from tension or stress (McCaffery, 1979). It is a state that may be present or absent throughout the body, affecting skeletal muscles, skin conductance, visceral functions like heart rate, respiratory rate, and blood pressure, and cerebral activities such as thoughts, perceptions and emotional states. It is possible for tension to exist in one area of the body while relaxations occur in another part, although relaxation in one location tends to promote or encourage relaxation in other areas (McCaffery, 1979).

Relaxation is an essential element in the maintenance of physical and mental health, and as such it is significant to nursing. Relaxation theory, incorporated into our knowledge base, will enable nurses to more effectively use the tools or training techniques to produce the desired feeling state or behavior change. Sweeney (1978) suggests that "relaxation is an adaptive coping process which lends itself to nursing interventions designed to promote and enhance health and ultimately, the quality of life" (p. 243).

A review of the literature reveals a growing body of evidence pointing to the clinical applicability of relaxation. Stovya and Anderson (1982) state that research primarily from the past decade "indicates that mastery of relaxation is a robust and clinically useful response" (p. 752). It becomes a difficult task to compare studies on the use of relaxation, because each researcher uses his or her own combination of techniques. To complicate the issue further, a particular skill like progressive relaxation may be taught by taped instruction, verbal instruction, using a "modified" Jacobson approach (which may or may not be described), or via the Bernstein and Borkovec manual (1973). Other variables, such as amount of practice of the specified relaxation technique, quality of the practice, feedback from the instructor, and relationship with the instructor are among the multitude of factors, often unaccounted for, that may influence outcome.

The physical state of relaxation is usually recognized by the absence of tension, measured either by physiological changes or by subjective self-report, or by a combination of both. Although many researchers have experimented with the effects of relaxation training and have studied the relative effectiveness of different methods with a variety of diseased and healthy populations, very few scientists have studied the phenomenon of relaxation itself. Four major models of theoretical frameworks were found and include: Edmund Jacobson's progressive relaxation; Herbert Benson's relaxation response; Hans Selye's general adaptation syndrome; and Davidson and Schwartz's psychobiology of relaxation.

THEORETICAL MODELS

Edmund Jacobson—Progressive Relaxation

The history of relaxation training began with the pioneering work of Edmund Jacobson, who started his work at Harvard University in 1908. As a result of his early investigations, Jacobson concluded that tension involves the effort manifested in the shortening of muscle fibers, that an individual experiences tension when he or she feels anxious, and that removing the tension can eliminate the anxiety. In his more recent writing, Jacobson (1970) states that indications of "anxiety tension" are not limited to the skeletal neuromuscular system, but are associated with overactivity of the nervous system, thereby involving cardiac and smooth muscle end-paths. Using electroneuromyometry, Jacobson has demonstrated the involvement of the skeletal musculature during periods of anxiety. He states that if electrodes are attached in any section of skeletal musculature selected at random, "action potentials run amazingly high" (Jacobson, 1929, p. 17). Chronic anxiety can lead to a variety of physical conditions including cardiac problems (valve disease, defects, hypertrophy), pylorospasm, and spastic colon. In all cases of chronic anxiety, x-ray exams have revealed spasticity of the digestive tract (Jacobson, 1970).

Impulses along efferent nerve fibers proceed from motor brain centers to striated muscle fibers, resulting in contraction. When muscle contracts, nerve fibers then carry impulses back to the central nervous system. Jacobson believes that the impulse can originate in either the brain or the muscle, causing the individual to experience tension. When the muscle relaxes, the corresponding brain center simultaneously discontinues the innervation with both afferent and efferent nerve fibers. Jacobson (1970) states that "muscles and brain proceed together in one effort circuit, active or relaxed" (p. 34).

Healthy individuals vary daily in their characteristic patterns of action potentials. In a highly anxious or panic state, however, individuals show similar high readings in all skeletal muscles. Jacobson's clinical observations, as well as his laboratory studies, show that responses to danger are reflected in perception as well as musculature. What a person believes and how he or she evaluates a threatening situation will then determine adjustment and ultimately survival.

These kinds of observations led Jacobson to develop a method of inducing relaxation that he termed *progressive relaxation*, in order to differentiate his treatment from rest or recreation. His system involved a series of tension-release muscle exercises that will be described in more detail (see "Techniques"). His technique results in the achievement of increased discriminative control over skeletal muscles until one can induce very low levels of tension in the major muscle groups. Due to Jacobson's awareness of the cognitive aspects of relaxation, he actively prevented premature muscle training by instructing patients as follows:

1. Without relaxing, determine the issue or problem.
2. Without relaxing, identify and localize the tension image patterns of anxiety about the issue or problem.
3. Relax the reaction patterns (Jacobson, 1970, p. 373).

Jacobson also teaches his patients to expect to use this process repeatedly throughout their lives. In his first book, *Progressive Relaxation*, published in 1929, Jacobson speaks of helping patients to cultivate "muscle-sense," an awareness of the sensations associated with the contraction of their muscles. Jacobson's system is both a problem-solving and a coping skill tool, and one that patients can incorporate into their daily lives. His model and writings generally focus more on treatment, evaluation, and explanation of his findings than on development of a theoretical construct of relaxation. Past and current research, however, has repeatedly demonstrated the effectiveness of his techniques in both their original and their modified or shortened versions.

Herbert Benson—The Relaxation Response

Herbert Benson (1975) constructed a model that he calls the *relaxation response*. He describes the relaxation response as an integrated hypothalamic response accompanied by a decrease in sympathetic arousal, and characterized primarily by decreased muscle tonus. The relaxation response is the body's "natural and innate protective mechanism" (p. 18) to counter the potential harmful body effects of the stress response. The stress response, also referred to as fight-or-flight, is the body's involuntary response to threat or change. The physiological components of the stress response have been demonstrated and well documented. These include an increase in blood pressure, pulse rate, respiratory rate, blood flow to the muscles, and secretion of adrenalin.

Benson (1975) believes that the more often the stress response is elicited, the greater is the likelihood for hypertension to develop, especially if circumstances do not allow one to fight or flee. Certainly many other diseases and symptoms have been associated with stress, namely headaches, peptic ulcers, arthritis, colitis, diarrhea, asthma, cardiac arrhythmias, sexual problems, and circulatory problems. Presumably the body uses the relaxation response as a protection, but Benson does not describe how this mechanism is activated other than by the intervention of a relaxation therapy. Physiologically, the relaxation response results in a *decrease* in oxygen consumption, carbon dioxide production, respiration rate, heart rate, arterial blood lactate, pH and base excess levels; and an *increase* of electroencephalographic alpha and theta waves and skin resistance. To summarize, there is a generalized *decrease* in sympathetic nervous system activity and a possible *increase* in parasympathetic activity. In the brain, the relaxation response is activated in the anterior hypothalamus and is believed to be a protective mechanism against overstress belonging to the trophotropic-endophylactic system. Alpha waves are associated with feelings of well-being and relaxation, and these increase in amplitude and regularity during meditation.

The major physiological change associated with meditation is a decreased metabolic rate. Oxygen consumption decreases in both sleep and meditation, but during sleep decreases gradually to 8 percent lower than wakefulness after 4 to 5 hours of sleep. During meditation the oxygen consumption decrease averages 10 to 20 percent and occurs during the first 3 minutes of meditating (Benson, 1975). Lactate is produced by the metabolism of skeletal muscles and is of particular interest due to its association with anxiety. Blood lactate levels have been shown to decrease rapidly in the first 10 minutes of meditation and remain at low levels throughout the meditating procedure, a finding consistent with a generalized decrease in central nervous system activity. According to Benson (1975) these physiological changes occur equally in individuals practicing simple forms of meditation and in highly trained and experienced practitioners of yoga or zen meditation. Benson therefore developed his own simple form of meditation (see "Techniques").

To test Benson's theory, 17 healthy subjects were studied after teaching themselves Benson's meditation and practicing for just 1 hour. Beary, Benson, and Klemshuck (1974), using these subjects as their own controls, were able to demonstrate a significant decrease in oxygen consumption, carbon dioxide production, and respiratory rate during periods of prescribed relaxation compared with periods of sitting quietly with eyes closed. The oxygen consumption decreased 13 percent, carbon dioxide 12 percent, and respiration decreased 4.6 breaths per minute below control values.

Benson (1975) recommends that regular use of the relaxation response "will offset the harmful effects of the inappropriate elicitation of the fight-or-flight response" (p. 69). Research is sorely needed to confirm Benson's findings and to give support to the claims of healthful and therapeutic benefits of the elicitation of the relaxation response. Benson himself and his colleagues declare that "only preliminary objective data exist at the present time which establish the place of the relaxation response in medicine" (Benson, Beary, & Carol, 1974, p. 44).

Hans Selye—The General Adaptation Syndrome

The two models just presented deal with the concept of relaxation in relation to stress. Relaxation is seen as the mechanism to protect the body from the potentially harmful effects of prolonged or repeated stress. Selye's theoretical model is included here because it further indicates the relationship between stress and relaxation. Selye (1982) defines stress as the nonspecific or common result of any demand on the body, whether the effect is mental or physical.

Selye describes what he terms the *general adaptation syndrome*, comprising three stages, namely alarm, resistance, and exhaustion. Selye believes that out stores of adaption energy are limited, and that sleep and rest can restore resistance and adaptability. The question, still unanswered, remains—what are the carriers of the alarm that signals the need for adaptation? We know that the hypothalamus is stimulated, probably via the nervous or circulatory system, which in turn links with the endocrine system, and adrenocorticotrophic hormone (ACTH) is discharged into the circulation. A series of corticoids provide the needed energy for adaptation as well as other responses such as suppression of immune reactions and inflammation. Stressors can be a variety of agents or demands including emotions (fear, joy, anger) as well as thoughts. To assist in the adjustment to life's demands, Selye recommends a daily period of complete rest with eyes closed and muscles relaxed, using one of the many relaxation techniques available.

Davidson and Schwartz—Psychobiology of Relaxation

Davidson and Schwartz (1976) confirm this author's conclusion of a lack of research and theory-building on the actual process of relaxation. Their theory is a multiprocess theory focusing on the interaction of various factors consistent with current neurophysiological research on perception, memory, and consciousness. Most definitions of relaxation include the cognitive and somatic elements; Davidson and Schwartz (1976) believe that a third, the *attentional* component, interacts with the other two. Depending on the technique, attention may be focused in a manner to restrict awareness as in concentrative meditation, or attention may be passive and receptive as in zen meditation, which results in an openness to all incoming stimuli.

To complicate the picture further, we are reminded to consider the influence of the brain hemispheres. A person suffering with delayed sleep onset insomnia may experience anxiety in the form of racing thoughts, preoccupation, or what Davidson and Schwartz (1976) refer to as "unwanted verbal cognitions" (p. 402). Another person might instead experience visual and spatial images, a disaster fantasy image of cancer invading the body, or of dramatic failure in a public performance. This latter process is associated with the right hemisphere of the brain, whereas the former cognitive process is thought to be left-hemisphere mediated. In the same way, global or diffuse body tension is thought to be right brain, whereas nervous pacing or foot tapping may be associated with left brain, which is dominant for voluntary motor output. The significance of this differentiation lies in the desire to propose a relaxation technique that will have the desired effect on the form of anxiety to be treated, whether it be manifested in a somatic or cognitive mode.

Somatic relaxation is defined as "both reduced peripheral muscle activity and reduced efferent motor commands" (Davidson & Schwartz, 1976, p. 411). In contrast to Jacobson's early hypothesis that the mind is relaxed when the body is relaxed, Davidson and Schwartz maintain that a distinction exists between muscular and mental relaxation: "It appears that one may not necessarily depend on the other, although when both are present, the experience of relaxation will probably be more profound" (Davidson & Schwartz, 1976, p. 412). These researchers have attempted to classify relaxation procedures according to the locus of attentional focus and the active or passive requirements of the technique. They have also proposed a typology of relaxation therapy on the basis of hemispheric specialization; some of this material will be incorporated into the description of techniques. It is recommended, for example, to employ visualization techniques to engage in right hemisphere cognitive system in order to block anxiety originating there. It is hypothesized that the left hemisphere is generally involved with cognitive anxiety, while the right hemisphere is associated more with somatic anxiety.

Based on a thorough literature review and their own findings, Davidson and Schwartz (1976) conclude that relaxation procedures differ in effectiveness depending on whether the tension or anxiety is experienced in a cognitive or somatic mode. They recommend teaching patients to recognize and treat their own kinds of anxiety. Two general principles derived from this theory are as follows:

1. Self-generation of behaviors (including voluntary focusing of attention) in a given mode will reduce or inhibit unwanted activity in that specific mode.
2. Self-generation of behavior in a given mode may, to a lesser degree, reduce unwanted activity in other modes. (Davidson & Schwartz, 1976, p. 432)

Although research is needed to test the theory, the Davidson and Schwartz system brings us closer to the establishment of a theoretical rationale for the use of designated relaxation techniques. A study comparing the effects of progressive relaxation and meditation showed more similarities than differences between the two techniques, but progressive relaxation produced larger decreases in forearm electromyogram (EMG) in response to stressful stimulation and a greater decrease in trait anxiety (Lehrer, Woolfolk, Rooney, McCann, & Carrington, 1983). Meditation appeared to be more motivational for most subjects; they practiced it more and reported being more involved in the technique (Lehrer et al., 1983). Transient anxiety, however, was reported to be elicited more by meditating subjects than by those using progressive relaxation by Lehrer et al. (1983). This finding was contradicted by Norton, Rhodes, Hauch, and Kaprowy (1985), who showed some physiological arousal in both techniques. The latter authors suggest that their results confirm the Davidson and Schwartz (1976) hypothesis described in this chapter's theoretical models, namely that a person's ability to relax is a function of the interaction between somatic, cognitive, and attentional dimensions. It is apparent that more research is necessary to predict the most appropriate technique.

CLINICAL APPLICATIONS FOR RELAXATION TRAINING

Anxiety

According to Wolpe (1973), "the autonomic effects of deep relaxation are diametrically opposed to those characteristics of anxiety" (p. 99). Wolpe's systematic desensitization is a counterconditioning treatment of fear responses. He developed a modified or shortened Jacobson relaxation technique based on his theory that the state of muscular relaxation is incompatible with anxiety. Once the patient is in a relaxed state, the therapist then repeatedly presents the feared stimulus in order to desensitize the fear or anxiety associated with the image. The technique of systematic desensitization, dating back to Wolpe's work in 1948, is now a well-established behavioral therapy, particularly in the treatment of phobias.

The description of systematic desensitization is offered here because this therapy has a body of literature using relaxation. The technique has been used with individuals and in groups. Wolpe (1973) refers to the use of group relaxation and desensitization to treat the common fear of public speaking, and group relaxation training has been successful in treating tension headaches, essential hypertension, sexual problems, and for patients with somatic problems (Johnson, Sheroy, & Langer, 1981; Obler, 1973).

In a population of 16 patients with greater than 15 percent of body burns, Wernick, Jaremko, and Taylor (1981) report using a combination of autogenic training, muscle relaxation, imagery, and skill rehearsal while imagining dreaded treatment of bathing, debridement, skin grafts, and dressing changes. In comparison with a no-treatment control group, the randomly assigned treatment group showed a significant increase in the ability to tolerate and control pain on nine measures, including anxiety, number of pain medication requests, and self and staff ratings. Weinstein (1976) describes a case study of a 10-year-old severely burned child in which two sessions of in-vivo desensitization combining relaxation and imagery resulted in the extinction of screaming and hitting behaviors during bathing.

Reduction of general anxiety has been successful using combined techniques in a healthy population (Charlesworth, Murphy, & Beutler, 1981; Sherman & Plummer, 1973), and in clinical populations of phobic patients and psychotic adults and children (Mathews and Gelder, 1969; Zeisset, 1968). Mathews and Gelder (1969) hypothesize that the lowered state of arousal that they demonstrated in relaxation-trained patients may prevent the autonomic response to the phobic stimuli, or the calm state perceived by the relaxed patient may lead to a change in attitude toward the feared object or situation. Zeisset (1968) showed that significant anxiety reduction in hospitalized psychiatric patients occurred with differential relaxation and desensitization as compared with an equivalent amount of individual attention or the mere passage of time in a therapeutic milieu setting.

Johnson and Spielberger (1968), studying 48 hospitalized psychiatric patients, learned that progressive relaxation training decreased the level of anxiety state or subjective anxiety, but had no effect on trait anxiety (refers to characterological anxiety proneness). Some evidence indicates that anxious individuals take longer to decrease physiological arousal following stimulation than normals (Raskin, Johnson, & Rondestvedt, 1973). Biofeedback or progressive relaxation can teach chronically anxious persons to be aware of internal cues of arousal, thereby reducing stress arousal and possibly preventing stress-related illness. Rasking, Johnson, and Rondestvedt (1973) found that the average training period was 6 weeks, with longer training needed most in those patients who responded initially with intense anxiety. In comparing biofeedback with concentration of muscle relaxation without tension-release in the treatment of psychiatric patients diagnosed with anxiety neurosis, Cantor, Kondo, and Knott (1975) found biofeedback to be superior in producing larger reductions in muscle activity and relief in anxiety symptoms.

Hypertension

Studies as far back as the 1930s have confirmed positive results indicating the reduction of blood pressure readings with relaxation therapy. Benson (1975) suggests that the relaxation response may lower blood pressure by the same action as some antihypertensive drugs that interrupt sympathetic nervous system activity. Relaxation does not replace or substitute for pharmacologic treatment, but may facilitate a reduced dosage or reinforce other medical treatment.

Southam, Agras, Taylor, and Kraemer (1982) report impressive results with their study of 42 patients diagnosed with essential hypertension. After eight 30-minute sessions of progressive relaxation, scanning, and recall, patients trained in relaxation demonstrated significant decreases in systolic and diastolic blood pressure that were maintained throughout the workday, even with stress, and persisted for 6 months after the training. Deabler, Fidel, Dillenkoffer, and Elder (1973) also showed reductions in systolic and diastolic blood pressure both in drug and no-drug groups using muscular relaxation and hypnosis, while the control group showed no significant reduction. Comparing biofeedback with progressive relaxation, Shoemaker and Tasto (1975) conclude that a successful treatment program for hypertension "ought to include training in muscle relaxation" (p. 41). Taylor, Farquhar, Nelson, and Agras (1977) demonstrated a significant decrease in systolic blood pressure (−20.6 mm Hg) in a group of hypertensive patients treated with progressive relaxation and imagery posttreatment of six training sessions, but the effects diminished in 6 months. Taylor et al. (1977) suggest that practice is needed to maintain the positive effects of relaxation training, and they also conclude that relaxation is of particular benefit to patients whose blood pressure is not well controlled by medication.

Insomnia

Insomnia is a single term representing a variety of sleep problems. Insomnia in hospitalized patients frequently represents a chronic health problem and a stressor related to hospitalization; in outpatients sleep disturbances may be a symptom of depression, anxiety, or grief reaction. The literature shows the successful application of progressive relaxation, visual imagery, and autogenic training in the treatment of insomnia (Bernstein & Borkovec, 1973; McCaffery, 1979).

Borkovec, Kaloupek, and Slama (1975) demonstrated progressive relaxation to be superior to relaxation without tension-release exercises, placebo, or no-treatment control, in treating latency to sleep onset (a type of insomnia referring to delay in falling asleep). The effects persisted with improvement at a 5-month follow-up. Improvement was noted even in the counterdemand period early in the training sessions when subjects were told not to expect improvement, in the group using the Bernstein and Borkovec method of progressive relaxation.

Somewhat contradictory findings are reported by Woolfolk and McNulty (1983), who studied 44 subjects and found the visual imagery with attention focusing to be superior to progressive relaxation in reducing latency of sleep onset and fatigue. A significant difference was found at the 6-month follow-up, where again the imagery group showed 66 percent reduction in latency of sleep onset from pretreatment levels, and fewer nocturnal awakenings. These conflicting findings may be explained by the Davidson and Schwartz (1976) theory presented earlier in this chapter, which would suggest that subjects with cognitive anxiety might respond more to the visual focusing treatment, while those with somatic distress might be treated more effectively with a somatic technique like progressive relaxation.

Pain

Pain is a symptom that nurses confront with all too frequent regularity, whether acute or chronic in nature, organic or psychic in origin. Fear, anxiety, and muscle tension may accompany painful procedures or arise in anticipation of such. Nursing interventions aimed at pain relief attempt to alter one or more of these multiple factors that influence the process of pain, because secondary anxiety and muscle tension can cause an increase in the perceived intensity of pain and in the individual's tolerance for pain (McCaffery, 1979).

McCaffery suggests that relaxation alone may not be an effective pain relief measure, but "there is little doubt that relaxation may enhance the effectiveness of many different types of pain relief measures" (p. 143). The literature demonstrates pain relief with the use of relaxation during labor and delivery, for tension headaches, muscle cramping during hemodialysis, acute and chronic pain, postoperative pain, and anticipatory pain in burn patients related to bathing or "tanking" (Clum, Luscomb, & Scott, 1979; Flaherty & Fitzpatrick, 1978; French & Tupin, 1974; Kitzinger, 1979; McCaffery, 1979; Weinstein, 1976; Wells, 1982; Wernick et al., 1981).

According to Stoyva and Anderson, "Studies are virtually unanimous that relaxation procedures act to decrease the amount of headache pain" (1982, p. 752). Biofeedback has been shown an effective tool in treatment and prevention of headaches, although two researchers find that verbally induced relaxation works as well and is less costly (Stovya & Anderson, 1982). Cox, Freundlich, and Meyer (1975), in a controlled study with 27 adults, found biofeedback and progressive relaxation equally superior to placebo in decreasing headaches and frontalis EMG, and noted that additional bonus effect of fewer somatic complaints and less medication.

A very simple Jacobson technique of rhythmic breathing, letting the jaw drop slightly, and keeping the tongue quiet was taught to a randomly assigned treatment group of patients prior to their first postoperative attempt at getting out of bed following cholecystectomy, herniorrhaphy, or hemorrhoidectomy (Flaherty & Fitzpatrick, 1978). Reported incisional pain, body distress, and 24-hour narcotic intake, in addition to decreased respiratory rate, were significantly lower in the treatment group. The Flaherty and Fitzpatrick (1978) findings corroborate other research data that show that patients who use systemic relaxation have less postoperative pain, report feeling more comfortable, and have shorter hospitalizations.

The successful use of mindfulness meditation (see description in "Techniques") was reported with 90 chronic pain patients as part of a stress reduction and relaxation program. Careful testing with a variety of measurement tools showed significant improvement in present-moment pain, negative body image, degree of inhibition of everyday activities, medical symptoms, and psychological symptoms including somatization, anxiety, depression, and self-esteem (Kabat-Zinn, Lipworth, & Burney, 1984). The patients fell into two classes of outcome: those with greatly reduced or eliminated pain in which headache sufferers predominated, and those reporting unchanged pain but improving coping, the latter reported by more low back pain patients. Although the Kabat-Zinn et al. study (1985) was descriptive rather than randomized, it suggests that active participation by individuals in a meditation program, thereby making use of a full range of internal resources, may improve quality of life for chronic sufferers. With the current emphasis on cost effectiveness in health care delivery, it is worth noting that groups of up to 30 patients were easily trained in the above study, with improvement maintained up to 15 months after the training.

In using taped relaxation instructions with 30 open-heart surgery patients, Aiken and Henrichs (1971) found 32 percent fewer postoperative complications than expected in the treatment group. The researchers also identified a decrease in surgical stress factors such as hypothermia, time on the bypass, anesthesia time, and units of blood required, after patients used the relaxation tape four times per day for 3.5 days prior to surgery. It should be noted that a nurse specialist spent 15 minutes to 1 hour daily with the treatment group patients to supervise the exercises and discuss concerns related to the surgery, a practice that may well have affected the study results. These positive findings were confirmed by Wells (1982) who found less postoperative distress in postcholecystectomy patients using a Benson relaxation technique, biofeedback from the rectus abdominus muscle, a shortened Jacobson exercise, and a mental device to decrease distracting thoughts. Although a study like Wells's does not differentiate which technique achieved the results, the accumulated evidence points to usefulness of relaxation techniques in reducing pain by decreasing anxiety, providing a sense of control over the pain, diverting attention, and reducing both cognitive and somatic tension.

Cancer

There is an increasing number of studies in the literature using relaxation techniques for adults and children with malignancies. Burish and Lyles (1981) taught progressive relaxation and guided imagery in a controlled study of patients who had developed negative conditional responses to chemotherapy for cancer. Patients in the treatment group reported feeling less distressed and nauseated and showed less physiological arousal than patients in the control group. These findings were confirmed in an exploratory study with children experiencing distress during venopunctures for chemotherapy (Dahlquist, Gil, Armstrong, Ginsberg, & Jones, 1985) and again in a descriptive study by Hall (1983). The latter describes individualized imagery used with children and parents and family practice sessions for the ill children with their siblings. A poignant example is a description of a visualization of a favorite family vacation taught to a mother with her 5-year-old child experiencing separation anxiety, panic states, and sleep and digestive disorders in response to chemotherapy. The attachment experience in fantasy appeared to enable mother and child to tolerate periods of separation at a conscious level. Hall (1983) states that effective imagery must bridge the gap between the psyche and the soma; he reports that children relate to the "white knights" description of the white blood cells doing battle with the cancer cells.

Dixon (1984) reports a study of 55 nutritionally at-risk cancer patients who were randomly assigned to one of four intervention groups receiving (1) nutritional supplementation, (2) relaxation training, (3) both supplementation and relaxation, and (4) control. Weight gain was greatest for the relaxation group, which was taught deep abdominal breathing, autosuggestion, progressive relaxation, and imagery. Biweekly home visits by research nurses over the 4-month intervention period may have contributed to the positive study results.

Fifteen patients suffering from secondary insomnia due to cancer showed a reduction from 124 to 29 minutes in mean sleep onset latency after progressive relaxation training as compared with means of 116 to 104 minutes in a control group receiving routine care (Cannici, Malcolm, & Peck, 1983). The authors hypothesize that pain distraction or the patient's bed becoming a discriminative stimulus for relaxation may have contributed to the success of this particular study. In summary, it seems clear that relaxation techniques are a valuable tool in reducing the negative conditioning effects of chemotherapy in adults and children, and in improving nutritional status and general well-being.

Others

A variety of other disorders have been treated with relaxation therapy, suggesting widespread use of these techniques. Moore (1965) has shown improvement in respiratory functioning in the treatment of bronchial asthma using progressive relaxation. In a population of 178 clinically depressed patients, McLean and Hakstian (1979) made random assignment to psychotherapy, behavior therapy, drug therapy, or relaxation therapy groups. Behavior therapy was superior at the end of the treatment, although less so in a 3-month follow-up, and progressive relaxation therapy proved in this case to be superior to drug therapy due to high treatment structure, a goal-focus leading to graduated self-mastery, and externalized interest to avoid preoccupation with mood.

A 4-year follow-up of 192 adults with two or more coronary risk factors (i.e., hypertension, elevated cholesterol, smoking habit) demonstrated that the randomly assigned relaxation group reported significant reductions in blood pressures that were maintained after 4 years, while the control group subjects had higher incidence of angina, hypertension, ischemic heart disease, and fatal myocardial infarction (Patel, Marmot, Terry, Carruthers, Hunt, & Patel, 1985). It should be noted that the treatment group met 1 hour weekly for 8 weeks and were taught breathing exercises, deep muscle relaxation, meditation, and stress management, and were loaned a tape recording for home practice. Reductions in smoking behavior noted at 8 weeks and 8 months were not maintained at 4 years. Reductions in systolic and diastolic blood pressures appeared to correlate with subjects who changed their behavioral or cognitive style of coping, i.e. they were cognitively or physically relaxing in their everyday life. The success of Patel et al. (1985) appears to be at least partly related to their approach of teaching a variety of relaxation techniques within a cognitive framework or what Yalom (1975) refers to as meaning attribution, a factor that correlates with highly positive outcome in group work.

An innovative use of relaxation training to enhance memory in the elderly is reported by Yesavage (1984), who taught a group of 39 adults with a mean age of 76 years a standard mnemonic technique to improve face and name recall. Significant improvement on performance measures of name and face recall in addition to decreased anxiety scores were demonstrated by the experimental group receiving relaxation training before learning the mnemonic. Control group subjects actually became more anxious before testing, a finding that is consistent with observations that anxiety interferes with the ability to concentrate. Yesavage points out that the relaxation was an adjunct to the cognitive intervention; it was the synergistic effect of both that appeared to yield the positive results.

A variety of clinical populations of children have been shown to benefit from relaxation training as a means of coping with illness and coping with stress and anxiety in the classroom. These populations include children with cystic fibrosis who had greater ease sleeping and decrease in intensity and duration of hyperventilation episodes (Spirito, Russo, & Masek, 1984) and hyperactive children (Raymer & Poppen, 1985; Richter, 1984). Even young children can learn stress management techniques as demonstrated by LaMontagne, Mason, and Hepworth (1985) with a group of 46 second graders. It appears that children benefit in ways similar to adults in learning means of coping with stress and anxiety, a finding that has important implications for future adjustment and prevention.

Summary

In summary, the literature on relaxation demonstrates repeatedly the clinical usefulness of relaxation therapy. More research is needed to enable the practitioner to discriminate one technique from another and to know when a specific technique is indicated or contraindicated. The techniques of progressive relaxation and meditation have been used more often in controlled studies yielding data in support of their use.

It has been increasingly acknowledged that severe stress weakens the effectiveness of the immune response, thereby increasing an individual's vulnerability to illness. The same stress reaction that protects or prepares the individual for coping can become maladaptive when maintained after the threat has passed. Considerable evidence has accumulated that relaxation therapy can facilitate recovery from stress arousal. We know that nurses work in stressful settings with distressed populations. It seems, therefore, that knowledge and use of relaxation theory and techniques need to be part of every nurse's repertoire. Relaxation is a preventive measure, a treatment, and a coping skill. It is to be hoped that this presentation has provided new directions for health and wellness, for research, and for education.

TECHNIQUES

Overview

Relaxation therapy can be considered a general or umbrella term encompassing a variety of specific procedures. Techniques are used in various combinations, often involving the somatic together with cognitive interventions (e.g., Jacobson's use of muscle relaxation followed by imagery) and mechanisms responsible for the therapeutic effects may overlap. Paul (1969) asserts that relaxation therapy and all standard hypnotic induction procedures share the following characteristics: placing limits on sensory intake, limiting bodily activity, restricting attention, providing narrow stimulation, and altering the quality of body awareness. Both techniques may also include motivational instruction and suggests of relaxation. With imagery, relaxation, and related techniques the patient is aware, participating, and cooperating in the process.

Several different relaxation techniques will be described. For more detailed instructions and variations, excellent manuals and other sources are available (Bernstein & Borkovec, 1973; Clark, 1981; Davis, Eshelman, & McKay, 1982; Jacobson, 1970; Kroger & Fezler, 1976; McCaffery, 1979; Steinmetz, Blankenship, Brown, Hall, & Miller, 1980). Relaxation is a learned skill and requires practice. Recommendations for practice vary, but usually include two or more daily practice sessions for a period of at least 2 weeks, followed by a program of maintenance or advancement. Hillenberg and Collins (1983) demonstrated the effectiveness of home practice assignments, especially during the application period.

Training at home may be achieved through the use of taped or written instructions. The initial training is usually achieved with live instruction since the literature suggests that taped instruction is less successful (Beiman, Israel, & Johnson, 1978; Paul & Trimble, 1970). It is suggested that a present instructor is able to check the muscle relaxation and monitor the appropriate progression according to the client response. In comparing live and taped instructions in hypnosis and self-relaxation, Paul and Trimble (1970) found hypnosis and self-relaxation unaffected by the use of tape, but progressive relaxation was significantly inferior when instructed by tape on all counts except self-report. Borkovec and Sides (1979), on the other hand, reviewed 25 studies of the physiological effects of progressive relaxation training and concluded that subject control over treatment progress appeared to be the more critical factor. This inconsistency may be explained by the importance for some patients, or simply the presence of their therapist.

It is important to try to match and individualize the technique for your particular patient. Someone who has an auditory or kinesthetic orientation may have difficulty with visualization. A psychotic patient may experience increased anxiety with meditation, yet respond well to the structured task of progressive relaxation. A hospitalized patient with a need to exert some control over his or her environment will appreciate learning or choosing a tool to achieve relaxation that can be used independently. Some relaxation techniques, especially those with a meditative passive approach, may increase a patient's awareness of pain or other internal stimuli such as breathing or heartbeat (McCaffery, 1979). It is therefore just as important to recognize when a particular technique is contraindicated as it is to know when to proceed. The following discussion will attempt to provide guidelines for choosing the most appropriate and useful techniques.

Uses of Relaxation Therapy

A literature search identified multiple uses of relaxation with different populations and for a variety of objectives. To summarize, relaxation may be used to (Kitzinger, 1979; McCaffery, 1979):

* Decrease anxiety
* Promote sleep
* Assist in stress management
* Serve as a coping device or skill
* Reduce pain or the perception of pain
* Reduce or prevent the physiological and psychological effects of stress.
* Alleviate muscle tension
* Increase suggestibility
* Combat fatigue
* Energize
* Enhance the effectiveness of pain relief measures
* Warm or cool parts of the body
* Slow the heartbeat
* Decrease blood pressure

Progressive Relaxation

Progressive relaxation is the tool most commonly taught and universally used, both in treatment and in research. The following is a description of a well used and tested model of progressive relaxation. For best results it should be carried out in a quiet setting with indirect lighting. Bernstein and Borkovec (1973) suggest that the patient should be in a reclining chair that completely supports his or her weight and ideally includes arm and leg supports, although any chair or bed may be used. Patients may use the same chair for each practice in order to increase the potential for the setting becoming a stimulus cue for relaxation. The procedure is explained to the patient as a technique involving the tension and relaxation of a certain sequence of muscle groups as well as attention to the feelings related to the tension and relaxation. The patient is instructed to tighten a specific muscle group, hold the tension for 5 to 7 seconds, and then release all the tension. After 30 to 40 seconds of relaxation, the instruction is repeated. Each muscle group is tensed twice, and the sequence is taught and practiced in a given order with 45 to 60 seconds of relaxation in between each muscle group.

Bernstein and Borkovec (1973) use the following 16 muscle groups:

1. Dominant hand and forearm—make a tight fist
2. Dominant biceps—push elbows down against arm of chair
3. Nondominant hand and forearm
4. Nondominant biceps
5. Forehead—lift eyebrows
6. Upper cheeks and nose—squint eyes and wrinkle nose
7. Lower cheeks and jaws—bite down and pull corners of mouth back
8. Neck and throat—pull chin downward without touching chest
9. Chest, shoulders, and upper back—deep breath, hold, and pull shoulder blades back
10. Abdominal region—make stomach hard
11. Dominant thigh—push back of knee into bed or chair
12. Dominant calf—flex foot or pull toes up toward head
13. Dominant foot—turn foot inward, point and curl toes
14. Nondominant thigh
15. Nondominant calf
16. Nondominant foot

During the tensing of muscles, the therapist helps the patient focus on the feelings with statements like "feel the tightness in your muscles" or "notice what the tension feels like." Similarly, during the longer relaxation period, the therapist helps the patient focus on sensations by comments such as "pay attention to the feelings in your arm as it becomes more and more relaxed." Once the 16 muscle groups are mastered, the groups may be condensed into seven and then four groups (e.g., muscles of both arms and hands comprise one group).

Tension can be observed by tightening and bulging of muscles. If the patient has difficulty, the instructions can be altered (e.g., "make a frown" or "grit your teeth"). The patient is alerted to tension in muscles other than those directed by the therapist's repetition of relaxation instructions or by comparison ("are the muscles of your right hand and forearm as relaxed as those of your left hand and forearm?"). Some therapists have clients use hand signals during training rather than words. In a modified form of progressive relaxation in childbirth education, the father-to-be or labor coach is often taught to lift arms and legs and observe and check for tightness or looseness of muscles. It is advisable to evaluate each session with the patient in order to identify problem areas or any untoward symptoms experienced, such as dizziness or cramping. Excessive tightening may cause muscle cramping, and caution is advised particularly in the neck, back, and legs. The therapist may also make note of the patient's own words describing sensations of warmth or calmness and incorporate these into taped instructions or future sessions.

Edmund Jacobson's system of progressive relaxation originally involved 15 muscle groups and extended daily practice sessions for each group. Jacobson's 1970 study has an appendix that illustrates the body positions for each exercise and includes six groupings (arm, leg, trunk, neck, eye region, and speech region). If the patient experiences tension in a particular area of the body, as in the eyes, the therapist could consider using Jacobson's techniques, which combine specific and detailed tension-release directions with visualization.

Once the nurse decides to use progressive relaxation training with a patient, he or she is advised to confer with the patient's physician in order to elucidate any medical contraindications of the procedure. For example, it may be more advisable to strengthen certain muscles than to learn to relax them, as in some cases of low back pain. The nurse may also wish to confer with the doctor regarding medications, since Bernstein and Borkovec (1973) suggest that relaxation skills are more easily learned and more beneficial in the absence of tranquilizing drugs. At other times, learning is facilitated when the patient has been medicated for pain and is comfortable but alert.

Chapter 3 of the Bernstein and Borkovec manual (1973), "Targets for Relaxation Training," describes uses of the tension-release method with case examples as illustrations. I highly recommend the whole manual to anyone interested in working on progressive relaxation with patients, because it guides the practitioner with very specific and practical instructions and advice. The techniques are easily adapted and can be used with all ages of patients from preschoolers to geriatrics, in settings varying from hospitals to community centers, to patients' homes.

My first exposure to relaxation training was in 1960 during a student nurse experience at a tuberculosis sanitorium where progressive relaxation instructions were broadcast over the PA system every afternoon to facilitate bedrest. I have since used relaxation training in teaching preparation for childbirth classes, in treating students and faculty at a college health service (e.g., for test anxiety and migraine headaches), with a variety of hospitalized patients, and am currently using it in conjunction with systematic desensitization for phobic patients. I have learned that your best first subject is yourself (or a compliant family member or friend). The most effective therapists develop their own style or presentation and incorporate any combination of the techniques presented relevant to their own practice.

Variations of Progressive Relaxation

Differential Relaxation

Differential relaxation is a commonly used variation of basic progressive relaxation. It is a technique that reduces tension in muscle groups that are not necessary for a particular task, and therefore leads to comfortable arousal even in stressful situations. Differential relaxation has three advantages (Bernstein & Borkovec, 1973, p. 39):

(1) increased practice and improvement in relaxation skills; (2) lowered arousal throughout the day, which is useful for patients with chronic tension; and (3) relaxation in specific situations.

The patient is instructed to define muscle groups that are essential for a particular activity and those that are nonessential. Homework is assigned that combines the activity with variations in position, activity level, and situation, for example, sitting alone in a quiet room, sitting with others in a quiet lounge, sitting in a noisy cafeteria, sitting while typing or writing, sitting and typing in a busy office with phones ringing and frequent interruptions. The patient is instructed in each situation to identify and release tension in all nonessential muscle groups. The process of recall may be used regularly or when needed.

Recall

Recall is a mental exercise and does not involve physically tensing and releasing muscle groups. Using recall, the patient focuses attention on each of the four muscle groups (arms and hands, face and neck, trunk, and legs and feet), identifies tension, and then relaxes by recalling the feelings of relaxation. It is an advanced technique and useful in generalizing the skill of relaxation to daily life. The therapist collaborates with patients to identify their individual stressful situations, such as board meetings, the dentist's office, or grocery shopping. Recall may be used in these situations, first through imagination and finally in vivo.

Meditation

Meditation is defined as a contemplation or reflection and has historically been associated in most cultures with seeking inner peace and harmony. Although often considered a religious practice or discipline, meditation can be practiced independently by anyone as a means of reducing inner discord and increasing self-knowledge (Davis, Eshelman, & McKay, 1982). With practice, the discipline of meditation has been shown to increase concentration, enhance effectiveness in setting and achieving goals, and improve self-esteem. Moreover, meditation can effectively create a state of deep relaxation in a relatively short time (due to the narrow focus and decreased internal and external stimuli). Metabolic changes during meditation include decreased oxygen consumption, carbon dioxide production, respiratory rate, heart rate, blood pressure, and lactic acid production (Benson, 1975; Davis et al., 1982). Davidson and Schwartz (1976) recommend meditation for patients with low cognitive and low somatic anxiety. In other words, only individuals experiencing generally low anxiety in both modes should choose meditation as a form of relaxation. Meditative techniques alone may not be useful for patients in distress, with pain, or with high anxiety or generalized anxiety.

Benson's Technique

Benson (1975) believes that no single method is unique in eliciting the relaxation response. He suggests four important characteristics of meditation, regardless of particular technique: (1) a quiet environment with decreased environmental stimuli; (2) a mental device—an object to dwell on (work, sound, object, or feeling); (3) a passive attitude; and (4) decreased muscle tonus—a comfortable position, so that minimal musclar work is required. A passive attitude is considered the most essential ingredient in producing the relaxation response. The therapist instructs the patient to "let it happen" and to not be concerned with performance or self-evaluation, which can increase anxiety or tension. The therapist might say "let your thoughts or distractions drift in and out, and return to your focus" (be it a special word or breathing). If the basic components are included, a modification of the more traditional transcendental meditation will still produce the same physiological results. The technique developed by Benson's group at Harvard's Thorndike Memorial Laboratory includes the following set of instructions:

1. Sit quietly in a comfortable position.
2. Close your eyes.
3. Deeply relax all your muscles, beginning at your feet and progressing up to your face. Keep them relaxed.
4. Breathe through your nose. Become aware of your breathing. As you breath out, say the word "one," silently to yourself. . . . Breathe easily and naturally.
5. Continue for 10 to 20 minutes. You may open your eyes to check the time, but do not use an alarm. When you finish, sit quietly for several minutes, at first with your eyes closed and later with your eyes opened. Do not stand up for a few minutes.
6. Do not worry about whether you are successful in achieving a deep level of relaxation. Maintain a passive attitude and permit relaxation to occur at its own pace. When distracting thoughts occur, try to ignore them by not dwelling on them and return to repeating "one." With practice, the response should come with little effort. Practice the technique once or twice daily, but not within 2 hours after any meal (Benson, 1975, pp. 114–115).

Mindfulness Meditation

A recently reported variation and extension of Benson's technique is called *mindfulness* or *awareness meditation*, in which the attention is given to a changing field of objects. Concentration on one object, usually the flow of breath, then expands to include all mental and physical events, that is, all thoughts, sensations, feelings, and fantasies with an attitude of detached self-observation. A notable difference according to Kabat-Zinn (1982) is that mindfulness meditation requires attending to unpleasant and painful sensations when these are present, as opposed to ignoring or escaping from same. Pain might then be simply observed as one separate object in the field of awareness, leading to a reduction of suffering. Kutz, Borysenko, and Benson (1985) suggest that patients with somatization disorder have shown enhanced awareness of bodily sensations and an ability to differentiate underlying rage or fear through the continued use of mindfulness meditation. This technique purports to increase self-awareness, patience, relaxation, and an ability to live more in the present moment.

Mantra Meditation

Many variations of meditative techniques can be found in the literature. Davis et al. (1982) describe ten different exercises; among these are awareness techniques such as focusing on all the sounds in the surrounding environment and in the internal environment, like the breath. Another is a mantra meditation in which a special word or phrase is changed in a rhythm, over and over, while the relaxation deepens and the chanting softens to a whisper or hum.

A typical chant is "Om," meaning "I am," and may be used by an individual or a group, chanting simultaneously. Meditation can occur while quiet or in motion, for example, walking through a place of natural beauty, or swimming laps with a focus on the movement, the rhythm, and the breath.

Contemplation

Contemplation is a form of meditation involving knowledge of an object through sensory attention rather than thought. The patient chooses an object like a stone or a piece of jewelry, looks at it, feels it, and keeps bringing his or her attention back. The goal is to learn to discipline the mind to focus attention on one thing at a time. This exercise, like all the other techniques described, should be practiced daily. A relaxed state is usually achieved within 20 minutes. A more advanced version is the contemplation of a yantra, an image or symbol of something important to the patient, which is visualized with eyes closed.

Breathing

Breathing itself can be an antidote to stress. Breathing normally has a natural rhythm that can be used to soothe, comfort, and achieve relaxation. In yoga, the breath is associated with cleansing and purifying, and with spiritual development. The breath may also signal anxiety, as in the deep and rapid breathing symptomatic of hyperventilation. Patients with a history of asthma, air hunger, or hyperventilation may not find breathing exercises relaxing.

Davis et al. (1982) describe 11 different variations of breathing exercises. A simple one to teach is deep breathing:

> Lie down on the floor with knees bent and spine straight. Scan body for tension. Inhale slowly and deeply, feeling your abdomen slightly rise with each inhalation. Inhale through your nose, and exhale gently through your mouth making a relaxing whooshing sound. Continue deep breathing for 5–10 minutes, focus on the sound of your breath, the gentle rise and fall of your abdomen, and the deepening sense of relaxation. Let other thoughts or distractions pass in and out of your mind. Practice daily and use whenever you feel tension.

Autogenic Training

Autogenic training refers to voluntary self-regulation. A method of silent repetition of phrases such as "my left arm is heavy," it is designed to teach the body and mind to relax. Autogenic training originated with research on hypnosis conducted by Oskor Vogt, a physiologist working at the Berlin Institute during the 1890s. Subjects reported feeling warm and heavy when their tension lifted. Dr. Johannes Schultz, a German psychiatrist, discovered that his patients could create a state similar to a hypnotic trance by concentrating on feelings of warmth and heaviness in the legs. Schultz published his work in 1932 and later Luthe (1970) continued the work using formulas producing an "autogenic state" that seeks to normalize mental and physical functional deviations. Six standard exercises are taught, beginning with feeling heaviness in the limbs to promote relaxation of striated muscle, followed by feeling warmth in the limbs to achieve peripheral vasodilation. The last four commands are "my heartbeat is calm," then "it breathes me," "my solar plexus is warm," and lastly, "my forehead is cool."

Autogenic training has been used to treat asthma, gastrointestinal disorders, high blood pressure, Raynaud's disease, and headaches. It is being increasingly used with biofeedback in stress reduction and at holistic health centers across the United States. Variations may be added to treat specific problems such as "my shoulders are warm" or "my feet are warm." At the end of each session, statements like the following are added: "I feel quiet and I am at ease. I feel serene and still."

Biofeedback

Biofeedback provides information about such processes in the body as muscle tension, blood pressure, heart rate, and skin conductivity. The goal of biofeedback training is to gain control over a body function and then to generalize this knowledge in daily life. If relaxation is the goal, biofeedback is usually done by electromyogram (EMG). Progressive relaxation, imagery, or autogenic training may be used with biofeedback in order to facilitate relaxation. If a patient learns deep breathing and autogenics in order to relax, biofeedback can provide information about physiological muscle relaxation, heartbeat, or blood pressure.

Biofeedback has been used to treat tension and migraine headaches, hypertension, insomnia, spastic colon, epilepsy, anxiety, phobias, asthma, stuttering, and teeth grinding. Alyce and Elmer Green (Davis et al., 1982) pioneered the clinical application of biofeedback in the late 1960s. Three muscles that typically respond to stress are the frontalis (forehead), the masseter (jaw), and the trapezius (shoulder). Any muscles can be monitored, but these three can be measured without much interference from other muscles. Monitoring devices such as the thermograph, which measures minor fluctuations in body temperature, can be purchased for home use. Since skin temperature lowers when one is anxious, using feedback from a thermograph on a finger, hand, or foot can train one to voluntarily raise skin temperature. One way to achieve the desired change is to image or visualize a hot sun beating down or immersing the body part in a hot tub of water. This kind of temperature training has been very successful with migraine headaches and vascular problems associated with cold hands and feet.

Others

Many other techniques have been identified in stress reduction, although little research is available to compare the effects. Clark (1981a) includes centering, massage, baths, humor, dance, music, poetry, and "inner shouting" in her list. I would add exercise, particularly those exercises that create a rhythm in harmony with the breath like walking, running, or swimming.

A very simple technique that I have used with patients is one borrowed from dance therapy and is called *grounding*. It makes use of the physical force of gravity in relation to our connection with the earth. Some people experience feelings of depersonalization or derealization when under great stress or when feeling anxious. They may express feeling "spacy," floating, or disconnected. These symptoms cause further distress or secondary anxiety, raising the question silently, "am I losing my mind?" Depending on the patient's orientation (visual, auditory, or kinesthetic sense) they may report seeing your mouth move without hearing the words, being unable to get "a handle" on things, or seeing the rest of the world as if through a thick glass or fog. The technique is as follows:

> Use a comfortable reclining or resting position. Inhale and exhale slowly. If sitting, focus on the chair accepting the weight of your body. Feel the arms of the chair supporting your arms, feel the chair behind your back and under your seat. Your chair is on the ground. You can depend on the ground to support you. If lying, focus on the bed or floor supporting all of your body weight. If standing, focus on the feet and legs in contact with the ground. Feel the solid ground underneath, taking all of your weight. Point out that the earth is a constant; it is always there for us to lean on, to lend security and support.

Behavioral Relaxation Training (BRT)

A patient's self-report of relaxation does not always corroborate physiological findings; we therefore need assessment tools in addition to our patient's perceptions. Schilling and Poppen (1983) reported in the literature a procedure to train overt relaxed behaviors that they call behavioral relaxation training (BRT). Schilling developed the training when working with learning-disabled boys who did not respond to progressive muscle relaxation. The focus on observable behaviors as opposed to the subjective states of tension and relaxation was far more effective for this population. In comparing the use of BRT with biofeedback, progressive muscle relaxation, and a music focusing control, Schilling and Poppen (1983) report similar improvements on the self-report scale in all four groups.

BRT includes ten instructions, listed below, and can be used by an observant practitioner as a tool for assessing relaxation. The items include:

1. Breathing—relaxed if less than baseline rate
2. Voice quiet—no vocalizations
3. Body—no movement of trunk
4. Head—in midline, supported by recliner
5. Eyes—closed with smooth eyelids

6.   Jaw—dropped with lip parted in center
7.   Throat—no movement or swallowing
8.   Shoulders—sloped and even, no movement
9.   Hands—curled in resting posture
10.   Feet—pointed away from each other, forming 90-degree angle

Schilling and Poppen (1983) suggest that simply demonstrating these ten behaviors can be a quick and effective method of teaching relaxation. They could also be incorporated into other techniques, by adding observations and giving feedback to raise your patients' awareness. Raymer and Poppen (1985) suggest the use of BRT with hyperactive children, particularly in situations where they are likely to display hyperactivity as in a classroom study period. These authors showed results in conjunction with the use of a bean bag chair.

REFERENCES

Aiken, L., & Henrichs, T. (1971). Systematic relaxation as a nursing intervention with open heart surgery patients. *Nursing Research, 20*, 212–217.

Beary, J. F., Benson, H., & Klemchuck, H. (1974). A simple psychophysiological technique which elicits the hypometabolic changes in relaxation response. *Psychosocial Medicine, 36*, 115–120.

Beiman, I., Israel, E., & Johnson, S. A. (1978). During training and posttraining effects of live and taped extended progressive relaxation and electromyogram biofeedback. *Journal of Consulting and Clinical Psychology, 46*, 314–321.

Benson, H. (1975). *The relaxation response.* New York: William Morrow.

Benson, H., Beary, J. F., & Carol, M. P. (1974). The relaxation response. *Psychiatry, 37*, 37–46.

Bernstein, D. A., & Borkovec, T. D. (1973). *Progressive relaxation training: A manual for the helping professions.* Champaign, IL: Research .

Borkovec, T. D., Kaloupek, D. G., & Slama, K. M. (1975). The facilitative effect of muscle tension-release in the relaxation treatment of sleep disturbance. *Behaviour Therapy, 6*, 301–309.

Borkovec, T. D., & Sides, J. K. (1979). Critical procedural variables related to the physiological effects of progressive relaxation: A review. *Behavior Research and Therapy, 17*, 119–125.

Burish, T., & Lyles, J. (1981). Effectiveness of relaxation training in reducing adverse reactions to cancer chemotherapy. *Journal of Behavioral Medicine, 4*, 65–78.

Cannici, J., Malcolm, R., & Peck, L. A. (1983). Treatment of insomnia in cancer patients using muscle relaxant training. *Journal of Behavior Therapy and Experimental Psychiatry, 14*, 251–256.

Cantor, A., Kondo, C., & Knott, J. (1975). A comparison of EMG feedback and progressive muscle relaxation training in anxiety neurosis. *British Journal of Psychiatry, 127*, 470–477.

Charlesworth, E., Murphy, S., & Beutler, L. (1981). Stress management skill for nursing students. *Journal of Clinical Psychology, 37*, 284–290.

Clark, C. C. (1981a). *Enhancing wellness: A guide for self care.* New York: Springer.

Clark, C. C. (1981b). Inner dialogue: A self healing approach for nurses and clients. *American Journal of Nursing, 81*, 1191–1193.

Clum, G. A., Luscomb, R. L., & Scott, L. (1982). Relaxation training and cognitive redirection strategies in the treatment of acute pain. *Pain, 12*, 175–183.

Cox, D., Freundlich, A., & Meyer, R. G. (1975). Differential effectiveness of electromyograph feedback, verbal relaxation instructions, and medication placebo with tension heaches. *Journal of Consulting and Clinical Psychology, 43*, 892–898.

Dahlquist, L., Gil, K., Armstrong, D., Ginsberg, A., & Jones, B. (1985). Behavioral management of children's distress during chemotherapy. *Journal of Behavior Therapy and Experimental Psychiatry, 16*, 325–329.

Davidson, R. J., & Schwartz, G. E. (1976). The psychobiology of relaxation and related states: A multi-process theory. In D. I. Mostofsky (Ed.), *Behavior control and modification of physiological activity.* Englewood Cliffs, NJ: Prentice-Hall.

Davis, M., Eshelman, E. R., & McKay, M. (1982). *The relaxation and stress reduction workbook* (2nd Ed.). Oakland, CA: New Harbinger.

Deabler, H., Fidel, E., Dillenkoffer, R., & Elder, S. (1973). The use of relaxation and hypnosis in lowering high blood pressure. *The American Journal of Clinical Hypnosis, 16,* 75–83.

DiMotto, J. W. (1984). Relaxation. *American Journal of Nursing, 84,* 754–758.

Dixon, J. (1984). Effect of nursing interventions on nutritional and performance status in cancer patients. *Nursing Research, 33,* 330–335.

Flaherty, G. G. & Fitzpatrick, J. J. (1978). Relaxation technique to increase comfort level of postoperative patients: A preliminary study. *Nursing Research, 27,* 352–355.

French, A., & Tupin, J. (1974). Therapeutic application of a single relaxation method. *American Journal of Psychotherapy, 228,* 282–287.

Hall, M. D. (1983). Using relaxation imagery with children with malignancies: A developmental perspective. *American Journal of Clinical Hypnosis, 25,* 143–149.

Hillenberg, J. B., & Collins, F. L. (1983). The importance of home practice for progressive relaxation training. *Behavior Research and Therapy, 21,* 633–642.

Jacobson, E. (1929). *Progressive relaxation: A physiological and clinical investigation of muscular states and their significance in psychology and medical practice.* Chicago: University of Chicago Press.

Jacobson, E. (1970). *Modern treatment of tense patients including the neurotic and depressed with case illustrations, follow-ups, and EMG measurements.* Springfield, IL: Charles C. Thomas.

Johnson, C., Shenoy, R.S., & Langer, S. (1981). Relaxation therapy for somatoform disorders. *Hospital and Community Psychiatry, 32,* 423–424.

Johnson, D. T., & Spielberger, C. D. (1968). The effects of relaxation training and the passage of time on measures of state and trait-anxiety. *Journal of Clinical Psychology, 24,* 20–23.

Kabat-Zinn, J. (1982). An outpatient program in behavioral medicine for chronic pain patients based on the practice of mindfulness meditation: Theoretical considerations and preliminary results. *General Hospital Psychiatry, 4,* 33–47.

Kabat-Zinn, J., Lipworth, L., & Burney, R. (1985). The clinical use of mindfulness meditation for the self-regulation of chronic pain. *Journal of Behavioral Medicine, 8,* 163–190.

Kitzinger, S. (1979). *Birth at home.* New York: Oxford University Press.

Kroger, W., & Fezler, W. (1976). *Hypnosis and behavior modification: Imagery conditions.* Philadelphia: J. B. Lippincott.

Kutz, I., Borysenko, J., & Benson, H. (1985). Meditation and psychotherapy: A rationale for the integration of dynamic psychotherapy, the relaxation response, and mindfulness meditation. *American Journal of Psychiatry, 142,* 1–8.

LaMontagne, K., Mason, K., & Hepworth, J. (1985). Effects of relaxation on anxiety in children: Implications for coping with stress. *Nursing Research, 34,* 289–292.

Lehrer, P. M., Woolfolk, R. L., Rooney, A. J., McCann, B., & Carrington, P. (1983). Progressive relaxation and meditation: A study of psychophysiological and therapeutic differences between two techniques. *Behavior Research and Therapy, 21,* 651–662.

Luthe, W. (Ed.). (1970). *Autogenic therapy: Dynamics of autogenic neutralization* (Vol. V). New York: Grune & Stratton.

Mathews, A. M., & Gelder, M. G. (1969). Psychophysiological investigation of brief relaxation training. *Journal of Psychosomatic Research, 13,* 1–12.

McCaffrey, M. (1979). *Nursing management of the patient with pain* (2nd ed.). Philadelphia: J. B. Lippincott.

McLean, P., & Hakstian, A. R. (1979). Clinical depression: Comparative efficacy of outpatient treatments. *Journal of Consulting and Clinical Psychology, 47,* 818–836.

Moore, N. (1965). Behavior therapy in bronchial asthma: A controlled study. *Journal of Psychosomatic Research, 9,* 257–279.

Norton, G. R., Rhodes, L., Hauch, L., & Kaprowy, E. A. (1985). Characteristics of subjects experiencing relaxation and relaxation-induced anxiety. *Journal of Behavior Therapy and Experimental Psychiatry,*

16, 211–216.

Obler, M. (1973). Systematic desensitization in sexual disorders. *Journal of Behavior Therapy and Experimental Psychiatry, 4*, 93–101.

Patel, C., Marmot, M., Terry, D., Carruthers, M., Hunt, B., & Patel, M. (1985). Trial of relaxation in reducing coronary risk: Four year follow-up. *British Medical Journal, 290*, 1103–1106.

Paul, G. L. (1969). Physiological effects of relaxation training and hypnotic suggestion. *Journal of Abnormal Psychology, 74*, 425–437.

Paul, G. L., & Trimble, R. W. (1970). Recorded vs. "live" relaxation training and hypnotic suggestion: Comparative effectiveness for reducing physiological arousal and inhibiting stress response. *Behavior Therapy, 1*, 285–302.

Raskin, M., Johnson, G., Rondestvedt, J. (1973). Chronic anxiety treated by feedback-induced muscle relaxation. A pilot study. *Archives of General Psychiatry, 28*, 263–267.

Raymer, R., & Poppen, R. (1985). Behavioral relaxation training with hyperactive children. *Journal of Behavior Therapy and Experimental Psychiatry, 16*, 309–316.

Richter, N. C. (1984). The efficacy of relaxation training with children. *Journal of Abnormal Child Psychology, 12*, 319–344.

Schilling, D., & Poppen, R. (1983). Behavioral relaxation training and assessment. *Journal of Behavior Therapy and Experimental Psychiatry, 14*, 99–107.

Selye, H. (1982). History and present status of the stress concept. In L. Goldberger & S. Breznitz (Eds.), *Handbook of stress: Theoretical and clinical aspects*. New York: The Free Press.

Selye, H. (1976). *The stress of life* (2nd ed.). New York: McGraw Hill.

Sherman, A. R., & Plummer, I. L. (1973). Training in relaxation as a behavioral self-management skill: An exploratory investigation. *Behavior Therapy, 4*, 543–550.

Shoemaker, J. E., & Tasto, D.L. (1975). The effects of muscle relaxation on blood pressure of essential hypertensives. *Behavior Research and Therapy, 13*, 29–43.

Southam, M. A., Agras, W. S., Taylor, C. B., & Kraemer, H. C. (1982). Relaxation training: Blood pressure lowering during the working day. *Archives of General Psychiatry, 39*, 715–717.

Spirito, A., Russo, D. C., & Masek, B. J. (1984). Behavioral interventions and stress management training for hospitalized adolescents and young adults with cystic fibrosis. *General Hospital Psychiatry, 6*, 211–218.

Steinmetz, J., Blankenship, J., Brown, L., Hall, D., & Miller, G. (1980). *Managing stress before it manages you*. Palo Alto, CA: Bull Publishing.

Stovya, J., & Anderson, C. (1982). A coping-rest model of relaxation and stress management. In L. Goldberger & S. Breznitz (Eds.), *Handbook of stress: Theoretical and clinical aspects*. New York: The Free Press.

Sweeney, S. S. (1978). Relaxation. In C. Carolson & B. Blackwell (Eds.), *Behavioral concepts and nursing interventions* (2nd Ed.). Philadelphia: J. B. Lippincott.

Taylor, C. B., Farquhar, J. W., Nelson, E., & Agras, S. (1977). Relaxation therapy and high blood pressure. *Archives of General Psychiatry, 34*, 339–342.

Wells, N. (1982). The effect of relaxation on postoperative muscle tension and pain. *Nursing Research, 31*, 236–238.

Weinstein, D. J. (1976). Imagery and relaxation with a burn patient. *Behavior Research and Therapy, 14*, 481.

Wernick, R., Jaremko, M., & Taylor, P. Pain management in severely burned adults: A test of stress inoculation. *Journal of Behavioral Medicine, 4*, 103–109.

Wolpe, J. (1973). *The practice of behavior therapy* (2nd ed.). New York: Pergamon.

Woolfolk, R., & McNulty, T. (1983). Relaxation treatment for insomnia: A component analysis. *Journal of Consulting and Clinical Psychology, 51*, 495–503.

Yalom, I. (1975). *The theory and practice of group psychotherapy* (2nd ed.). New York: Basic Books.

Yesavage, J. A. (1984). Relaxation and memory training in 39 elderly patients. *American Journal of Psychiatry, 141*, 778–781.

Zeisset, R. (1968). Desensitization and relaxation in the modification of psychiatric patients interveiw behavior. *Journal of Abnormal Psychology, 73*, 18–24.

BIBLIOGRAPHY

Alexander, A. B., Miklich, D. & Hershkoff, H. (1972). The immediate effects of systematic relaxation training on peak expiratory flow rates in asthmatic children. *Psychosomatic Medicine, 34*, 388–394.

Coates, T. J., & Thoreson, C. E. (1979). Treating arousals during sleep using behavioral self management. *Journal of Consulting and Clinical Psychology, 47*, 604–605.

Donovan, M. (1981). Study of the impact of relaxation with guided imagery on stress among cancer nurses. *Cancer Nursing, 4*, 121–126.

Edelman, R.I. (1970). Effects of progressive relaxation on autonomic processes. *Journal of Clinical Psychology, 26*, 421–425.

Goleman, D. J., & Schwartz, G. E. (1976a). Meditation as an intervention in stress reactivity. *Journal of Consulting and Clinical Psychology, 44*, 245–466.

Goleman, D. J., & Schwartz, G. E. (1976b). Meditation as an intervention in stress reactivity. *J. of Consulting and Clinical Psychology, 44:3*, 456–466.

Green, K., Webster, J., Beiman, I., Rosmarin, D., & Holliday, P. (1981). Progressive and self-induced relaxation training: Their relative effects on subjective and autonomic arousal of fearful stimuli. *Journal of Clinical Psychology, 37*, 309–315.

Hartman, E. L. (1973). *The functions of sleep.* New Haven: Yale University Press.

Haynes, S. N., Woodward, S., Moran, R., & Alexander, D. (1974). Relaxation treatment of insomnia. *Behavior Therapy, 5*, 555–558.

Hock, R. A., Rodgers, C. H., Reddi, C., & Kennard, D. W. (1917). Medico-Psychological interventions in male asthmatic children: An evaluation of physiological change. *Psychosomatic Medicine, 40*, 210–215.

Ivancevich, J. M., & Matteson, M. T. (1980). *Stress and work: A managerial perspective. Glenview, IL: Scott Foresman.*

Lader, M. H., & Mathews, A.M. (1970). Comparison of methods of relaxation using physiological measures. *Behavior Research and Therapy, 8*, 331–337.

Lazarus, A. A. (1963). The treatment of chronic frigidity by systematic desensitization. *The Journal of Nervous and Mental Disease, 136*, 272–278.

Lazarus, A. A. (1971). *Behavior therapy and beyond.* New York: McGraw-Hill.

Madsen, D. H., & Ullman, L. P. (1967). Innovations in the desensitization of frigidity. *Behavior Research and Therapy, 5*, 67–68.

Masek, B.J., Russo, D.C., and Varni, J.W. (1984). Behavioral approaches to the management of chronic pain in children. *The Pediatric Clinical of North America, 31*, 1113–1131.

Nicassio, P. M., & Brotzin, R. R. (1974). Comparison of progressive relaxation and autogenic training as treatment for insomnia. *Journal of Abnormal Psychology, 83*, 253–260.

Pelletier, K. R. (1977). *Mind as healer, mind as slayer: A holistic approach to preventing stress disorders.* New York: Dell.

Schumann, M. J. (1981). Neuromuscular relaxation—A method for inducing sleep in young children. *Pediatric Nursing, 7*, 9–13.

Shagass, C., & Malmo, R.B. (1954). Psychodynamic themes and localized nuscular tension during psychoterhapy. *Psychosomatic Medicine, 16*, 295–313.

Wadden, T. (1984). Relaxation therapy for essential hypertension: Specific or non specific effects? *Journal of Psychosomatic Research, 28*, 53–61.

Wallace, R. K., Benson, H., & Wilson, A. (1971). A wakeful hypometabolic physiologic state. *American Journal of Physiology, 221*, 795–799.

3

IMAGERY

ROTHLYN P. ZAHOUREK

OVERVIEW

We can hear the sound of our child's voice, see a loved one's face, smell a fish, taste a lemon, feel our feet buried in warm sand, and sense our bodies swimming in cool water. Imagery is mental representations of both reality and fantasy, including not only mental "pictures," but also mental representations of hearing, touch, smell and taste, and movement.

Research and literature on mental imagery as a phenomenon and an intervention have increased markedly in recent years. This explosion in knowledge reflects the movement away from a mechanistic approach to an integrated perception of mind and body interrelatedness. The study of imagery is an important link in this evolution.

The aim of this chapter is to provide the health care giver with both a theoretical and a research background about this rapidly expanding field of knowledge. Guides for implementing imagery interventions and clinical applications comprise the second part of the chapter. This second section discusses these potential uses from a broad historical and research perspective. The final section provides specific forms of intervention. An emphasis throughout is that imagery interventions spring from a strong theoretical base and are utilized within the context of a broader therapeutic relationship and often to augment other interventions.

Definitions

Imagery refers to "quasi-sensory or quasi-perceptual experiences of which we are self-consciously aware and which exist for us in the absence of those stimulus conditions . . ." (Richardson, 1969, p. 2). We recreate and modify reality through the

53

imaginative process. Imagery is also, according to Horowitz, "memory fragments, reconstructions, and reinterpretations or symbols which stand for objects, feelings, or ideas which enable us to create, to dream, and to know" (in Singer, 1978, p. 43).

Through a private, nonobservable inner process involving a neural activity within the brain associated with memory, perception, and thinking, images arise from both internal and external stimuli. These in turn stimulate physiological and behavioral responses. Because physiological reactions occur, imagery is employed as an effective tool in the maintenance of health and well-being and in the treatment of illness and the management of stress and pain.

Imagery occurs spontaneously, during periods of reverie, listening to music, relaxation, or during light sleep. People can also purposefully imagine. Creative ideas and unconscious material surface to stimulate novel solutions to old problems. Occurring often with primary process thinking, imagery may be associated with the emergence of unconscious material. It is not just free floating primary process, however, but is often combined with secondary process thinking, or the use of rational thought and words (Hilgard, 1979, p. 491). Imagery then may be either nonverbal or aligned with the use of words. Words stimulate pictures and the pictures are then interpreted through language and logic.

An important part of psychological development, imagery becomes a familiar mental mechanism in early childhood. It is part of the way people think, remember, and process new information. During ego development attachments are made by forming mental pictures of loved ones (the development of object relations). Following a loss, detachment occurs; mental pictures play a vital role in successful resolution of the grief process (Collison & Miller, 1987).

Many seeking to understand and explain imagery have discussed images in categories. The following describe several methods of classifying images found in the literature (see Table 3–1).

Horowitz's System

According to Horowitz (1983) images can be classified by *vividness, context, interaction with perception*, and *content*. Images vary in intensity and clarity. The most vivid is called the *eidetic* image. The eidetic image ". . . is seen inside of the mind . . . and this seeing is accompanied by certain somatic events as well as a feeling of meaning" (Ahsen, 1977). It is a special, highly detailed image that remains in the visual field as long as attention is directed to it. Other images categorized by vividness include hallucination, pseudohallucination, thought images, and unconscious images.

Images are often related to the continuum of states of consiousness from sleep to wakefulness. These contextual images include hypnogogic or hypnopompic, dream or nightmare imagery, psychedelic, flashback, and flickering images. *Hypnogogic* and *hypnopompic* images are closely related to sleep and are often mentioned in the literature as important states for suggestibility. According to Kosbab, hypnogogic, or *affective*, imagery is preconscious and preverbal thinking in pictures. It is characterized by symbol content, changing thematic scenes, motion, color, autonomy, and meaningful feelings (Kosbab, 1974, p. 283). Hypnogogic imagery straddles the threshold between

Table 3–1.   Classification of Images

Horowitz:
> *Vividness*: hallucinations, eidetic, pseudohallucination, thought image, unconscious images
> *Context*: hypnogogic, hypnopompic, dream, psychedelic, flashback, flickering images
> *Interaction with Perception*: illusion, synesthesia, déjà vu, negative hallucination, perceptual distortion, after-images
> *Content Images*: memory, eidetic, imaginary images, body image, phantom limb, paranormal hallucination, imaginary companion

Achterberg:
> *Perverbal Transpersonal*

Ashen:
> *Image* (I)
> *Somatic Response* (S)
> *Memory* (M)

sleep and wakefulness and resembles dreams. It is like an eidetic image because it is "of such vividness, clarity, and detail that it approaches sensory realism, appearing suddenly to someone in a drowsy state just before sleep" (Holt, 1964, p. 254). Hypnopompic imagery is the similar phenomena that occur just prior to awakening.

Illusion, perceptual distortion, synesthesia, déjà vu, negative hallucinations, and after-images are examples of images that interact with perceptions. When categorized by content, images are called memory and eidetic images, imaginary images, entroptic, body image, phantom limb, paranormal hallucinations, and imaginary companion.

Many of these types of images are familiar to health care workers. It is not the intent to define each of these but rather to sensitize the reader to the numerous frames of reference that exist and have been studied.

Achterberg's System

Achterberg classified images as *preverbal* and *transpersonal* (Achterberg, 1985). In preverbal imagery the imagination communicates directly with tissues, organs, and cells. This kind of imagery evolves prior to the development of language, can be used deliberately and can be measured physiologically. Transpersonal imagery occurs between people and requires channels of information not yet identified by science, falling instead into the realm of shamanic healing (Achterberg, 1985, p. 5).

Ahsen's System (I.S.M.)

Ahsen's scheme breaks down any imagery experience into three components that may occur in any order and are always present: (1) imagery or imagination (I); (2) somatic response or feeling (S); and (3) meaning (M) (Ahsen, 1986). This system illuminates the complexity of any imagery experience in a simple easy-to-remember format, I.S.M.

Images are not isolated pictures or representations but are related to each individual's specific experience. For example, if you ask a group to visualize a house, each member will visualize something different. Some may visualize a house from childhood while others a house of their dreams. These images, furthermore, will tend to be integrated into more complex response patterns that are dependent on the stimulus and will generate a variety of emotional and physiological responses (Sheikh, 1983, p. 85). Some, for example, will smell specific odors associated with the house while others will see the house in their mind. Individuals will react physiologically in varying ways as well. When visualizing "house" one person may have an increased pulse rate, another increased perspiration, and yet another an increase in relaxed diaphramatic breathing.

How the caregiver understands imagery as a concept will influence its therapeutic use. Imagery is not a simplistic mental event but rather one that is multidimensional and develops throughout the life span. The following theoretical foundations illustrate several approaches to the understanding of the imagery phenomena. These include: (1) images as part of the operations and development of the self, and (2) structural and functional theories.

THEORETICAL FOUNDATIONS

Images: Mediators and Interpreters of Self and Others

What is the "self"? This question has plagued both philosophers and psychologists through time. Self concept is the sense, knowledge, and beliefs one has about oneself. This sense is shaped and continuously modified by internal images that begin development first in infancy as a primitive composite sense of self. This self consists of a sense of one's body (body image) and several psychologically oriented self images.

Imagination provides a bridge between the different levels of the self (Pelletier, 1977, p. 251). It mediates between past experience and future projections. This process creates a unique and personal perception of any present experience.

While not always conscious, images can be the mode through which we perceive and regulate our daily lives. A positive self image is important for health. The following theoretical frameworks explain self image, body image, and the impact of past and future images on a sense of self.

Self Image

Karen Horney (1950) described a concept of self that includes three separate images: the *real*, the *actual*, and the *idealized self*. These self image constructs are explained so they can be applied to assessment and intervention.

The *real self* image consists of ideas and feelings about how we see ourselves. Horney believes that this real self is the "unique alive force" within us all. It includes the "clarity and depth" of real feelings, thoughts, wishes, interests, and special talents (Horney, 1950, p. 17). This real self incorporates a sense of integration as well as the faculty of spontaneous self-expression. The real self is what we see when we do an honest appraisal of ourselves, including strengths, weaknesses, faults, and talents. The real self grows toward realization if neurotic strivings toward unrealistic perfectionism (the "search for glory") do not interfere. The imagination can play a crucial role in this process by either fueling the development of neurosis or promoting growth (Horney, 1950).

The *actual self* is the sum total of the individual's life experiences, the perception of those experiences, and the image we have of how we think others see us.

The *ideal self* image is what we want to become—how we picture ourselves having reached our goals and aspirations in any sphere of our lives (work, relationships, etc.). The unrealistic strivings and idealized pictures of how we should be that become compulsive and joyless can also be classified with the ideal self. To those utilizing behavior therapy, cognitive therapy, hypnosis, and hypnotic techniques the ideal self is utilized therapeutically to help an individual set goals and develop hope that these aspirations can be realized. Developing a realistic ideal self image counters the sense of immobilization common in depression by enhancing an individual's sense of potential power, enjoyment, and ability to control negative thoughts.

These self images affect how we live, feel about ourselves, and relate to others, as well as how we formulate goals for the future. They are the basic elements of mental health.

Body Image

Body image is a mental and kinesthetic representation of how we look, how we move, and how we believe our appearance is perceived by others. It is a "hypothetical construct of usually unconscious images that operates as a specialized, internal, analog data center for information about the body and its environment" (Horowitz, 1983, p. 23). We have a sense of different parts of our bodies and how well-integrated those parts are, or are not, as well as how those body parts relate to the environment. Our body image can be accurate, distorted, or disrupted. We probably consist of a series of body images that have altered over time. Some body images are preconscious, while others are entirely unconscious. When a body image becomes conscious, the vividness will determine its type. For example, when an individual anticipates an unusual task, *thought images* generally occur about how that individual will use his or her body. Sensory and kinesthetic imagery might also augment this perception. If an injury takes place, the person may experience *pseudohallucinatory images*. When this happens, the person experiences his or her body as it once was and may have difficulty adjusting. When stress, sleep deprivation, drugs, or overstimulation cause altered states the individual may experience a sense of dissociation or an *out-of-body experience*. *Phantom limb* is another imagery experience related to both disrupted body image and neurophysiological remembrance of the amputated part.

Nurses work with these concepts daily as they prepare patients for surgery, counsel overweight or underweight individuals, help patients cope with the loss of a body part or limb, or work with patients who have little self-confidence because of the way they look.

Past and Future Images

A smell stimulates a series of remembrances and influences our present state. A mental picture of the future helps us make decisions. Most of us can visualize the house where we grew up, a special birthday, the first day of school, and so on. The images may be distorted, fragmented, or illogical, but when explored and understood in the therapeutic process, images communicate thematic meaning.

These past, present, and future images affect our experience of today. They stimulate feelings and provide valuable information for making both simple and more complex decisions. Through images of the future, we "practice" what it will be like to have a family, to work a different job, or to experience the death of a loved one. These times of reverie are all associated with pictures, sensations, and feelings, and they influence how we make major life decisions. We might tell a prospective bride or groom, for example, to visualize what it might be like to live with a person for 20 years. This can provide a realistic picture for when the potential partner is no longer young or as attractive, prompting a healthy evaluation of the other's more important personality attributes.

These images (self, body, past, and future) all reflect the "self." In working with people, each image needs to be considered, although at one point one aspect may be emphasized over another.

Self Development Through Images

Imagery plays an important role in the psychological development of *object constancy*, in which the image of an absent other or a missing external object substitutes for its physical presence. As the child develops, these internal representations provide comfort during separations. In this context, new experiences are also interpreted. When a new experience or object is encountered, similarities and differences with past images are determined and an interpretation is made. If object constancy is developing normally the child matures, secure in the past, and is capable of learning and enjoying new encounters.

Margaret Mahler (1975) in her classic work on object constancy described the role of internal mental representations in phases of separation-individuation that occur when very early symbiosis is resolved. During the symbiotic phase (1 to 5 months) the infant perceives himself, his mother, and the world as indistinguishable and as one. The separation and individuation phase (5 months to 2½ years) is divided into four subphases that move the individual along two tracks: (1) the *separation* or the intrapsychic awareness of separateness, and (2) the *individuation*, which is a sense of unique identity (Mahler, 1975, p. 292). The four subphases as they relate to the imagic process are reviewed as follows:

Differentiation: (5–9 months) Through visual and tactile exploration of the mother's face and body the infant begins demarcation of self and other. A primitive body image develops and pleasure related to self and outside world is experienced and expressed in close proximity to mother (Mahler, 1975, p. 289).

Practicing: (9–14 months) The infant moves away from mother and crawls or walks back. The environment is explored but the sense or image of mother cannot be maintained for long.

Rapproachment: (14–24 months) Mother is rediscovered as a different individual; a beginning sense of separateness along with vulnerability is experienced. Mother is held somewhat longer as a mental image. The toddler wants to be both away from and close to mother. This can result in intense reactions, i.e., temper tantrums or the rapproachment crisis (Mahler, 1975, p. 292).

Consolidation of Individuality and Emotional Object Constancy: This phase begins toward the end of the second year and can be open-ended. Separation of self and objects are clearly differentiated; mother is separate and at the same time is an internal representation (image) in the child's mind that can be maintained over long periods of time.

Tower (1983) described the role of imagery for the toddler. Because the child actively explores, the environmental and interpersonal experiences stimulate psychophysiological development. As the child accommodates to social reality, new objects and experiences are mentally matched with old ones. By 2 years, the child has stored images of how things are, or should be, what he is or is not, and what he can or cannot do (Tower, 1983, p. 233). Imagination develops as the child creates new images and matches them to the old. Images become familiar and result in pleasure; "On the one hand the affect of interest fuels differentiation; on the other, joy motivates integration" (Tower, 1983, p. 227). Imagining becomes more elaborate and important in the child's life. The child projects symbols onto objects (a block becomes a truck) and later the whole body becomes involved and role playing develops (arms become wings). Still later the child becomes able to create alternate selves (the child becomes a king or queen) (Tower, 1983, p. 230).

Imagery evolves into an adaptive mechanism, which depends on positive, supportive, and shared early experiences. Good role models for imitation, imaginative playmates, enough time to be alone, stimulating toys, and a space free of interference enhance this process. According to Tower, as these adaptive processes develop, the child gains the following:

1. Increased discrimination between self and others,
2. A broadened sense of the world as full of emotional and social possibilities,
3. Increased sensitivity to the physical expression of feeling from others, an awareness of his or her own feelings, and an articulated body concept,
4. Broader avenues for emotional expression,
5. High levels of self-control, positive affect, coping abilities, self-confidence, and security,
6. High levels of concentration and an ability to be alone.

Play is an essential ingredient for developing an imaginative child. Imaginative play and fantasy are further carried into adult life as an adaptive mechanism for dealing with stress and conflict and for pleasure. Erik Erickson explains that dramatic or imaginal play is an "infantile way of thinking over difficult experience" (Erickson, 1940, p. 130).

Additional values of imaginary play are listed by Peller (1971). Some of particular relevance are:

* imitating a loved one,
* mastering a fear by assuming a role,
* assuming the role of a loser and gaining mastery over that experience,
* "incognito indulgence,"
* clowning to exaggerate mistakes and embarrassments,
* deflecting or exaggerating vengeance,
* anticipating retaliation,
* furnishing a happy ending to a traumatic experience, and
* creating magic (Peller, 1971, p. 115).

Pediatric nurses are particularly familiar with encouraging imaginative play to alleviate fears and anxiety with children. Allowing children to play with surgical masks, bandages, syringes, and other tools used in a hospital to helps their adaptation to illness and hospitalization. In adulthood we see these functions of imagination in fantasy role playing. This is an important function for health in enabling the individual to mentally enact or experience future events. In making important decisions this is usually positive; in anticipating surgery it might be a liability needing more positive direction by the caregiver.

In summary, Tower explains that imaginative children (and I would add adults) are sought out because of their good ideas, lower aggression, and better abilities to cooperate. They are more open, more flexible, and more empathic. Furthermore, they develop an intrinsic set of standards and are better able to learn from the experience of others by organizing and integrating diverse stimuli (Tower, 1983, pp. 239–242).

Structural Theories

Introduction

Over the years structural, chemical, neurological, metaphorical, and philosophical theories have been used to explain the imagination and the imagery process. Both research and theory development have been closely allied with the study of learning, memory, and perception, and finally with therapeutic endeavors such as behavior therapy, hypnosis, and cognitive approaches. The following section describes various structural and functional theories related to imagery. These theories have been utilized to understand both the nature of thinking as well as the imagination.

In the last ten years, as theorists have struggled to define and explain the process of imagery, theories have become increasingly complex. In the early days of theory development, Paivio (1971) emphasized that the brain stored information in two ways: pictoral and verbal. He demonstrated that concrete words were better remembered than abstractions, and pictures (images) were recalled better than words. Pictures and words are the primary tools of thinking. Imagery can, however, also be preverbal and the depot of primitive, as well as sophisticated, thought.

The brain is a "health care system" regulating the body's responses to change (Schwartz, 1978). The environment places demands on an individual and, depending on those demands, some body functions will be activated while others may be suppressed; homeostasis will be maintained until the demand is so great that tissue damage results.

Negative stresses set up a negative feedback loop, and the individual experiences discomfort and pain, forcing the brain to reconsider and modify its direction. The adaptive brain, according to Schwartz, learns from its mistakes and develops a capacity to anticipate the needs of the organism more efficiently. A healthy brain monitors many of its thoughts and images to promote health and well-being.

Triune Brain

Margaret Armstrong, a prominent nurse scientist, studied the nature of brain function, pain, and altered states of awareness. In 1977, she discussed brain anatomy and function in relation to altered states of consciousness and the truine brain theory. The triune brain theory, developed by Paul Maclean (1975), describes a tri-level organization of the brain. The inner level, incorporating brain stem activities, generates reflex functions and survival activities. It is the primitive part of the brain. The intermediate level, or limbic system, is concerned with emotions and behavior. Imagery, as well as other states of altered awareness, supposedly emanates from this level. The top level, the cortex, is responsible for higher conscious functions, e.g., verbal activities.

Laterality

Right and left brain laterality theory has created great interest in recent years and deserves discussion regarding the definition and understanding of imagery. Research supports cerebral asymmetry; one half of the brain controls the opposite side of the body. Sounds to the left ear, images to the left visual field, and sensation on the left side of the body are projected to and interpreted in the right hemisphere.

The right hemisphere, associated with imagery, is linked to visual/spatial tasks of mental rotation of objects in space and detection of tactile patterns. It is considered the locus of emotions and nonrational thinking, fantasy, curiosity, intuitive thought, and feeling. This right hemisphere processes information in a nonlinear, diffuse manner; it reasons inductively and is experience-centered. Nonverbal images, e.g., body image, are lateralized in the right hemisphere (Achterberg, 1985, p. 122). The right hemisphere is holistic, and diverse emotional stimuli including reactions to speech, music, and facial expressions are likewise interpreted here. It is now believed that images and strong emotions are connected and have a direct effect on the autonomic nervous system (Achterberg, 1985).

For right-handed, and most left-handed people, the language and logical processes occur in the left hemisphere. (Only 15–35 percent of left-handed people are right hemisphere-dominant for language.) The left hemisphere is the logical, sequential language processor. It is linear, focused, deductive, and analytically goal-directed. The left is also discriminative, intellectual, and rational. Because our interest is imagery, the right-sided functions are emphasized in this book, but adequate function of both sides is important for healthy behavior and thinking.

Some emotional states seem to be associated with hemisphere interferences and each hemisphere participates in utilizing different emotions. Patients receiving electroconvulsive shock therapy (ECT) had depressive moods following left-hemisphere intervention; following right-hemisphere disturbance from ECT, euphoric or indifferent moods occurred (Robertson & Inglis, 1977). Other research shows that the right side is associated with negative emotions while the left is associated with positive. The implications of this are unclear; whether there are unilateral or bilateral hemispheric effects on emotions continues to be controversial. Even with the controversy, most agree that emotions are primarily within the realm of the right hemisphere (Ley, 1983, pp. 256–257).

In understanding the relationship of emotions, the imagic process, the stimulation of the autonomic nervous system (ANS), and hemispheric involvement, Achterberg hypothesized that a message must undergo translation by the right brain into nonverbal, or imagerial, terminology before it is interpreted by the autonomic nervous system. Before the images can be interpreted into meaningful logical thought they must be processed in the left hemisphere. If the connections between the hemispheres are severed, then images would continue to affect the ANS and physiology but without the ability to be logically interpreted (Achterberg, 1985).

Considering that most of our therapeutic methods involve the use of words (left brain) to help people identify their feelings (right brain) and to explore creative ways for solving problems (right brain), it seems logical (left brain) to develop right-brain activities (emotions and creativity) through methods that include a right-brain approach (imagery, hypnosis, and so on).

Nursing has been cognizant of these right-brain functions of late with the increasing emphasis on diagnosing and treating human cognitive and emotional *responses* to health and illness and with the advent of innovative techniques in nursing practice that are aimed at promoting health, comfort, and self growth. Such techniques recognize the influence of inner processes on health and healing. Mechanical and chemical approaches are no longer sufficient.

Horowitz's Modes of Thought

Horowitz described three modes of cognition: imagic, lexical, and enactive (Horowitz, 1978). The *imagery mode*, he explained, adds a "sensory character to ideas and feelings" and allows for the continual processing of information in dreams, fantasies, and images. It originates from the right side of the brain and includes visual, auditory, tactile-kinesthetic, and olfactory-gustatory subsystems and is primary process thinking. This imagic mode is represented by introjects such as body image, self image, the relationship between self and objects, and specific fantasized images of others such as an omnipotent parent.

The *lexical mode* originates from the left side of the brain and encompasses language and verbal abilities. Words and grammar describe objects and enable us to think in several languages and to represent ideas mathematically. This mode integrates diverse phenomena into language.

The *enactive mode* is motoric and behavioral, originating in the motor cortex and limbic system. It expresses itself through skeletal and visceral muscles, in gestures, facial expressions, postures, psychosomatic symptoms, and nonverbal behavior.

According to Horowitz, "In ordinary wakeful thought, these modes blend richly; reflective awareness seldom distinguishes one from the other" (1978, p. 38). A balance of these modes is essential for health. When one mode is especially dominant, the other two can be encouraged to develop. For example, a highly verbal individual states he understands all aspects of his problem but cannot seem to change either his behavior or feelings. He can be encouraged to form images and to become aware of how his body expresses the problem. For a full description of these modes and their use in therapy see Singer and Pope's book, *The Power of Human Imagination* (1978), or Horowitz (1983).

The Holographic Model

The holographic model developed by Pirbram (1982) and explored further by Epstein (1986) proposes that the brain is like a hologram in how it receives, transmits, and stores information. Because each nerve cell has the capacity of stimulating several other neurons biochemically at the synaptic cleft, and many thousand synapses are possible, nearly an infinite number of patterned associations are possible. Like a hologram, when any part is stimulated the whole is reproduced. For example, a word can trigger a set of sensations; a smell stimulates a whole visual memory set. This model has been based on sophisticated statistical and mathematical theories as well as neuroanatomy and physiology.

The metaphor to holographic photography is fascinating when thinking about images in our brains; the storage of the image is everywhere at once and has no space/time dimension (Achterberg, 1985, p. 133). This model helps explain such phenomena as phantom limb; it is not necessary to have a limb to sense it, it is only necessary to have once had that limb, or to have thought about having that limb. The holographic model also exlains our abilities to recreate complex memories of past events. The memory is not only a visual picture but also a set of feelings and physiological responses. The memory itself will stimulate neurotransmitters and subsequently hormone production and finally the complex related physiological response.

Functional Theories—The Process and Physiology

The Biochemistry

Several biochemical processes are associated with both thinking and imagery. These will be discussed only briefly and the interested reader will be referred to more in-depth physiology sources. Images stimulate biochemical reactions in the brain that then affect several master glands that in turn influence feeling states and behavior. Neurotransmitters (serotonin and dopamine) relay information from the hypothalamus to the pituitary. The pituitary then stimulates release of hormones from such glands as the adrenal and the ovaries. Epinephrine, norepinephrine, and acetylcholine are secreted by adrenals. Often associated with the fight or flight response, these chemicals influence thinking, feeling states, and actions. Images can cause these chemicals to be secreted and utilized; this process then continues to influence feeling states, imagery, and behavior. Levels of these neurotransmitters and hormones and the brain's ability to produce and utilize them have been implicated in studies of schizophrenia, manic depressive illness, stress, depression, and anxiety, as well as other disorders including alcoholism and eating disorders.

In addition to the transmission of impulses, the chemicals of comfort and pleasure have been studied and written about in relation to imagery. The neuroregulators (endorphines and enkephalines) are the body's endogenous opiates. Endorphines are influenced by the imagination and are responsible for such phenomena as the placebo effect, the proliferation of T-cells, and subsequently the adequate functioning of the immune system (Achterberg, 1985, p. 140).

The Array Theory

The *array theory* (reviewed in Pinker & Kosslyn, 1983) associates imagery with active, visual long-term memory. An array-like medium in the brain serves visual perception, mimics coordinate space perception, and provides for active memory. Just as the matrix of computer memory is composed of elements whose organization and distribution produce a picture on the computer screen, selective, activating cells in the "array" depict objects in the brain. Researchers hypothesize that the process occurs in the following manner. An external sensation or internal memory is believed to elicit three kinds of processes: (1) a "mind's eye" process (similar to pattern recognition in visual perception) interprets patterns depicted in the array and associates these patterns with symbolic descriptions; (2) a process fills the array with contents from long-term memory files; and (3) the data are shifted from cell to cell producing mental rotations, size scalings, and translations, etc. (Kosslyn, 1981). The "pictures" people report are generated by this system. Trehub enlarged on these theories and explained the action of the array on a neurocellular level (Trehub, 1977).

P. J. Lang's Bioinformational Theory

P. J. Lang (1979) proposed that images are both structural and functional coding systems and processes in the brain. When a stimulus is perceptually processed, it is done through sensory detection of that stimulus. That sensory processing is accompanied by visceral and somatomotor activities as well as subsequent behavior. The kind and quality of somatovisceral response will be related to the specific content of the image. For example, imagining warm sand on your body will increase body temperature and cause diaphoresis. This process is influenced by the following: (1) the person is instructed to image something, (2) the person receives directions about what is to be imaged, and (3) the person is instructed to be active in the imagery situation (Mast, 1986, p. 119).

The brain, furthermore, contains biochemical networks (or memories) about how stimuli are related to responses. Responses are related to past experience and are not only motor and behavioral but also physiological as well. To illustrate, a person runs from a previously feared object or experience. A simultaneous physiological arousal will occur with mental images of a feared outcome. Remembering and visualizing a fearful experience will also produce the same physiological arousal. Mast, in reviewing Lang's work, stated that while many of the findings on stressful imagery and physiological correlates are equivocal, for some the repeated memory or the stereotyped processing of emotionally stressful situations might result in chronic pathophysiological responses, e.g., hypertension (Mast, 1986, p. 120) This theory might also explain why imagery can successfully override past conditioned responses and counter some pathophysiologic conditions.

Epstein's Theory: Imagery Is "Real"

A contrasting, nonphysiological theory on imagery appeared in a recent issue of *Advances*. Epstein (1986) described imagery as "real" although it cannot be perceived by others. Imagery is not metaphorical; "the imaginal experience is always concrete, directly apprehendable by the senses. The senses at work here are the same ones we use to ascertain the external world-seeing, hearing, tasting, touching, smelling, kinesthetic and proprioceptive perception" (Epstein, 1986, p. 23). Senses are purposefully turned inward for the purpose of exploring inner processes in imaginal activities. In this context, the image happens outside linear time, is objectless, and can only be approximated in words. As a novel experience, it often has no precedent or antecedent. The image is plastic, boundless, and infinitely changeable. This mental image is like a three-dimensional hologram and like a hologram a part contains the whole. Understanding this system depends on inductive, rather than deductive reasoning. As Epstein explained, "Image is the interface between the concrete world of everyday reality and the non-substantial world that informs it . . ." (p. 28). The image therefore helps us know ourselves and our possibilities and directs us toward another reality, "the reverse of everyday reality." Images ". . . are not produced by the brain but rather are an inner reality amenable to discovery through the functioning of the brain and inward turning senses" (Epstein, 1986, p. 28).

Epstein related these theories to how imagery affects healing. Movement towards entropy—disorder and disease—takes place in physical time. Healing—the movement toward integration and "negentropy"—is reversing time and an experience unattached to physical and spatial dimensionality. Only human beings have the capacity to use the imagination to turn from the physical to the intangible freedom from terminable time. This is "the power consciously to will an instant of freedom" (Epstein, 1986, p. 27) and is how imagery can heal.

Summary: Theory-Based Research

David Marks (1983) summarized some of the characteristics and theories about imagery. Both imagery and perception share conscious awareness and are represented by the same neural pathways and networks in the brain; both are based on the "encoding of features extracted from the environment using scan paths that vary in degree of consistency across subjects" (Marks, 1983, p. 124). This encoding takes place through a neural network from which conscious images are formed. A higher nonconscious level acts as an executive of the abstraction and controls the activity of image production.

Interest in brain biochemistry and physiology is stimulating research in what many consider the last and most important frontier in both science and psychology. We know now that thought, memory, learning, and perception all relate to the firing of neurons and the ability of neurotransmitters to either conduct messages over preexisting pathways or form new ones. The quality and quantity of experience and thought depend on the amount of these chemicals as well as the blockade or enhancement of the transmission and the areas of the brain that are activated or deactivated. Biochemical discoveries and hypotheses are being generated from the study of pain (endorphins and enkephalines), addictions, depression, and schizophrenia, as well as the study of perception and memory. It is not the intent to review all of this work but to introduce the concepts and to encourage the reader to keep abreast of new data as they emerge in the literature.

Numerous recent studies demonstrate that not only does the imagination arise from physiological processes, but it in turn stimulates physiological responses. For example, imagining a lemon stimulates salivation (Barber, Chauncey, & Winer, 1964); heart rate increases with arousing imagery (May & Johnson, 1973); and changes in electromyograms occur from active visualization (Craig, 1969; Jacobsen, 1929; McGuigan, 1971). In addition, the following alterations in physiological functions have been demonstrated in response to directed imagery: pupillary size increased and decreased (Simpson & Pavio, 1966); blood glucose increased; gastrointestinal activity decreased; gastric acidity altered; skin temperature modified; and formed skin blisters (Barber, 1961, 1969, 1978). Studies in biofeedback are replicating these results and applying them in clinical situations to treat such disorders as migraine headache and hypertension.

Pinker and Kosslyn (1983) summarize the recent research on imagery and identify two trends. First, theorizing is increasingly precise and generalizable. The imagination is now known to be correlated with biological functions and the architecture and evolution of visual systems in higher mammals. The computer, holographic photography, and geometry as well as cellular biochemistry are current popular models for understanding human cognition (Finke & Kosslyn, 1980; Sheppard, 1978; Trehub, 1977). More controlled research is showing us where images are generated, through which cells, and by which chemicals. New theories explain how we transmit an external representation through the eye (a sense organ) into a three-dimensional representation that can be recalled at will, directed, or emerge spontaneously in the imagination.

Gary Schwartz (1978) emphasizes that as we are learning more about the structure and neurophysiology of the brain we must remember that the whole is greater than the sum of its parts and that a *qualitative* rather than *quantitative* understanding is necessary. Perception is dependent on the organization of the brain and on its chemical reactions as well as on still undiscovered mechanisms. The probabilities for unique expression are endless. Whether measured on an electroencephalogram (EEG) or through complex biofeedback equipment and computers, we know people imagine and thereby change their attitudes, physiology, and the course of their lives.

CLINICAL APPLICATIONS

Introduction

Many researchers believe images are goal-directed and motivate behavior. Individuals act more on the basis of what they visualize will happen than on considering the actual consequences. A patient, convinced he will die in surgery, is plagued by mental pictures of his grieving relatives standing around his coffin. These images are resistant to modification even when the probabilities are intellectually discussed and he receives emotional support to express his feelings.

Images alter the perception of words and elicit a specific emotional response, and ". . . images make it possible for us to preserve an emotional attitude towards absent objects" (Sheikh, 1983, p. 393). Such rememberings precipitate either positive or negative consequences. Remembering how it feels to be with a loved one during separations provides comfort, while visualizing the details of a negative encounter with an old friend causes pain.

Numerous opportunities for planning and executing interventions exist when considering this model. For example, when a young man was scheduled for a liver biopsy, the procedure was explained and the wrapped biopsy tray placed beside his bed. Hours later he was seen in rounds. Highly anxious and fearful, he sat perspiring and stiff watching everyone who passed his room. To him "biopsy" meant suspected cancer and in his mind's eye he saw painful, mutilating procedures and a lonely death. While waiting he visualized the hidden equipment as huge needles, probes, knives, and other instruments of torture. Klinger (1980) explains that images are stimulated not only by words such as *biopsy,* but also through other cues in the environment (e.g., the wrapped tray). With multiple stimuli the individual is therefore more likely to experience a full range of emotions, which in the example above, was to the patient's detriment rather than benefit.

Daydreams and imagery may produce results without interpretation, intellectual understanding, or insight. Imaginary rehearsal promotes responses that are then generalized to future reactions and behaviors. The young man above could have been asked to picture what the word *biopsy* meant and to imagine what was in the covered pack. Unrealistic, detrimental images could then be changed to beneficial ones through education; for example, an uncovered pack could have been shown to him. With guided imagery he might see himself experiencing the procedure with comfort, relaxation, and a minimum of stress. This likewise could help him anticipate how he would react if the results were positive or negative.

Meichenbaum (1978) explains that clinically, imagery procedures generate: (1) the feeling of control gained by monitoring and rehearsing various images; (2) a modified inner dialogue that precedes, accompanies, and replaces maladaptive responses or behavior; and (3) mental rehearsal of various responses and reactions that increases coping skills. The implications for nursing and health care are obvious.

Applications

As adjunctive treatment for many physical and psychological disorders, as well as for the enhancement of healthy functions, imagery techniques have numerous applications. Medical conditions for which imagery has been helpful include stress reactions, acute and chronic pain states, cancer, arthritis, diabetes, burns, obesity, and immunologic disorders. Imagery techniques have also been used in natural childbirth, stress management, enhancement of the immune system's function, preoperative teaching, and health education. Among the primarily psychological disorders whose treatment imagery may facilitate are phobias, anxiety states, alcoholism and substance abuse, habit disorders, acute and chronic depression, and acute crises. Outside the range of pathology imagery techniques serve many functions that can promote good health and well-being. Some such functions that have been augmented by the imagic process are decision making, conflict resolution, increasing coping skills, stress management, and promoting self growth. All these do not exhaust the list of implications for nurses and other practitioners.

Interventions that utilize imagery include autogenics, hypnosis, guided affective imagery, biofeedback, behavioral therapy, cognitive therapy, desensitization, death imagery, eidetic psychotherapy, guided imagery, inner dialogue, inner advisor technique, psychosynthesis, rational emotive therapy, oneirodrama, and psychoanalysis.

IMAGERY: HISTORICAL PERSPECTIVES*

The use of the imagination for health and healing is as old as human history. It has been well known to and an integral part of the practice of shamans (folk healers) from primitive cultures. Modern medicine is now exploring the processes used by these healers to learn more about what seems to precipitate spontaneous cures and remissions.

Prior to Descartes' separation of the mind and body, this holistic tradition permeated beliefs about humankind and health and illness care.

Mental images were believed to have powerful influences on bodily functions;

> When an image became an obsession it pervaded the body, bound up the heart, clutched at the sinews and vessels, and directed the flesh according to its own inclination. Soon its essence became manifest in its victim's complexion, countenence, posture and gait. Imagination had greater powers of control than sensation, and thus anticipation of a feared event was more damaging than the event itself . . . (McMahon, 1976, p. 181)

In general medicine this became an outmoded belief as more sophisticated theories developed from anatomic studies and the acceptance of the germ theory. Mental processes were seen as less influential than the environment or physiology in the development of disease.

---

*For a history of imagery and healing dating back to the beginning of human experience, see Achterberg, 1985.

In psychology and philosophy mental processes were always of interest. Prior to 1900 Freud used imagery extensively. In fact, he abandoned the use of hypnosis to work with imagery, believing it was a process more under the patient's conscious control. Freud pressed on a patient's forehead and told him or her to observe the images that appeared when he relaxed the pressure. Patients saw, in rapid succession, scenes that were related to their central conflict. These scenes frequently surfaced spontaneously and chronologically. Around 1900, he abandoned this procedure for the more verbal forms of psychoanalysis and free association, emphasizing that his therapy now was oriented toward eliminating these pictures. He also believed imagery was a form of resistance to free association and a defense against unacceptable impulses. He also believed imagery was primary process thinking and therefore primitive. Many speculate today that Freud may have been overwhelmed with the amount of primitive material he was able to obtain from both hypnosis and imagery. Words, secondary process, or rational thinking provided a safety valve to a patient's potential flood of emotion.

Other analysts, however, like Carl Jung, recognized the symbolic nature of hypnogogic imagery and its value in exploring early childhood memories and pre- and unconscious material. The disagreement between Jung and Freud about imagery continues to influence both theory and practice of psychotherapy. Whereas Freud regarded imagery as primitive, Jung believed imagery was an essential creative part of the psyche, which should be utilized and developed. As Jung explained, the

> psyche consists essentially of images. It is a series of images in the truest sense, not an accidental juxtaposition or sequence, but a structure that is throughout full of meaning and purpose; it is a "picturing" of vital activities. And just as the material of the body that is ready for life has a need of the psyche in order to be capable of life, so the psyche presupposes the living body in order that its images may live (Jung, 1960, pp. 325–326).

Imagery then was a means of perceiving mind-body unity. Fantasy (encouraged by classical analysts), according to Jung, was of the individual's own invention and remained on the "surface of personal things and conscious expectation." "*Active imagination*," a Jungian psychotherapy technique, utilized images because they had a life of their own, developing within the framework of their own logic, particularly if conscious reason did not intervene.

Because of Freud's rejection and the popularity of behaviorism, the study of imagery in the United States was ignored from the early 1900s to 1960, but a strong tradition of exploring its relevance in psychology persisted in Europe. Pierre Janet (1898) encouraged patients to substitute one image for another. This helped hysterical patients who had "idées fixes." Alfred Binet (1922) encouraged his patients to converse with their images while in an introspective state.

Other than pre-Cartesian clinicians, Eastern practitioners, and indigenous healers, the first modern therapeutic approach based largely on imagery was developed in Germany in the 1930s by Carl Happich (1932). He expanded Binet's induction of images by encouraging muscular relaxation, passive respiration, meditation, and predetermined scenes to stimulate the patient's imagery process. He speculated that a "meditative zone" existed between the conscious and unconscious mind where un-conscious productions mature and become visible to the mind's eye. Others, at this time, began to practice imagery with relaxation techniques. Schultz and Luthe (1959) developed "autogenic training," which combined both systematic relaxation and the encouragement of either spontaneous imagery or guided imaginary scenes.

While imagery and hypnosis had lost favor with Freudian analysts, many other analysts in Europe continued imagery therapy. One approach developed in Italy was called *psychosynthesis*; it was considered holistic and eclectic, employing imagery to reorganize the total personality. Many of these early clinicians believed conflict resolution occurred in the imaginary state and, when the solution solidified, it was ex-perienced in a physiological sense of balance and harmony.

In the United States, imagery techniques were resurrected when in the 1960s, the moratorium was lifted on the study of inner experiences. Researchers outside the mainstream of psychology in engineering psychology studied sensory deprivation and sleep. Neuropsychological research and the "third force," or the humanistic revolution, all stimulated the study of imagery as a viable aspect of the human personality and a tool for therapy.

Within the framework of humanistic psychology, inner psychic experience be-came paramount. Greater access to various states of consciousness and the expansion of one's imaginative potentials were goals. The drug culture of the 1960s and 1970s contributed both positively and negatively. Imagery experiences were sought first through chemical means (hallucinogens) and later through natural means as a method to understand one's self, monitor bodily functions, and to live more meaningfully. Ges-talt and cognitive therapists also incorporated the imagery process. Assertiveness train-ing, inner dialogue, experiential focusing, and Beck's (1970) conditioning effect of repetitive fantasy, or cognitive affective restructuring, all depended on various forms of visualization to change a maladaptive affect or behavior.

Behavior therapists used systematic desensitization (Wolpe & Lazarus, 1966) that depended on both relaxation training and visualization to cure phobias and fears and alter physiological anxiety states. Hard data on the efficacy of relaxation and imagery to monitor body processes were being generated and continued to grow with the ad-vent of biofeedback.

Hypnosis once again intrigued practitioners from analytic, behavioral, and physiological orientations, and they began to explore those theories and to integrate the techniques into both practice and research.

The study of brain laterality, as well as brain chemistry, has expanded imagery research; it is now common knowledge that the brain and the body are intimately con-nected and interdependent.

Uses of Imagery in Health Care, Nursing, and Nursing Research

Pat Heidt, speaking at the second annual conference on Imagery and Fantasy Process in 1978 (Achterberg, 1985), stated that creative imagery serves three main functions in working with patients in a general hospital:

1. Imagery helps the caregiver form a close relationship with a patient in a short period of time.
2. Imagery facilitates the expression of feelings about being in the sick role.
3. Imagery enhances the patient's belief in his or her ability to participate in the healing process (Achterberg & Lawlis, 1980, p. 49–50).

Nurses' interest in the imagery process has flowered over the last few years. This increased attention has occurred, in part, as a reaction to the increased mechanization of care and the desire to provide noninvasive and often nonchemical support to patients (clients) seeking help for physiological or psychosocial difficulties. Nurses are implementing imagery techniques with adults, children, and the aged (Griffin, 1986). In recent years, chapters in textbooks (McCaffery, 1979; Snyder, 1985), articles, scholarly papers on the science of imagery (Mast, 1986), and research reports have extensively covered the use of imagery in specialty practice areas.

These beginning nursing research efforts confront a consistent problem of evaluating a highly personal experience and the effect of that experience. Numerous techniques and approaches have been investigated using a variety of standardized as well as nonvalidated instruments. Frequently the perceived positive and growth-enhancing effect of imagery is reported in the research; this qualitative rather than quantitative phenomena is not easily measured.

At present research has not advanced sufficiently to determine absolutely what kind of imagery works best with which kind of patient, symptom, or with which diagnostic category. The wealth of clinical case descriptions and attempts at controlled clinical studies are growing and adding to the scientific basis for utilizing specific techniques and processes.

Regarding the scientific aspects of imagery, Achterberg states,

In order for the imagination to move from its current adjunctive role in medicine . . . two factors must be in place: (1) a body of solid, convincing research must be generated to support the role of the imagination in total health; (2) those who heal in the imaginary realms must also understand and speak the language of the scientist in order to establish credibility and be embraced in the total medical community" (1985, p. 75).

Nursing research is beginning to contribute along with other disciplines to that end.

Application: The Imagery Process

Imagery intervention techniques occur within a process. This process can defined according to the following models: (1) assessment (preparation and diagnosis), (2) intervention (treatment and mental rehearsal), and (3) evaluation (feedback and planning) (Achterberg, 1985, p. 76). Highly individualized and based on an adequate assessment of the client (patient), the process is built on a thorough understanding of the problem or disease, the client's coping skills, past and present, the client's method of processing information (representational systems) (Knowles, 1983), and an assessment of the client's unique imagery system.

The following guidelines have been devised from a variety of sources: (1) Achterberg and Lawlis's (1980, pp. 63–70) work with patients suffering from illnesses such as cancer, diabetes, and arthritis; (2) Margo McCaffery's (1979) guidelines for using imagery in her classic book on pain, and (3) a system devised by the author. This process can be applied to both ill and well populations.

I. Assessment
   A. The Illness/Problem: Diagnosis
      1. Assess the symptom(s)
         a. Collect as much data from patient, chart, and coworkers as possible
         b. Obtain a clear description of the symptom(s) from the patient. Encourage metaphor, i.e, "does it have color and/or shape, is it like an animal or a plant?" Have patient draw pictures of self with the illness or symptom
         c. Determine what makes the problem better and what makes it worse
      2. Assess disease imagery
         a. Vividness
         b. Strength/weakness
         c. Ability to persist
      3. Assess treatment imagery
         a. Vividness
         b. Strength or weakness
         c. Potential effectiveness
      4. Assess person's potential ability to fight disease
         a. Strength/weakness of image
         b. Symbolic nature of image chosen
   B. Assess the Self System
      1. Body image
         a. Body integrity
            1. Is the body perceived as intact or in pieces?
            2. Is the body boundary closed and protected or open to growth or assault?
         b. Personal sense of space and privacy
         c. Internal body image
            1. Has a part been removed or added?
            2. What is the meaning of that part?
            3. How severe is the sense of loss and disruption?
      2. Self image
         a. Real self image
            1. "What kind of person are you?"
            2. "What are your strengths and weaknesses?"
            3. "What important roles do you play?"
            4. "What personality characteristics do you value, e.g., independence, strength?"
         b. Actual self image
            1. "How do others see you?"
            2. "How would your family describe you?"

          3. "How would your friends describe you?"

          4. "How would your coworkers describe you?"

    c. Ideal self image

          1. "What would you like to be when you grow up?"

          2. "What kind of person do you want to be?"

          3. "What ideals do you strive to obtain?"

          4. "What are your goals?"

  4. Assess representational systems

    a. How the person processes information—auditory, visual, kinesthetic—by:

          1. predicates; e.g., "I see what you mean"

          2. eye movements; e.g., up indicates visual process

  5. Assess person's experience

    a. Past experience images

          1. "What have you experienced in the past that might relate to this? What pictures or sensations do you experience when you close your eyes?"

          2. "What images occur to you just before you go to sleep or just before you awaken?"

          3. "What traumatic experiences have you had in the distant or recent past?"

          4. "What past experiences of friends or family might be coloring this present one?"

    b. Future images

          1. "What does this current experience mean to your future as a person, a family member, a worker?"

          2. "What do you picture for the future, both immediate and distant?"

    c. Present images:

          1. "What are your day and night dreams like?"

          2. Draw a picture of:

            a. Your illness

            b. Yourself

            c. Your situation

            d. Your treatment process

II. Implementation; Treatment

  A. Prepare the Patient for the Procedure

    1. Explain the procedure to the patient

    2. Make sure you have the patient's attention; call by name, stand in clear view, touch, use clear words and neutral voice.

    3. Establish rapport; determine what the patient needs prior to getting relaxed; e.g., help the patient into a more comfortable position

    4. Explain how relaxation and imagery has helped patients with the same problem and can help him or her as well

    5. Explain the importance of the patient's cooperation and willingness to participate

6. Emphasize that the patient has ultimate control over the process
7. Explain that the technique will increase comfort and be pleasurable
8. Explain that the procedure will augment and not replace other regimens that are being followed to help
9. Answer any questions

B. Choose a Technique
1. Learn what imagery the patient has found helpful
2. Decide whether imagery should be oriented away from or toward the body. (Sometimes this is done on a trial-and-error basis. Patients in pain sometimes react better when the imagery is distracting and away from the body, e.g., going to a relaxing place. Other times the patient may find it useful to go into the pain, explore it, modify or redirect it)

C. Initiate the Technique
1. Ask the patient if he or she would like to close his or her eyes
2. Have the patient take a nice relaxing breath
3. Guide patient through a scene or allow patient to develop by self. (If patient is in acute distress guiding them seems to be most effective)
4. Do a relaxation technique such as muscle relaxation, calm, restful, rhythmic, monotonous speech
5. If describing a scene, paint a clear and elaborate picture using all of the senses—sight, smell, touch, and taste
6. Ask the patient to add anything that will increase pleasure and relaxation
7. Use the suggestion that as relaxation increases so will comfort and a sense of security and control
8. Give the patient feedback that he or she is doing well. Comment on obvious signs of relaxation even if the change is slight
9. Use a soothing voice, monotone and occasional repetition

D. Termination
1. Count from 1 to 5. Tell the patient to open his or her eyes, feeling alert, and rested
2. Wait until the patient seems alert and oriented

III. Evaluation and Continuation
A. Get feedback from the patient about the experience
B. Explain how the patient did well and how motivation and cooperation helped the process
C. "Was there anything that could have made the experience better?"
D. Encourage the patient, if appropriate, to practice: take deep breaths, relax, visualize a pleasant scene or return to former pleasant places, experience pleasant sensations in a part of the body that is easily accessible such as a finger or hand
E. Teach family and other staff to encourage the patient and to work with him or her in a similar fashion
F. If indicated, plan a new image based on your evaluation
G. If appropriate, make an agreement to work with the patient again

Several aspects of this process need highlighting. First, a *cooperative relationship* defines the process. The patient has ultimate control over imagination and can choose whether to share the content with the caregiver. Second, caregivers are encouraged to focus on their own internal images and to comment on those to the patient. For example, "Mr. Jones, you look as if you have a dark cloud over your head today. How are you feeling?" In one instance a patient who had chronic pain mentioned he liked science fiction movies. I asked him if he had seen Walt Disney's movie *TRON*. He had not, but had seen articles about the special effects. I explained that the picture of the characters with brightly colored energy flowing through their bodies kept occurring to me as we talked. He liked the image, and we used it later in the session. Third, the process is evaluated with the patient and modified to suit the patient's needs. Fourth, other individuals can assist the patient with visualization. Fifth, other techniques can be added to this process. For example, biofeedback tension measuring devices, tapes of relaxation procedures, or relaxing music or sounds might be used. Patients can also be asked to draw pictures of themselves, their pain, or their symptoms. Through these projective techniques data can be obtained to more fully understand the patient, implement the imagery technique, and then evaluate the results. According to Achterberg (1985) this technique produces valuable diagnostic information as well as clues for therapeutic intervention. Sixth, these techniques are fun for both the patient and practitioner. Often images stir pleasant memories or are humorous, and laughter enhances physical and mental healing. Seventh, the patient's sense of control is emphasized. Whether or not imagery will be used, in what situations, by which technique, and how the image might be changed are all the patient's prerogative. Eighth, teaching the patient imagery techniques when he or she is as comfortable as possible aids in promoting an early success and continued motivation. Ninth, varying the "painted picture" and developing all representational systems keeps the process fresh and stimulating.

Finally, some patients state that their imagination is poor or that they seldom think in pictures. The clinician can then ask about their daydreams and what they experience while reading an involving book or listening to music. To further convince them they do have the power of imagination the following brief exercise may help:

> Imagine a big bright yellow lemon. Notice the skin of the lemon. Sometimes it's rough and sometimes quite smooth. Feel the skin. Sniff the lemon. Cut the lemon in half and notice how the color is much lighter than the outside skin. Also notice the incredible organization of the inside. There are sections and within the sections tiny pouches of succulent juice. Sniff the lemon again and then squeeze it. Taste the sour juice!

Usually people picture the lemon, pucker and salivate when the fantasized juice is tasted.

Whenever an imagery exercise like the one above is used the nurse must remember the patient's language abilities, level of intelligence, and attention span. If a patient speaks poor English or has an organic impairment, simple words, short phrases, and simple scenes are in order. Likewise when the attention span is short using a brief exercise helps. An imagery exercise can enhance concentration but if signs of restlessness or distraction occur the technique should be changed or stopped and the experience discussed. If an image is chosen that elicits discomfort then it should be modified. For example, experiencing an imaginary beach and ocean for an individual who fears water can be upsetting and counterproductive.

This process implies a long-term relationship, but on many occasions nurses must intervene in a crisis. The process can be applied in an abbreviated form and the nurse needs only know the rudimentary facts that have precipitated the emergency. Briefly explaining that a technique exists to reduce stress will generally focus the patient's attention and enlist cooperation. Similarly, reassuring the patient that any essential knowledge will be communicated fosters confidence and indicates that the nurse will be an available advocate. The nurse can ask how the patient generally copes with stress and then explain the value of distraction or deep breathing. Telling the patient to take a deep breath (if appropriate medically and the patient is able), and then instructing him or her to go to a very relaxing imaginary place are usually the first steps after establishing rapport. In a crisis the nurse should be directive, painting a detailed picture and encouraging the patient to experience the scene through as many senses as possible. Suggestions of peace, calmness, relaxation, and security augment the effectiveness. All of this can be accomplished in a relatively short time and integrated into routine procedures.

In a longer-term relationship, or in situations where problems are more complex, the nurse needs to evaluate the patient more extensively.

Specific Applications: Examples of Therapeutic Imagery

Images That Promote Relaxation

Many images are described in the literature that promote relaxation and reduce stress. A person might be encouraged to experience a visit to a favorite vacation spot, the mountains, a fantasy place, or his or her most relaxing spot at home. Drawing on a past positive experience or reminding a patient that he or she has experienced previous relaxing times vivifies the scene. If a beach is visualized (a popular image for many people), the nurse instructs the patient to "see" the color of the water and the sky, to notice the "smell" of the salt air, and to "hear" the birds singing and the surf hitting the shore. A sense of relaxation is encouraged and other bodily sensations mentioned such as "feel the warm sun on your back and how the sand feels as it slips through your toes." Using words such as "relax", "comfort," "peace," and "soft" all develop sensory responses to the images.

An anxious burned patient experiencing pain and unable to sleep went, mentally, to a lush green meadow. The sky was blue with puffy clouds that made interesting shapes. The mountain air was fresh and crisp, the birds were singing and in the distance a brook babbled. She rested on grass that felt like green velvet puff pillows, and watched the clouds drift by. Warm and secure, her cares were left behind. Relieved and less tense, she slept.

Altering Physiological Responses

An individual can imagine increased blood flow bringing warmth and healing to a particular area of the body. Mental hand warming techniques have been successful in biofeedback to aid people with migraine headaches and with other peripheral vascular dysfunctions (Maslach & Zimbardo, 1972; Sargant, Walters, & Green, 1973). Encouraging anxious patients to imagine regular waves of the ocean gently hitting the shore or a metronome clicking can reduce hyperventilation and rapid pulse rate. A man with hypertension visualized the movie character *ET* with his warm glowing chest. This pulsing image promoted warmth in his own chest and allowed his pulse rate to decrease and become more regular.

Healing Imagery

Imagery is often associated with the promotion of healing. Increasing blood flow to an area and sending "healing energy" throughout the body or to a specific part are imagery techniques now known to the lay population. When using such imagery the nurse needs to be cognizant of the pathologic process. For example, an inflammation might be increased if warm increased blood flow is sent to a part. If a pain is of a constricting spastic nature, then relaxed open rhythmic images should be utilized. Healing images can indeed be helpful but the nurse must be aware that unrealistic expectations in the patient might promote failure if dramatic results are not forthcoming. Positive future images activate positive physical changes, enhance healing, and are often associated with surprising remissions or spontaneous cures. These positive images are strengthened by positive self-talk or inner dialogue such as, "I can feel good, vital, and happy."

The Simmontons (1978) are well-known for their imagery work with cancer patients. Their patients, who also received radiation, chemotherapy, relaxation techniques, and often psychotherapy, were encouraged to visualize their immune system as actively attacking the cancer cells and destroying them. White knights attacking evil or good monsters eating up bad ones are images that have been associated with their dramatic reports of remissions and cures with some of their patients.

Achterberg and Lawlis described several healing images with cancer patients, those with burns, diabetes, arthritis, heart disease, and so on. They developed a physiological framework supporting the healing qualities of imagery (1978). Epstein (1986) also described both a theoretical framework and case examples of imagery and healing.

Ego Building

Often we use images to describe feeling states and views of self, for example, "I'm limp as a dishrag; mad as a hatter; wiped out; drained; empty; in a black mood; happy as a clown." Ego-building techniques develop positive self images and promote self-confidence. These techniques developed by Hartland (1966) encourage the individual to see himself or herself as a growing, strong, and capable person. The image of an internal rose developing from a tightly closed bud to a beautiful glorious flower graphically aids in ego development. Picturing oneself as strong, capable, and motivated to change using self-affirmation techniques is, likewise, an ego-building technique (Brallier, 1982; Clark, 1981; Gawain, 1978; Knowles, 1982). As in positive thinking techniques, the individual is encouraged to say to himself or herself such things as "I can accomplish my goals"; "I am competent"; "I am a dynamic loving person." These self-affirmations, said repeatedly to the self in a relaxed receptive state, operate like positive suggestions and therefore potential for realization is greater. Similarly picturing oneself in the desired way can profoundly impact behavior. Athletes now imagine themselves performing with grace and competence. These techniques have been so successful that many major teams now incorporate visualization techniques as part of training.

Visualizations are also important in assertiveness training. A young woman needed to tell her boss that he was working her too hard. She feared his anger and rejection. Through imagery she was able to see herself dressed in her favorite outfit, feeling confident and relaxed. In her mind she heard herself asking assertively for what she wanted. She pictured her boss looking nervous and tired sitting in his office in his underwear. Vulnerable in the fantasy, he granted her whatever she wanted. She continued to feel strong and relaxed and confident, silently giggling to herself about his compromised position.

Pain Reduction

People naturally use imagery to describe their pain. It's like a "hot poker," "a vice," "raging fire," "icy grip," or "twisted stretched rubberbands." These are cues to the clinician about how to modify the patient's experience. A woman metaphorically described her headache as like a bright, cold, jagged lightning bolt that shot through her head. Following brief relaxation, she imaged that lightning bolt first straightened, then softened, and finally warmed to a rosy color. Her headache was gone.

Imagery to Explore Inner Processes

Imagery can be used to understand a therapeutic issue more fully, to explore unconscious motivations, to clarify a conflict, develop insight, or solve a problem. These techniques vary in style and often are more indirect, allowing the patient's fantasy to dominate. An individual might explore the house where he or she grew up or a special event in the past. He or she might fantasize several future outcomes, experimenting with what feels best. These techniques are often used in psychotherapy by experienced psychiatric nurses and other therapists but can be used by other specialists to aid clients (patients) in decision making and problem solving.

Redreaming a dream may enhance the psychotherapy process. A young woman in psychotherapy for depression and inability to make choices about her life related this dream: "I'm in a cave and I'm being prepared for an important rite. You are there and so are several old cronies. I'm being wrapped in a shroud, and I'm going to be submerged in water to go through a tunnel; it's because of all my hard work that I can go through this ritual." During the therapy session, she redreamed the dream. Feeling she was being reborn, the dream was a positive rather than frightening experience. Following this, she began to make major decisions about her work and her relationships. Soon, she terminated treatment feeling she could continue her growing process on her own.

Because imagery stimulates inner processes and elicits emotional reactions, it can augment problem solving (Samuels & Samuels, 1977). The inner dialogue technique described in detail by Clark (1981) (and in her chapter in this book) allows for mental conversations arguing both sides of an issue. An inner advisor might be chosen to be a creative and wise mediator. New insights emerge about the problem and its solutions. Likewise, mental pictures of potential results propel one toward the decision most desired.

A patient, contemplating chemotherapy, which was predicted to extend his life for two years, could not decide if he wanted to put up with the side effects for some extra time. Visualizing the potential outcome of both decisions helped him make a decision that seemed right to him and he had no regrets. He contemplated what he could do with two extra years even though he would occasionally be very ill. He wanted to see his son graduate from college and hoped to finish some long-term business commitments. He elected to have the chemotherapy.

Behavioral Rehearsal

Behavioral rehearsal is often used to treat phobias and other anxiety states. While in a relaxed state, the individual imagines experiencing a dreaded event; relaxation is coupled with the event rather than anxiety and subsequently the phobia is eliminated (Wolpe, 1966). The individual is then able to act without the fear. This can be useful for patients anticipating surgery or other distasteful procedures, for students with test anxiety, and for individuals who want to change an old habit or behavior. It is often used by athletes, public speakers, and actors to practice an event or performance in a relaxed state.

A middle-aged divorced woman had been a good tennis player. She was dating for the first time since her divorce and had recently met a man who played tennis. Although she wanted this to be a shared activity, she was anxious because she hadn't played in years. Their first match was a disaster. Her therapist encouraged her to mentally sit down and see a small card file. She looked through it until she found the card marked "tennis." The card was magical in that when it was placed in a projector, she would both see and feel herself playing tennis as well as before. In the relaxed imaginary state she played beautifully. That afternoon she played an adequate game and both she and her new boyfriend were delighted.

Death Imagery

Imagery has also been utilized successfully with patients and families anticipating a death. Imagining the future provides meaning and a sense of potential and actual control to both the ill person and those anticipating the loss. This is described by Collison and Miller (1987) as facing the dual task of "identity preservation" and "relationship redefinition." Negotiating these tasks for both the dying and the family increases the likelihood of successful grief resolution, and the work is augmented by the imagery process.

Anticipating one's own death through imagery has been used with terminally ill patients, their families, and with those who work with them to sensitize everyone to the dying patient's experience. Often visualizations (and imagery exercises) encourage a behavioral rehearsal of tasks needed to be completed in the final stage of life. Such tasks may included disengagement from others and completion of unfinished business. Often visualizing the actual dying is experienced as a peaceful and pleasant transition to an afterlife. Such imagery experiences can promote calm and comfort. (For detailed case examples see Chapter 8).

Storytelling and Metaphor to Enhance Imagery

Most of us grew up learning from stories. The messages in fables, myths, fairy tales, and stories create powerful images and metaphors for the rigors of growth and development. These stories have for centuries guided people through the complexities of growing up, including building interpersonal relationships and dealing with such painful experiences as sibling rivalry, poverty, and the death or loss of a parent.

Well-known characters become examples or role models for everyday living. Dorothy in *The Wizard of Oz*, for example, always had the power to alter her plight and return home; she simply needed to recognize she had it at her "toe tips" and how to use it effectively.

Metaphors promote learning through subtle images and have numerous implications in health care. Changes of the seasons can be used as metaphors for describing individual growth and development. Nurturance can be discussed by describing the care that plants and pets need; wound cleaning can be metaphorically described as similar to weeding a garden, the weeds like dead tissue needing to be removed to allow for new growth.

Sharing with a patient an actual or made-up story about someone in similar circumstances can enhance the positive image and expectation that he or she will experience the same results. The 12-step self-help programs such as Alcoholics Anonymous structure their meetings around telling stories (qualifications). Members identify with the storyteller's experience of the disease as well as the process of recovery. Possibilities expressed in the story bypass censorship of conscious control and exert a powerful, yet subtle, impact. Therapeutic stories can be brief and simple or more complex. The possibilities for tales, analogies, and metaphors are endless and can be developed through both the patient's and nurse's repertoire of experience.

The use of therapeutic stories is a unique and creative opportunity for providing intervention for numerous problems and situations. Recently several books have been published that provide clinical examples and theoretical bases for these techniques (Barker, 1985; Wallis, 1985) (see Chapter 5).

SUMMARY

Many imagery techniques are available and relevant to all areas of health care. While initially the process may take longer than administering a pill or referring the patient to another caregiver, imagery can enhance efforts to solve complex problems by maximizing the patient's involvement and sense of control. The major changes created by the imagery experience can be long-lasting in contrast to a pill whose effectiveness may be limited to a few hours.

From childhood to death we are a kaleidoscope of images that lighten and change as we, our environment, and our perceptions move and are manipulated. These images color how we feel about ourselves, our bodies, our past, present, and future. Images can foster self-esteem and a sense of well-being or precipitate a lack of self-confidence, depression, and anxiety. Our images are not fixed, but dynamic, plastic, and responsive to internal and external changes. Like holding and turning the kaleidoscope, we can focus and change images at will, creating an infinite number of patterns.

Imagery is a naturally occurring phenomenon that in the hands of a caring and well-trained practitioner can be harnessed as a powerful therapeutic tool.

REFERENCES

Ahsen, A. (1977). Eidetics: An overview. *Journal of Mental Imagery, 1*, 5–38.

Achterberg, J. (1985). *Imagery in healing: Shamanism in modern medicine*. Boston: New Science Library.

Achterberg, J., & Lawlis, G. F. (1978). *Imagery and disease*. Champaign, IL: Institute for Personality and Ability Testing.

Achterberg, J., & Lawlis, G. F. (1980). *Bridges of the body mind: Behavioral approaches to health care*. Champaign, IL: Institute for Personality and Ability Testing.

Armstrong, M. (1977). Use of altered states of awareness in nursing practice. *AORN, 25*, 49–53.

Barber, T. X. (1961). Physiological aspects of hypnosis. *Psychological Bulletin, 58*, 390–419.

Barber, T. X., Chauncey, H. M., & Winer, R. A. (1964). The effect of hypnotic and non-hypnotic suggestion on parotid gland response to gustatory stimuli. *Psychosomatic Medicine, 26*, 374–380.

Barber, T. X. (1969). *Hypnosis: A scientific approach*. New York: Van Nostrand.

Barber, T. X. (1978). Hypnosis, suggestion and psychosomatic phenomena: A new look from the standpoint of recent experimental studies. *American Journal of Clinical Hypnosis, 21*, 13–27.

Barker, P. (1985). *Using metaphors in psychotherapy*. New York: Brunner Mazel.

Beck, A. T. (1970). Role of fantasies in psychotherapy and psychopathology. *Journal of Nervous and Mental Diseases, l50*, 3–17.

Binet, A. (1922). *L'Etude experimentale del intelligence*. Paris: Gostes.

Brallier, L. (1982). *Transition and transformation: Successfully managing stress*. Los Altos, CA: National Nursing Review.

Clark, C. C. (1981). *Enhancing wellness: A guide for self care*. New York: Springer.

Collison, C., & Miller, S. (1987). Using images of future grief work. *IMAGE: Journal of Nursing Scholarship, 19*, 9–11.

Craig, K. D. (1969). Physiological arousal as a function of imagined, vicarious, and direct stress experiences. *Journal of Abnormal Psychology, 73*, 513–20.

Epstein, G. (1986). The image in medicine. *Advances, 3*, 22–3l.

Erickson, E. H. (1940). Studies in the interpretation of play. *Genetic Psychology Monographs, 22*, 557–671.

Finke, R. A., & Kosslyn, S. M. (1980). Mental imagery acuity in the peripheral visual field. *Journal of Experimental Psychology: Human Perception and Performance, 6*, 126–39.

Gawain, S. (1978). *Creative visualization*. Berkeley: Whatever.

Griffin, M. (1986). In the mind's eye. *American Journal of Nursing, 86*, 804–806.

Happich, C. (1932). Das B ildbewvsstsein als ansatzstelle psychischer behandling. *Zbl. Psychotherapy, 5*, 663–667.

Hartland, J. (1966). *Medical and dental hypnosis*. Baltimore: Williams and Wilkins.

Hilgard, J. R. (1979). Imaginative and sensory-affective involvements in everyday. In E. Fromm & R. E. Shor (Eds.), *Hypnosis: Developments in research and new perspectives*. New York: Aldine.

Holt, R. R. (1964). Imagery: The return of the ostracized. *American Psychologist, 19*, 254–264.

Horney, K. (1950). *Neurosis and human growth*. New York: W. W. Norton.

Horowitz, M. J. (1978). Controls of visual imagery and therapeutic intervention. In J. L. Singer & K. S. Pope (Eds.), *The power of human imagination*. New York: Plenum.

Horowitz, M. (1983). *Image formations and psychotherapy*. New York: Jason Aronson.

Jacobson, E. (1929). Electrical measurements of neuromuscular states during mental activities: 1. Imagination of movement involving skeletal muscles. *American Journal of Psychophysiology, 91*, 567–608.

James, W. M. (1890). *Principles of psychology*. New York: Holt.

Janet, P. (1898). *Neuroses et idées fixes*. Paris, Alcan.

Jung, C. G. (1960). *The structure and dynamics of the psyche*. (R. F. C. Hull, Trans.) *Collected works* (Vol. 8). Princeton: Princeton University Press. (Originally published 1926)

Klinger, E. (1980). Therapy and the flow of thought. In J. E. Shorr, G. E. Sobel, P. Robin, & J. A. Connela (Eds.), *Imagery: Its many dimensions and applications*. New York: Plenum.

Knowles, R. D. (1982). Affirmations. *American Journal of Nursing, 82*, 615.

Knowles, R. D. (1983). Building rapport through neurolinguistic programming. *American Journal of Nursing, 83*, 1011, 1014.

Kosbab, P. (1974). Imagery techniques in psychiatry. *Archives of General Psychiatry, 31*, 283–290.

Kosslyn, S. M. (1981). The medium and message in mental imagery: A theory. *Psychology Review, 88*, 46–66.

Lang, P. J. (1979). A bio-informational theory of emotional imagery. *Psychophysiology, 6*, 495–511.

Ley, R. (1983). Cerebral laterality and imagery. In A. A. Sheikh (Ed.), *Imagery: Current theory, research and application*. New York: Wiley.

Maclean, P. (1985). *A triune concept of the brain and behavior*. Toronto: Toronto Press.

Mahler, M. F. P., & Bergman, A. (1975). *The psychological birth of the human infant: Symbiosis and individuation*. New York: Basic Books.

Marks, D. (1983). Mental imagery and consciousness: A theoretical review. In A. A. Sheikh (Ed.), *Imagery: Current theory, research and application*. New York: Wiley.

Maslach, C. M. G., & Zimbardo, P. G. (1972). Hypnotic control of peripheral skin temperature: A case report. *Psychophysiology, 9*, 600.

Mast, D. E. (1986). Effects of imagery. *IMAGE: Journal of Nursing Scholarship, 18*, 118–120.

May, J., & Johnson, H. (1973). Physiological activity to internally elicited arousal and inhibitory thoughts. *Journal of Abnormal Psychology, 82*, 239–245.

McCaffery, M. (1979). *Nursing management of the patient with pain* (2nd ed.). Philadelphia: J.B. Lippincott.

McGuigan, F. J. (1971). Covert linguistic behavior in deaf subjects during thinking. *Journal of Comparative and Physiological Psychology, 75*, 417–420.

McMahon, C. E. (1976). The role of imagination in the disease process: Pre-Cartesian history. *Psychological Medicine, 6*, 179–184.

Meichenbaum, D. (1978). Why does using imagery in psychotherapy lead to change? In J. L. Singer & K. S. Pope (Eds.), *The power of human imagination*. New York: Plenum.

Olson, M. (1987). The out-of-body experience and other states of consciousness. *Archives of Psychiatric Nursing, 1*, 201–207.

Paivio, A. (1971). *Imagery and verbal processes*. New York: Holt.

Peller, L. W. (1971). Models of children's play. In R. E. Hutton & B. Sutton Smith (Eds.), *Child's play*. New York: Wiley.

Pelletier, K. R. (1977). *Mind as healer; Mind as slayer*. New York: Delta.

Pinker, S., & Kosslyn, S. (1983). Theories of mental imagery. In A. A. Sheikh (Ed.), *Imagery: Current theory, research and application*. New York: Wiley.

Pirbramin, K. (1982). What the fuss is all about. In K. Wilber (Ed.), *The holographic paradigm and other paradoxes*. Boulder: Shambala.

Richardson, A. (1969). *Mental imagery*. London: Routledge and Kegan Paul.

Robertson, A. D, & Inglis, J. (1977). The effect of electroconvulsive therapy on human learning and memory. *Canadian Psychology Review, l8*, 285–307.

Samuels, M., & Samuels, N. (1975). *Seeing with the mind's eye.* New York: Random House.

Sargant, J. D., Walters, E. E., & Green, E. E. (1973). Psychosomatic self regulation of migraine headache. *Seminars in Psychiatry, 5*, 415–427.

Schultz, J. H., & Luthe, W. (1959). *Autogenic training: A physiological approach to psychotherapy.* New York: Grune & Stratton.

Schwartz, G. (1978). Psychobiological foundations of psychotherapy and behavior change. In S. Garfield & A. Bergin (Eds.), *Handbook of psychotherapy and behavior change* (2nd ed.). New York: Wiley.

Sheikh, A. A. (1983). *Imagery: current theory, research and application.* New York: Wiley.

Sheikh, A. A. (1984). *Imagination and healing.* New York: Baywood.

Sheppard, R. D. (1978). The mental image. *American Psychologist, 33*, l25–137.

Shorr, J. (1974). *Psychotherapy through imagery.* New York: Intercontinental Medical.

Simmonton, C., & Simmonton, S. (1978). *Getting well again.* San Francisco: J. P. Tarcher.

Simpson, H. M., & Paivio, A. (1966). Changes in pupil size during an imaginary task without motor involvement. *Psychonomic Science, 5*, 405–406.

Singer, J. L. (1979). Imagery and affect psychotherapy: Elaborating private scripts and generating contexts. In A. A. Sheikh & J. T. Shaffer (Eds.), *The potential of fantasy and imagination.* New York: Brandon House.

Singer, J. L., & Pope, K. S. (1978). *The power of human imagination.* New York: Plenum.

Snyder, M. (1985). *Independent nursing interventions.* New York: Wiley.

Tower, R. B. (1983). Imagery: Its role in development. In A. A. Sheikh (Ed.), *Imagery: Current theory, research and application.* New York: Wiley.

Trehub, A. (1977). Neuronal models for cognitive processes: Networks for learning and imagination. *Journal of Theoretical Biology, 65*, l4l–169.

Wallas, I. (1985). *Stories for the third ear: Using hypnotic fables in psychotherapy.* New York: W. W. Norton.

Wolpe, J., & Lazarus, A. (1966). *Behavior therapy techniques.* New York: Pergamon.

BIBLIOGRAPHY

Marks, D.F. (1986). *Theories of image formation.* New York: Brandon House.

McKay, M., Davis, M., Fanning, P. (1981). *Thoughts and feelings: The art of cognitive stress intervention.* Richmond, Ca: New Harbinger Publications.

Squires, S. (1987). The power of positive imagery: Visions to boost immunity. *American Health 6*: 56-61.

Vines, S. (in press 1988). Imagery in managing pain and stress. *Holistic Nursing Practice Journal.*

4

THERAPEUTIC SUGGESTION

DOROTHY M. LARKIN

INTRODUCTION

The thin body of literature on therapeutic suggestions pertains almost exclusively to their use in hypnosis, although the principles of suggestions are also applicable in imagery and relaxation techniques. Because it is difficult to clearly differentiate between the processes of hypnosis, relaxation techniques, and imagery, it is worthwhile to refine and implement the contributions of each modality. Imagery tends to focus more on visual internal experiences, relaxation techniques emphasize kinesthetic responses, and hypnosis might include both of the above combined with suggestions for perceptual/behavioral change, personal development, insight, appreciation, and generalized improvement. In teaching patients imagery and relaxation techniques, several principles of hypnosis can be incorporated. Relaxation and imagery are frequently taught to patients as hypnotic induction methods. Patients who prefer to learn meditation techniques can be additionally offered education interspersed with imagery, relaxation, and hypnosis. Essentially, many of the differences among the techniques pertain to semantics. Regardless of which modality is offered, the incorporation of therapeutic suggestions will augment the benefits.

The following is revised from the author's contributions in Zahourek's "Clinical Hypnosis and Therapeutic Suggestion in Nursing" (1985). The principles of hypnotic suggestions are applicable for relaxation techniques, imagery, and guided meditations.

Additional case studies that emphasize therapeutic suggestions, relaxation, and imagery are provided, as well as a special section of contributions from two colleagues.

As one becomes attuned to the patterns and forms of therapeutic suggestions, it becomes apparent that all communication is essentially suggestive in nature. The therapeutic use of suggestions, interspersed in daily conversations with patients, can highly augment their sense of comfort and participation in their healing process. This chapter will introduce the basic principles of this form of communication.

DEFINITIONS OF SUGGESTION

The term *suggestion* has been traditionally defined as a stimulus that evokes uncritical acceptance of an idea. This definition implies that the subject is a passive recipient void of a capacity to reason. The phrase "uncritical acceptance," misinterpreted, belittles the potential of each subject. The unconscious mind is capable of rejecting any inappropriate or immoral suggestion, but the conscious mind, with all its learned limitations and prejudicial biases, frequently needs to be opened to alternative ideas. This is what effective suggestive communication can do.

Field (1979) compared the former definition to molding plastic in a machine, and hence refers to it as the mechanistic meaning of suggestion. Passive recipient individuals subjected to direct authoritative suggestions typically attribute their success to the power of the facilitator. This impression does not afford the subjects their warranted personal credit or discovery of their own potential.

Another meaning of suggestion refers to hinting, indirection, or intimating (Young, 1931). Field called this the humanistic aspect of suggestion because it emphasizes the transactional, mutual aspects of communication. Individuals are described as artists who respond to suggested themes and ideas in order to creatively restructure reality (Field, 1979).

Milton Erickson is credited with introducing many of the concepts and freedom of indirect suggestions. He ascribed to the tapping of the doctor within each individual in that "Hypnotic suggestion . . . results in the automatic evocation and utilization of the patient's own unique repertory of response potentials to achieve therapeutic goals that might have been otherwise beyond reach" (Erickson & Rossi, 1981, introduction). His suggestions were frequently permissive, open-ended and replete with options. Most of the Ericksonian literature consists of case studies, since individualized suggestions, inductions, and treatment are difficult to standardize for traditional research.

THEORETICAL FOUNDATIONS

Three "Laws of Suggestion" were popularized in 1923 by Emil Coué and then gained further recognition when Kroger republished them in 1976. Although the resilient nature of these principles might imply authenticity, many clinicians consider any law in hypnosis faulty because it does not account for or encourage unique capacities and variations of subject response. Mention is given to these laws because they can enable the modern practitioner to extend basic principles of suggestion beyond preconceived limitations.

The first "law of concentrated attention" consists of the premise that "whenever attention is concentrated on an idea over and over again, it spontaneously tends to realize itself" (Kroger, 1976, p. 48). Many creative visualizations and affirmations are based on this principle, and many people report positive results from this process. Repetitive radio and television commercials are also typical examples of this law, but it should be acknowledged that such repetition can backfire, yielding tendencies to avoid buying items advertised with repellent redundancy. Proponents of Ericksonian hypnosis consider such repetition insulting to the individual's intellect and unconscious mind.

These practitioners might instead choose to capture appropriate "concentrated attention" via hints and subtle implications. Many successful advertisers have also reverted to this approach.

The second "law of reversed effect" implies that the "harder one tries to do something, the less chance one has of success" (Kroger, 1976, p. 48). Kroger reported that continual negative thoughts can lead to their realization because of the belief and expectation that they will happen. This can be true; however, negative thoughts can also lead to creative preventive solutions, and a subject could benefit from viewing a potentially ominous situation in a different and more positive light (see reframing, p. 88). This law also implies that trying too hard can impede progress. Many of the benefits of hypnosis, imagery, and relaxation techniques result from allowing the unconscious mind to lead the way, and conscious attempts to help are frequently perceived as interference.

The third "law of dominant effect" is based on the principle that a strong emotion tends to replace a weaker one. Since "strong" and "weak" are relative concepts, suggestions that effectively divert attention can change their perceptual degree of importance.

Coué is also credited with the early acknowledgment that generalized, nonspecific suggestions are received with less criticism or resistance and therefore are more successful. This generalized tendency is exemplified in his famous phrase "Everyday, in every way, I am getting better and better" (Coue, 1923). His patients, who were encouraged to repeat this phrase several times a day, were free to choose how they might create desirable change.

Kroger described suggestions as "a process by which sensory impressions are conveyed in a meaningful manner to evoke altered psychophysiologic responses" (Kroger, 1976). Suggestions provide sensory input via verbal, nonverbal, intraverbal (voice modulation), and extraverbal communication (implication of words). The adept practitioner will utilize each form of communication and offer suggestions in a congruent manner.

Effective suggestions are a composite of three processes: the emotional rapport between subject and facilitator, the acceptance of the suggested idea, and the effect created by the idea once it has been incorporated within the personality (Jones, 1948).

Individuals respond to suggestions in two different ways (Weitzenhoffer, 1980): some experience their response as voluntary, whereas others perceive the suggested effect involuntarily, and without conscious participation. When suggestions bypass higher cortical processes and elicit a nonvoluntary response, it is presumed that unconscious acceptance and participation has been secured.

Kroger (1976) emphasized that suggestibility tendencies are significantly determined by the way a subject learned to respond to suggestions in the past. Hence, children, nonassertive adults, and hospitalized patients who have adopted a passive role might initially respond better to direct, authoritative suggestions. Clinicians can introduce these subjects to the pleasures of independent thinking by gradually offering more suggestions that include choice and require active decision-making.

Motivation, cooperation, and the capacity to be receptive to new ideas also influence acceptance of suggestions. The impact of these variables is subject to change depending on how the suggestions are presented. Therapist ingenuity can ultimately be a more dependent factor in securing subject compliance.

Suggestibility

The scientific literature on suggestibility in hypnosis is extensive and frequently contradictory. Most of the early studies used direct, standardized inductions, and consequently resultant theoretical conclusions are considered potentially valid indicators only when similar direct inductions are utilized.

An important study by Alan Shulik (1979) found that third-person indirect grammatical suggestions significantly increased hypnotic compliance as compared to the traditional second-person direct grammatical suggestions. A standardized susceptibility scale was used to evaluate subject response to second-person grammatical suggestions. A typical example of this type of suggestion is "You cannot move your arm." The same standardized scale was utilized for comparison, except this scale had the second person "you" changed to third person "she" or "he." Hence the former mentioned sample suggestion would be changed to "She/he cannot move her/his arm." The statistically significant results imply that indirect wording of inductions facilitates the hypnotic state more than the typical direct inductions. Shulik reasoned that indirect techniques bypass the subject's conscious attitudes and resistances and hence directly influence subject compliance. Milton Erickson similarly utilized this type of indirect technique when he told patients third-person stories that contained relevant solutions to their presenting clinical problems.

Waking Suggestibility and Nursing Implications

Waking suggestibility consists of an individual's capacity to respond to suggestions without a preliminary trance induction. Although research indicates that suggestibility tends to increase from waking to hypnotic conditions (Hilgard & Tart, 1966; Weitzenhoffer & Sjoberg, 1961), the reported high correlation of responsiveness implies that "waking suggestibility may reside within the domain of hypnosis" (Bowers, 1976, p. 89). Furthermore, responding to suggestions can of itself induce a hypnotic trance (Tart, 1970). These results have important implications for the overburdened nurse who might mistakenly believe that suggestive benefits are realized only when time is available for a formal hypnotic induction. Waking-hypnotic suggestions can be interspersed in any nurse-patient conversation, no matter how brief, and tend to compound benefits of other therapeutic interventions.

The nursing literature attests to the brevity and ease of utilizing waking suggestions, and emphasizes nurses' capacity to enhance patient compliance and comfort (Holderby, 1981; Larkin, 1985; Orndorf & Deutch, 1981). Rogers (1972) described how hospitalized patients are frequently hypersuggestible. Nurses are encouraged to utilize this state of receptivity so patients can be introduced to ideas of a therapeutic and healing nature. She reported that "a patient whose attention is already intensely focused on himself may be in a hypnoidal state during which his suggestibility is so increased that ideas presented to him act like posthypnotic suggestions" (Rogers, 1972, p. 715). Whether it's spontaneous or deliberate, this trancelike state can be recognized when the patient exhibits a sudden fixation of attention and possibly a faraway stare. This is a period when suggestions are more readily accepted because the patient's conscious critical faculties are reduced. The nurse can utilize this receptive state by offering therapeutic suggestions, reassurance, and health-promoting education. Continual assessment will need to be observed, so if the subject's attention suddenly shifts, the nurse can concurrently change the offered therapeutic strategy to meet the patient's needs and altered perceptions. When the patient's attention is again secured, suggestions of a different nature can be offered to further direct awareness toward a therapeutic goal.

Suggestions are often used in nursing communication for "*reframing*" (Erickson, Rossi, & Ryan, 1985), or changing the meaning of a situation so it can be viewed more favorably. An example from the author's work in a burn center was when patients complained about their itching burns, they were congratulated and told that itching is a great sign of healing skin. The reframing occurred when they associated future itching with healing, instead of the formerly perceived irritant. Additional suggestions were frequently offered to change their perception of itching, perhaps to "tingling," for a more gentle reminder of their healing progression.

FORMULATING SUGGESTIONS

It is initially important to comprehend the difference between direct and indirect suggestions. Most of the traditional inductions available in general hypnosis texts utilize the direct form of suggestion. Direct suggestions are often effective in a crisis situation and when working with passive subjects. Minor linguistic changes can transform direct suggestions of an authoritarian character to create indirect suggestions that will bypass the potential of resistance. The following examples can demonstrate this principle.

   1.   Direct: Close your eyes and see a beautiful ocean beach. Feel yourself resting on this beach, getting more and more relaxed.
   2.   Indirect: When you close your eyes, you might see a beautiful beach. You can feel yourself resting on this beach, getting more and more relaxed.
   3.   Indirect: It might be interesting to notice that when you close your eyes, you

can see a beautiful, relaxing scene. Some people prefer to see a perfect beach scene, hear the waves and the sounds of the birds, smell the salt, and feel the warmth of the sun. Others enjoy the peace of the mountains, with the sounds and smells of nature. I don't know what place gives you more comfort and relaxation, or how that relaxation develops, perhaps at the top of your head first, or maybe noticing the changes as they develop somewhere else . . . , I don't know and it doesn't even matter how you enjoy the progression of relaxation and the peace of that place. And to know that you can create this comfort whenever you need or want to, perhaps by taking a few deep breaths . . .

The initial indirect change just consisted of rephrasing the suggestion to be more permissive, with the terms "can" and "might." The second, more developed indirect suggestion conveys a variety of options as to how the subject might experience imagery and relaxation. In order for the subject to notice how the implied changes develop, it is necessary to focus inward, which is a desired hypnotic response. The permissive nature of suggestions that are replete with options is termed *fail-safe*, since any response can be considered appropriate.

Other methods of phrasing permissive suggestions are offered in the follow ing examples: "You *might* be surprised to discover . . ."; "*Perhaps* you've already noticed . . ."; "You *can* think of *any pleasant place or time* . . . ."

SAMPLE SUGGESTION TECHNIQUES

Truisms (Erickson & Rossi, 1980) are simple, undeniable statements about behavior that the patient has experienced or is currently experiencing: "You woke up this morning . . ."; "You are sitting in a large chair . . ." These statements ensure acceptance and are typically combined with other suggestions for the promotion of a receptive, accepting state of mind.

Contingent suggestions (Erickson & Rossi, 1980) are offered by commenting on something that is indisputably true and linking it with something you would like the patient to perceive or experience: "*As* you take that next breath (the patient will, hopefully, indisputably take a next breath), *you can begin to notice* further relaxation in that arm."

Conjunctive suggestions (Bandler & Grinder, 1975) similarly link two (or three or four) statements but use the term *and*: "You're sitting in the chair (indisputably true comment) *and* you can notice something pleasantly different happening to your left hand."

Presupposition suggestions (Bandler & Grinder, 1975) assume and presuppose a desirable response: "*Perhaps you're already noticing* a developing sense of numbness in that hand."

Conversational postulates (Bandler & Grinder, 1975) typically utilize questions to instruct client behavior: "Can you find a comfortable spot on the wall to focus on?"; "Will you sit in this chair to be comfortable?"

Implied directives (Erickson & Rossi, 1980) consist of a time-bound, implied, or assumed suggestion for a behavioral response: " . . . *when* you sit in that chair and be comfortable, . . ."; "I'm not sure *when* your eyes will close"; "Any time after this you can use these learnings . . ."

Dissociative suggestions (Erickson & Rossi, 1980) can evoke a local analgesia by separating perception of a body part or parts: "While *that* leg over *there* continues to heal, you can rest comfortably in the bed"; "You can *take your mind* to any pleasant relaxing scene while we take care of that wound"; "You can discover a variety of ways to *reorient from the head up.*"

Interspersed suggestions (Erickson, 1966) consist of direct suggestions that are interspersed within the framework of a permissive comment or an unrelated statement, such as "You can *keep on relaxing, George*, while I . . ." or "I enjoy sailing too, and it *feels so good, George, so comfortable*, just drifting along wherever the wind might take you." Erickson's interspersal technique (1966, 1980) as an induction process is an exquisite testimony of the potential of such suggestions. Readers are encouraged to peruse the reference.

Generalized referential index (Grinder, Delozier, & Bandler, 1977) describes an actual or hypothetical situation that has direct relevance to the patient and then provides generalized options that the patient can mentally develop. Therapeutic solutions tend to be conveyed in third-person grammatical form and are relayed through stories, metaphors, and analogies (Erickson & Rosen, 1982; Gordon, 1978; Larkin & Zahourek, in press; Mills & Crowley, 1986). For example, if the patient is a baseball player, a story about another baseball player can effectively secure the patient's attention. Indirect suggestions can then be offered in the form of describing what the first baseball player did to promote comfort and accelerate the healing process. Erickson frequently prefaced such suggestions with the phrase "I had a patient once who . . ."

A metaphor offered by the author to a patient suffering from severe hypertension described how one learns to drive. Suggestions for maintaining a healthy blood pressure were interspersed throughout the conversation. This example is abbreviated as follows:

> Initially, one needs to consciously think about *pressing the brakes* at the *right time* and when to *accelerate properly* so one can arrive *safely and comfortably* at the desired destination. But soon the driving *becomes automatic*, with the foot *slowing down* the car or speeding up the car *as appropriate to the situation*, and one can *trust this automatic capacity while enjoying* music on the radio or conversing with a good friend. Now, New York taxi drivers are sometimes silly, in that they speed up quickly only to stop and wait at all the red lights. It seems so much more reasonable to *move along at the proper designated pace* which *when properly timed*, can capture all the green lights *comfortably* . . .

Subsequent hourly vital signs indicated normal blood pressure for the remainder of the shift, and the patient gleefully reported that she learned how to make it automatic. Since her medications were ordered according to specific blood pressure parameters, it wasn't necessary to secure a prescription change.

Listening to stories naturally evokes imagery, i.e., "A little girl and her dog ran into a red house" invites development of the unsaid specifics, the features of the house, dog, and girl are created by the listener's imagination.

Imagery, metaphor, and storytelling forms of communication are believed to be processed in the right brain (left brain for those who are left-handed). Additionally, the creation of psychosomatic symptomatology is believed to be a function of the right brain (Mills & Crowley, 1986). Erickson and Rossi have theorized that such "symptoms are expressions in the language of the right hemisphere" and "the use of metaphorical language communicates directly with the right hemisphere" (Erickson & Rossi, 1979, p. 144). Hence, communication with the cerebral area that houses the problem could have more impact in suggesting potential change.

Mills and Crowley (1986) have elaborated on Erickson's form of "two-level communication" or communicating simultaneously with the conscious and unconscious mind (Erickson & Rossi, 1976, 1980; Erickson, Rossi, & Ryan, 1986). "While the conscious mind is provided with one message (in the form of concepts, ideas, stories, and images) which keeps it 'occupied,' another therapeutic message can be slipped to the unconscious mind via implication and connotation" (Mills & Crowley, 1986, p. 18). Erickson's method of integrating interspersed suggestions throughout the larger context of a story/metaphor "can be understood as exerting their powerful effects through the same mechanism of activating unconscious association patterns and response tendencies that suddenly summate to present consciousness with an apparently 'new' datum of behavioral response" (Erickson & Rossi, 1976, 1980, p. 448; Mills & Crowley, 1986, p. 18). This would explain the more gradual behavioral shift and emotional change that frequently follows the telling of therapeutic stories. Storytelling with therapeutic suggestions interspersed throughout theme development can metaphorically mirror the patient's problem, reframe its meaning, and suggest forms of resolution.

Erickson's initial discovery of the use of metaphor and interspersed suggestions (Erickson, 1966) involved a terminally ill florist named Joe, who suffered from intractable pain and opposed any overt form of "hypnosis." Erickson told him a lengthy story with much imagery about how a tomato plant can grow comfortably, and interspersed the story with such suggestions as "the rains that *bring peace and comfort*, and the joy of growing to flowers and tomatoes, . . . ; *you can really feel happy* looking at a tomato seed, thinking about the wonderful plant it contains *asleep, resting, comfortable, Joe . . .*" (Erickson, 1966, 1980, p. 271). Following the tomato plant story, Joe lived his remaining 3 months in comfort, at his home, with his family, and gardening.

Full description of the therapeutic use of metaphors and stories with imagery, although still in its infancy, is beyond the scope of this chapter (See Chapter 5). Mills and Crowley (1986) provide an exceptional description and interpretation of the process of creating therapeutic metaphors individualized to match and reframe the patient's presenting situation. Additionally, they have published a beautifully designed comic book for Childhelp USA, entitled *Garden Stones: Fred Protects the Vegetables*. This story metaphorically, through injured vegetables in a garden, mirrors child abuse and prepares a child for placement in a foster home, while the "gardener" goes to school to learn how to care for growing vegetables. The comic book also uses the child's imagery to reframe his or her response to his or her abusive experience by drawing how the hurt looks when it's smaller.

Posthypnotic suggestions are suggestions offered during hypnosis that are intended to be carried out in the subsequent waking state. The suggested response is usually elicited by an associated cue, and tends to spontaneously reinstate a brief hypnotic trance (Udoff, 1981). Posthypnotic suggestions can be direct or indirect. An example of a direct posthypnotic suggestion is "This medication will make you more comfortable in a few minutes so you will be able to sleep." An indirect posthypnotic suggestion might be "When the doctor comes to check that wound, you might be surprised at how quickly you relax and become comfortable . . ."

Suggestions for reorientation from trance should reverse any suggested effects that are not appropriate for maintaining in the waking state. "As you reorient, that numbness can change to comfort, and it can stay that way as long as proper healing continues." (This suggestion safely ensures comfort, unless healing is not progressing properly, in which case the subject will need to attend to the resultant lack of comfort and seek proper medical attention.)

Since the hypnotic state is so pleasant, subjects frequently appreciate a few minutes of "world time" to reorient: "Take two or three minutes of world time to comfortably finish for now what you've already begun, knowing full well that you can return to this state at any proper time, perhaps just by taking a few deep breaths. After that world time, you can reorient alert, refreshed, and perhaps curious about how much you have already accomplished . . ."

CLINICAL APPLICATIONS

Therapeutic Suggestions in an Emergency Room Setting

The variety of patients seen in emergency rooms provides many opportunities for utilizing therapeutic suggestions. Every conversation can include some form of therapeutic suggestion. For example, patients usually come to the ER with fear and anxiety. On initial assessment the nurse can ask why they came to the ER and then, while taking their vital signs, tell them something about their body that is properly functioning, for example, "Your pulse is a good rate, nice and steady"; "You've got a good healthy blood pressure"; or "That bleeding has been cleaning out that wound properly, so it can heal better." The rationale for these comments is consistent with Milton Erickson's utilization technique. This approach implies accepting and utilizing something the patient is doing appropriately, and then leading the patient with perhaps a conjunctive clause, such as "and when you have this gown on with the opening to the back, you can sit here and be comfortable and the doctor will see you shortly." This suggestion includes the implied directive "when you put this gown on," the permissive "you can," and an interspersed direct suggestion "sit here and be comfortable." Patients that receive this simple type of introduction generally are more compliant and patient while they wait in the ER.

All drugs can be given with suggestions for their effective therapeutic action. For example, "Mr. Smith, this medication will help open up the blood vessels in your heart so more oxygen will nourish the area, and you should begin to feel more comfortable very soon."

Therapeutic interventions should also be offered with suggestions, for example, "This neck brace will help remind you to keep your muscles relaxed and comfortable while they heal properly."

When an uncomfortable procedure needs to be done the nurse can explain the rationale for the process with suggestions for a healthful outcome. Suggestions for relaxation or imagery can be easily interspersed, for example, "George, I'm going to gently clean these burns so the area can heal more quickly . . ." A metaphor with implied suggestions for healing is as follows: "It's sort of like tending a lawn, and weeding out anything that might interfere with a healthy growth of grass. This cleansing will help make the area fertile for new cells to grow, just like the seeds of grass that need to be tended, . . . and as they grow and heal properly, nourished by the oxygen in the blood, like how the grass loves the rain, those cells can grow comfortably . . ." (See Erickson's interspersal technique, 1966, 1980).

Asthmatic patients frequently present to the ER in acute physiological and psychological distress. As an adjunct to the traditional medical treatment of oxygen, epinephrine, alupent treatments, and possibly amniophylline drips, patients can be taught how to breathe diaphragmatically. Typically the conversation begins with a discussion of the research that is being conducted in San Francisco (Peper, in press); "patients are being taught to *breathe this way* (demonstrate with hand on stomach, pushing out abdomen with each inhalation), and then somehow, *those tubes* that bring air to your lungs *open up*" (form tube with hand and enlarge for visual demonstration). The patient should join the nurse in this breathing, with his or her or a parent's hand on the stomach "to show you how to *do it right*, so those *tubes can open up and give you more air.*" The nurse can diaphragmatically breathe with the patient, observe and comment about what he or she is doing right, and offer further clarification as needed. The patient is then asked to practice and demonstrate later "how well *you can do it*," and "to *notice the feelings as those tubes open up.*" They are left with the generalized referential index suggestion that "People who breathe this way usually find it relaxing too." Later the patient should be asked for a demonstration, and when they are breathing correctly, offered the double-bind future oriented suggestion that "I don't know whether your stomach will tell and show your mind when you need to breathe this way first, or perhaps your mind will direct your stomach to breathe this way and open up those tubes . . . It probably doesn't even matter how you choose to breathe this way, because *you know how to do it*, and *you can do it whenever you need to*, maybe without even thinking about it . . ."

I have utilized variations of this basic conversation with patients ranging from age 4 to age 79. Most patients who correctly demonstrate diaphragmatic breathing seem to have a significant reduction in wheezing in a shorter than medically expected time frame. As these are subjective observations, research is warranted for objective verification of these therapeutic benefits.

Therapeutic Suggestions and Imagery for the Control of Bleeding

A 4-year-old girl with leukemia was admitted to the pediatric oncology ward with an uncontrollable nose bleed. Her emergency medical treatment consisted of nasal packing and immediate platelet transfusion. The following night she suddenly developed another nosebleed. I was in charge and responded when her mother frantically cried "It started again!".

I entered the girl's room, got down to her eye level, and emphatically told her I would apply pressure on her nose to help *stop the bleeding*. I then began to gently stroke her cheek to match the rhythm of her breathing. This is a technique similar to Erickson's utilization approach called "pacing," which implies accepting and utilizing the patient's rhythms. When the subject and facilitator's rhythms are matched, the nurse can then "lead" the patient, which I did, by slowing the stroking of her cheek. She responded by slowing the rate of her breathing to match my stroking. Concurrently, I spoke to her about how "*some children* know how to *go inside their mind and see cartoons . . .* Now I don't know if when you *look inside your mind you see Bugs Bunny or Donald Duck.*" The girl's eyes were closed, I waited a moment while still pacing and leading my stroking with her breath, and she whispered "Bugs Bunny." I utilized her response with "that's right, and Bugs Bunny looks like he's exploring all around the corners in there, and I don't know if *you can see* what he's hiding behind his back, so I'll tell you, *he's got some 'Krazy Glue'* . . . Do you *see it now?*"

She slowly nodded her head. I said, "And now, maybe you can tell me when *Bugs Bunny finds that little hole and patches it up with the Krazy Glue so it doesn't leak anymore* . . . Has he found it yet?" She nodded, and I said, "OK, and now you can just *watch him put that strong glue in and watch it dry,* but I'm not going to take my finger off your nose until *you know it's absolutely dry* . . . Is it dry yet?" She slowly shook her head. I reassured her, "OK, you can let me know when *it's strong and dry,* I know *that stuff works fast* . . . Is it *dry now?*" She nodded. I released the pressure and her bleeding had stopped. As she opened her eyes to meet mine, I continued to pace and stroke her cheek, and offered a future-oriented suggestion: "And you can *do that whenever you need to, Bugs Bunny will be there with the Krazy Glue.*" She nodded, I looked at her shaken and confused but smiling mother, and she also nodded. The remainder of the night was relaxed and uneventful. When I returned to the floor later in the week, she had already been discharged.

A directive and active approach characterized the interaction during the crisis. This approach captured the patient's attention and cooperation and subsequently reduced both her and her mother's anxiety. The italicized interspersed suggestions were emphasized by a change in voive modulation prefaced by permissive or qualifying comments such as "you can . . . " and "when . . . " These comments encourage active participation of the patient and help avoid resistance to the therapeutic suggestions provided. A consistent direct and implied message continued to be that she could control and stop the bleeding.

Suggestions Go Everywhere

Therapeutic suggestions communicated to one individual can also evoke beneficial responses from persons overhearing the conversation. Such suggestions can actually be intended for present persons to whom the nurse is not overtly speaking. The following is an example from my work with a 12-year-old girl with chronic renal problems and an intravenous technician.

While receiving morning report, the highly competent technician distressingly reported that Julie's IV needed to be restarted and she didn't think she could do it. She relayed that Julie has terrible veins, and she couldn't start the IV last time. She then emphatically stated that she would only try three times, and then the doctors would have to start it.

I entered Julie's room on morning rounds while the IV technician was setting up the necessary equipment. I had not met Julie before, and walked up to her bed to introduce myself. To establish rapport, I lowered to her eye level and gently squeezed her arm where the IV would likely be inserted. The following conversation occurred:

"Hi Julie, my name is Dorothy and I hear you need a new IV. Why don't you *make those veins big so she can get it in on the first try*? I bet you didn't know *you could do that*, did you? You can *tell me later how well you did it.*"

Julie looked a bit surprised and then nodded. The IV technician overheard our conversation with the interspersed suggestion "she can get it in on the first try." The interspersed direct suggestion for Julie to "think those veins big" was prefaced by my permissive comment of wondering if she already knows how to do it. This implication that it can be done is followed by the interspersed suggestion "you could do that." The final comment implies future satisfaction for a job well done.

Ten minutes later the IV tech rushed up to me and joyfully announced that she got it in on the first try! I congratulated her and then returned to Julie's room to extend further congratulations. When I greeted the beaming Julie with my thumbs up, I offered the future-oriented suggestion, "And now that you know how to do it, *you can think those veins big anytime you need to*, and isn't that good news?" She nodded vigorously, with an obvious sense of warranted personal pride.

Perioperative Education

Preoperative and postoperative education offers many opportunities for utilizing therapeutic suggestions. Merely educating the patient as to what to expect postoperatively is an implication that the patient will make it through surgery. Preoperative suggestive education greatly facilitates postoperative comfort, voiding, coughing, and reorientation, and seems to accelerate healing. "Blood works to nourish cells and clean wounds as they heal properly and comfortably, and deep breaths will replenish the oxygen in the blood, which will feed those healing cells and help them grow strong" is an easily incorporated positive suggestion. To teach preoperative patients how to splint abdominal muscles for coughing, a positive suggestion could be, "This will give you support, so when you cough and clean out your lungs, it can be more comfortable, and more oxygen can get to the cells to speed your healing." Effective suggestive preoperative education also helps relax patients prior to surgery, because some of their fear of the unknown has been alleviated by specific information of how surgery takes place.

The following case studies are provided by Jennifer White, BSN, RN, from her work in an ambulatory surgery unit.

CASE 1: Bladder Catheterization

A 19-year-old female required catheterization of the bladder. The patient was tense and fearful. Before I could begin explaining the procedure, she asked, "Are you going to shove that thing into my bladder?" I replied, "Oh no, I'm just going to gently slide the tube in." The patient relaxed and the tube slid in, uneventfully. This is an example of reframing, or interpreting a situation differently, in a more therapeutic manner.

CASE 2: Postoperative Voiding

A 53-year-old male was postoperative in a day surgery unit following arthroscopy. The physician's assistant (PA) came by to check the status of the patient and to recommend a time for a follow-up appointment. She inquired of the patient whether he had voided since surgery. When he responded, "No," she offered him the negative suggestions that "sometimes *after spinal anesthesia the bladder is still numb and patients are unable to void.*" The patient appeared anxious and asked what would happen if he could not urinate. The PA replied, "We would have to stimulate the bladder." I then informed the patient that his bladder was already receiving stimulation (utilizing and reframing the PA's information) via the IV that was infusing. I further suggested that his bladder would know when (implied directive) the sensation had returned and that he would be able to urinate (interspersed suggestion) when the stimulation and sensation reached the perfect balance. We discussed the timing of his first postoperative ambulation. I suggested that when the sensation and movement had fully returned to his legs, I would assist him in ambulation (implied directive). I informed him that from my experience, most patients (generalized referential index) are able to ambulate to the bathroom and urinate whether or not they are aware of the urge to urinate (double bind). Approximately 1 hour later, I assisted the patient in ambulation at which time he urinated without difficulty.

CASE 3: Recovering from Anesthesia

A 16-year-old female underwent eye surgery under general anesthesia. She returned to the day surgery unit very groggy, but arousable. She remained stable throughout the postoperative course, but maintained a state of grogginess or sleep for the next 4 hours. The patient's mother was at the bedside during the patient's recovery period. She verbalized concern over her daughter's "slow" recovery, as she had observed many other patients in the unit who had recovered more rapidly and had been discharged home. She felt her daughter should be admitted for an overnight stay. Discussing the situation with the patient's mother, I reassured her that an overnight stay was a possibility, but we would continue to monitor the patient's recovery for at least 1 more hour before making such a decision. Still within the patient's hearing range, I discussed the individuality of a patient's recovery from anesthesia (suggestions go everywhere). We reviewed the range of possibilities from a very gradual recovery to a sudden coming to alertness after a long period of sleeping (this double bind implies that the question is not 'if' the patient will recover today but 'how' the patient will recover today). Fifty minutes later the patient sat upright in bed and was totally alert. She announced she felt "much better" was hungry, and felt ready to be discharged.

Parenting and Pediatrics

Other situations that benefit from the use of therapeutic suggestions are parenting and managing/teaching young children. The following case examples were provided by Lissa Armstrong, LPN, and these principles can be easily applied to pediatric nursing situations. She has integrated therapeutic suggestions for her 4- and 2-year-old children since birth. She has found indirect, contingent, interspersed, and implied directive suggestions to be most helpful with young children, and emphasizes that a relaxed state is not necessary when suggestions are given with a calm controlled tone of voice.

Suggestions are initially formed by "pacing," or accepting and utilizing some aspect of the ongoing situation, followed by "leading," when suggestions for future behavior are offered. For example, "The noise is very loud in here (pacing and utilizing). I'm sure it will be more fun and relaxing for all of us when it's quieter (implied directive). Let's see how quiet we can be (leading with interspersed direct suggestions)."

Suggestions for requesting bedroom/toy clean-up might include: "It's good you're dressed (acceptance and utilization) . . . I think you'll enjoy picking up your room (leading with interspersed direct suggestion) . . . It might be now or perhaps in another minute, I'm not quite sure when (double bind with either option acceptable) . . . but you will be happy and proud when you finish picking up your room (implied directive for future behavior)."

One night the 2-year-old woke up with a bad dream: "The cows scare me in my room." Her mother responded with, "Remember when we go to the farm? . . . The cows are big there but a strong fence is there to keep the cows away and you are safe." (utilization of an imaged memory combined with the interspersed direct suggestion "you are safe") . . . Let's imagine a big, strong fence around you here, so you can be safe and still comfortable in your cozy, warm bed (conjunctive and interspersed suggestions)."

When the children were sick, their mother rocked them, sang a lullaby, and offered concurrent suggestions such as, "this song always helped my tummy feel better when I was little, too . . . " This generalized referential index suggestion prompts the child to associate the lullaby with feeling better.

When the 4-year-old had trouble falling asleep, his mother stroked his forehead and asked him to "feel right here . . . now close your eyes, relaxing even more and watch the colors in your mind . . . Maybe they spin and dance, they might even make a soft, quiet music to help you sleep." When she asked him later, postsleep, about the colors in his mind, he said, "I see a pretty rainbow." She asked him, "Do the colors swirl and do you hear the soft music?" He said, "No, Mama, they are breaking out (break dance music)." Since indirect suggestions encourage personal choice, people should hear their own music.

NONTHERAPEUTIC SUGGESTIONS AND COUNTERING MEASURES

Practitioners will also discover various opportunities to counter nontherapeutic suggestions. Frequently, these hurtful suggestions are given to patients by well-meaning health practitioners who are unaware of the potential maladaptive impact of their communications. A professional's benevolent intent of truthfully conveying to patients probable perceptions of medical procedures is legally warranted and ethically appropriate, but too often the negative potential response is emphasized at the expense of potentially positive or neutral responses. For example, in working with burn patients, it is necessary to dress the wounds with an antibiotic that was frequently perceived as uncomfortably hot. Other nurses often warned patients with, "Get ready, because this dressing is going to burn." Naturally, the patients apprehensively paid attention to the predicted burning sensation, and subsequently complained or grimaced when the heat was felt. When the author dressed patients' wounds with this topical antibiotic, patients were truthfully told, "This dressing is going to feel wet" (a simultaneous perceptual experience). The occasional patient that reported discomfort from excessive warmth would have that experience accepted and acknowledged. His or her attention could be suggestively redirected to another, different, truthful perceptual experience, perhaps toward the concept of time, for example, "Yes, but most patients say the heat lasts only a short time, and I wonder how soon yours will quit (interspersed suggestion for brevity of discomfort)."

Another burn patient was scheduled for his first postoperative burn cleansing tank immersion procedure. His attending physician loudly announced within the patient's hearing range, "Get the thrombin ready, *he was just debrided and he's going to lose a lot of blood.*" To counter this nontherapeutic suggestion, I calmly but emphatically stated at his ear level, "Although, I wonder how interesting it might be to *notice how little you need to bleed*, perhaps *just the amount needed to cleanse the burns properly*, so they can *heal even quicker.* After all, you have been *stopping the bleeding* all your life, and even if you don't fully know how to do it, *you do know how to do it*, and maybe you could just watch to *see how it's done properly this time . . .*" These suggestions were subtly reemphasized throughout the tanking procedure and were interspersed with suggestions for relaxation, deep breathing, and enhanced comfort. The patient was compliant, relaxed, and required very little thrombin.

Another example of countering nontherapeutic suggestions was when a 9-year-old dying leukemic boy encumbered with a variety of intravenous lines, Swan and Arterial monitors, respirator, and chest tube needed to be logrolled and weighed. An attending nurse informed the boy that she was sorry, but this was going to hurt him. The patient responded with a grimace and a moan. I then commented that "Sometimes it can *be more comfortable if one moves slowly, carefully, and gently*, and maybe *takes a few slow, deep breaths, which can really help.*" The patient's furrowed brow relaxed, he took a deep breath and began to assist us by slowly moving one arm and leg. The other nurse responded with, "Oh no, there's no way you can be comfortable logrolling with a chest tube. *Chest tubes always make you hurt.*" The boy's frown and grimace returned. I countered with, "I'm not so sure about that, but it might be really interesting to find out *how comfortable it could be . . . with deep breaths*, and *slow, careful movements, right now . . .* so maybe *the hurt won't even need to bother him . . .*" The patient's forehead again relaxed and he proceeded to assist us further. The other nurse was verbally persistent in maintaining her position that comfort could not exist, and the conversation continued to offer the patient opposing suggestions (to which the patient correspondingly alternated relaxed and furrowed brow) until I chose to monopolize the conversation. The procedure was completed with willing patient participation and minimal nonverbal indications of discomfort.

CONCLUSION

The scope of this chapter permits only a preliminary introduction to the process of formulating effective suggestions to augment imagery and relaxation. A more comprehensive form of education will occur as the nurse observes patients' verbal and nonverbal responses to therapeutic suggestions. That is when the value of this adjunctive tool truly becomes apparent.

REFERENCES

Bandler, R., & Grinder, J. (1975). *Patterns of the hypnotic techniques of Milton H. Erickson, M.D.* (Vol. 1). Cupertino, CA: Meta.

Bowers, K. (1976). *Hypnosis for the seriously curious.* Belmont, CA: Wadsworth.

Cooper, L. M., & London, P. (1976) Children's hypnotic susceptability personality and EEG patterns. *International Journal of Clinical and Experimental Hypnosis, 24,* 140–148.

Coué, E. (1923). *How to practice suggestion and autosuggestion.* New York: American Library Service.

Diamond, M. J. (1974). Issues and methods for modifying responsivity to hypnosis. *Annals of the New York Academy of Sciences, 296,* 119–128.

Erickson, M. (1966). The interspersal hypnotic technique for symptom correction and pain control. *American Journal of Clinical and Experimental Hypnosis, 3,* 198–209.

Erickson, M. (1966/1980). The interspersal hypnotic technique for symptom correction and pain control. In E. Rossi (Ed.), *The collected papers of Milton H. Erickson on hypnosis. Innovative hypnotherapy* (Vol. 4) (pp. 262–278). New York: Irvington.

Erickson, M., & Rosen, S. (1982). *My voice will go with you.* New York: W. W. Norton.

Erickson, M., & Rossi, E. (1976/1980). Two-level communication and the microdynamics of trance and suggestion. In E. Rossi (Ed.), *The collected papers of Milton H. Erickson on hypnosis. The nature of hypnosis and suggestion* (Vol. 1) (pp. 430–451). New York: Irvington.

Erickson, M., & Rossi, E. (1979). *Hypnotherapy: An exploratory casebook.* New York: Irvington.

Erickson, M., & Rossi, E. (1981) *Experiencing hypnosis—Therapeutic approaches to altered states.* New York: Irvington.

Erickson, M., Rossi, E. L., & Ryan, M. O. (Eds.) (1985). *Life Reframing in Hypnosis.* New York: Irvington.

Erickson, M., Rossi, E. L., & Ryan, M. O. (Eds.) (1986). *Mind-body communication in hypnosis.* New York: Irvington.

Field, P. B. (1979). Humanistic aspects of hypnotic communication. In E. Fromm & R. Shor (Eds.), *Hypnosis: Developments in research and new perspectives* (2nd Ed.) (pp. 609–610). New York: Aldine.

Gordon, D. (1978). *Therapeutic metaphors.* Cupertino, CA: Meta Publishing.

Grinder, J., Delozier, J., & Bandler, R. (1977). *Patterns of the hypnotic techniques of Milton H. Erickson, M.D.* (Vol. 2). Cupertino, CA: Meta Publications.

Hilgard, E. R., & Tart, C. J. (1966). Responsiveness to suggestions following waking and imagination instructions and following induction of hypnosis. *Journal of Abnormal Psychology, 71,* 196–208.

Holderby, R. (1981). Conscious suggestions: Using talk to manage pain. *Nursing, 11,* 44–46.

Jones, E. (1948). The nature of auto-suggestion. In *Papers on psycho-analysis* (5th Ed.). Baltimore: Williams & Wilkins.

Kroger, W. S. (1976). *Clinical and experimental hypnosis* (2nd Ed.). Philadelphia: J. B. Lippincott.

Larkin, D. M. (1985). Therapeutic suggestions. In R. Zahourek (Ed.), *Clinical Hypnosis and Therapeutic Suggestion in Nursing.* Orlando, FL: Grune & Stratton.

Larkin, D., & Zahourek, R.P. (1988). Therapeutic storytelling and metaphor in holistic nursing. *Holistic Nursing zzzpractice* (Spring, 1988).

Mills, J. C., & Crowley, R. J. (1986). *Therapeutic metaphors for children and the child within.* New York: Brunner/Mazel.

Orndorf, R., & Deutch, J. (1981). The power of positive suggestion—persuading patients to cooperate. *Nursing, 11,* 73.

Rogers, B. (1972). Therapeutic conversation and posthypnotic suggestion. *American Journal of Nursing, 72,* 714–717.

Rossi, E. (1986). *The psychobiology of mind-body healing.* New York: W.W. Norton.

Shulik, A. M. (1979). Right versus left hemispheric communication styles in hypnotic inductions and the facilitation of hypnotic trance. *Dissertation Abstracts International, 40,* 2445-B.

Tart, C. J. (1970). Self-report scales of hypnotic depth. *International Journal of Clinical and Experimental Hypnosis, 18,* 105–125.

Udolf, R. (1981). *Handbook of hypnosis for professionals.* New York: Van Nostrand Reinhold.

Weitzenhoffer, A. (1980). Hypnotic susceptibility revisited. *American Journal of Clinical Hypnosis, 22,* 130–146.

Weitzenhoffer, A. M., & Sjoberg, B. (1961). Suggestibility with and without induction of hypnosis. *Journal of Nervous and Mental Disease, 132*, 205–220.

Young, P. C. (1931). Suggestion as indirecton. *Journal of Abnormal and Social Psychology, 26*, 69–90.

Zahourek, R. (Ed.) (1985). *Clinical Hypnosis and therapeutic suggestion in nursing.* Orlando, FL: Grune & Stratton.

5

THERAPEUTIC STORYTELLING

EMILY M. BORNSTEIN

EDITOR'S PREFACE

Therapeutic use of stories has numerous implications in nursing practice. Patients naturally "tell their stories" as nurses take health histories. Seldom, however, are these stories consciously pursued or developed for therapeutic ends. This chapter describes the use of fairy tales and other forms of stories in psychotherapy, but numerous implications exist for the practicing nurse. While the process described in this chapter is relatively complex, nurses can use stories to explain procedures and to evoke hope for a "happy" or successful ending. For example, using a simple story that describes successful completion of "trials and tribulations" can be a metaphor for undergoing difficult diagnostic tests or procedures. Similarly, telling a story about another patient who survived or grew from a similar experience subtly engenders optimism.

Stories also provide valuable diagnostic information. Descriptions elicited from comments like "Tell me about your pain. Could it be an object, have a color, or even be an animal? How does it behave?" can be used to develop a scenario that promotes therapeutic results. Similarly, valuable psychological information can be obtained by learning what an individual's favorite stories were when he or she was a child.

Because stories can have such potent therapeutic value, readers are encouraged to think about their own repertoire of "favorite stories" that might be used with their particular patient population. Such therapeutic stories are presented throughout this book.

See, for instance, Chapter 7, "The Difficult Patient" and Chapter 10, "Relaxation/ Weight Loss."

THEORETICAL FOUNDATIONS: STORYTELLING AND METAPHOR

A man who was living in comfortable enough circumstances went one day to see a certain sage, reputed to have all knowledge. He said to him:

"Great Sage, I have no material problems, and yet I am always unsettled. For years I have tried to be happy, to find an answer to my inner thoughts, to come to terms with the world. Please advise me as to how I can be cured of this malaise."

The sage answered:

"My friend, what is hidden to some is apparent to others. Again, what is apparent to some is hidden to others. I have the answer to your ailment, though it is no ordinary medication. You must set out on your travels, seeking the happiest man in the world. As soon as you find him, you must ask him for his shirt, and put it on."

This seeker thereupon restlessly started looking for happy men. One after another he found them and questioned them. Again and again they said, "Yes, I am happy, but there is one happier than me."

After traveling through one country after another for many, many days he found the wood in which everyone said lived the happiest man in the world.

He heard the sound of laughter coming from the trees, and quickened his step until he came upon a man sitting in a glade.

"Are you the happiest man in the world, as people say?" he asked.

"Certainly I am," said the other man.

"My name is so-and-so, my condition is such-and-such, and my remedy, ordered by the greatest sage, is to wear your shirt. Please give it to me; I will give you anything I have in exchange."

The happiest man looked at him closely, and he laughed. He laughed and he laughed and he laughed. When he had quieted down a little, the restless man, rather annoyed at this reaction, said:

"Are you unhinged, that you laugh at such a serious request?"

"Perhaps," said the happiest man, "but if you had only taken the trouble to look, you would have seen that I do not possess a shirt."

"What, then, am I to do now?"

"You will now be cured. Striving for something unattainable provides the exercise to achieve that which is needed: as when a man gathers all his strength to jump across a stream as if it were far wider than it is. He gets across the stream."

The happiest man then took off the turban whose end had concealed his face. The restless man saw that he was none other than the great sage who had originally advised him.

"But why did you not tell me all this years ago, when I came to see you?" the restless man asked in puzzlement.

"Because you were not yet ready then to understand. You needed certain experiences, and they had to be given to you in a manner which would ensure that you went through them."

—FROM WORLD TALES, COLLECTED BY IDRIES SHAH (1979)

Folklore as Cultural Wisdom

Before people relied on the written word, cultural wisdom was passed from adults to children through storytelling. The history of the tribe, descriptions of the world and how things work, and stories about tribal heroes and their adventures were included in storytelling sessions around the campfire. When young people asked questions about life and its meaning, the tribal elders often answered with a story. Today, however, the majority of the people of the world no longer live in the tribal situation, and access to the special wisdom contained in fairy tales and myths is confined to books (often labeled as children's books), movies, and television. Some children's movies, such as *The Black Stallion* or *The Wizard of Oz* do portray growth and development in a fairy-tale way, but many of our modern myths, such as *Star Wars*, overemphasize technological mastery as opposed to psychological growth and development.

Metaphor and Symbolism as Language of the Unconscious Mind

Myths and fairy tales are powerful and compelling because their characters represent the projected contents of the unconscious mind. The listener automatically recognizes the psychological truth of the tale without subjecting it to critical scrutiny. Carl Jung was perhaps the first psychological theorist to observe and write about the power of metaphor and symbolism in directing and reflecting human conscious and unconscious processes (Jung et al., 1964), but artists, composers, and poets have recognized for centuries that metaphor and symbolism provide a direct avenue to the imaginations and emotions of their audiences. Stories are innately fascinating to most people because they stimulate the imagination as well as contain useful information.

PSYCHOTHERAPY AS A PROCESS OF PERSONAL GROWTH AND EDUCATION

People often seek psychotherapeutic treatment for symptom removal or to resolve a crisis in psychological functioning. Regarding the therapist as an expert in diagnosis and treatment, they often have magical expectations for quick cures.

Many neurotic people have unrealistic attitudes about the amount of hard work, self-discipline, endurance, and exercise of initiative required to achieve mastery in a given arena of human endeavor. Many have suffered deprivation, neglect, and frustration in childhood and adolescence, and have not learned now to handle frustration through creative problem-solving. They often believe that others are more competent than they, and the therapist is viewed as one who has "the answers."

The Therapist as a Teacher and Guide

Enter the therapist, who functions as a benevolent parent, a knowledgeable teacher, and a constructive critic in helping the patient to view himself or herself more realistically. Guiding explorations of internal lives and personal histories, like the sage in the "Happiest Man in the World" story, the therapist arranges experiences that will help the patient learn what is necessary to lead a healthy life.

The therapist helps patients examine the everyday events of their lives for feelings, attitudes, and personal meaning. As a teacher, the therapist imparts the basic principles of human behavior and development, and helps patients to practice new behaviors, new coping strategies, and new perceptions of personal difficulties. Storytelling is built into the process of psychotherapy, as patients unravel their histories and therapists help them review and recognize the important events of their lives. Neurotic behavior patterns emerge in the story, including the origins, maintenance, and reinforcement of these patterns over the years.

Constructing a Psychotherapeutic "Map"

The story of a particular symptom provides a psychotherapeutic "map," or an outline of steps to be taken in psychotherapy. The map helps patient and therapist identify developmental "snags," places where attitudes and behavior seem to be stuck in an earlier phase than would be indicated by the current chronological age.

Other problems that need to be "mapped" include unresolved conflicts, neurotic behavior and attitudes, lifestyle unsuitable to the patient's natural temperament, intellectual or social underachievement, and interpersonal relationship difficulties. As the personal history of the patient unfolds, the diagnosis, prognosis, and probable course of treatment become apparent, and the therapist must decide how best to communicate this information and understanding to the patient. Most therapists try to help patients see for themselves what needs to take place in order for positive changes to occur.

For most adult patients, the therapeutic relationship has a regressive aspect, which is reflected in the universally observed phenomenon of transference. Therapy encourages dependence on the therapist for emotional support, and in acting out transference patients often expect the therapist to "read" their minds, tell them what to do or how to remove symptoms. Some regression in psychotherapy is necessary for the patient's emotional, intellectual, and symbolic integration of formative experiences. This integration prepares for learning new and more effective ways of adjusting and coping with life.

The Use of Unconscious Processes in Psychotherapy

Many therapists teach their patients to use the productions of the unconscious mind to guide their behavior through interpretation of dreams and use of hypnosis and imagery techniques. Most therapists also teach the examination and interpretation of behavior by learning to understand unconscious motives. There are some therapists who rely exclusively on the use of unconscious processes to bring about change, but most utilize a combination of conscious and unconscious thought in processing therapeutic issues.

ERICKSONIAN APPROACHES TO THERAPEUTIC COMMUNICATION

Milton Erickson and his associates have contributed enormously to the body of practical knowledge about utilization of unconscious processes to bring about psychological growth. Erickson believed that one could circumvent the patient's resistance to change through the use of indirect, or covert suggestion, rather than by mobilizing resistance through direct confrontation or appeal (Zeig, 1985).

Experience by Analogy

Erickson emphasized that change results from experience, and the therapist must find a way to persuade the patient to experience certain curative events as in the "Happiest Man" story. These curative experiences may take place in the patient's inner world, through the use of imaging, or in everyday external reality. In either case, the Ericksonian therapist primes the patient so that he or she is ready to learn from the experience when it happens. Erickson himself commonly achieved this effect by telling a metaphorical story or anecdote that presented a description of the experience by analogy. Often the stories contained an element of paradox, designed to create confusion and cognitive disorientation. The story might stop abruptly, and Erickson would ask the patient to "find" the ending or resolution. Any kind of direct or cognitively recognizable statement of the message was avoided so the patient felt no need to defend against threatening content.

Psychological Rapport

At the heart of Ericksonian psychotherapy is psychological rapport. This is achieved through careful and deliberate observation of the patient, including his or her cognitive style, temperament, muscular tension, style of movement, chronological and developmental age, psychoneurologic orientation, intelligence, and education. The therapist subtly adapts his or her own style to that of the patient by mirroring the movements, breathing pattern, and verbal style of the patient. Therapeutic communication is often achieved through nonverbal means such as eye contact, gesture, touch, and vocal or respiratory pacing.

Although numerous techniques are employed by the Ericksonian therapist to achieve rapport, the most important is the total mental and physical concentration he or she directs toward the patient during the therapeutic interaction. The patient feels that the therapist is attuned to his or her needs and experiences the therapist as an ally and guide.

THERAPEUTIC APPLICATIONS: FAIRY TALES AS PSYCHOTHERAPEUTIC "MAPS"

Example: "The Desolate Island"

There was once a very wealthy man, who was of a kind and generous disposition, and who wanted to make his slave happy. He therefore gave him his freedom, and also presented him with a shipload of merchandise.

"Go," he said, "and sail to various countries. Dispose of these goods, and whatever you may get for them shall be your own."

The freed slave sailed away, across the wide ocean. He had not been long on his voyage before a storm blew up. His ship was driven onto the rocks and went to pieces, and all on board were lost except the former slave himself. He managed to swim to a nearby island and drag himself ashore.

Sad, despondent, lonely, and naked and with nothing to his name, he walked across the land until he came to a large and beautiful city.

Many people came out to meet him, crying, "Welcome! Welcome! Long live our King!"

They brought him a rich carriage and, placing him in it, escorted him to a magnificent palace, where many servants gathered around him. He was dressed in royal garments, and they addressed him as their sovereign: they expressed their complete obedience to his will.

The ex-slave was, naturally enough, amazed and confused, wondering whether he was dreaming, and all that he saw, heard, or experienced was merely passing fantasy.

Eventually he became convinced that what was happening was in fact real, and he asked some people around him, whom he liked, how he could have arrived in this state.

"I am, after all," he said, "a man of whom you know nothing, a poor, naked wanderer, whom you have never seen before. How can you make me your ruler? This causes me more amazement than I can possibly say."

"Sire," they answered, "this island is inhabited by spirits. Long ago they prayed that they might be sent a son of man to rule over them, and their prayers have been answered. Every year they are sent a son of man. They receive him with great dignity and place him on the throne. But his status and power end when the year is over. Then they take the royal robes from him and put him on board a ship, which carries him to a vast and desolate island. Here, unless he has previously been wise and prepared for that day, he finds neither subject or friend, and he is obliged to pass a weary, lonely and miserable life. Then a new king is selected, and so year follows year. The kings who came before you were careless and did not think. They enjoyed their power to the full, forgetting the day when it would end." These people counseled the former slave to be wise, and to allow their words to stay within his heart.

The new king listened carefully to all this, and he felt grieved that he should have wasted even the little time which had passed since he came to the island.

He asked a man of knowledge who had already spoken:

"Advise me, O Spirit of Wisdom, how I may prepare for the days which will come upon me in the future."

"Naked you came among us," said the man, "and naked you shall be sent to the desolate island of which I have told you. At present, you are King, and may do whatever you please. Therefore, send workmen to the island, and let them build houses and prepare the land, and make the surroundings beautiful. The barren soil will be turned into fruitful fields, people will go there to live, and you will have established a new kingdom for yourself. Your own subjects will be waiting to welcome you when you arrive. The year is short. The work is long; therefore be earnest and energetic."

The king followed his advice. He sent workmen and materials to the desolate island, and before the end of his term of power, it had become a fertile, pleasant, and attractive place. The rulers who had come before him had anticipated the end of their time with fear, or smothered the thought of it by amusing themselves. But he looked forward to it with joy, for then he could start upon a career of permanent peace and happiness.

And the day came. The freed slave who had been made a king was stripped of his authority. With his royal robes he lost his powers. He was placed naked on a ship, and its sails were set for the island. When he approached its shore, however, the people whom he had sent ahead came forward to welcome him with music, song, and great joy. They made him ruler, and he lived ever after in peace.

—FROM WORLD TALES, COLLECTED BY IDRIES SHAH (1979)

This story is an allegory designed to teach and is not a true fairy tale. The elements of the story are simple and straightforward, but it does contain most of the basic patterns that are commonly found in fairy tales. It is therefore a useful example to demonstrate how stories and tales can be utilized for therapeutic impact.

Developmental Characteristics of Fairy Tales

As with most fairy tales, the hero of "The Desolate Island" is involved in a process of transition. His servitude at the beginning of the story is like adolescence, when the child is thrust out into the world with "goods" provided by the parents. The adolescent has no personal power, only that which has been "borrowed" from the master (parents). In fairy tales, the hero is always involved in a developmental transition.

Separation and individuation are common themes, with the main character having to earn his or her own place in the world. In adapting to the outside world, many people find that the things they learned back home don't apply in the new living situation, and they must learn new coping mechanisms. Thus, in "The Desolate Island," the hero has to give up the borrowed riches of his master and has to enter a strange new land naked and alone. As with most fairy tales, the consequences of avoiding growth and development are disastrous. In this story, the rulers who had come before the hero represent avoidance behavior, while in other stories this theme is represented by the protagonist's arrogant siblings. Thus the general themes of leaving home, relinquishing the dependent child identity, forging a new adult identity, and learning new skills are common to most fairy tales.

Whether the fairy tale's main character is a prince or princess or, as in "The Desolate Island," a hero of common origin, most tales end with the character becoming a king or a queen—a metaphor for personal power and mastery over one's own fate. The underlying message of this common theme is that individuals who demonstrate a willingness to undergo life's difficulties with courage, perseverance, and an attitude open to learning, can become rulers of their own lives. Furthermore, in becoming kings and queens, these characters must exercise choice and judgment to avoid getting stuck in passivity and stagnation.

Externalization of Internal Conflicts

Because fairy tales and stories are experienced as external phenomena, the story takes place "out there," and people are less likely to react defensively to disturbing content. Certain conventions of expression in fairy tales are designed to distance the story from the context of everyday life, such as "once upon a time," "in a land far away," or "the thrice ninth land in the thrice tenth kingdom."

Use of Unconscious Processes

The language and imagery of fairy tales create a dreamlike atmosphere, where ordinary concerns of rationality and logic do not apply, and important messages are conveyed through symbolism. When people listen to these stories, they willingly suspend disbelief, as they would in nocturnal dreaming or daydream activities: strange coincidences, morphologic transformations, and other magical phenomina are accepted as normal events. Symbolism is the language of the unconscious mind, and imagery is more emotionally evocative than language-based thought. Thus people are drawn into the stories and become emotionally and mentally engaged very rapidly.

In "The Desolate Island," the image of the shipwreck and the hero being washed up on shore, naked and alone, conveys at once the emotions and perceptions of people in severe crisis. Adolescents and others involved in major life transitions often feel this way—shipwrecked—forced to leave behind many of the familiar old ways of perceiving, doing, relying on the judgment of others. "Shipwreck" as an evocative image is far more powerful than the more logical "forced to leave behind" or "loss of familiar old ways." Thus the tale effectively uses metaphor to provide a new experience, which helps the listener absorb the content of that experience by engaging the unconscious mind.

Promoting a State of Internal Absorption

Because of their dreamlike quality and the appeal to the unconscious mind, fairy tales evoke a very internal orientation. The writer has observed that patients often close their eyes when listening to a fairy tale, even when there has been no verbal suggestion to do so. Patients also display slowed breathing and other physical signals that indicate relaxation. Occasionally they spontaneously lie down on the therapeutic couch when they know they are about to hear a story. These behavioral signals indicate that people are experiencing a shift in orientation from an external focus to an internally directed state in which they are more receptive to the unconscious messages embedded in the story. The therapeutic impact of the story is powerfully enhanced when the therapist chooses a tale that is precisely relevant to the therapeutic issue at hand.

Some novels, films, plays, and other works of art contain psychological material of great developmental value that can be used metaphorically, but for practical reasons these narratives cannot be easily adapted for use within a therapy session, primarily due to time limitations. One practical advantage of a typical fairy tale is that most of them can be read in a relatively short period of 10 to 15 minutes.

Levels of Meaning

Because of the many levels of meaning in most fairy tales, listeners can simply "tune in" to the scenes or symbols that seem to be most relevant. The therapist can use the fairy tale as a psychologist uses a projective test, discovering the patient's cognitive style, primary concerns, level of developmental achievement, and important conflicts. In listening to the story of "The Desolate Island," for example, one can attend to the surface meaning: a man learns how to be kind, after living as a slave. One might also "hear" the developmental themes of transition from adolescence to adulthood, or the spiritual message dealing with the journey of the soul through life. Most importantly, the story can be understood as a metaphor for psychotherapy itself: a man (patient) finding himself shipwrecked and abandoned (emotionally disturbed individual seeks therapy during periods of crisis) is given a year of borrowed power and sustenance (the therapeutic process) to set his house in order and learn how to rule his own kingdom (the self). With the assistance of a sage (the therapist) he matures, and eventually goes off to lead his own life more fully prepared and confident. Thus the rich symbolism of fairy tales is ideal for conveying developmental information in a way that can be absorbed according to the needs of the individuals.

Common Developmental Themes

Truth and Paradox

Truth can be paradoxical, and appearances deceiving. Examples: the happiest man in the world wears no shirt; the "beast" is really a handsome prince. Sometimes we have to give up illusions before we can perceive reality more accurately.

Personal Autonomy

Individuation and the development of personal autonomy are necessary for healthy adult functioning. Fairy tales describe heroes and heroines learning practical skills of self-care and survival that lead to personal autonomy. Characters learn self-assertion, self-esteem, emotional self-nourishment, strategic thinking, self-discipline, authenticity of behavior, and self-realization so they can fulfill their own destinies and utilize natural talents and abilities.

Crisis and Personal Growth

Traumatic incidents in life can lead to personal growth and development. Many fairy tales begin with the hero's loss of of a parent through death or separation, while in others the hero sets out on a journey, encountering frightening and traumatic situations along the way. The key to personal growth often lies in the way that the heroic character responds to the loss, threat, or challenge by developing self-reliance, good judgment, perseverance, and using his or her wits to solve problems.

Emancipation from Family of Origin

Children must develop their own autonomy and growth away from the family of origin; the heroic characters must often embark on long journeys to achieve psychological emancipation. In some stories, the family of origin is neurotic and destructive, with parents and siblings engaging in harmful and destructive behavior toward their offspring. In these cases, the hero must look elsewhere for guidance and assistance in growing up and must leave behind the unhealthy emotional climate.

Nonfamilial "Guides"

Since people often need help to understand themselves and life, many heroes obtain assistance from benevolent nonfamilial helpers such as fairy godmothers, wise women, dwarfs, talking animals with special powers, and magical objects. A common method of portraying this need to accept guidance is for two siblings of the hero to fail in achieving their objectives because they ignore the advice of a guide character. The third brother or sister will achieve the intended goal, after listening to the advice and following the instruction. These themes can emphasize the need for a strong therapeutic alliance.

Maturity Precedes Marriage

Men and women achieve psychological maturity before they can find an appropriate mate, or maintain a healthy marital relationship. In many fairy tales, this truth is emphasized through the temporal arrangement of events: the hero does not marry the intended spouse until the end of the story. If the two do meet and marry early in the story, they are often separated during the narrative, so that each can acquire the skills they lack and achieve the psychological growth they need to be ready for marriage. One common symbol of emotional readiness for marriage is emancipation from the family of origin, and most marriage counselors are familiar with the plight of couples who have unsuccessful spousal relationships because one or both members still have emotional energy invested in the family of origin.

The Importance of Psychological Balance

Psychological balance within the personality is essential for health and productivity. In fairy tales, we see people who are passive learn to be assertive, people who are arrogant learn to be humble, those who are timid learn to be courageous, people who are dependent learn to be independent, and those who disconnect with femininity during the process of masculinization must reconnect with the feminine, and women cut off from their masculinity must find it again. In the familiar story of "Beauty and the Beast," the beast is transformed only after Beauty has learned to appreciate his "beastliness" (masculine aggression and sexuality). On one level, the story is about the transformative power of love, but on another, it is about restoration of balance within the personality: Beauty must accept her own masculinity rather than fear it, because she needs this aspect to emancipate from her father, who wished to keep her with him at home.

Perseverance and Optimism

Life can be difficult and confusing at times, but people can overcome obstacles to self-realization through struggle and perseverance. This underlying optimism, which is part of all fairy tales, engenders feelings of hope in those who read or listen to them. This optimism is neither shallow nor superficial, but is based on the principle of facing problems directly and learning how to deal with them effectively.

Taking Risks and Personal Growth

Personal growth requires taking risks and experimenting with new behaviors and attitudes. Many fairy tale heroes must encounter dangerous beasts, expose themselves to enchantments, or enter into combat with figures of demonic power. The Jungians identify these figures as representing the dark side of human nature, the "shadow" self, while a religious view might hold that these are personifications of evil. A more psychodynamic interpretation might be that these figures are projections of our own sadistic, murderous, or otherwise negativistic impulses. However we interpret the nature of the forces represented by the monster figures, they are always dangerous to people, and the hero must maintain his or her own integrity in the face of onslaught or pressure from these entities.

Sometimes the arena of combat is physical, while at other times the battle may be psychological, but the hero is clearly exposed to danger and must often take great risks to fulfill his or her mission. Once the monster is vanquished, the power of the fallen foe is integrated into the hero, as in the story of Perseus, where the hero uses the paralyzing power of Medusa's head to defend himself after decapitating her. When young women are the heroic characters, they often use intelligence and intuition to defeat the demonic forces rather than engaging them in physical combat, but the outcome of the encounter is always new growth and development for the central character. The parallel with psychotherapy is evident: the patient cannot achieve a new level of psychological integration without taking risks and exposing himself or herself to "dangerous" situations that may have been previously avoided.

Gaining New Perspectives

The solution to a personal problem can often be discovered by looking at the situation from a different perspective. In the "Happiest Man" story, the searching hero is able to accept the teaching of the master because he has a different perspective at the end of his journey. Often the hero undergoes an experience of injury or even death before being reborn with new insight and capability.

STORYTELLING TECHNIQUES

The Mutual Storytelling Technique

Dr. Richard Gardner (1971), a child psychiatrist, uses a mutual storytelling technique to communicate with his young patients. The stories, made up by the children, are presumed to contain important diagnostic material about the interests and concerns of the individual child. After careful consideration of the content, Gardner constructs a new story, using the same symbolic elements, which contains a psychological resolution to the problem posed in the child's story. While this method is similar to the traditional play therapy in the focus on reflection of the child's feelings and wishes, the didactic quality of the stories constructed by the therapist is designed to present novel solutions in a metaphorical way (Stoner, 1985; Chapter 4, "Therapeutic Suggestion").

Fairy Tales as Vehicles of Learning for Children

Bruno Bettleheim, another child therapist, emphasizes the importance of fairy tales as vehicles of learning for children in *The Uses of Enchantment* (1976). Fairy tales have been used to teach about life because they "direct the child to discover his identity and calling, and they also suggest what experiences are needed to develop his character further." Because fairy tales are metaphorical stories about human growth and development, the listener can observe from a distance the externalization of internal psychological events. Fairy tales make use of the same daydreaming process that most children and adults use to cope with psychological pressures, and because the stories are entertaining, the messages embedded in characters and plot are accepted by the listener without resistance.

Psychodiagnostic Storytelling

Psychological examiners have long recognized the usefulness of storytelling as a diagnostic strategy. Tests such as the "Thematic Apperception Technique" (TAT) (Murray, 1943) and the children's version (CAT) (Bellak, 1972) sample the subject's fantasy life. The subject is asked to make up stories about ambiguous pictures. The resulting stories are presumed to reflect unconscious concerns, important developmental themes, and clues as to the actual behavior and attitudes of the individual being evaluated. (For a case example, see Stoner's chapter of mutual storytelling in *Clinical Hypnosis and Therapeutic Suggestion in Nursing*, Zahourek, 1985.) In analyzing the stories, the examiner looks for significant recurring themes, as well as mood tone, level of complexity, and organization. These tests are called *projective techniques* because the subject is presumed to project some of the content of his or her own internal life onto the scenes portrayed in the pictures.

Therapeutic Metaphors: Specially Constructed Stories Tailored to Convey Prescriptive Problem Resolution

Milton Erickson, Richard Bandler, and John Grinder (Neurolinguistic Programming), Phillip Barker (1985), David Gordon (1978), and Lee Wallas (1985) have all described the utilization of specially constructed therapeutic stories. An effective metaphor is designed to "meet the client at his model of the world" (Gordon, 1978). The purpose of the metaphor is to change the patient's internal representation of the problem experience in such a way that the essential events of the story lead to different emotional or behavior consequences. Successful metaphors increase the number of perceived choices and may even suggest which of the available choices would be most advantageous.

To design a story that ensures that the patient will identify with the metaphor, the therapist must have a thorough understanding of the patient's world view and of his or her preferred mode of processing information. All important elements of the problem need to be included: characters, dynamics, language, representational patterns, and preferred mode of communication. If a desired outcome or resolution is presented in the story, there must be a "connective strategy" (Gordon, 1978) included to bridge the gap between the problem and its solution. If the connective strategy is missing, the patient may reject the story or simply emulate the solution without achieving new learning or insight. Construction of effective metaphors is complex, requiring the therapist to use sophisticated analysis of human communication patterns, thorough diagnostic understanding, and knowledge of personality dynamics.

The Use of Fairy Tales in Psychotherapy

Selection of Stories

Symptomatology.   In order to employ this method successfully, it is necessary for the therapist to be familiar with as much of the vast fairy tale literature as possible, selecting for use those stories that best capture particular developmental issues or particular neurotic conflicts and problems, such as "Allerleirah" (see p. 19), which deals with the effect of an incestuous father-daughter relationship on the daughter. Others deal with specific neurotic conflicts. In the familiar tale of the "Fisherman and His Wife," a man suffers terrible internal conflict and gives up personal power as he tries continually to satisfy a narcissistic, demanding wife.

Presentation of healthy role-model behavior.   Stories can present healthy role-model behavior. In "The Desolate Island" the hero recovers from the effects of his devastating loss and takes advantage of an opportunity. When a patient identifies with a hero who demonstrates desirable behavior, the effect is similar to that of behavior rehearsal—the patient practices the new behavior in a safe way through the use of imagery. Since psychological autonomy is emphasized in most fairy tales, patients can expose themselves to new ways of behaving simply by hearing the story and identifying with the main character.

Portrayal of growth process.   Fairy tales portray the change process itself and convey current psychotherapeutic tasks symbolically. It is a way for the therapist to say, "Here is something we really need to be working on" without overwhelming the patient. After the task has been presented metaphorically, the therapist can then point out the parallels in the patient's own life. For example, the author has used the story of "Beauty and the Beast" to help women who are fearful of intimate relationships with men. The story provides tools for learning to be comfortable in such a relationship, and the potential rewards of tackling the problem as opposed to avoidance.

Introduction of Method to Patients

Patients should be introduced to this method gradually, with consideration given to individual need, receptivity, and the patient's basic world view and psychological orientation. Generally, those who rely on verbal, rational modes of processing information take longer to feel comfortable with the imagistic, non-rational aspects of fairy tale narratives. Initially, they often try to reduce the message of fairy tale to a common-sense type of lesson. This tendency can be gently discouraged by the therapist in the interpretive discussion that follows the presentation of the story.

Introverted people adapt to the use of fairy tales easily, while extroverts have to learn the value of the internal focus. People who are very inhibited and tense may have more difficulty letting go of their defenses long enough to hear the stories, although at times they do relax in spite of themselves. Accurate diagnosis is always important, but especially with paranoid patients, who may develop fantasies about mind-reading or psychic invasion if the method is introduced too early in the treatment. Generally, it is not recommended to use this method with persons who are experiencing acute psychosis, although it can be used very effectively with nonpsychotic individuals in psychological crisis.

Those patients who are less educated or sophisticated about psychological matters are actually more accessible through the use of the storytelling method. They are more likely to "catch" the meaning of a particular story than the educated individual who wants to show off his or her intellectual prowess by analyzing the tales. Because imagery "speaks" without the need for verbal analysis, people who have difficulty with verbal expressions do well with this method.

Presentation of Stories

Initially the therapist may ask the patient to identify which scenes in the story seem most vivid, and what emotions were evoked. After establishing the important scenes, it is useful to peruse the personal meaning of these particular scenes, as well as the patient's attitudes toward important characters. Can the patient imagine himself or herself behaving in the way that the hero has done? If the patient can grasp the relevance of the story line to his or her personal history, the therapist can ask that patient to place himself or herself developmentally on the story line. In this way the therapist can help the patient to diagnose himself or herself and to identify developmental hurdles that need to be addressed in the therapeutic process.

The therapist may simply ask, "Would you like to hear a story?" at some point during the therapeutic interview. The ideal timing is at a point in the session when the introduction of a new perspective would be helpful. The surprise of introducing a story suddenly and without warning may create some confusion, perhaps making the patient more receptive to the message of the tale. The story idea can be casually mentioned in conversation before actually introducing a particular tale. Even in the initial interview, the therapist can ask about previous storytelling experiences.

The bedtime story is often a positive memory, although some patients report that their parents did not read to them. It is useful to elicit from patients their associations with the storytelling, and to inquire about a favorite childhood story. A discussion of the meaning of the favorite story can be an effective way of introducing the topic.

Initially, the therapist may simply ask the patient to listen carefully to a story, without asking for any other mental preparation. After the patient is more comfortable and accustomed to the story experience, hypnotic induction or relaxation can be used as a preparation for listening to the story. The hypnotic trance, which brings about a state of deep relaxation and receptivity in the patient, is ideal for fairy tale work, but is not essential for effective use. The therapist can instruct the patient to let the unconscious mind help him or her take notice of the parts of the story that are most important at the present time. After the story is finished, the therapist can either rouse the patient from the relaxed state and discuss the patient's memory of the story or, continuing in the deeply relaxed modality, help the patient to explore further important images that have been generated by the narrative.

Creating the Proper Atmosphere for Storytelling

Relaxation and receptivity.   Eliciting relaxation and receptivity is very important and can be achieved in a variety of ways. For example, when asking whether the patient would like to hear a story, the therapist can smile in an encouraging way. If the patient indicates anxiety, the therapist can suggest that he or she "just sit back and relax" while listening. Some highly rationalistic or judgmental individuals may worry about having the proper understanding of the story, but the therapist can emphasize the richness of the stories, and the fact that no particular interpretation is the "right" one. Having a comfortable place for the patient to sit or lie down and soft rather than bright light are preferable. If the patient has indicated positive association with bedtime story experiences in childhood, the therapist suggests that he or she listen as though he or she were a child again.

Use of hypnosis.   While not necessary, hypnosis increases the patient's receptivity. In general, most people experience more vivid imagery in the hypnotic state. While listening to a fairy tale in a hypnotic state, patients find it easier to merge identities with the central character, thus achieving greater emotional resonance with the narrative process. Although psychological defenses may still operate, the need to defend is lessened because of the underlying sense of security and trust that is engendered through hypnosis. A simple hypnotic induction, followed by the instruction "Please listen carefully to the following story" is generally adequate for this purpose. It should be noted that while listening to a story, many will spontaneously enter a trance.

Non-verbal communication.   In reading or telling stories, the therapist may use nonverbal communication to convey meaning. If the therapist wants the patient to notice certain scenes, ideas, or verbal messages embedded in the story, he or she can underline these passages with nonverbal signals. If the patient is listening with eyes open, the therapist makes eye contact at the point in the narrative needing emphasis. Pauses are effective, as well as repeating a significant image or phrase. The therapist can put emotion into the story at appropriate points through intonation, facial expression, and gesture. Interestingly, repetition of key themes is built into the writing of most fairy tales, and nonverbal techniques are employed universally by effective storytellers.

Resistance.   Resistance to this method is most common among highly verbal, rational people who rely heavily on intellectual processing. Persons fearful of dependency or experiencing negative transference with the therapist will also tend to be resistant. Several fairy tales deal with each of these issues and may be employed to help work through the resistance at the unconscious level. While it is generally not advisable to give lengthy explanations (of the fairy tale method), it can be helpful to explain briefly the basic rationale. A small number of people also have difficulty producing mental imagery of any kind, and they may need to proceed more slowly with assistance in practicing provided by the therapist. The Autogenic therapists, J. H. Schultz and Wolfgang Luthe (1969), have described in detail methods for training persons who have difficulty with imagery production.

Numerous experts on hypnosis and guided imagery have singled out the obsessive compulsive personality as being especially resistant and nonresponsive. The author agrees but finds that once these patients allow themselves to relax enough to participate, they are capable of extraordinarily rich experiences.

Interpretation of meaning. Bruno Bettleheim (1976) advised little or no interpretive discussion when using fairy tales with children but advised letting the unconscious mind assimilate the story and process its meaning. With adults, however, it is often useful to help them bridge the gap between imagistic and verbal thought with some interpretive discussion. Interpretation promotes assimilation of the message at several levels of awareness and establishes a therapeutic metaphor that can be referred to at later points in treatment.

Follow-up use of established metaphor. Generally there will be one or two stories that seem to capture the essence of a given patient's predicament. The patient will feel a very strong connection with these stories and may be able to verbalize this identification. Using the story line as a map, the therapist and patient then generate an outline for the process of therapy, including conflicts that must be resolved, emotional factors that need to be explored, skills or new behaviors that the patient must acquire, and changes in lifestyle that may be indicated. Therapist and patient can then begin to work together as a team rather than as adversaries, with the patient resisting as the therapist tries to drag him or her along toward growth. As therapy progresses, the relevant metaphor may change, and a new fairy tale motif may be introduced. Some stories are more developmentally advanced than others, and the timing is very important in terms of the usefulness of a given story to a particular patient. The use of the fairy tale as a structure for guided imagery is a very powerful way to help the patient integrate the learning at a deep psychological level.

Use of fairy tales in guided imagery. Fairy tale story themes can be utilized in guided affective imagery (Leuner, 1984) or oneirotherapy (Frétigny and Virel, 1968). The patient, in the relaxed state, enters into the story line and subjectively experiences the narrative. Generally, patients will freely adapt the basic story to their own needs, generating the narrative from internal sources.

When the therapist encourages a patient to place himself or herself in imaginary behavioral situations, he or she can experiment with his or her own behavior and learn new ways of coping in specific situations. Thus a woman who is fearful of men might, as Beauty did, journey to the castle of the Beast. Her unconscious mind will adapt the story to her own needs, producing vivid, challenging, and informative imagery experiences that have the power and intensity of nocturnal dreams. If, in her imagery adventure, she engages in new behavior or experiences new perceptions, the effect will be similar to performing the same act in everyday life.

Competent guided imagery therapy requires a great deal of sensitivity and skill on the part of the therapist. Although fairy tales can provide a framework, there are no formulas for successful imagery work. The therapist must enter into the patient's imaginary experience and at times guide the flow of the imagery. Thus a close rapport between patient and therapist is essential in order for treatment to be successful. The therapist must have a thorough understanding of patterns of symbolism as they relate to psychodynamic issues, as well as functional familiarity with the individual patient's symbolic system.

These methods can be utilized effectively in long- or short-term psychotherapy.

Fairy tales can be introduced early in the treatment process to help reorient the patient's view of treatment and to assist in the development of appropriate therapeutic goals. Extensive use of guided imagery may come late, when the patient is ready to accept change at a deeper psychological level.

Clinical example: The use of "Allerleirah" in the treatment of victims of incest. The Greek myth of Oedipus is the most influential story about incest in western culture, but the profound fatalism and pessimism of the myth make it a poor candidate for therapeutic use. In contrast to the tragic outcome of the Oedipal myth is the German fairy tale, "Allerleirah" (Furskin), in which a young princess refuses to be trapped in an incestuous marriage with her father and runs away from home.

Wearing an unusual fur coat made of many different animal skins, she disguises herself as a "hairy animal" (*Grimm's Fairy Tales*, 1944). She is sleeping in a hollow tree in the forest when she is discovered by the servants of a young king and is then taken to his palace to live. At the palace she lives a life of misery and servitude as a cook's helper, staying hidden in her little den under the stairs when she is not working in the kitchen. Eventually she is transformed back to her true nature as a beautiful princess, in part through the recognition and appreciation given to her by the perceptive young king. When she is ready to do so, she assumes her proper place as queen of the new kingdom.

Some patients have worked through their own emotional conflicts via dramatization of specific scenes from Allerleirah through guided imagery. At times they are encouraged to observe the princess undergoing her process of transformation, while in other instances a more subjective mode of experience is encouraged. In my experience the most effective approach to the treatment of incest has included guided imagery exploration of real-life traumatic memories, alternating with exploration, confrontation, and resolution at the metaphorical level, using the fairy tale as a map. At the most basic level, this fairy tale helps the incest victim to be relieved of her terrible isolation by recognizing that this problem is an ancient one. She can also hope for a positive outcome if she identifies with the fairy tale.

SUMMARY

Storytelling can be a powerful and effective tool of psychological intervention. By using metaphorical stories and fairy tales, the therapist can communicate important diagnostic and prescriptive information to the patient in a way that speaks directly to the unconscious mind. The patient absorbs the developmental lessons that are embedded in the story and utilizes the story line as a map for future growth and development.

The use of stories can help the patient to develop understanding of the importance of psychological balance and the relationship between psychological crisis and personal growth. Stories can be utilized for greater impact in a brief therapeutic encounter or to provide structure and goals for long-term psychological development.

REFERENCES

Bandler, R., & Grinder, J. (1975). *Patterns of the hypnotic techniques of Milton Erickson, M.D.* Cupertino, CA: Meta.

Barker, P. (1985). *Using therapeutic metaphors in psychotherapy.* New York: Brunner-Mazel.

Bellak, L. (1952). *The children's apperception technique.* Larchmont, NY: C.P.S. Inc.

Bettleheim, B. (1976). *The uses of enchantment.* New York: Alfred A. Knopf.

Frétigny, R., & Virel, A. (1968). *L'imagerie mentale.* Geneva: Mont Blanc.

Gardner, R. A. (1971). *Therapeutic communication with children.* New York: Science House.

Gordon, D. (1978). *Therapeutic metaphors.* Cupertino, CA: Meta.

Grimm, J., & Grimm, W. (1944). *The complete Grimm's fairy tales.* New York: Pantheon.

Jung, C. G. (1964). *Man and his symbols.* Garden City, NJ: Doubleday.

Leuner, H. (1984). *Guided affective imagery.* New York: Thieme-Stratton, Inc.

Murray, H. (1943). *The thematic apperception technique.* Cambridge: Harvard College.

Schultz, J. H., & Luthe, W. (1969). *Autogenic therapy* (vol. I). New York: Grune & Stratton.

Shah, I. (1979). *World tales.* New York: Harcourt Brace Jovanovich.

Sheikh, A. (1983). *Imagery: Current theory, research, and application.* New York: John Wiley & Sons.

Stoner, M. (1985). Use of mutual metaphor with a disturbed chold: A case study, in *Clinical Hypnosis and Therapeutic Suggestion in Nursing.* Orlando, FL: Grune & Stratton.

Wallas, L. (1985). *Stories for the third ear.* New York: W. W. Norton.

Zahourek, R. P. (Ed.) (1985). *Clinical hypnosis and therapeutic suggestion in nursing.* Orlando, FL: Grune & Stratton.

Zeig, J. D. (Ed.) (1985). *Ericksonian psychotherapy* (vol. I). New York: Brunner-Mazel.

PART II

CLINICAL APPLICATIONS

6

STRESS AND COPING

CAROLYN CHAMBERS CLARK

FRAMEWORKS FOR STRESS ASSESSMENT

In 1914 Cannon described the fight or flight response or "emergency reaction" that prepares the individual to fight or run. Physiological changes for this response include increase in blood pressure, heart rate, metabolism, respiration, blood glucose, epinephrine, peripheral vascular construction, dilation of the pupils, and decreased testosterone levels (Benson & Klipper, 1976; Cannon, 1914; Selye, 1956).

Some stress is necessary for life and cannot be avoided. Individuals also vary greatly in their psycho-social-physiological responses to life events. What is defined as "stressful" by one individual may not be by another.

With chronic stress, the immune system is weakened, leading to lowered resistance and disease (Zeagans, 1982). Temporary conditions can become permanent ones under chronic stress: for example, transient high blood pressure can become hypertension, and stomach upset may turn into colitis or ulcers. Stress has been related to many diseases and ailments including headaches, peptic ulcers, colitis, arthritis, asthma, diarrhea, sexual problems, cardiac arrhythmias, muscle tension, circulatory problems, and cancer (Davis, McKay, & Eshelman, 1982, p. 6).

It is not possible (or wise) to turn off innate fight/flight responses to threat. It is possible and wise to learn to interpret and label experiences differently, thus lowering negative stressor impact.

The first step in reducing stress may be to assess the major stressors. The Holmes "Schedule of Recent Experience" was developed by Thomas Holmes at the University of Washington School of Medicine in Seattle, Washington. It gives a value for each life event and allows the respondent to obtain a total score. Typical items include change in financial state, death of a spouse, divorce, sexual difficulties, and vacation. The assumption underlying the schedule is that the more change individuals have to adjust to, the more likely they are to become ill. Holmes found that 80 percent of the persons he studied who had a score over 300 were apt to become ill in the near future.

Critics of the schedule claim that some changes are not stressful and may even be pleasant. For example, according to the schedule, a job change is stressful. There may be certain conditions when a job change is less stressful than it would be to stay in a dead-end job that is draining and results in ongoing resentment. Following is a list that presents information for assessing and reducing stressful life change.

1. Identify sources of stress for you. List changes in the following areas that are affecting you now.
     * School:
     * Close relationships with friends, family, and significant other people or pets:
     * Work:
     * Life style (include nutrition, fitness, etc.):
     * Living arrangements or place of residence:
     * Finances:
     * Amount of worry about the future:
     * Sudden challenges:
2. Identify which changes seem to be negative (stressful) by placing a minus sign (−) in front of them and which seem to be positive (helpful or neutral) by placing a plus sign (+) in front of them.
3. Identify the negative (−) changes and decide on a procedure for limiting the effects of the stress. (Refer to the rest of this chapter for appropriate procedures to use.)

One method of identifying stressors is the Stress Awareness Diary. Clients make note of times that a stressful event occurs in the diary and also note the occurrence of physical or emotional symptoms. In time, it is possible to recognize the connections between the stressful event and the symptom. Clients will learn body areas where they store tension. With increased awareness, clients can learn to use procedures for releasing tension in those areas and preventing further physiological damage. The diary can also serve as a record of progress, reinforcer for success, and identification of issues that require additional practice.

A wellness model (Fig. 6–1) examines the interactive effects of nutrition, stress, fitness, the environment, interpersonal relationships, self-care, and value systems (Clark, 1986).

Stress can result from under- or overnutrition, lack of fitness or overexercising, over- or understimulating environments, negative or unsatisfying interpersonal rela-

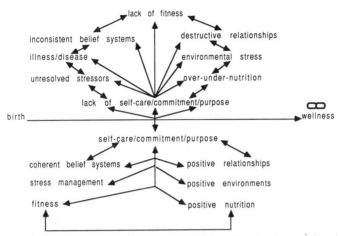

Figure 6–1. The Wellness Continuum.   The continuum is interactive, developmental, and unidirectional toward wellness. Disability, illness, or dying do not necessarily interfere with movement toward wellness and can occur at any point on the way to wellness. Copyright, Carolyn Chambers Clark, 1987.

tionships, insufficient self-care procedures, conflicting values, or any possible combinations of these factors.

This chapter will examine stress reduction from the viewpoint of relaxation and imagery frameworks and procedures. It is well to keep in mind that stress may also be reduced by intervening in any other wellness dimension since each dimension affects the total wellness of an individual.

Physical symptoms may have physiological sources, so it is unwise to assume that all symptoms are completely stress-related. Once it has been established that stress is the major source of the symptom, a stress management procedure can be chosen. Two types of procedures can be used: those that focus on relaxing the body and those that focus on handling stress in a new way. Often it is useful to use at least one approach from each category. For example, progressive relaxation may be used to calm the body and refuting irrational ideas may be used to reduce negative perspectives on events that increase stress (Davis, McKay, & Eshelman, 1982, p. 15).

RELAXATION METHODS

Progressive relaxation was developed by Jacobson in 1938. The procedure involves tightening and relaxing the muscle groups of the body, beginning with the hand and moving to the upper and then the lower arm, the forehead, eyes and nose, mouth, neck, upper back, abdomen, buttocks, thigh, calf, and foot for 5 to 7 seconds. The client is encouraged to check for relaxation prior to moving to the next major muscle group. A signal can be agreed on prior to inducing relaxation so the client can let the helper know if relaxation has been attained without interfering with the relaxation process.

There are a number of other methods of attaining relaxation besides progressive relaxation. Some clients relax more readily with one approach than another; it is up to the helping person to observe and collaborate with each client to find the relaxation technique (or combination of techniques) most useful for attaining a relaxed state.

Initially, the helping person may read a prepared relaxation script, play a relaxation audiotape,* or repeat a useful relaxation monologue. A relatively simple and quick way to attain relaxation by altering the client's consciousness state is to help the client become aware of sensations that are usually not consciously noted. The clinician makes comments to put the client in touch with what is being experienced through various sensory modes that are out of total awareness (Grinder & Bandler, 1981). For example, the helper may say, "You can become aware of the feeling of your hands on your thighs and the sensation of your feet on the floor."

A second method involves imagery and assists the client to take an inner journey to a peaceful, quiet, relaxing place. A helping person can say, "Close your eyes and take yourself in that place, smelling the smells, hearing the sounds, seeing what there is to see, feeling all the sensations available to you there." The client is then not interrupted for 3 to 5 minutes while he or she redirects the client back to the present by saying, "Keeping that sense of peace and relaxation, bring yourself back in time and space to the present and focus on . . . ."

Although the helping person provides the content for the relaxation at first, by the end of the first session, the client has been taught an appropriate method and has been encouraged to practice relaxation out-of-session. Some health care professionals have made audiotapes for clients to use between sessions, while others give clients relaxation scripts or encourage them to develop their own regimens for daily practice. Whichever method is used, it is suggested to the client that relaxation is a learned skill that requires regular, systematic practice.

Relaxation Assessment

Scandrett and Uecker (1985, p. 33) suggest that a careful assessment of the client is essential prior to employing relaxation techniques. Symptoms need to be identified, and an anxiety scale or anxiety symptom checklist is completed. Baseline (pretreatment) and posttreatment vital sign measures will validate physiological changes associated with relaxation. The following components for the pretreatment phase include assessing:

* Client identification of the most bothersome symptom
* Onset, duration, and full description of symptoms

---

*One source of tapes is *The Wellness Newsletter*, 3451 Central Avenue, St. Petersburg, FL 33713.

* Family history of similar complaints
* Interventions tried by the client and results
* Reasons for seeking help now
* Current and recent prescription and nonprescription medications
* Physical limitations and illnesses
* Previous experience with relaxation training
* Use of alcohol, nicotine, and mind-altering drugs
* Dietary patterns, especially use of caffeine and sugar
* Sleep patterns
* Exercise patterns
* Daily stressors
* Psychiatric history, especially major depressive or psychotic disorders
* Willingness to learn and practice at home

USE OF SUGGESTION FOR STRESS REDUCTION

Suggestion can be used in two ways to relieve stress. The first includes the following steps: (1) obtain data regarding the client problem, (2) agree on an individualized stress reduction suggestion with the client, (3) assist the client to a relaxed state, and, (4) repeat or ask the client to repeat the stress reduction suggestion.

The second approach includes the same steps, but reordered and modified. The client is helped to a relaxed state at the beginning of the session. Prior to beginning the relaxation procedures, the helper and client agree on finger signals, for example, asking the client to "raise the index finger of your right hand when you feel completely relaxed," and "raise the little finger of your left hand when you feel yourself becoming less relaxed."

While in a relaxed state the assessment questions are asked with finger signals indicating relaxed or tense responses. This approach allows the helper to stop assessment questions that induce stress and proceed directly to a relaxation procedure until stress is reduced and assessment can continue. This procedure alone is often helpful in reducing client anxiety sufficiently to preclude the use of further intervention. The helper uses the consistent suggestion during this procedure of increasing relaxation.

The order of intervention chosen is based on a number of factors, including (1) level of client resistance to use of suggestion, (2) level of client comfort with each order of intervention, (3) level of helper resistance to use of suggestion, and (4) level of helper comfort with each order of intervention.

Once the stressor has been identified, it may be necessary for the helper and client to spend some time deciding which portion of the situation to focus on and how the suggestions can be worded most effectively for that client. For example, for a student who becomes highly anxious while taking an examination, the suggestion could emphasize physical relaxation, reducing the threat of the examination questions, environment, or both. Suggestions that may be appropriate include, "I will pass this exam" (self-focused); "These questions are questions I know the answer to" (environment-focused); "I can become more relaxed and focus on the exam questions" (both).

Designing Stress Reduction Suggestions

To get the flavor of how stress reduction suggestions can be formulated, examine the stressful client situations below and think of a suggestion to use for each one.

1. Fear of being alone in the house at night.
2. Feeling anxious about work or school deadlines, but being unable to concentrate.
3. Being unable to get to sleep.
4. Feelings of being inferior to classmates or work peers.
5. Worry about being rejected for a job, a grade, or a date.

Now, examine some possible suggestions for the above situations:

1. It's getting easier and easier to stay home alone at night.
2. I'm getting more and more relaxed about getting my work done or It's getting easier and easier to concentrate on the task at hand.
3. I'm gradually becoming more drowsy and in a few minutes I'll be able to fall asleep.
4. Each time I'm with _____, it's getting easier and easier to feel relaxed and good about myself.
5. By letting my breath flow through me, I can feel confidence flowing throughout my whole body.

(For additional use of suggestion see Chapter 4 "Suggestion and Therapeutic Communication.")

Teaching Clients to Use a Stress Reduction Hierarchy

Relaxation can be combined with imagery to reduce the threat posed by stress through the use of a stress reduction hierarchy (Wolpe, 1969). As with other approaches, effective relaxation skills form the basis for use of stress reduction hierarchies. Once the client is able to relax at will a stress hierarchy is formulated. For example, suppose the dreaded event is participating in an interdisciplinary conference. The end goal is speaking up in the conference. However, there are a series of preceding steps the client must move through in order to be relaxed in the target situation.

Step 1: Attain total body relaxation.

Step 2: Picture myself waking up and remembering today is the day to speak up in the interdisciplinary conference.

Step 3: Check for decreased relaxation; if anxiety has risen, stop that image and return to total body relaxation until relaxation is attained, then move back to step 2 and proceed.

Step 4: Picture myself getting out of bed and thinking about speaking up in the interdisciplinary conference.

Step 5: As in Step 3.

Step 6: Picture myself dressing and thinking about speaking up in the conference.

Step 7: As in Step 3.

Step 8: Picture myself on the way to the interdisciplinary conference.

Step 9: As in Step 3.

Step 10: Picture muself approaching the door of the conference room.

Step 11: As in Step 3.

Step 12: Picture myself entering the room and being seated.

Step 13: As in Step 3.

Step 14: Picture myself waiting for my chance to speak up in the conference.

Step 15: As in Step 3.

End Goal: Picture myself speaking up in an interdisciplinary conference while feeling relaxed.

Initially, the helper assists the client to learn the hierarchy process as follows:

1. Agree on finger signals for increased and decreased relaxation.
2. Assist the client to a relaxed state.
3. Move from one step to the next only when the client signals a deep state of body relaxation.
4. Whenever decreased relaxation is signaled, assist the client to attain a deeply relaxed state, watching the client's finger signals to indicate when to move to the next step.
5. Work back and forth between assisting the client to relax and moving closer to the end goal until the client feels relaxed imagining the goal.
6. Suggest to the client that now body, thoughts, and feelings are integrated in a relaxed whole, making it easier and easier to relax in the actual situation when it occurs.

Clients will develop individualized hierarchies based on the content that is important to them. The content will change, but the process of working through the anxiety remains the same. Fewer steps may be needed or more added, depending on the level of stress attached to the event. In this approach, as in the others mentioned, the helper should check back and forth with the client to ensure the appropriate number of steps are used and words relevant to the client's experience are chosen. Once clients learn their hierarchies, they can work on them out-of-session.

COPING SKILLS PROCEDURES

Another stress reduction approach that can also be used by clients for self-care purposes is teaching stress coping thoughts (Davis, McKay, & Eshelman, 1982). Their approach is based on cognitive psychology theory, which holds that thoughts rule feelings. The way the future or present is imagined intensifies or decreases the feelings experienced.

For example, if a bus is missed, the person can negatively interpret the situation thinking, "Oh, dear, now I'm late, I'll never get all my work done," or positively interpret by thinking, "Well, now I have a few minutes to relax and enjoy the scenery and the people." The first interpretation will probably lead to knots in the stomach, increased heart rate, and so on. The second interpretation will probably lead to decreased heart and respiratory rate and feelings of calmness, if not enjoyment.

When working to reverse negative thoughts, there are suggestions the client can use at each phase of the stressful situation. Anticipating the stressful event, the client could say: "I'm going to be all right," "I won't let this upset me," or, "I've handled this situation before and gotten through it all right." At the beginning of a stressful situation, suggestions such as the following can be used: "I'll take this one step at a time," "I'm doing my best and I'll be okay," and, "I'm getting tense and so I'll focus on taking some deep, relaxing breaths." When the situation ends, the client can say, "I got through it and I did well," "I'm able to handle this situation," or, "I'm going to tell one other person how well I did."

The most effective coping thoughts are probably those developed by the client. These suggestions can provide guidelines for formulation for future activities. Once coping thoughts have been formulated, clients can write them on 3×5 cards, carry them with them, and read them when confronted with a stressful situation.

Coping skills training grew out of relaxation and systematic desensitization procedures that were expanded and refined by Meichenbaum and Cameron (1974). The procedures include a combination of progressive relaxation and stress coping self-statements that are used to replace the defeatist self-talk called forth in stressful situations.

Coping skills procedures can be used to rehearse via the imagination for real life events deemed stressful. First, a stressful situation is called forth. Next, progressive relaxation is practiced. Finally, coping skills statements are repeated until the situation can be thoroughly completed in rehearsal without feeling stressed.

The procedures enhance the reduction of general anxiety and interview, speech, and test anxiety and appear to be effective in the treatment of phobias, especially the fear of heights. David, McKay, and Eshelman (1982, p. 120) reported the effects of 2-year follow-ups of hypertense, postcardiac clients showing that 89 percent were still able to achieve general relaxation using coping skills training, 79 percent could still generally control tension, and 79 percent were able to fall asleep sooner and sleep more deeply. According to the researchers, coping skills procedures can be mastered in approximately 1 week, once progressive relaxation has been learned (1–2 weeks for mastery).

THOUGHT STOPPING

In the late 1950s Joseph Wolpe and other behavior therapists adapted Bain's thought stopping method for the treatment of stressful obsessive and phobic thoughts. Thought stopping involves concentrating on the unwanted thoughts and then suddenly stopping and emptying the mind. The command "STOP," a loud noise, or an image of the thought being stopped are generally used to interrupt unpleasant thoughts. Thought stopping is thought to work because the command "stop" serves as punishment, distractor, and can be followed by thought substitutions and reassuring or self-accepting statements. It has been well documented that negative and frighteneing thoughts precede negative and frightening emotions. By controlling the thoughts, overall stress levels can be reduced (Davis, Eshelman, & McKay, 1982, p. 91)

Mastery of the techniques requires regular practice for 3 to 7 days. The client chooses the problematic thought for focus. Some clients may require assistance in prioritizing interfering thoughts. The negative thought is then brought to attention. Clients are then asked to close their eyes and imagine a situation during which the stressful thought is likely to occur. The next step is to interrupt the nagging thought with an alarm clock, snap of the fingers, or an image or verbalization of the word, "STOP."

When clients are able to conjure up and dispense with the nagging thought at will, positive, assertive statements are used to replace the nonconstructive ones, for example:

* Fear of attack: "I am safe if I use the approaches I have learned to protect myself."
* Fear of flying: "This is a beautiful view from up here."
* Food obsession: "My body is using the food I have already eaten to sustain me."
* Fear of failure: "I have already succeeded by conquering my fear of failure."

Clients who experience failure with the approach can choose a less intrusive thought to begin with; once success is achieved, more troublesome thoughts can be attempted. Distressful thoughts may return in the future, especially during times of stress; the procedure can be repeated in these cases.

REFUTING IRRATIONAL IDEAS

Human beings engage in almost continuous self-talk during their waking hours. Self-talk is the internal language we use to describe and interpret the world to ourselves. When self-talk is accurate and realistic, stress is reduced and wellness enhanced; when it is irrational and untrue, stress and emotional disturbance occur.

Albert Ellis (Ellis & Harper, 1961) developed a system to attack irrational ideas or beliefs and replace them with more realistic interpretations and self-talk. According to Ellis, at the root of irrational thought is the idea that something is being done to the person; rational thought is based on the idea that events occur and people experience these events. Irrational self-talk tends to lead to unpleasant emotions; rational self-talk is more likely to lead to pleasant feelings and a positive interpretation of experiences.

A common form of irrational self-talk includes statements that "awfulize" experience by making catastrophic, nightmarish interpretations of events. Interpreting a momentary chest pain as a heart attack, a grumpy word from a supervisor as intent to fire, or silence as negative criticism, are examples of "awfulizing."

Goodman (1974) developed guidelines for turning irrational thinking into rational thought:

1. The situation does not do anything to me; I say things to myself that produce anxiety and fear.
2. To say things should be other than they are is to believe in magic.
3. All humans are fallible and make mistakes.
4. It takes two to argue.
5. The original cause of a problem is often lost in antiquity; the best place to focus attention is on the present and what to do about the problem now.
6. People feel the way they think; the interpretation of events leads to emotions, not the events themselves.

HELPING CLIENTS REFUTE IRRATIONAL IDEAS

Davis, McKay, and Eshelman (1982) suggest the following format for refuting irrational ideas:

1. Write down the event that led to a loss of sense of mastery (e.g., "Mr. Reuben failed me on my exam").
2. Write down any rational ideas about the event that indicate understanding another point of view, or the blamelessness of the situation (e.g., "I didn't study" stated as a neutral fact).
3. Write down any irrational ideas that indicate that something is being done to you or that loss of control, confidence, or self-esteem has occurred (e.g., "The teacher is out to get me").
4. Write down any feelings that resulted from the irrational ideas (e.g., "I feel angry and depressed").
5. Challenge any irrational ideas (e.g., "I'm not the only one who failed so he can't be out to get just me; I've talked myself into getting depressed; the worst thing that can happen is I won't get an A in the course, but it doesn't mean I'm a bad person.").
6. Make concrete plans for dealing rationally with the situation (e.g., "I'll have to

study harder to get a better grade; I'll treat myself to a good dinner and then talk with a friend awhile until I feel better. I'm beginning to feel better already").

USING GUIDED IMAGERY WITH CLIENTS

There are three basic ways to use imagery with clients (Samuels & Samuels, 1975):

1. Receptive—to help become more aware of feelings, dissatisfactions, tensions, and images that are affecting body functioning.
2. Healing—to help erase bacteria or viruses, build new cells to replace damaged ones, make rough areas smooth, hot areas cool, sore areas comfortable, tense areas relaxed, drain swollen areas, release pressure from tight areas, bring blood to areas that need nutriment or cleansing, make moist areas dry or dry areas moist, bring energy to fatigued areas, and enhance general wellness.
3. Problem solving—to consult with one's intuitive source of wisdom in a structured way.

Each of these will be discussed in turn.

Receptive Guided Imagery

Research* was conducted by the author to investigate whether clients have intuitive knowledge about their bodies that is not currently being assessed by traditional nursing assessment procedures. Diagnostic guided imagery was the tool used to measure this intuitive knowledge in student nurses coming for help to the nurse-managed clinical practice unit.

Diagnostic guided imagery can be used as an assessment procedure, but can also help clients become aware of feelings they have been "holding" in body areas, creating undue stress on body tissues. A number of research studies have shown that inhibiting emotions about traumatic events results in increased autonomic activity including increases in skin conductance, increased heart rate, and blood pressure (Fowles, 1980; Gray, 1975). Selye (1956) and others (Davies, 1970; Jones, 1960; Kissen, 1966) have examined the long-term effects of stress and failure to confide in others about traumatic experiences (Pennebaker, 1985). It appears that diagnostic guided imagery has potential for assisting clients to uncover hidden feelings and provides a context within which to discuss them.

Since the conscious mind is bypassed when using imagery, this approach may stimulate strong emotional reactions. Thus, an occasional client may seem confused by the strong feelings experienced. It is wise to suggest to clients that they need only be-

*This research was supported in part by a grant from the Robert Wood Johnson Foundation Grant to the Lienhard School of Nursing for Research in the Clinical Practice Unit, and by a Pace University scholarship research grant.

come aware of feelings they feel comfortable handling at that time. Such a comment reduces resistance to becoming aware of feelings they feel comfortable handling at that time and also gives clients permission to protect themselves from painful feelings they are not yet ready to face.

Some questions that have been used during the research process to assist clients to develop diagnostic images and that can be used clinically to help elicit feelings, dissatisfactions, tensions, or unhealthy images are:

1. Close your eyes and go inside yourself. Locate where any feelings of anger or resentment are in your body. Tell me what you see. Anything else?
2. Where in your body are there feelings of guilt? What are you picturing? Anything else?
3. Where in your body are there any feelings of sadness? What do you see? Anything else?
4. Now scan your body once more for any feelings or images you might have missed. Describe what you see now.

During this procedure clients may become aware of strong feelings that they were not aware of previously or may discover the image of their body is misshapen or of distressing color or texture. Some clients may comment that they knew about some of the feelings or images but had not been able to integrate them into an understandable whole until using the imagery approach.

Sometimes it is useful to ask clients to picture how the feelings are affecting their muscle tension, blood flow, hormonal secretions, or general body functioning. Some clients describe these effects spontaneously; one client reported, "Tightness in my breathing in my chest—I see a blue plastic band like the ones around broccoli—I want to cut it."

Results suggested that clients do offer an entirely different order of information about their perceived health problems when asked to use diagnostic guided imagery as opposed to when they are asked traditional intake questions such as, "What brought you here today?" Some comparisons may prove useful in differentiating the two types of information.

Traditional Assessment Responses:

1. Lack of confidence in school and social situations

2. No callus formation on fractured humerus

3. Anxiety about exams

Diagnostic Guided Imagery Responses:

1. "My stomach is contracted, shrunken like a balloon, sucked in, oozing HCL and in spasm."

2. "I see the ends of two broken chicken bones; the plates are screwing metal and cold, but the bone ends are jagged. I feel anger in my fist; I'd like to punch the doctor who put in the plates without asking me. My stomach is tightening like a vice, all green and prickly. Sadness is in my heart. I want to cradle it with my right arm and bend my head over to take care of it."

3. "My professor is writing on the board but there's nothing written there. I see a big cave with a light at the end. I'm not afraid, but I'm dwarfed by how large the chamber is. It's tedious, monotonous trip, but beautiful at the end."

4. Angina

4. "My heart is tense and fibrillating; tight, working too hard, snapping."

5. Sore back muscle

5. "The muscle is torn and ragged, redder at the ends, instead of pink. I hurt myself lifting a piece of furniture with my brother—the one I'm always angry at."

6. Stuttering

6. "My throat is moving around, never still. Trachea is huge and it sticks out, white and hard. My lungs are scarred, they're too small for the space they're in."

7. Overeating

7. "There is an animal consumed in flames some place between my stomach and throat. There are tentacles reaching into my trunk and GI tract, downwards to my knees and up past my shoulder. It has no head or much of a body."

8. Agitated depression

8. "Tightness in my intestines, anger is tightening in my shoulders, tautness in the middle of my back, sadness in my heart; I can only see one lung, chaotic mess of tubes and blood vessels in my chest."

Healing Guided Imagery

The clinicians can choose the therapeutic image for the client, ask the client, "How would the area look if it were healthy?", or the two can collaborate to develop an individualized healing image. The author's experience is that it is more efficient and effective when the client chooses a healthy image. The therapeutic images developed for the problems assess via diagnostic guided imagery and reported in the preceding section were:

Diagnostic Guided Imagery Problem:

Therapeutic Image:

1. Stomach contracted, shrunken, sucked in, oozing HCL, spasm.

1. Stomach full, relaxed, healthy.

2. Plates metal, cold bone ends jagged.

2. Plates are warm, soft, bone ends are connecting.

3. Can't read professor, trip is tedious, monotonous, beautiful at end.

3. Reads what professor has written on board; journey becomes less tedious and monotonous.

4. Heart tense, fibrillating, working too hard, snapping.

4. Heart beating nicely.

5. Torn, ragged red muscle.

5. The torn edges of the muscle are moving together, color changing to pink, anger is placed in a container and put away.

6. Throat moving around; trachea huge, sticking out, hard, white; lungs too small; scarred.

6. Throat at rest, trachea smoothing and softening, lungs expanding to fill available space.

7. Animal consumed in flames; tentacles, no head and little body.

7. Flames die out, the life force is gone, no center remains, the animal deflates, lies in a puddle, leaves body as waste.

8. Tightness in intestines, anger tightening shoulders and back, heart/lungs chaotic and partial.

8. Loosening and widening of muscles in gut, shoulder, back; standing back from body to be able to see other lung; heart and lungs are pink, expanded, orderly.

Another way to form therapeutic images is to ask the client to think of images of love, peace, joy, and harmony and to picture each one's effect on muscle tension, blood flow, hormonal secretion, and body functioning.

Some images that can be used (or adapted) for health or stress problems include (Bry, 1972; Samuels & Samuels, 1975; Simonton, Simonton & Creighton, 1978):

Health/Stress Problem:	*Therapeutic Images:*
1. Headache	1. Picture a hole in your head near the area of the headache; on exhalation, imagine the pain going through the hole as a color.
2. Nasal or sinus congestion	2. Imagine tubes opening and draining like a sink unclogging.
3. Hemorrhoids	3. Imagine the pelvis becoming warm as you picture blood flowing into it; see your anus cool, and becoming cooler, perhaps sitting in a cool relaxing bath.
4. Anger	4. Locate the place(s) in your body where you see the anger. Now choose a container of some sort. Put all the anger in the container, cover it, and put it some place where it cannot affect you.
5. Sadness or ending a relationship	5. Locate all your feelings of sadness or ending in your body that you want to get rid of. Put all the anger in the container, cover it, and put it some place where it cannot affect you.
6. Excessive gastric secretion	6. Picture the texture and dryness of blotting paper in your stomach area; picture absorbant dryness.
7. Gynecological or menstrual problems	7. Picture your pelvis warm and healthy.
8. Ineffective immune system	8. Picture healthy white blood cells moving in to attack invading viruses or bacteria; see the white blood cells carrying the weakened viruses or bacteria away, out of your body.

Another way to use healing guided imagery is to picture the entire body healthy, whole, and relaxed. This kind of image can be used universally, despite the symptom or problem. It is most useful as a preventive image. Clients can be asked to picture their bodies healthy, whole, and relaxed several times a day, each day. A good time to use preventive imagery is when taking a shower or bath. The water provides the relaxation and the task allows for nearly total concentration on the therapeutic image.

Problem-Solving Guided Imagery

Imagery can be used in a number of structured ways to assist clients to solve problems.

The Closed Box (Bry, 1978)

Picture yourself locked up in a giant wooden box with a securely tied lid. Picture what you would do to get out of that box. (This exercise can be used to help clients discover what's wrong with their lives and how to change it. As clients begin to picture how to get out of the box, new insights about how to change their lives will occur to them.)

The Blue Frames (Bry, 1972)

Clearly define the problem. Place it in a blue frame. Pretend you're telling the problem to a friend. Be very specific about all aspects of the problem. See the solution to the problem in a white frame. It is suggested that a client ponder the following questions prior to attempting to solve the problem: Do I really want to know the answer to the problem?; Do I feel I deserve an answer to this problem?; Am I willing to accept the solution even if it's not what I'd hoped for?

HELPING CLIENTS CONTACT THEIR INNER ADVISER

Inner dialogue is based on the idea that everyone has an intuitive aspect that knows what to do to be healthier and happier. There are a number of different ways to get in touch with this intuitive, self-healing aspect (Clark, 1981). One way is to enter into a dialogue with an archetypal or mythical figure. The dialogue focuses on physical symptoms and what they represent and on ways to reorder one's life, thereby releasing oneself from the symptoms (Bry, 1972). The theoretical basis of this approach is that the body is the battleground for conflicting attitudes, beliefs, and ideas. Once the client dialogues about the conflict, that conflict changes form and there is potential for a healthier body.

Dr. Irving Oyle, a proponent of this approach, helps clients deeply relax their bodies and then directs them to go to a lake in their mind's eye and wait for a figure or animal to appear to them for the purpose of dialogue. Another way to use inner dialogue is to ask a client to depict his or her inner adviser in whatever shape or form that seems right. In time, each person will visualize an adviser form that has helpful qualities. Perseverance and honesty are necessary to be successful with this approach.

Initially, clients may be skeptical about this procedure For this reason, some people may try it only after many other approaches have failed to bring relief. As with other solutions, the helping person needs a positive attitude to assist the client in learning and using the technique. One way to feel more positive about the technique is to try it prior to using it with clients. This may help forestall any difficulties that might be encountered in working with a client since the helper will be familiar with the process.

This technique is not meant to be a substitute for needed medical care. However, many clients have symptoms that cannot be helped by medical intervention, such as colds, pain that does not respond to medication or for which there is no organic basis, and to receive reassurance. Some examples may help to explain the use of the inner adviser.

Example 1

Beth, a young nurse, had been proclaimed cured of breast cancer following surgery. However, she did not seem to heal or to be interested in life. She described severe, continuing pain in her back, "like a tiger clawing at me." Pain medication did not help. A nurse on the unit taught Beth the inner dialogue approach. Beth learned how to relax her body and then went in search of her inner adviser. She met a tiger by a stream who told her he had been trying to get her attention by clawing at her. The tiger told Beth she had never wanted to be a nurse but had gone through nursing school to please her parents. Resentment and unfulfilled dreams had led her to cancer. The tiger told Beth to decide what she wanted to do with her life and do it and then her pain would be bearable. After several sessions of dialogue, Beth reported less pain.

Example 2

Warren is a teacher who recently bought a house with his wife. He worked every evening on the house after teaching all day. Recently he had incurred several injuries including a pulled back muscle, a sprained thumb, and a broken toe. His wife read about the inner dialogue technique and asked him to try it to find out why he was getting so many injuries. Warren laughed at first, but finally agreed. With persistence he was able to contact his inner adviser, an American Indian woman who told him he was being pulled in so many directions that he was injuring himself. The inner adviser told him to slow down and not try to do so much work on the house at once and that life is to enjoy. After Warren cut his time on the house in half, he incurred no further injuries.

Before using the inner adviser approach, clients can prepare themselves by asking a series of questions.

1. If I had an inner adviser, what would he, she, or it look like?
2. What characteristics would my inner adviser have that would be helpful to me?
3. What is the best way to communicate with my inner adviser?
4. What familial body vulnerabilities might I be getting messages about? (For example, do people in my family tend to show conflict by getting colds, backaches, diarrhea, or some other symptom?)
5. What are my usual body symptoms that may be giving me messages about imbalances in my body/mind?
6. In what ways have I been misusing my body/mind lately?
7. In what direction is my life going that I do not want it to go?

The answers to these questions provide valuable clues about what to expect and provide the beginning experience for inner dialogue. Following this preparatory stage, the client is helped to engage in a relaxation exercise.

Suggestions for consulting an inner adviser include the following:

1. Choose a time when you are not rushed. Relax your body completely using a relaxation exercise.
2. Totally focus on picturing your inner adviser. Go to a place where you are comfortable and at peace. Wait peacefully and expectantly for your inner adviser to appear.

3. Picture very clearly what your inner adviser looks like, including size, shape, age, dress.
4. Find a comfortable physical distance between you and your inner adviser.
5. Begin to communicate with your adviser. Find out what kind of an adviser you have. Ask questions about your health or life problems.
6. Realize that communication with your inner adviser may seem silly or stilted at first or that it may be perfectly natural; take whatever happens in stride. Give yourself permission to continue and to work toward optimum communication with your inner adviser.
7. When you have obtained answers to your questions, return to the here and now.
8. Allow yourself to feel good about your progress and what you have learned.
9. Make a plan for using what you learned and be confident you can change.

Inner dialogue may be of the most help to clients with psychosomatic symptoms. They are usually the least aware of the meaning of their symptoms. If they were more aware of their inner conflicts, they may not have developed the symptoms in the first place. Inner dialogue may also be of great help to clients who are unable to verbalize their thoughts and feelings directly. Clients who use self-blame or guilt may find help through inner dialogue too; it is a structured way of providing positive new direction without focusing on self-destructive feelings that may interfere with wellness.

Inner dialogue can also be used to solve problems. Health care professionals may turn to their inner advisers for intuitive help with a client problem. Clients who want to solve a work-related problem can turn to their inner work adviser. Inner dialogue can be carried on with aspects of the social, work, intimate, student, family, or political self. As many inner advisers as needed can be consulted about everyday or emergency situations.

SUMMARY

This chapter has examined the following topics: frameworks and tools for stress assessment, relaxation methods, the use of suggestion for stress management, methods for designing stress reduction suggestions, suggestions for teaching clients to use a stress reduction hierarchy, coping skills procedures, thought stopping, refuting irrational ideas, helping clients refute irrational ideas, using guided imagery with clients, receptive guided imagery, healing guided imagery, problem-solving guided imagery, and helping clients contact their inner adviser.

ACKNOWLEDGMENT

Some of the material for this chapter appeared in Clinical Hypnosis and Therapeutic Suggestion (Grune & Stratton, 1985), but it has been revised and updated.

REFERENCES

Benson, G., & Klipper, M. (1976). *The relaxation response.* New York: Avon.

Bry, A. (1972). *Directing the movies of your mind* (pp. 131-164). New York: Harper & Row.

Cannon, W. (1914). The emergency function of the medulla in pain and the major emotions. *American Journal of Physiology, 33*, 283, 287.

Clark, C. C. (1981). Inner dialogue: A self-healing approach for nurses and clients. *American Journal of Nursing, 81*, 1191-1193.

Clark, C. C. (1986). *Wellness nursing: Concepts, theory, research and practice.* New York: Springer.

Davies, M. (1970). Blood pressure and personality. *Journal of Psychosomatic Research, 14*, 89-104.

Davis, M., McKay, M., and Eshelman, E. (1982). *The relaxation and stress reduction workbook* (2nd Ed.). Oakland, CA: New Harbinger.

Ellis, A., and Harper, R. (1961). *A guide to rational living.* North Hollywood, CA: Wilshire Books.

Fowles, D. C. (1980). The three arousal model: implications of Gray's two-factor theory for heart rate, electrodermal activity and psychopathy. *Psychophysiology, 17*, 87-104.

Goodman, D. (1974). *Emotional well-being through rational behavior training.* Springfield, IL: Charles C. Thomas.

Gray, J. A. (1975). *Elements of a two-process theory of learning.* New York: Academic Press.

Grinder, J., & Bandler, R. (1981). *Trance-formations, neurolinguistic programming and the structure of hypnosis* (pp. 14-15). Moab, UT: Real People Press.

Jacobson, E. (1938). *Progressive relaxation.* Chicago: University of Chicago Press.

Jones, M. M. (1980). Conversion reaction: Anachronism or evolutionary form? A review of the neurological, behavioral, and psychoanalytic literature. *Psychological Bulletin, 87*, 427-441.

Kissen, D. M. (1966). The significance of personality in lung cancer in men. *Annals of the New York Academy of Science, 125*, 820-826.

Meichenbaum, D., and Cameron, R. (1974). Modifying what clients say to themselves. In M. Mahoney & R. Cameron (Eds.), Self-control: Power to the person. Monterey, CA: Brooks/Cole.

Pennebaker, J. W. (1985). Traumatic experience and psychosomatic disease: Exploring the roles of behavioral inhibition, obsession, and confiding. *Canadian Psychology, 26*, 82-95.

Samuels, M., & Samuels, N. (1975). *Seeing with the mind's eye* (pp. 156-238). New York: Random House.

Scandrett, S., & Uecker, S. (1985). Relaxation training. In G. Bulecheck & J. McCloskey (Eds.), *Nursing interventions: Treatments for nursing diagnoses* (pp. 22-48). Philadelphia: W. B. Saunders.

Selye, H. (1956). *The stress of life.* New York: McGraw-Hill.

Simonton, O.C., Simonton, S., & Creighton, J. (1978). *Getting well again* (pp. 131-139). New York: J. P. Tarcher.

Wolpe, J. (1969). *The practice of behavior therapy.* Oxford: Pergamon.

Zeagans, L. (1982). Stress and the development of somatic disorders. In L. Goldberger & S. Brezwitz (Eds.), *Handbook of stress: Theoretical and clinical aspects.* New York: Free Press.

7

THE DIFFICULT PATIENT

ROTHLYN P. ZAHOUREK

INTRODUCTION

Diane, labeled a "crock," "histrionic," "psychosomatic," a "malingerer," "border-line psychotic," and "noncompliant," was a chronic pain to the emergency room staff, the mental health team, and all who worked with her. As her psychotherapist, I had worked with her through many medical and psychiatric admissions. She had begun to improve, was working full time, managing her two small daughters more effectively, was abusing drugs and alcohol less, and had stopped visiting the emergency room with confusing complaints and minor injuries. One night she was admitted to intensive care having burned her upper torso, arms, and face in a cooking accident. She was acutely ill with second and third degree burns. Her old problematic behaviors returned. She drove the staff crazy with her continuous complaints and demands. She was fascinated with how grotesque she looked, she slept little, and she demanded large amounts of pain medication from which she experienced little relief. The staff was at the end of their rope and I was at a loss as to what to do for either the patient or them. In desperation one afternoon, I remembered Lamaze (focused relaxation training) techniques from obstetrics and imagery techniques I had learned in a behavior therapy workshop. I decided to try these, thinking if they worked for women in labor and people suffering from intense fears associated with phobias, that they might help Diane as well. I also knew that tension and anxiety made pain worse and that her abilities to cope with these feelings had in the past been maladaptive.

I asked her if she wanted to try something different to be more comfortable and she enthusiatically said "yes." I told her to close her eyes and take a nice relaxing breath, and that then we would take a fantasy trip far away. The trip would help her relax and feel better. I suggested that when she relaxed her pain medication would last longer, act more quickly, and provide more relief. After a brief talk about relaxing her muscles and breathing more slowly and regularly I had her visualize a meadow— green, lush, and comfortable. Then I asked her to lie down on the lush green grass that felt like warm velvet. I told her, "It's warm (she suffered from always being cold). Listen to the birds and smell the fresh air. You can rest and watch the clouds float by." I continued describing this picture and for the first time in three days she fell into a restful sleep. Both the staff and I were amazed. When she awakened later she felt refreshed and more comfortable. I continued working with her in this way, adding places for her to visit and suggestions that related to her present problems. I taught the staff these simple techniques and they began to work with her in a similar manner particularly during painful dressing changes. Diane looked forward to my visits, began to eat and sleep better, and became more cooperative and less demanding. The staff reinvolved themselves with her; both the staff and Diane felt more in control. Although Diane died three months later of unexpected complications she managed to increase her pain tolerance, to rest, and to relate more positively to all involved with her care. She also managed to teach me much about how well these techniques work with difficult patients. I worked with Diane nearly 20 years ago; she was my first patient to use relaxation/imagery (R/I) techniques.

This chapter describes the use of R/I techniques with a multi-problem patient (client) group. The "problem patient" is defined and described generically and psychodynamically. Cases have been chosen to illustrate the integration of R/I into a therapeutic process. Examples include patients with chronic pain, AIDS neurosis, and those with demanding and manipulative behavior. The complex nature of the development of a problematic relationship between staff and patient is also emphasized in relation to the use of R/I techniques.

Who is this "Problem Patient"?

Nurses commonly confront patients who exhibit more than one complex medical or behavioral problem at once. They also struggle when patients do not follow prescribed treatment regimens, seem never to feel comfortable, or do not recover from standard interventions. Often new medications or procedures are tried. Staff conferences or consultants may be called. Some patients, however, continue to be chronic nonresponders, or earn labels such as "noncompliant" or "malingering." One problem complicates another so that staff become increasingly frustrated and hopeless about the patient's relief or recovery and their own abilities to potentiate this process. Caregivers complain they have tried everything and have run out of ideas. This then results in staff's judgmental attitudes, hopelessness, and withdrawal.

In an unpublished study done in a large metropolitan hospital the nursing staff was surveyed by the mental health nurse consultant to learn what kinds of patients caused them the most difficulty. The chronically ill patient with deteriorating conditions, dying patients, neurotic or psychotic patients, the patient with chronic pain, and the relapsing substance abuser or alcoholic with complicated medical/surgical problems were all noted. Several behavioral constellations identified included the demanding and manipulative patient, the overly dependent patient, the chronically crying patient, and the chronically depressed patient (Zahourek, 1974).

According to Sarosi, the patient who is labeled "bad" by the staff is emotionally unstable, highly anxious, depressed, hostile, aggressive, impatient, unappreciative, nonconforming to regulations, and unsympathetic to the nurse's point of view. Because communication is unclear he or she challenges the nurse's actions and may ask countless questions (Sarosi, 1968). The problem patient's behavior provokes staff rejection and avoidance (Parsons, Farber, Hilger, Selg, & Stetzer, 1971). Demanding, hostile behaviors that cause stress for staff usually result from the patient's: (1) need for control, (2) threatened self image, (3) loss of independence due to hospitalization, (4) difficulties with expenditure of time and energy, and (5) helplessness (Parsons et al., 1971).

Psychodynamically, the problem patient's actions express the following conflicts: (1) control and mastery versus helplessness; (2) pain versus comfort; (3) isolation versus connectedness; (4) fear versus security; and (5) threatened versus secure self and body image. Frequently the behavior is born out of a patient's defense system and while seeming maladaptive is actually a means of coping and maintaining a sense of self and well being. If the nurse views the behavior in this context, that it is a manifestation of a struggle or conflict and a coping mechanism, the first step in countering potential nurse rejection and withdrawal is accomplished and the process of assessment and intervention can begin. Assessing how the patient's imagery system* is affected by the illness or hospitalization becomes a framework that explains both staff and patient behavior.

"I am out of control, I'm unlovable, dependent, and inadequate" are statements that illustrate how a patient's self image may be disrupted. "I am half a person," "I have no space," and "Cover me up" similarly tell us that he or she is feeling mutilated, exposed, or invaded. When the staff listen for temporal (past, present, and future) images, they learn from where intense often unrealistic behaviors spring. Such images include ideas learned from previous experiences: "All people I've ever heard of with this illness die a horrible death." Images also influence the present, "I can picture that long needle entering my chest and killing me"; and mental pictures alter the perception of the future, "I'm never going to be productive or happy again."

All these thoughts are accompanied by vivid images, feelings, and physiological responses. Because the imagination is so tightly hooked to these responses, logic and reason are seldom able to dispel them entirely. The patient remains chronically anxious and fearful and behaves in ways that may seem adaptive to the patient but cause problems for the staff and subsequently the patient.

Imagery System refers to the ability to image as well as the content and quality of the imagery.

TABLE 7-1. Summary: Problem Patient Dynamics Interplay with Caregiver and Imagery

Characteristics	Patient Images
Problem Patient	
Noncompliant, nonresponsive, dying, denying, self-destructive, abusive, angry, demanding, dependent, a failure, whining, in unrelieved pain, alcoholic, or substance abuse relapse, manipulative	Self image disrupted: I am out of control, unlovable, unworthy, inadequate
Patient feels fearful, out of control, needy, anxious, sad, angry, dependent	Body image distorted: I am mutilated, exposed, have no privacy; I am too big, too little; no body awareness; body a shell; denial of sensations
	Past images: People with same problem always die or suffer a great deal or go crazy
	Future images: Will I ever be the same again? How can I function without my limb, body part, job, or substance
Nurse	Present images: I'm falling apart, a mess
Nurse wants to help, wants to teach, wants to control for positive ends	Nurse's self image: I am a good and giving helper able to promote health and well-being
Patient resents nurse's efforts, withdraws from nurse's efforts, attacks nurse's efforts	Patient's self-image: I am a bad patient; I must fight to survive; If I give in I'm vulnerable, the staff are terrible.
Nurse feels a failure, hopeless, helpless, and angry	Nurse believes: I'm a bad nurse; the patient is terrible; I can't handle the situation and need to withdraw
Patient remains the same or gets worse, gets discharged, well, or dies	
Nurse feels lousy about self, patient, work; possible burnout	

Table 7–1 summarizes some of the problems of the difficult patient and the interaction with the caregiver. It also demonstrates the interlocking of the imagery systems between caregiver and client. This process is summarized as follows: a situation charged with feelings, images, and thoughts precipitate, coping behaviors by both the patient and the nurse.

The following cases demonstrate this process with several problematic patients. The examples illustrate the complexity of treating chronic pain and substance abuse, severe medical and psychiatric problems, demanding behavior, poor healing, and the inability to let go of an intense reality-based fear.

DEMANDING SCREAMER

Ms. M was well known and dreaded by the staff each time she had to be admitted to the hospital. She had suffered from chronic juvenile rheumatoid arthritis for most of her 28 years. The disease had left her crippled, confined to a wheelchair, and in chronic pain. Numerous related emotional and medical problems complicated her adjustment to the disability. She was notably noncompliant outside the hospital and demanding and complaining in the hospital. She was also obese, weighing close to 300 pounds. This hospital admission was for the surgical repair of a bowel obstruction, but she did not heal postoperatively and had a large gaping abdominal wound that needed packing several times a day. During packing and dressing changes her screams of pain became so severe that the staff had begun to draw lots to determine who would take care of her. In between dressing changes she was demanding, hostile, insulting, and verbally abusive to the staff. She refused to do even the minimum in self-care and complained strongly when she had to be out of bed.

In desperation the staff called the mental health nurse consultant to "make it better." During a staff conference it was decided to include relaxation and imagery techniques as part of an overall plan of intervention in hopes of reducing Ms. M's stress and making her more comfortable. The consultant agreed to provide the treatment and encouraged the staff to observe, reinforce, and learn the process so they could help her during all shifts. Openly the staff wished she would become a less demanding and more cooperative and pleasant person. They also hoped she would soon heal and get out of their hair.

When the consultant approached the patient proposing to help her with the stress and pain of dressing changes she was curious but expressed negativism and hopelessness that anything could help, "Nothing is ever going to make me better; I'm only going to get worse and worse." Taken literally these comments were true—she had a progressive disease that was going to continue to worsen. The consultant acknowledged the severity of her progressive illness but added that while the illness might progress, her response to it and to her current situation could vary: "I'm sure you are aware of days when you feel better and accomplish more and other days when you are more likely to let the illness get the better of you. Judging from what the staff has told me you do not like having things get the better of you. I know having this wound that has not healed yet has been a good example of how much you would like things to be different." Through these comments the consultant hoped to establish rapport and reframe the patient's current experience. The patient's reality as well as her defenses and wish for things to be different were all utilized. The consultant explained she would work with Ms. M to help her relax and the relaxation would help her feel more comfortable during dressing changes.

The consultant also emphasized that she had worked with several other patients who had severe pain from burns. These patients had been particularly successful being comfortable during dressing changes and even skin grafts. Ms. M was impressed with the example of the work with burned patients and then asked several questions about how the process worked and what she would have to do. She informed the consultant she didn't have much energy because she was both very sick and depressed. The consultant explained about the effect of muscle relaxation on discomfort and that imagery provided a chance for distraction and could even promote blood supply to an area and aid in healing.

Because this patient had enormous dependency needs, the consultant told Ms. M she would see her each day; the staff would also become involved so that they could help her at other times. Ms. M was also told that while the consultant would do much of the work the patient would need to cooperate as best she could and that practicing other times made the technique even more successful. As part of these instructions Ms. M was also told she could change the process or the images while she practiced; this could be fun for her. The patient agreed to work with the consultant, adding that she didn't know how successful it would be, but that "anything would be better than how I am now."

First, Ms. M's pain and stress were assessed. She described abdominal wound pain as different from her arthritic pain, which was like chronic aching hot, stiff muscles. The wound pain was a sharp, digging "red hot poker" that was most unbearable and intense during dressing changes. She also experienced continued pain following the procedure and felt unable to control crying and screaming. Watching television and changing position helped but did not reduce the pain to a tolerable level. Medication was also only marginally helpful.

The consultant taught Ms. M progressive relaxation during two visits. She stated she liked the technique, that it made her feel "good" and more comfortable, but she couldn't do it on her own. Imagery of a pleasant place was added as well as images of cleansing new blood flow to her wound. During each visit the consultant spent some time talking with her about how she was feeling, how she was getting along with the staff, and how she was reacting to the hospitalization.

Several relaxing visual scenes were used to help this patient. One was a tropical island that had brilliant colors, another was a warm fluffy feather bed into which she sank deeply and comfortably. Images were also used of changing the red hot poker into a blunt, soft, cool, and pink healing material that dissolved into her and provided comfort and healing. These were direct methods added to suggestions that she was "more and more able to cope" as she relaxed "more and more" and was "more and more" able to visualize herself in a relaxing pleasant place. As she visualized another place, she could transport herself and could change her feeling state.

This patient was seen for a total of 18 visits. The work was shared by another consultant and the nursing staff and was not easy or smooth. It had been clear to all who worked with her that the chronic course of the arthritic pain, in addition to the acute illness, was complex because secondary gain from the pain was an issue. Although she had alienated the staff, her difficult behavior was an attempt to both control and get help. In addition, this woman had long-term hostile dependent personality problems. She was also lonely, crippled, and had no hope of her illness or her disabled living and working conditions improving. She was angry about having to spend the majority of her 28 years in a wheelchair or hospital; her ability to function as her peers had always at best been limited. Needing attention and nurturing, she was fearful that if she obtained much relief or got any better, she would lose the new added contact with the consultant and staff.

After several visits the patient began to improve. First, she reported she was sleeping better at night and that it was easier for her to sit in a chair for longer periods of time. The high doses of morphine she required for dressing changes began to decrease as did the screams and curses during dressing changes. Remarkably, after five sessions she noted she was becoming more able to practice on her own and that on many occasions she was feeling pleasant tingling sensations instead of pain. The wound was finally healing nicely. She stated she was most successful practicing when she heard the consultant's voice in her head. The consultant told her this was not uncommon and that she was making good progress.

The staff began to report an improvement in her attitude and cooperation both during dressing changes and in her behavior throughout the day. Her capacity to do progressive relaxation and visualization developed. She admitted that although she thought all of this was a "bunch of bull" she was feeling better. Ms. M was remarkably difficult, resistant, negativistic and miserable. Relief, while not as rapid or dramatic as is sometimes observed, did occur. Although negativistic, this patient wanted the involvement of others. By staying involved with her and continuing to support her progress she developed more comfort and more independence. When the staff began using the technique with her they found that she was more often receptive and cooperative—even friendly. As a result they stopped avoiding her as much and while she never became a 'favorite' patient she was accepted and worked with more empathically.

In summary, Ms. M was difficult. The use of R/I provided both a new context for staff-patient interaction as well as a comfort producing set of procedures for the patient. She responded in her characteristic personality style—demanding and negativistic. While she responded positively it was hard for her to admit that anything was helping. This case demonstrates the value of the symptom and that modifying rather than seeking to eliminate Ms. M's chronic pain is important so that intense resistance is diminished.

THE SIMMERING POT*

Mr. S, a 60-year-old widower, had multiple physical problems, some of them a result of chronic alcoholism. He suffered from reflex esophagitis and had a history of pancreatitis and several episodes of gastrointestinal (GI) bleeding. Another complicating problem was an inoperable thoracic anuerysm, hypertension, and atypical angina. In addition to all of these problems, Mr. S experienced episodes of severe depression since his mother's death when he was 15 years old. The depression became chronic in 1969 when his wife and son were killed in an automobile accident while he was driving.

This patient was first seen after he had been hospitalized in a psychiatric unit for management of his health problems and treatment for depression. He suffered from epigastric and chest pain and had frequent thoughts of suicide.

---

*This case example supplied by Elizabeth Mudd, RN CAC, Alcoholism Counselor, St. Vincent's Hospital, New York City.

The initial request was for alcoholism counseling, and as an experiment during the second week the alcoholism counselor began teaching him relaxation techniques. During this time this sad man gave the distinct impression of a simmering pot that could boil over at any time; his aneurysm could rupture, or he could have a gastrointestinal bleed. His temper also flared on occasion. He usually kept the lid on by appearing to be a mild mannered, proper gentleman, in his words, "a good patient." During the assessment phase he was asked what he thought would help him the most; he answered, "I want out; my life is over. I have nothing to live for." During the next several sessions his feelings were talked about and a half hour of each meeting was spent practicing progressive relaxation. Visualizations were gradually introduced by describing a scene in New England where he grew up. He often remembered times when he was young, vigorous, and healthy. At first he was resistant to imagery related to pain, saying, "the pain must have to get worse it has something to accomplish." When talking about this he would draw in his shoulders and cross his arms across his chest. Specific pain-relieving imagery was not incorporated until he seemed more comfortable learning the relaxation techniques.

By the eighth visit a relationship of trust had been established with the counselor. Whenever she arrived on the unit, he would light up with a smile. Practicing the relaxation on his own morning and evening time, he now reported reduced pain, an improved appetite, and being able to sleep better. Gradually, touch was integrated into the sessions; the counselor first put her hands on top of his shoulders and then on the back of his neck and head, which encouraged the upper torso to release. This human contact served to calm him, since it was the only physical contact he had with anyone.

The relaxation exercise included images of lightness, softness, and a porous sensation. He was like a sponge and pain could exit through his pores and good feelings be soaked up. Each time images of a trip to New England were included with varying scenes: a mountain lake, a pine forest, a farm meadow. At this time Mr. S spontaneously reported that he was making up his own visualizations. He pictured himself as a boy of eight bringing the cows in from pasture at evening. He pictured a favorite place high on a hill where he could look down at the meadows. There was a cool waterfall that dropped down into a pool.

After 6 weeks direct imagery was included to reduce pain. He described the pain as "red or white hot" and "sharp as a sword." When asked what might cool the pain to coral or pink, and he responded, "my waterfall." From then on the image of the waterfall became a part of the work for pain reduction. Mr. S became quite creative with ways the cool waterfall helped the pain; he began to be more active in his visual journeys.

At this writing, the alcoholism counselor has worked with Mr. S for 4 months. He is sleeping and eating better. He has relief from some of the pain whenever he uses the techniques he has learned. His feelings of depression are less; he is also expressing some of his frustration, anger, bitterness, and fears that formerly he thought were "unspeakable" and made him a "bad patient."

The most striking and gratifying event during his therapy was the day he announced that "I want to live and to spend the rest of my life in New England."

When the time finally came for discharge, Mr. S received a placement in a skilled nursing facility. The week of discharge he was seen twice in order to facilitate the transfer and preparation for termination. After 15 minutes of relaxation the author read him a story, "The Little Plum Tree" (Wallas, 1985). This beautiful, brief story about the life cycle of a plum tree deals with separation anxiety. At the end, a seed from the heart of a plum finds warmth and nourishment in the earth away from the parent tree. The seed grows and flourishes and as time passes becomes a strong new tree (Wallas, 1985 p. 65–66).

This case demonstrates the value of individualized imagery techniques with clients. In addition, the importance of new technique for an old seemingly hopeless problem cannot be underestimated. Through imagery this patient rediscovered pleasurable aspects of his life that in recent years had been forgotten. This ability, to again experience pleasure, seems to have reduced both his chronic pain and his depression and has enhanced his ability to participate in discharge plans. To date he is doing well in his new setting.

AIDS NEUROSIS

Patients in numerous health care settings have psychosomatic symptoms and may develop unrealistic attitudes about their health. Dynamically, these symptoms can express unresolved conflicts and needs that the individual has not been able to express in any other way. The following case example demonstrates the therapeutic process with a patient who developed an AIDS neurosis.

Paul, a 45-year-old homosexual chronic alcoholic patient, had been treated in an alcoholism program for 2½ years He was attending school, and doing well. AIDS was just beginning to be news when he developed a sore throat and swollen glands. Although reassured by his physician that he had a nonspecific infection, he was convinced he had developed AIDS and was going to die.* The meaning of the symptom was discussed: having a terminal illness would make him "special" and provide him with a great deal of attention. Feeling guilty for recent promiscuous sexual behavior, AIDS would be the ultimate punishment. He could delay thinking about the future that, for the first time in his life, promised to be productive. He feared success, and he knew that being sick would get him out of projects at school. During past drinking and drug taking binges he had made several suicide attempts. Now sober, he had made no suicide attempts; this crisis confirmed his belief that he wanted to live and feared death.

When asked what might help relieve his fears he responded, "I want to spend a *year waiting* to see if I get AIDS; I'm too anxious to do anything else." The following R/I process utilized his need to wait and incorporated both direct and indirect suggestions. This abbreviated dialogue demonstrates the complexities inherent in working with a multi-problem patient.

---

*This occurred prior to the availability of blood tests and the vast amount of information available now on AIDS. "AIDS neurosis," however, continues to be a problem particularly in the gay community and with other at-risk populations.

Therapist: Close your eyes, take a deep breath, relax, and imagine how you are going to wait.

Paul: (surprised) What?

Therapist: Where are you going to wait for the year?

Paul: In Joe's apartment.

Therapist: Where are you in the apartment?

Paul: (smiles and giggles) I'm in the kitchen at the table in my bathrobe.

Therapist: What are you doing?

Paul: I'm going over my body looking for swollen glands, rashes, and sores.

Therapist: What else are you doing?

Paul: Drinking coffee.

Therapist: Is anyone else with you?

Paul: No, I'm alone.

Therapist: It's the end of the summer and fall is coming. Notice how things have changed. It's cooler and crisp and you are still sitting at the kitchen table examining yourself, in your bathrobe and *drinking coffee*. (Emphasis to help maintain sobriety) (Pause) Now it's winter and it's cold and snowy, but you are still sitting at the kitchen table examining yourself *and drinking coffee*. (Pause) It's summer again, and it's hot and muggy. You're at the kitchen table, in your bathrobe, examining yourself *and drinking coffee*. The year has passed. Two things can now happen, and we will look at each one. *First*, you discover you have AIDS. You have large swollen glands, rashes all over, and horrible sores. You're exhausted and have no energy; you realize that you are going to die. (Pause) (Paul's breathing increased, and he looked more distressed.) Become aware of how you are feeling. *Next*, (Pause) as if by magic you are healthy, you have no symptoms and you're absolutely fine and healthy. (Pause) Become aware of how you're feeling. (Pause) *Now you are healthy*. Now open your eyes and we can talk about how you felt and what you experienced.

Paul: Well that was interesting. I could see the marigolds outside my window change with the seasons (smiling and no overt signs of anxiety). I realized that I felt better when I had AIDS than when I didn't. I was almost disappointed when I didn't. I felt relieved and that people would take care of me and give me a lot of attention. I also felt I was *right* and I'll show them I *did* get AIDS after all. I feel kind of let down and ashamed to admit all this.

His need to suffer and to show "them" all up was discussed and a directive was given attempting to use his need for obsessional thinking.

Therapist: I want you to do something in between appointments that will help you understand. Twice a day for 10 minutes each imagine your future. You can imagine anything but it *must* be *positive*. (This directive allowed the obsessive thoughts to continue but reframed them more positively).

Paul: Gee, do I have to tell you?

Therapist: No, of course not, unless *you want* to or *you feel they're important*. (Imbedded command to tell the therapist what he fantasized but giving him the freedom to privacy if he really wanted).

Paul: You know I feel guilty letting those other thoughts go and doing something that's fun; I worry about letting my guard down.

Therapist: Okay, the rest of the day excluding these 20 minutes you can obsess as much as possible about AIDS and what will happen if you get it. Is twenty minutes a day too much to ask for positive thoughts?

Paul: No. (laughs)

Several aspects of this session illustrate general principles of R/I techniques and suggestion. The patient's own imagery, spending a year thinking about his problem, was chosen as the arena for visualization. The intent was to produce a sense of time distortion and behavioral rehearsal by having him live that year of waiting in the space of a few minutes. Hopefully he would find it boring and unsatisfying. The repetition of the image (sitting at the table examining himself) was an attempt to create boredom with the symptom. When in the exercise he felt relief with the AIDS diagnosis a new feeling became clear. *"Now I've got you experts. I was right all the time and you were wrong."*

The purpose of the task was to encourage a period in the day when he consciously focused his thoughts and experienced the opposite of what he was generally feeling and thinking. This encouraged his sense of control and the realization that he could experience positive thoughts and feelings. Because he was fearful of losing the symptom, the therapist encouraged its continuation for the remaining hours in the day and, in fact, he was encouraged to intensify it.

Following other sessions using R/I, the obsessional thinking about AIDS decreased. He decided he wanted to drop out of school for the rest of the year. Because of his anxiety he had fallen behind and the pressure was building. He felt this was a good decision for him. Later this patient droppped out of treatment and to date no further medical care has been recorded at our hospital.

Clearly the treatment was directive; pleasure was encouraged to combat hopelessness. While the meaning of his symptoms never was completely clear, positive hope was communicated. Therapeutic tasks assigned as homework were reminiscent of school and encouraged his active participation in developing a more positive and realistic outlook. The "homework" was modified with his input.

Summary

Within the context of a long-term counseling relationship and lengthy sobriety, the imagery, indirect suggestions, and therapeutic tasks helped Paul make a decision that "felt very right." His unrealistic fears were recognized as serving an important purpose within his personality structure. It became clear early on that attacking these fears directly and rationally was not going to accomplish relief. Allowing the symptom and encouraging his obsessional thinking about AIDS in a more prescribed and controlled manner enabled him to gain a new sense of control. No longer was he at war with himself; now he was able to focus on the real issues of guilt, feeling overwhelmed, fear of success, and the need to be cared for.

Through the imagery exercise Paul realized he needed more time to complete school. He feared other's reactions and that he might *either* succeed or fail. In the past, drunkenness anesthetized his feelings and flirting with death through suicide attempts had brought caregivers to his rescue. Now he realized he needed new mechanisms to cope.

With the recent increase in cases of AIDS, people in the high-risk categories are at risk for AIDS neurosis as just described. Judging from recent lay news articles and reports from hotlines, this neurosis is common and characterized by panic, depression, and psychosomatic symptoms resembling AIDS. Some high-risk individuals when experiencing a virus infection and the usual signs of an increased immune response become depressed and convinced they will die a painful death; some suicides have even been reported. Helping patients cope using relaxation and visualization can reduce anxiety and promote receptivity to information being given during a diagnostic work-up that at times is lengthy.

RELIGIOUS PAIN

Mr. T, a 50-year-old recovering alcoholic, had suffered from crippling cerebral palsy since childhood. With some pride he reported having had 40-plus surgeries to correct his badly deformed feet and legs. An active member of a religious order, he described himself as someone who, while committed to helping others, suffered from chronic debilitating pain that compromised his ability to work and stay sober and perpetuated his diazepam intake.

It is not unusual to work with alcoholic patients who become chemically dependent as a result of chronic pain or who because of the alcoholism develop an illness or sustain an injury that results in a chronic pain syndrome. The pain seriously impairs their abilities to stay sober and avoid other mind-altering drugs. I began seeing Mr. T for help with pain. This, in addition to his regular group and individual alcoholism treatment, was enthusiastically supported by his orthopedic surgeon and was proposed by his counselor who encouraged him to take advantage of this "extra" treatment.

During the initial assessment Mr. T was verbal and clearly descriptive about his symptoms. He graphically described his pain and explained what exacerbated and relieved it. The pain was a bunch of "tight rubber bands that twisted and pulled" in his legs and feet. These rubber bands felt like "red hot pokers" that were relieved only by muscle relaxants and going to bed. Sometimes distraction and praying decreased the pain; he also noticed that when he was helping others solve their problems he was relatively comfortable or, "at least I don't think about it that much."

Rapport was established easily. Positive expectations had preceded our first contact. An intellectual discussion of the value of relaxation and imagery during which his questions were answered further established a collaborative working relationship. At this point he had managed 3 continuous months of sobriety but was still taking large doses of diazepam daily.

After describing his pain, he began talking about what it had meant in his life. He poignantly told of not being able to do what other kids did as he was growing up and always having to fight hard for everything he was able to accomplish. As was every physical step, each step in development was painful.

During the initial assessment interview it was clear by the number of scientific questions he asked that he was highly intellectual in his approach to life and to his recovery. While spiritual as well, his capacity to imagine could be enhanced. To bypass some of the intellectualization I asked him to draw a picture of himself and his pain. Verbally very expressive of his feelings and able to describe his pain metaphorically, when he was asked to concretize it in a drawing he confessed he was stumped and didn't feel he could even try. I explained it could be a very simple drawing and offered him paper and a set of various colored felt tip pens. Finally, he chose a black pen and drew a large circle with two tiny dots for eyes and a grimace for a mouth (Fig. 7–1). The circle had two simple lines for a neck and no body. He then drew several jagged horizontal lines at the bottom of the page to indicate what his pain might look like. He stated, "I can't believe how hard that was." The struggle in doing the drawing indicated that he was dissociated from his body and the content of the drawing demonstrated a distorted body image. The color he chose might also indicate depression and hopelessness. Using drawings can be a useful tool in the assessment process for evaluating both the symptom and how patients view themselves in relation to the problem. Drawings also describe more accurately than words how the patients are progressing during treatment and at termination. For Mr. T, it provided valuable insight about himself and his pain at the end of treatment.

Following the assessment, the process of relaxation and imagery was discussed and his questions answered. I emphasized that the technique was a psychophysiological process that produced muscle relaxation to provide relief from the spasms and mental distraction to promote comfort and enhance the relaxation. Mr. T explained that

may 16 1983

Figure 7–1. First drawing done during assessment (May).

a pleasant place to go in his imagination was a tropical island with a beautiful white sandy beach. Having his legs buried in the warm sand was a comforting thought. He explained that the warmth was different from the searing heat of the pain; warmth provided comfort, intense heat caused poker pain. He chose a key word to trigger the relaxation response: "monastery." He explained that a monastery was peaceful, quiet, and spiritual and that being there provided him great comfort.

Progressive relaxation was started at the top of his head because it was the lower part of his body affected with pain. The word "monastery" was used and a description of what it might be like to be there provided the initial part of the relaxation exercise. This was followed by a trip to the tropical island with its beautiful beach and lush jungle. The author asked him to picture himself relaxed and comfortable with his legs buried in the warm sand. He smiled as it was described. I explained he could do many things while he rested: watch the clouds make shapes in the sky; smell the soft salt air; and listen to the quiet, nearby village music or the gentle sound of the water.

Many images were employed with this patient that were built on his history, profession, and symptomatology. Over the course of treatment the actual images were tailored to his immediate needs and the feedback he provided.

It was clear from his drawings he had little sense of body integrity and his focus was on his head (his intellect). He often asked intellectual questions about how this process worked; answers were given that included research as well as theory. In the R/I exercise a sense of body integrity was encouraged.

To Mr. T, being able to work long hours, even with the pain, was extremely important. The ability to function even with discomfort is positive when planning for intervention with chronic pain and therefore needed to be integrated as well, i.e., "as you relax and feel more comfortable, your ability to work effectively will increase."

The relaxation exercise started at his head. Because he liked warmth and the color yellow he was asked to envision a bright yellow light (could be interpreted as a halo) above his head. As he was focused on relaxing those muscles this light spread warmth, relaxation, and energy from his head down his body and finally into his legs. The energy exited out his feet and entered the earth where it could recirculate as energy and return to his head, again refueling him with more energy, relaxation and comfort. A spiritual image, the description emphasized suggestions of body integrity, being one with the universe and the pain exiting out his feet, entering the earth and then returning to him as energy. His response after a couple of exercises was that the energy did not exit through his feet. The energy and pain exited through his knees. Was he doing it "right"? The therapist questioned how his feet and legs felt. They felt better. The therapist explained it was less important where the pain exited and more important that he felt more comfortable.

Mr. T found that the exercises helped and began practicing at home in a large comfortable chair. His use of muscle relaxants decreased. During one session he reported he was having trouble sleeping. Overtired, he had not taken the time to practice the relaxation exercises. His feet and legs were quite painful. He elected to take a diazepam and then decided he felt guilty and should do the relaxation exercise, which he did. Quickly he felt relief and was able to fall asleep immediately. With surprise and pride he realized the relaxation, not the medication, eased the pain and promoted sleep.

The use of drawings was an important adjunct to both the imagery and the therapeutic process. When he did the first drawing I pointed out that he had drawn himself with no body. At that time his reaction was neutral. A month after working together the drawing was repeated (Fig. 7–2). This time he drew a body with very prominent crutches that he sometimes used reluctantly. The face was not as grimacing. The drawings were briefly discussed and again his reaction was neutral. At termination he did another drawing (Fig. 7–3). This time the colors were varied, he integrated yellow and a warm brown; black was not used. He clearly now had a body and a cane. What previously had been lines to describe the pain were now lines to indicate new freedom in walking. The face was smiling and had a verbal caption, "I feel good." In showing Mr. T the drawings and asking for his reaction he clearly reacted. "I can't believe it. I was so disconnected from my body." At this point he became nearly tearful, saying, "For so many years I've struggled with my condition. I've hated my body and not wanted it to be a part of me. Now I feel whole. I can't believe it."

This patient was clearly a success. The process went more rapidly than usual with chronic pain patients. He was proud of his progress and enthusiastically agreed to make a videotape of the work we had been doing. His ability to share his success with others was important in cementing his recovery since this was an integral part of his life as a helper. The use of drawings were important in the therapeutic process; they provided the therapist with useful information that solidified a hypothesis about the patient's underlying problems with body image. During treatment and at termination the drawings demonstrated a measure of progress that was shared with the patient. This less intellectual process enabled him to have insight that was useful in both his management of chronic pain and sobriety.

Figure 7–2. Drawing #2 by Mr. T. (June). Done in yellow, not black, ink.

Figure 7–3. Mr. T's drawings 2 months after start of treatment (July).

SUMMARY

This chapter has focused specifically on working with multi-problem patients using R/I techniques as part of an overall therapeutic process. Often the addition of these techniques promotes a relationship that is both collaborative and nurturing. These approaches also provide something new in a process that has reached a stalemate. Both patient and therapist (caregiver) have an opportunity to look at the total situation in a new light and to work together on an approach that enhances comfort to the patient and a sense of satisfaction to the caregiver.

REFERENCES

Parsons, M.P., Farber, H., Hilger, N., Selg, M. J. S., & Stetzer, S. L. (1971). Difficult patients do exist: A study of six patients. *Nursing Clinics of North America, 6*, 173–187.

Sarosi, G. M. (1968). A critical theory: The nurse as a thoroughly human person. *Nursing Forum, 4*, 349–364.

Wallas, l. (1985). *Stories for the third ear: Using hypnotic fables in psychotherapy.* New York: W.W. Norton.

BIBLIOGRAPHY

Sloboda, S. (1977). Understanding Patient Behavior. *Nursing*, 74–77.

Ujhely, G. (1963). *The nurse and her problem patients.* New York: Springer.

Zahourek, R. P. (1974). Unpublished survey done at Denver General Comprehensive Community Mental Health Center with general nursing staff. Denver, CO.

8

IMAGERY AND RELAXATION AS A THERAPEUTIC INTERVENTION WITH THE DYING

MARCIA FISHMAN

For patients, their families, and their friends, dying is not an easy experience. It is often just as difficult for the caregivers to provide the physical and emotional support and comfort necessary for all involved. Nurses are in the unique and privileged position of being the most constant, accessible, and consistent caregivers during those difficult times.

Although it is usually physicians who give unwelcome news to the patient and to the family, they do not often remain to explain, comfort, or console. Nurses are more actively present during the illness, the lingering, the final hours, the death, and the postmortem period. Being in this position, nurses benefit by having more techniques available to assist in therapeutic communications and enhance their ability to assist dying patients and their families.

In this modern, highly technical state of the art society, death is overtly ignored. Death and many of the rituals have been removed from the home and, therefore, the family. Most people who are ill and dying are in hospitals—unfamiliar, depersonalized institutions. When death occurs, it is often surrounded by chaos and strangers. More often than not, loved ones have little chance for last goodbyes. The dead are quickly whisked away, while the rituals are performed by professional strangers. Rarely, do we as individuals and society have a chance to see and understand death as a part of daily life, the unfortunate exception being the daily violence depicted by the news media, television programs, movies, music, and so on. Our first encounters with death are often impersonal and our responses to it are often denial, fear, and anxiety. It is only when the individual faces imminent death or the imminent death of a loved one that the reality is so blatant. The fears and discomfort with death on the part of the patient, family, and caregivers often create an atmosphere of avoidance and isolation for all. Each tries to protect the other and themselves, creating blocks to open communication.

Besides being a death-denying society, western culture has long put the emphasis on finding, obtaining, and keeping. Whether it be possessions or relationships, letting go has not been encouraged. Still there comes a time when we all must let go, of things, events, relationships and the ultimate, life. Using imagery with patients and families is a way of helping them confront and cope with the "letting go." When relaxation and an altered state of consciousness are achieved, one's critical faculties are more easily put aside, helping the patient and family be more open and receptive to new ideas facilitating change.

A patient is understandably ambivalent regarding his or her death and may not have any idea what he or she wants or needs to face. In many instances, it is not until the patient is involved with the imagery process itself that he or she knows where it will lead. Because it is the patient's relationship with death and not the nurse's, the process is altered. There comes a point during the exercise when the nurse stops acting as the guide and allows the patient to completely take over. Yet it is vitally important that the nurse be there for whatever support is necessary. At times, the nurse might even have to give the patient permission to end the exercise.

In my own practice, I have had the privilege of working with a number of people who were dying. Some of them knew they had a terminal illness. Others were essentially healthy and death in the near future was not foreseen.

Imagery and relaxation were used to help both patients and their families confront and better understand their feelings regarding death. If the patient was agreeable, a family member or members participated in the session. These sessions can become extremely valuable in breaking the bonds of isolation and opening the way for families to talk and listen to one another. It also provides a way of integrating the family into the care of their loved one.

One last extremely important consideration, when assisting patients and their families in dealing with the final season of life, is the nurse's confrontation of self and his or her own mortality. As stated by Sheikh, Twente, and Turner, "Confronting death brings one to the threshold of life. By recognizing the finiteness of one's existence, one is able to muster the strength to cast off those extrinsic roles and to devote every day to growing as fully as possible" (1979, p. 151). Using imagery and relaxation can help nurses examine their fears and anxiety concerning their own death. Rather than turn away from death, the techniques provide a way to achieve a more positive understanding and acceptance of death as a part of life. This fosters an empathic insight, making it easier to care and share with those having the greatest need.

The following case studies depict how imagery and relaxation were used to assist patients confront their mortality and better handle their approaching death.

Barbara

Using imagery with Barbara was to be quite a different experience. First of all, Barbara was ready to accept her death. In fact, she looked forward to the time when pain and disease would no longer control her. She even requested all treatment be stopped. Unfortunately, her family and health care providers would not and could not accept her imminent death. When I finally used imagery experience with Barbara, it gave her the motivation to hang onto life long enough for her to openly confront her family with the seriousness of her illness, which would finally lead to her death.

Barbara was a 32-year-old wife and mother of two preteenaged daughters. Along with being a capable housewife, excellent cook, devoted parent and wife, she was expected to be physically attractive at all times. Her illness greatly interfered with all of her expected roles in life.

When Barbara first found the lump in her breast, 2 years before, she and her husband felt surgery would be too mutilating. For the next 6 months, they decided against any other medical interventions. Barbara became very ill. I met her when she finally began treatment. Unfortunately, over the next year and a half surgery, radiation, and chemotherapy did little to halt the progression of cancer. In fact, there was now bone, lung, and brain involvement.

On this particular morning, the physicians and nurses were trying to get Barbara to consent to one more round of therapy: "Couldn't she see it would make her better?"

Clinically and visually we saw the weight loss, fatigue, and spread of disease. Still we kept insisting she would get better. Barbara looked terrible. Worse, she appeared frightened and alone. Clearly it was time to put Barbara first. It was time for those of us who cared for her to acknowledge what was occurring as well as support Barbara in what she had already accepted.

I walked through the crowd, around the bed, took her hand and said, "Barbara, you look terrible this morning."

Stunned silence followed from the others. Only Barbara reacted.

Holding my hand very tightly, Barbara very angrily replied; "Are you crazy? Weren't you listening? Can't you see how much better I am? I'm getting stronger and stronger!" (She was now crying).

I ignored someone else's comment, "Barbara stop acting like a child!" Another remark was directed to me, "Nurse do you mind?"

I kept my attention fully on Barbara, and we continued holding hands. Our conversation went as follows:

Marcia: How do you feel?

Barbara: I feel terrible. I hate this place. I wish I could get away, just for awhile.

Marcia: If you could go anywhere else, where would that be?

Barbara: I want to be dead.

Marcia: But where do you want to be?

Barbara: I want to be dead and away from here, away from the pain and being sick.

Marcia: If that's what you really want, let's try and imagine what it would be like. (I realized everyone was looking at me as if I were crazy. There were also all retreating from the room except for her primary nurse who chose to remain). Barbara, let's make you more comfortable (I helped her move about until she seemed more relaxed). Now, I want you to close your eyes.

Barbara: What are we doing? (She was very calm).

Marcia: I'm taking you where you want to be. We're going to imagine it in our minds.

Barbara: Are you really going to let me see what it would be like to be dead?

Marcia: If you want. Is there some other place you would prefer to visit? (Inwardly, I admit I was hoping she'd say yes. However, Barbara didn't let me off that easily. This was to be my first death imagery experience, ready or not.) Are you ready? (She nodded) Okay, close your eyes, Take a slow, very deep breath—Good. Again. Very slow, very deep, and once more—Every time you exhale, feel yourself become more and more comfortable. Continue to breathe quietly—calmly—easily. Now, imagine yourself as you are. Can you tell me how you see yourself?

Barbara: (Hesitantly) I'm so skinny. I look like a living skeleton—I look terrible without hair—My hair used to be so beautiful—I don't even look like me—I look very ill.

Marcia: Barbara, how do you feel?

Barbara: Do you know, the pain never stops? Even the medicine doesn't help anymore—I even feel it when I'm trying to sleep—I'm so tired, I can't go on like this. I haven't got the strength to do anything for myself—I don't want to live like this. Why can't I just die? (She was now crying) (We were still holding hands).

Marcia: I know you are very ill.

Barbara: And the cancer is spreading, I'm getting worse and worse—I'm *not* getting better.

Marcia: Barbara, do you want to continue with this exercise?

Barbara: Yes, you promised.

Marcia: Can you imagine yourself as weak as you can possibly get? Try to imagine that your life is very near the end. Can you express how this might feel?

Barbara: It's the same as I just told you.

Marcia: Okay, let's continue. Imagine you are living the last few moments of your life—Your life is coming to an end—Try to feel all of your life forces coming to a stop—Can you imagine your soul and physical being leaving your body?

Barbara: It's very strange—Everything is so black. My body feels very heavy yet I'm floating—Wherever I'm going—It's different. I'm floating toward a very bright light. Can you see it? It's blinding. Can you see it?

Marcia: No I can't see it. This is your image of what you think your death will be like.

Barbara: I'm still floating. The light is quieter but it's beautiful here.

Marcia: What makes it beautiful?

Barbara: It's very safe. Everyone here understands. We have all been through the same thing.

Marcia: What have you all experienced?

Barbara: Dying!

Marcia: What else are you experiencing?

Barbara: I look healthy again. I feel strong. The pain is gone. There are people I know up here.

Marcia: Like who?

Barbara: My grandparents, my aunt, and some friends. They all died before me.

Marcia: Barbara, I realize you feel quite comfortable with this imaginary experience. I want you to carefully think, has there been anything, anything, at all you would want to do while you are still alive? (She remained very quiet for several minutes. Then suddenly she came out of the trance, opened her eyes and let go of my hand.)

Barbara: (very excited) Marcia, I can't die yet. No one has told my husband or children how sick I really am. They have to be told—I have to tell them. We can't pretend anymore. I have to ask my mother-in-law if she'd be willing to take care of the girls after I'm gone. My husband couldn't do it alone.

Marcia: How do you intend to do all of this? (She was very quiet, then she looked at her nurse and myself.)

Barbara: You're going to help me. I'll make a deal with you. I'll continue my radiation therapy (palliative treatment to help manage pain), if you two will give me moral support when I talk with my family.

Marcia:That will be a very emotional gathering. I'm not sure how much support I could be.

Barbara: I know, but you let me talk about dying and being dead. I've known for so long. No one else seemed to face it. It was very lonely with no one to help me. I just need you to be with me when I talk to my family—I really feel much better. Would you let me sleep for awhile?

Barbara slept soundly for several hours. Afterwards, she still felt comfortable. We realized the exercise helped manage the pain. Barbara also realized this and asked if we could to this more often. Her nurse wanted to use imagery, but we both felt the death experiences was not an appropriate visualization to continue.

I decided to speak with Barbara regarding the use of imagery to help manage her pain and generally add to her comfort. I asked her if there was a special place that gave her a feeling of peace and comfort. She replied immediately that whenever she was upset and troubled she'd take a walk through the woods near her house. This became the place we used for future relaxation exercises. Not only did her nurse learn the techniques, but her older daughter and mother-in-law also helped her to use this method for pain management.

We all met together, and I was with Barbara when she told her family and doctor she knew she was dying. After that, Barbara and her family seemed closer. She and her doctor were able to talk more openly.

Barbara decided she wasn't ready to die yet. She decided she wanted to live long enough to finish arrangements for her family. She also wanted to be around her for daughter's spring vacation. She felt they needed that time to be together as a family one last time.

This was a situation when relaxation and imagery helped one continue to live awhile longer. Barbara's relief helped all involved better cope with the death later on.

TWO CASE EXAMPLES

Preparing for Death

Some patients consciously ready themselves for death. Preparations for their death can be rather extensive, and it may seem incredible how much control they exert over the last season of their lives.

Mr. M was such a patient. Although this case study's focus is on the use of imagery with a patient who readies himself to die, his fight to overcome a recent illness played a vital part. Because he recovered from an acute illness, there was no apparent medical reason to expect Mr. M to die.

Mr. M and his wife, a vibrant, elderly, European, Jewish couple, had lived in my neighborhood for year. Mr. M had an angioplasty to relieve an arterial occlusion, and his family hired me to care for the wounds on his right foot and leg.

The blockage had necessitated the amputation of the middle toe and caused a large necrotic area (2½ inches by 3 inches) on the back of the calf. Weeks after surgery the leg still remained cold with barely audible pulses (by Doppler). Dressing changes and debridement were being done twice a day. Still necrosis of the tissue continued. Mr. M realistically feared more extensive amputation would be necessary.

Attempting to relieve Mr. M's tension and discomfort, I taught him relaxation and imagery. He enjoyed these sessions and found the techniques helpful.

After several weeks of conventional treatment on his leg, deterioration continued. I suggested we use imagery to help relax the blood vessels and increase blood flow to his right lower leg. I have to admit, Mr. M and his family were a bit skeptical. I reminded them of the positive effects Mr. M felt when he used it to lessen tension and decrease pain. I stressed we had tried almost everything else and felt it might help. It couldn't hurt to try.

It took several sessions to develop an image acceptable to Mr. M. Finally he selected the visual image of seeing all the blood vessels in his leg as an intricate highway system. The blood was seen as bright red cars driving up, down, and all around those highways. Mr. M conscientiously used the imagery every 2 hours for 10 minutes. During the dressing changes I reinforced the imagery. A day after we began using imagery, we saw the first sign of bloody drainage on the dressing. Over the next couple of weeks, the leg became warm with palpable pulses. Pink, granulating tissue was increasing in the wound areas. The improved blood flow meant Mr. M was able to have skin grafts to close the wounds. A long, hard battle for him, starting in spring finally ended in early winter.

I saw Mr. M several times after the skin grafts were done. He was strong and back working out of his home office as an editor of a newspaper.

Several months later, Mr. M asked me to again assist him in the use of imagery and relaxation, but he could not give a reason why. He also began talking about visiting the country of his birth and became increasingly preoccupied with this idea. It was frightening to his wife since they would be away from their children and grandchildren. Although fairly healthy, both Mr. M and his wife had several but well-managed medical problems.

I became suspicious that something else was going on as Mr. M gave off other clues. When I assisted him with relaxation, he insisted his wife stay with us. This was new; our sessions had previously been private. In retrospect, it was as if he wanted her to take part in his preparations. Mr. M became more withdrawn from his family and friends. A noticeable loss of appetite developed. Although he continued his work with the newspaper, he started talking about letting someone else take over. He constantly talked of visiting his birthplace.

Over a few short weeks Mr. M became thin and tired. His physician could find nothing physically wrong. He felt Mr. M was depressed. However, Mr. M denied being depressed or ill. He was not sure what he felt, "it was just different and odd."

During my next visits to Mr. M, he continued to speak of going back to visit his homeland. His need was very strong yet he could not give a reason. Because the reality of making such a trip seemed impossible, I finally suggested we use imagery to go back to Europe. Mr. M thought this was a good idea and looked forward to using imagery for this purpose.

After achieving a relaxed state, I instructed Mr. M to imagine himself in a large open field covered with beautiful wild flowers. There he would find a path that would lead him to the town where he was born, raised, and lived half of his life. At this point, I informed Mr. M I would not give any directions or suggestions. I encouraged him to tell us what he was seeing, doing, and feeling. Mr. M not only took us to his homeland but also vividly guided us through his life. (Life review is often a preparation for death.) We visited the house in which he was born and raised and finally would take his bride to live. There were visits with boyhood friends and teachers. He recalled school days, courting his girlfriend, getting married, and the joy at the birth of his first child. Then came the horror and grief of the Nazi invasion, the perseverance to survive and rebuild life after the war, the Communist takeover, and the decision to bring his wife and children to the United States.

It was after reaching the decision to immigrate that Mr. M became very quiet during the imagery exercise. I asked him if he wanted to return to the present. "No," he said. He had one more place to visit. "I want to go to the cemetery where my parents are buried."

Mr. M led us through the gates and to their graves. This time he excluded us. Silently, he nodded and gestured as if in conversation. Although he became tearful, he looked more relaxed and more at peace than he had in several weeks. After some very long minutes, I asked if he would share with us what was happening.

Quietly and calmly, he told us he had seen and talked with his parents. They were waiting for him.

I now realized why he had seemed withdrawn and had had the overwhelming desire to return one last time where his life had begun.

I asked Mr. M if he was unhappy about making the trip. He denied it. I asked if he wanted to join his parents. Smiling, he replied yes, he would join them soon. It was as if he finally understood what he had been going through these past several weeks. I asked him to think of his wife, children, and grandchildren. Did he really feel ready to leave his loved ones? Mr. M asked his wife to hold his hand. Holding it he replied, "It is time for me to go. I am so tired. I have survived the Nazis and Communists. I have lived through several heart attacks, and my recent illness. I've lived seeing my wife and children, safe, sound, and happy. I've had the joy of watching my grandchildren begin their lives. It is time."

I asked Mr. M why he had fought so hard during his recent illness? Why hadn't it been the right time then?

He answered, "I didn't want to have my leg amputated. I wanted to die a whole man. You and I know my circulation won't stay good much longer. The older I get, the worse it will become. It will be better this way."

Mr. M let me know he was ready to return to usual awareness. I suggested he again imagine himself in the field and a moment later, on the count of three, he would open his eyes and find himself back to the present.

When he opened his eyes, he talked about his own death. He had not realized he had been preparing himself until he saw and spoke with his parents. He wasn't afraid and although he loved his family dearly, he realized he would be leaving them soon.

Though his wife was upset by his talk of dying, she also had a sense that it would be soon.

Mr. M had always been a "take charge" gentleman, and he needed to maintain that control over his life to the very last. He knew there had been something going on within himself that he was not able to explain. The imagery enabled him to come to terms with his past life, as well as his oncoming death. Mr. M was not depressed by this but was able to ready himself and make the preparations he felt necessary.

Several weeks later, Mr. M died naturally in the arms of his wife with dignity, peace, and love surrounding him.

This case clearly demonstrates that working within the patient's framework might unearth unexpected understanding and provide dramatic and positive results. In a short period of time, Mr. M was able to utilize a previously successful process with a new problem, to face death with a sense of comfort and resolution. For Mr. M, visiting the country of his birth was what he wanted most. Unable to do this physically, he was able to accomplish it mentally and experience a peaceful review of his life.

Completion of Unfinished Business

Sam was an energetic, healthy gentleman, well into his eighties. For several weeks, he had experienced "a feeling" that he could not explain. It made him "feel uneasy and a little nervous." For some unexplained reason, he felt a need to go over his past life, but he had "trouble remembering."

I was already acquainted with Sam and his wife from their many visits to the home of their friend and my client. From their friend, they were aware of the help he felt he derived from imagery and relaxation. Through this friend, Sam got the idea that these techniques might help him.

When he came to me, I was not surprised that his wife had accompanied him. We talked for awhile about the process. I assured Sam that he would be able to communicate with me during the session. In fact, I asked him for the privilege of joining him in the experience and was hoping he would share his life with me. I reminded him that anything he wished to keep private he could. Sam asked if at any time he did not wish to continue, I would promise to stop. At this point, I reinforced the fact that "this is your life and if at anytime you want to discontinue, you may." I also emphasized that I was here to guide, help, and support him, rather than direct his experience.

Sam's wife spoke for the first time. She was not sure this would work but knew Sam had "never been able to remember the war years." She only knew he had lost his family but where and how he "could not" tell her. He remembered he and his family being arrested by the Nazis, then nothing, only finding himself in Israel some years later. There he met his present wife, a widow with children. They eventually became his present family. Sam acknowledged this with a nod, but made no further comment except to ask if we could proceed.

Sam settled into a comfortable chair of his choice. I had him focus his eyes on a point about a foot in front of him. The more he focused on that point, the heavier and more relaxed his eyelids would feel. Very soon he would find it more comfortable to close his eyes. With his eyes closed, he would find his body and mind become more and more relaxed. The more relaxed his body became, the more open his mind would be to the past. Sam was extremely receptive and visibly relaxed. At this point, I asked him to find the path that would lead him through his life. I asked Sam to let me know when he had found the path. A few moments later he informed me he had found his path.

I asked Sam if he would share the experience with his wife and me. He nodded yes but began speaking in his original German. I reminded him I didn't understand, would he be able to relate the events in English. He agreed. We proceeded down the path until Sam stated this was where he "had to begin."

He was an affluent German Jewish gentlemen, with two teenage boys and a wife. We progressed through several years of his life in detail and several conversations concerning the political situation were recalled. Sam did not feel anything would happen to them. Sam soon became visibly agitated. He again reverted to German. I asked if he wished to continue, but he did not answer. I asked him to tell me what was going on and reminded him to speak in English. He said the Nazis had come to arrest the family. The Nazis came while Sam, his wife, two sons, his parents, and his wife's parents were having a family celebration. He continued, still quite agitated. Sam never saw his parents or in-laws again. He was separated from his wife and his sons. He saw them once again, all dead. He found them among the dead he was required to remove from the gas chambers. Sam was now crying and extremely emotional. I spoke as calmly as possible to tell Sam I knew this was very upsetting to him. However, "these memories could no longer physically hurt him or his family. The memories would be painful but if he wished, sharing them could make it easier. Also, these were his memories, and he could choose to remember or forget whatever he wanted." Sam revealed he wanted to talk to his family. Over the next hour or so, he spoke with each one. It was a confession of love and grief for their loss, sorrow, and guilt for not being able to save them and shame and guilt for his own survival. From that point, Sam recalled being liberated, arriving in Israel, and being in a hospital for a long time.

Sam now asked if we could stop. I told him to take a few moments to collect himself. When he opened his eyes, he would feel "surprisingly relaxed and relieved."

Sam opened his eyes and stated he would now die in peace. Sam's wife, quite startled, asked what he was talking about. He said he now knew he was going to die soon, but he had to complete the unfinished business in his life first. Sam felt part of that had been remembering a forgotten past. The other part was settling the present. He wanted to get together with his (present) family, make a will, and get things in order. He was sure he would be around to conduct the family seder during the Passover holiday but knew he would not be alive much longer.

Sam spoke with a certainty and calm that was rather convincing. I asked Sam if knowing he was going to die soon was frightening. Sam was quiet for a moment then looking up at me smiled and asked why I asked. I told him many people who know they are going to die soon often express fear of the unknown and of death. Sam's wife said he was crazy, and she did not want to continue this conversation. Sam then looked at both of us, shaking his head, and said, "Why should I be afraid? Do you know of anyone who did not go when it was time to die? By the way, do you know of anyone who came back to tell you, you should not go?"

Sam lived for the next 3 months. He was healthy, vibrant, and proceeded to get everything in order. He did have seder with his family as usual. He died as he predicted.

Sam's need to remember an important yet painful part of his past was not an unusual wish as the conclusion of his life approached. Sam knew he lost his first family, but had been unable to remember how. Although the imagery experience had been traumatic, there was the need to resolve the turmoil within himself. Consciously, Sam had been unable to achieve this. However, using imagery and relaxation, Sam put aside his usual critical faculties and obtained a new perspective. Being in a safe and supportive environment, he was now able to face and put to rest many repressed and denied emotions. For Sam, this was a necessary achievement before he could peacefully face his own death.

THE POWER OF IMAGERY WITH A DYING CHILD*

Fear of death is extremely common, yet there are certainly ways in which the patient can be helped. Relaxation and imagery is one more tool to use with selected patients. The following case study was selected for several reasons. The primary one is its ability to show how a negative perception became positive. This case also proves age need not necessarily be a deterrent and how inclusion of the family potentiates the results. It also shows clearly the importance of taking the patient's input and integrating it into the process.

I am not a pediatric nurse. Dealing with seriously ill children leaves me emotionally and physically drained. I tell you this to give you some idea of what it was like to see Jimmy as a client.

---

*This case study is retold by permission from the Foundation of Thanatology, 630 West 168th St., New York, NY, where it has been previously published.

I was packing for a working vacation when I received a call from an extremely distraught father asking me to see his 7-year old son, who was dying of leukemia. I tried to explain that I did not handle children. The father insisted I try. Jimmy was at home because it was what he wanted and what his parents and physician felt best for him. Jimmy was at a point where he was in terrible pain and could not keep even minimal food or liquids down. Worse still was Jimmy's continuous fight against sleep because if he closed his eyes, he was afraid he would die. Not medication, nor being home, nor loving parents were able to console Jimmy nor stop his pain. His physician suggested hypnosis and steered the parents to me. I realized this would be a one-time attempt. I could not say no.

Jimmy was emaciated and dehydrated with a swollen belly and painful joints. His eyes were sunken, his skin yellow, and he was tachypneic. He was in a tight fetal position with fists tightly clenched. When I first laid eyes on him, I physically withdrew from him and verbally expressed my dismay—not the best way to establish rapport with a child. Jimmy was very aware of my presence and reaction. There was no retreat. I looked at this wide-eyed child and said, "I'm sorry, Jimmy, I didn't realize how sick you really are." He quickly acknowledged my explanation with a nod of his head.

I went on to explain who I was and that I was there to help him feel much better. Did he know how to pretend? Again, a nod. I asked him to close his eyes. Could he see a picture of a boat in his head? A nod. His favorite toy? A nod. His Mommy and Daddy? A nod. Open your eyes Jimmy. He did. "Jimmy, can you tell me what it's like to be sick?" He said, "It's cold, dark, lonely, and hurts a lot. I'm afraid. I'm very thirsty but if I drink anything I start to throw up and then I hurt more. I can't play any more. I miss my friends and school." Jimmy then showed me a picture he had drawn. It was on legal-sized paper, totally colored in heavy black crayon, except for one small square in the lower right-hand corner, where a simple picture of a stick figure in fetal position on a bed was drawn.

I said, "Jimmy, tell me where you would like to sit when we play 'Let's pretend.'" He chose his father's reclining chair, with a pillow behind his back so he could sit upright. His father carried him into the den and settled Jimmy into the chair. I assured Jimmy that Mommy and Daddy were going to be in the room, and we would not do anything to make him hurt more.

At this time, I asked Jimmy to close his eyes and to "slowly breathe in and out." Even though his breathing rate was very rapid, I maintained a slow, calm, rhythm and tone. After several minutes, when I saw his breathing begin to slow down a bit, I said, "Jimmy, can you breathe in through your nose and out through your mouth?" His eyes opened wide. "I don't know what you mean. Show me." Once I demonstrated, Jimmy said, "I can do that." He gave a return demonstration. Then I asked him to do it with his eyes closed. He promptly closed his eyes and proceeded to breathe evenly and calmly. Jimmy's breathing had markedly slowed down, maintaining the rhythm I set. His facial expression began to show a decrease in tension, but his arms and legs were still tightly flexed and his fists clenched. I wanted to see if he would continue to follow my directions. I asked him to breathe faster, and I speeded up the rhythm.

"Very good, Jimmy. Notice how much better you're beginning to feel. Now let's slow down your breathing. Nice and easy. In, out, in, out. You're doing wonderful. You're feeling so much better. Jimmy, can you feel your arms and legs getting looser and looser?" I continued reinforcing his feeling better and better and his legs and arms getting more relaxed and looser. After 3 or 4 minutes, he straightened his legs and let his arms rest at his sides. "Jimmy, can you tell me about your favorite toy?" With a great big smile, he said, "Dog." (Jimmy cuddled the toy as if he were really holding it.) "He's big, brown, soft, and warm, and he doesn't hurt." In actuality, "Dog" was in the room on the couch, a ragged, nondescript, stuffed toy.

I asked "How would you like to take Dog and go to the park with me?" Shaking his head yes, he put out his hand while still clutching Dog.

I said, "You're going to have to show me the way because I don't know how to get to the park."

As we walked down the street, he told me who lived in the different houses. He even gave me the name of the big dog on the corner. Jimmy assured me the dog didn't bite. The rest of the conversation went as follows:

Jimmy: Oh, boy! I see the swings.

Marcia: Would you like to get on the swings? (Nodding yes, Jimmy handed Dog to me.)

Marcia: Would you like me to push you?

Jimmy: No, I can do it myself.

Marcia: Very good. You are feeling stronger. Jimmy, you are going higher and higher. The higher you go the better and stronger you feel. (I let Jimmy play in the playground for about ten minutes. We watched his little body relax more and more.)

Marcia: Look how high you're going. You look much better. Do you feel better?

Jimmy: I don't hurt so much now.

Marcia: Jimmy, it's time to leave the park now. We have another place to go and visit. (I gave Jimmy time to slow down and get off the swing. Once off the swing, he asked for Dog back and again took my hand.) Now we're going to visit a different place. We're going to visit where death is and see what it's like. (Jimmy immediately withdrew his hand and again rolled into a tight fetal position.) Jimmy, remember this is just 'Let's pretend.' I promised nothing can hurt you. Mommy and Daddy are here. I am here and nothing will hurt you. (Jimmy relaxed a bit, took my hand and again straightened out in the chair.) Jimmy, tell me what death looks like.

Jimmy: I'm scared.

Marcia: Don't be frightened, it's only 'Let's pretend.' (Pause) Can you tell me what death is like?

Jimmy: It's very black and cold. I'm all alone and scared, and it makes me hurt.

Marcia: (I realized Jimmy's description of death was exactly the same as his earlier picture of what it was like to be very ill.) Jimmy I know what's wrong now. You are not seeing death. You are seeing what it was like being sick all this time. You're looking in the wrong place. Turn your head to the left. (He did.) Do you see the beautiful light? (He nodded yes.) Let's you and I go see where the light is coming from. Remember, nothing will hurt you, so you can peek in and see how different death is from being sick. (Jimmy held my hand tighter. In the other he clutched Dog. We walked through the dark and cold together.) Are we there yet? (Jimmy nodded yes) Okay, now push the door open and tell me what you see?

Jimmy: (Suddenly excited) Grandpa! Grandpa is smiling and waving to me (Jimmy's mother and father were surprised at this description). And my goldfish, they're here too! (He also described the park and its playground, even the swings. Then I noticed a change in Jimmy's face.)

Marcia: Jimmy, can you tell me what is wrong?

Jimmy: (Sadly) I don't see any other children here.

Marcia: (Knowing Jimmy liked school) I'll bet they're in school. (This seemed to satisfy Jimmy. He became very serious.)

Jimmy: When I die, Grandpa is going to meet me. But if I die, I'll leave Mommy and Daddy and my sister. (Jimmy's parents were on the edges of their seats. I motioned for them to stay there and tried to reassure them with quiet hand signals that all was okay. I felt it was something that could be handled.)

Marcia: Yes, Jimmy, you are going to leave them. But remember, they are going to know you and Grandpa are happy together. Mommy and Daddy will know that you are well and don't hurt any more. You and Grandpa will be able to watch over your Mommy,

Daddy, and little sister." (Jimmy appeared very relaxed and accepted my explanation with a simple "Yes." At this point, I felt very tired.) I think it's time we go back home now.

Jimmy: Hold my hand when we pass through the dark.

Marcia: Now that we're almost home, I will soon slowly count to three. On three, you can open your eyes. When you open your eyes, you will feel much better . . . . I'll bet you're hungry and thirsty from all this playing and walking.

Jimmy: Yes. Can I visit these places again?

Marcia: Yes, Mommy and Daddy will know how to help you with "Let's pretend." Playing this helped you feel much better, didn't it?

Jimmy: Yes.

Marcia: (Slowly) One . . . . two . . . . three . . . . You may open your eyes.

Jimmy opened his eyes and smiled. "I liked that. Can I have some milk?" Mommy and Daddy and I were all quietly crying. There was a remarkable change in Jimmy. When he saw us, he put his hand on his hip and shook his head in dismay, saying "I don't know why you're crying. I feel much better."

Jimmy had his snack and went to sleep for the first time in several days. His mother, father, and I sat together discussing what had been accomplished and how they could do the same. They were still shocked by Jimmy's having seen Grandpa. It was then I learned his beloved Grandpa had always lived with them. A little over a year before, Grandpa was suddenly rushed to the hospital by ambulance. The last time Jimmy saw his Grandpa was when the attendants carried him out of the house on a stretcher. Jimmy asked to visit Grandpa, but this was not allowed. Grandpa died in the hospital about a week later. Jimmy's parents told him of Grandpa's death. Jimmy did not ask questions. Mommy and Daddy did not think he would understand so they gave no explanation. Jimmy was not taken to the wake or funeral as his parents felt it would be too upsetting. Jimmy did not mention Grandpa again. Six months later, Jimmy was diagnosed with leukemia.

I left for my working vacation the following morning. When I returned two weeks later, his parents called to tell me Jimmy had passed away. His death had been at home and peaceful. Jimmy's parents used imagery over his last days to control much of the discomfort. Using imagery they took him to the park where he would go on the swings and seesaw, play with his friends and sister. This always reduced his pain and made him hungry and thirsty. Often, they did it before bedtime and gave the suggestion of his getting very tired. Jimmy was able to sleep more restfully. Whenever they did imagery, Jimmy and his parents would hold hands. Sometimes they let his little sister participate. The parents felt very positive about their experience. It gave them a way to help comfort their dying son and brought the family closer together. The parents also found it decreased their own anxiety and made it easier for them to handle the stress they were feeling. Most importantly, Jimmy and his sister were again able to share time together, including several good sibling fights. When Jimmy had been in severe pain, dehydrated, and without sleep, he had become very frightening to his little sister. That had stopped once he felt better.

Jimmy asked to visit death several more times before his death. Although a little uncomfortable at first, his parents did not deny him. They always had to pass through the cold and black first. Once there, Jimmy would peek in. He always saw Grandpa waiting for him. Sometimes he would see other children playing. They were smiling and waiting for him to come soon.

The night he died, he asked to visit "Grandpa" (not death). When his mother said she would take him, Jimmy stated, "It's okay, we don't have to play 'Let's pretend' tonight." Jimmy died quietly in his sleep that night.

I have been in touch with the family several times since then. They are all doing well. For me, it was difficult. I will never forget my first look into Jimmy's terrified eyes. But I will also never forget the change in Jimmy after our "Let's pretend."

This case example needs little summary, other than that it powerfully exemplifies the unique role a caregiver can play with the dying and their significant others. Imagery/relaxation can augment that role.

> "There are many similarities between . . . birth and death. In childhood, the conscious mind slowly emerges from the oceanic feeling of immersion in unconsciousness. As death approaches, the conscious personality seems to be reemersed gradually in the unconscious. Both processes are facilitated by the presence of a caring person" (Crasilneck & Hall, 1975).

Using imagery and relaxation provides the patient and their family with a way to face questions and fears regarding death. It also helps provide physical relaxation. These techniques often provide the vehicle that allows the client to approach unpleasant events in a more positive way. The clients are more open and receptive to affirmative suggestions be they from the therapist, significant other, or self suggestion.

Working with the dying and those fearful of dying can be extremely taxing. It stimulates our own fears of dying and losing loved ones, and often we avoid these patients when they need us the most. Caregivers are encouraged, therefore, to visit their own imaginary deaths to have a fuller appreciation for both their patients lives and for their own lives.

REFERENCES

Crasilneck, H.B., & Hall, J.A. (1975). *Clinical hypnosis: Principles and applications.* New York: Grune & Stratton.

Sheikh, A. A., Twente, G. E., & Turner, D. (1979). Death imagery: Therapeutic uses. In A. A. Sheikh & J. T. Shaffer (Eds.), *The potential of fantasy and imagination.* New York: Brandon House.

BIBLIOGRAPHY

Blake, S.L. (1977). Comforting each other, in *Dealing with death and dying: Nursing skillbook.* Jenkintown, PA: Intermed Communications.

Cohen, K.P. (1979). *Hospice: Prescription for terminal care.* Germantown, MD: Aspen Systems Corporation.

Gonda, T.A., & Ruark, J.E. (1984). *Dying dignified: The health professional's guide to care.* Menlo Park, CA: Addison-Wesley, Medical Division

Schoenberg, B., Carr, A. C., Peretz, D., & Kutscher, A. H. (1972). *Psychosocial aspects of terminal care.* New York: Columbia University Press.

9

THE CANCER PATIENT

SUSAN BERENSON

OVERVIEW

Cancer patients frequently comment, "I've lost control." Whether corporate executive, suburban housewife, or high school student, life has been, for the most part, predictable and has provided choices. When told that they have cancer, all of that changes. Suddenly they have a disease with ill-defined causes and temporary "cures." They suffer multiple changes and losses. Hair loss, scars, burns, mouth sores, and weight loss are some of the physical consequences of treatment. Emotional, financial, social, and existential issues may arise. Cancer patients see themselves as dependent on the physician, the nurse, and the hospital for treatment, and dependent on family and friends for ongoing support. Cancer can make a person feel like a victim: helpless in a hopeless situation. In the setting of total upheaval, relaxation and imagery offer the patient and the nurse a therapeutic strategy to help get back some control.

Cancer patients must cope with both physical and emotional stresses. These may result in anxiety, anger, depression, altered body image, insomnia, pain, fear of procedures, reactive and anticipatory nausea and vomiting secondary to chemotherapy, and a sense of helplessness in the presence of these.

Family members and significant others often experience a similar sense of helplessness. Relaxation and imagery offer patients and their families a new way of coping; once learned, this tool is something they can use for themselves the rest of their lives.

Victor Frankl wrote as an inmate of a concentration camp, living daily with deprivation, suffering, and death, ". . . everything can be taken from a man but one thing: the last of the human freedoms—to choose one's attitude in any given set of circumstances, to choose one's own way" (1959, p. 65). For survival, Frankl and other prisoners chose (1) turning to an inner life through the use of imagery, i.e., imaging past experiences, loved ones, future vision; and (2) finding some meaning in the suffering. Frankl saw some remain brave, dignified, and unselfish in the face of suffering and death and found this to be ". . . sufficient proof that man's inner strength may raise him above his outward fate" (1959, p. 67).

Frankl's observations and personal account of survival are inspiration for life with cancer. The cancer patient does have choices in attitude toward cancer and its treatment. It is the observation of this author that cancer patients who cultivate the inner life and come to some meaning of their suffering have more quality of life. Relaxation and imagery provide a useful vehicle for coming to quiet to get in touch with the inner life, specifically the inner strength and inner wisdom that every living human being possesses.

Theoretical Framework

Helplessness, Hopelessness, Depression, Anxiety

According to Massie and Holland, "The most common emotional distress experienced by cancer patients is depression" (1984, p. 27). Feelings of helplessness and hopelessness are usually experienced by cancer patients at some point or points during the course of their disease, i.e., diagnosis, relapse, failure of treatment, bleeding, or fever of unknown origin. This is a frustrating aspect of care for the nurse. How can one help a helpless, hopeless patient? The feeling of being out of control proportionately affects feelings of helplessness and hopelessness and subsequently the degree of anxiety and depression. Relaxation and imagery enhance control and subsequently reduce helplessness, hopelessness, anxiety, and depression.

Recently in the *New York Times*, a feeling of control was discussed as having consequences for physical and mental health (Goleman, 1986). Researchers have found that by increasing the sense of control among elderly residents in a convalescent home, the residents were happier, more alert, and lived longer. Goleman cited a theory developed by Richard deCharms, a psychiatrist at Washington University in St. Louis: ". . . people who feel they have little control over their circumstances come to feel like 'pawns,' while those who feel more in control experience themselves as 'origins' of power" (Coleman, 1986).

In an earlier work, Martin Seligman postulated the "learned helplessness" theory of depression (1972). People come to feel helpless and hopeless when faced with repeated traumatic events over which they have no control. This causation model of depression was based on animal research (Seligman, 1972, p. 407). Dogs exposed to repeated, uncontrollable, and inescapable electric shocks eventually stopped avoiding and passively accepted the shocks. They were also slow to learn adaptive responding or learning. Seligman's cure for the dogs' "learned helplessness" was "directive therapy" or literally dragging the dogs over the barrier so that changing the compartment terminated the shock. Seligman's prevention of "learned helplessness" was to give experience in controlling trauma.

Intervention based on the learned helplessness model focuses on (1) activating the patient in a realistic, goal-directed way to move toward adaptive coping; and (2) assigning therapeutic tasks mutually determined by the therapist and patient (Stuart & Sundeen, 1983, p. 321). The tasks should be simple and easily accomplished to insure success and to enhance self-esteem.

Relaxation and imagery (R/I) is a proposed intervention, not a cure, for helplessness/hopelessness. As a new adaptive coping mechanism or "directive therapy," R/I promotes a success, a sense of mastery, and control; and thereby enhances self-esteem. By teaching R/I to cancer patients, the experience of control is encouraged, and helplessness lessened or prevented.

Beck views depression and anxiety as cognitive problems (1976). Depression is dominated by a negative evaluation of self, the world, the future (Beck, 1976, p. 56). The patient explains adverse events as personal shortcomings and expects future adversity and failure to continue permanently. The patient feels hopeless because of a negative mind set. Intervention is aimed at: (1) modifying negative thinking and expectations by identifying the negative thoughts and conclusions and increasing positive thinking, i.e., focus on assets, accomplishments; (2) increasing the patient's sense of control over goals and behavior; and (3) developing self-esteem (Beck, p. 233–262). Anxiety is likewise viewed as a cognitive problem, with vulnerability as an essential ingredient. Patients feel as though something bad is going to happen that they will not be able to handle (Beck & Emery, 1983, p. 67, 68). Intervention focuses on exploring three basic questions: (1) "What's the evidence?"; (2) "What's another way of looking at the situation?"; (3) "So what if it happens?" (Beck & Emery, p.201). R/I will not cure anxiety, depression, helplessness, or hopelessness, but learning and mastering a self-help technique can counter anxiety and depression and give a sense of control and thereby increase self-esteem. Looking at negative thoughts and feelings, but also looking at accomplishments, can decrease feelings of helplessness and hopelessness.

This chapter will address the problems of the cancer patient and the use of R/I to enhance coping. It describes the work of a psychiatric nurse but the techniques can be used by other health professionals working with cancer patients. Specifically, the chapter will discuss (1) the Simonton approach, its problems and preferred approaches; (2) passive progressive muscle relaxation with imagery (PPMRI), its strength and its problems; (3) the particular adaptation of PPMRI to the problems of the cancer patient; (4) engaging the physician, nurse, and family as vital members of the patient's relaxation team; and (5) two complete cases illustrating the use of PPMRI.

SIMONTON VS. PREFERRED APPROACH

The Simonton Approach

In 1978, *Getting Well Again*, the popular but controversial Simonton book of self-awareness techniques for the treatment of cancer, was published. Eight years later,

Simonton has become a household word in the field of oncology, especially for non-traditional approaches to the treatment of cancer.

The Simonton approach gives full recognition to the mind/body connection and to the stress/illness link. The techniques are based on the premise that illness is not purely a physical problem, but rather a problem of the whole person, body, mind, and emotions (Simonton, Simonton, & Creighton, 1978, p. 9). It is the belief that, ". . . emotional and mental states play a significant role both in susceptibility to disease, including cancer, and in recovery from all disease" that is the innovative part of the Simonton work (Simonton et al., 1978, p. 9). More simply, attitude can make one susceptible to disease, as well as help one recover from disease. It is suggested that high stress and "giving up" on life can suppress the immune system and increase susceptibility to illness, especially cancer (Simonton et al., 1978, p. 63). On the other hand, it is also suggested that an active and positive participation can influence the disease, a successful outcome of treatment, and an improvement in the quality of life (Simonton et al., 1978, p. 11).

The suggestion that people can cause their own cancer and make themselves well is a very controversial premise. If one accepts that a patient's attitude plays a substantial role in the development of cancer and the response to treatment, then one logically might have to accept that patients are responsible for causing their own cancer or state of health; thus recognizing one's power over causing, controlling, and curing their cancer. It logically follows that if one has the ability to make oneself susceptible to cancer, then one can reverse the process and make oneself well again. The Simontons state that "It is not our intention to make anyone feel guilty or frightened," (Simonton et al., 1978, p. 63). Despite their intentions, some patients become fixated on having caused their cancer and thus immobilized with fear and guilt. This is not clinically productive.

The two components of the Simonton self-awareness techniques are (1) identification of the stressors and behaviors by which the person participates in the onset of their cancer, and (2) a program of relaxation and visualization. Essential to this technique is the patients' identification of their stressors and resultant behavior. They take responsibility for these as contributing to the onset of cancer. A plan of changed behavior can then be introduced along with a daily regimen of relaxation and visualization. Mental imagery is used as a self-directive method to visualize a desired outcome. Effective or "right" images are generally ones that view cancer cells as weak and confused, treatment as strong, and white blood cells as numerous, aggressive, and eager for battle. This relaxation/visualization regimen generally consists of:

1. Muscle relaxation with imagining a pleasant scene.
2. Visualizing the cancer.
3. Visualizing the treatment destroying the cancer.
4. Visualizing the body's natural defenses helping recovery.
5. Visualizing the cancer decreasing in size and the return to health.

Problems with the Simonton Approach

Some patients have read and interpreted the Simonton techniques without professional guidance and have assumed guilt for causing their cancer and fear that a negative attitude or expression of emotion might cause the cancer to return. This guilt and fear can be so overwhelming that they immobilize the patient. If this occurs, not only must cancer patients deal with their disease, but also with the responsibility for causing the cancer and the cure. When considering the numerous stressors faced by cancer patients, these additional burdens seem unfair. It should be noted that for some patients, personal responsibility is important because it may lead to an increased sense of personal control. The nurse has the important role of helping the patients interpret the Simonton approach and to have it best serve them without being an additional burden.

In brief, the problems with the Simonton approach to the treatment of cancer are as follows:

1. Patients may blame themselves for their cancer.
2. Patients may take responsibility for causing their cancer, thus adding guilt and fear to the burden of their disease.
3. Negative attitudes, stresses, and maladaptive behaviors are overemphasized as the cause of cancer.
4. Patients may be on guard mentally and emotionally so as not to fall into old patterns.
5. Patients may view relapse as a failure, that they didn't do their part, or that they didn't do their visualizations frequently or well enough.
6. Patients struggle with the idea of why they would want to give themselves cancer.
7. The Simonton approach needs careful explanation and guidance by a professional.

Achterberg and Lawlis—Image-Ca Technique

Achterberg and Lawlis worked with the Simontons and studied the role of the mind and in particular the role of imagery in disease and wellness states. They soon became aware of the power of positive images on the immune system and therefore on cancer (Achterberg & Lawlis, 1984, p. 16). Believing that images were the most important factor in disease response, they developed the Image-Ca technique, a psychological instrument to analyze the content of the imagery. The Image-Ca technique evaluates the effectiveness of the patient's imagery and predicts the future development of the disease (Hall, 1984, p. 162).

The Image-Ca assesses imagery by the following process: (1) patients achieve a relaxed state by listening to a tape; (2) patients receive a brief education on the immune system, disease process, and how treatment might work; and (3) patients are asked to imagine and to draw pictures of how these three factors pertain to them. Both drawings and the verbal explanations are then evaluated on fourteen dimensions, including vividness, activity, and strength of cancer cells; vividness, activity, and proportion of white blood cells (immune system) to cancer cells; size and strength of white blood cells and vividness and effectiveness of treatment (Achterberg & Lawlis, 1984, p. 26).

The Image-Ca technique has revealed that ". . . patients' imagery reflects their attitudes about their disease and treatment as well as any belief they might have in their innate ability to overcome the illness . . ." (Achterberg, 1985, p. 188). Thus, the Image-Ca technique is not only used to assess imagery but also to devise a plan to treat the cancer. Treatment includes helping patients alter or strengthen the images that are most likely to help them fight the cancer. The author feels more compatible with this approach because of the lack of focus on maladaptive behavior or negative attitudes.

Preferred Approach

This author prefers a positive approach that focuses on strengths and assists the patient in tapping into their inner resources with the use of R/I. Once the patient is feeling stronger and more positive, there is time for introspection and evaluation of behavior.

At the outset it is made clear that the patients did not cause their cancer. It is explained that we know from scientific evidence that stress compromises the immune system, but that other contributing factors such as viruses, genetic predisposition, and environmental factors must be present to cause cancer. Stress and compromised immune system alone do not cause cancer.

Part of the process of building on patients' strengths is to learn how they coped in the past. Remembering past successes reinforces the evidence of inner strength and wisdom and builds hope for future success. Often coping strategies that have worked before are not sufficient in the face of a cancer diagnosis and subsequent treatments. The caregiver can reinforce with the patient what has worked in the past, praising it, trusting it, and coupling it with R/I as a plan of action for the present.

In summary, the author's preferred approach emphasizes the following:

1. The patient is not responsible for his or her cancer or relapse of cancer.
2. Stress and a compromised immune system alone do not cause cancer, but may provide a milieu for abnormal cells to thrive; other contributing factors must also be present.
3. By learning and mastering relaxation, the patient can do something for himself or herself and therefore retrieve some lost control.
4. In a quiet, relaxed state, healing on all levels (physical, emotional, intellectual, and spiritual) can take place.

In conclusion, the author often utilizes specific methods developed by the Simontons, depending on the needs and desires of the patient. However, patients should be cautioned about adopting their approach without careful consideration of the concerns previously mentioned.

The following section describes an integrated R/I approach that was used by the author.

PASSIVE PROGRESSIVE MUSCLE RELAXATION WITH IMAGERY

A passive form of Jacobson's (1938) progressive muscle relaxation plus imagery (PPMRI) is successfully used by many cancer patients. This type of relaxation is appealing to cancer patients because, unlike the active form of PMR, it doesn't require muscle contractions. Therefore, it is less strenuous and the patient feels less self-conscious doing it. In addition, PPMRI allows the patient to mentally float off more easily. For patients who have difficulty concentrating, a more active muscle relaxation is recommended.

Relaxation/Centering for the Practitioner

For best results, the author recommends that the clinician practice relaxation on a regular basis. This helps maintain a relaxed state and acquaints the practitioner with the benefits and sensations of relaxation. Centering just prior to working with a patient is of a benefit. According to Krieger, "Centering oneself physically and psychologically; that is, finding within oneself an inner reference of stability" (1979, p. 35) may prevent one from identifying with and becoming a part of the patient's problem.

Approach

Once a patient is referred and the chart is reviewed, the patient is approached. An introduction as the "relaxation nurse" is followed by an assessment of the patient to determine (1) the willingness on the part of the patient; (2) the appropriateness of relaxation, (3) the ability of the patient to image including visual, tactile, auditory, or kinesthetic, and (4) to uncover pertinent information to decide the best relaxation method and most helpful images. The presenting problem, past medical history, personal and social history, coping style, previous experience with self-regulatory therapies, frequency of dreaming/daydreaming, and location and circumstances surrounding episodes of tension and discomfort are all a part of the initial assessment (see Table 9–1).

A brief explanation of the workings of PPMRI should emphasize the following:

1. When doing PPMRI, the patient is in control, able to move, able to stop, able to open his or her eyes.
2. The goal of relaxation is not to make the mind a blank but to quiet the body, which leads to the quieting of the mind.
3. By letting go of tension one saves or conserves precious energy for healing.
4. In a quiet, relaxed state, healing is potentiated—healing on all levels (physical, emotional, intellectual, and spriritual).
5. To learn relaxation takes time, motivation, practice, and even more important, patience and love towards oneself.

Table 9–1.   Assessment Sheet for R/I

Patient Name/Phone
Address/Birthdate
Diagnosis/Physician
Current Treatments (including psychiatric medications)
Presenting Problem
1. Past Medical History
2. Personal and Social History (including past psychiatric history, religion, family problems)
3. Past Coping Styles (try to incorporate that which is familiar and has worked in the past with the new R/I)
4. Previous experience with or understanding of self-regulatory techniques (e.g., hypnosis, biofeedback, yoga, meditation, guided imagery)
5. Frequency of Dreaming/Daydreaming (possible indicator of how imaginative and creative a patient might be)
6. Location of Body Tension/Discomfort
7. Circumstances and Frequency of Tension/Discomfort Episodes
8. Leisure Time Activities (hobbies, group commitments; what patient does for fun and feels committed to; good indicators for helpful images)

Setting Goals

Goals are set with the patient. The primary goal is to learn the technique of PPMRI, while the secondary goal is the application of PPMRI to the particular problem, whether it be anxiety, insomnia, pain, or nausea and vomiting. If learning the techniques is not the primary goal, patients may set themselves up for failure if PPMRI does not control their pain or nausea and vomiting at first trial.

Preliminaries

There are four items for the patient to consider before commencing practice of PPMRI: (1) quiet environment, (2) comfortable position, (3) an open attitude, and (4) an object or word to dwell upon (Benson, 1975, p. 110). Even as an inpatient, the interruptions or environment can be controlled. The phone can be taken off the hook. If sharing a room, the patient can ask the roommate for 10 to 15 minutes of quiet or lowered conversation/radio/television. It may be helpful to both parties to include the roommate in the relaxation instruction. Certainly the patient's nurse should be informed and plans made for the best time for relaxation to avoid interruptions.

Patients are encouraged to position and reposition themselves to enhance comfort. Good support for the head and shoulders is important; a small pillow under the knees helps break the locked knee joint. Frequent urination, bowel movements, and dry mouth can be overwhelming distractions. The patient should be encouraged to take care of his or her needs and then to resume practice of relaxation.

It is natural to compare one relaxation experience with another. Patients often report that they must be doing the relaxation wrong because they are unable to reproduce the same deep relaxation each time. The clinician reassures the patient that different experiences and intensities of relaxation are normal. The clinician also encourages an open attitude at the beginning of each relaxation—no judgments, no great expectations, no right or wrong way, and openness to the experience of that moment.

Since control is such an issue with cancer patients, it is important to emphasize that they are the ones doing relaxation for themselves. They may have a sense of floating or heaviness during relaxation but can move their limbs, open their eyes, and stop at will. Once comfortable, with eyes closed, the practitioner asks them to orient themselves to the room, with specific awareness of the position and placement of their body and sounds around them, and then to allow sounds and busy or worrisome thoughts to be more in the background.

A busy, worrisome mind is a source of great concern and aggravation. Relaxation is a gentle process, not a struggle to make the mind a blank. Rather, the goal is to quiet the body and quiet the mind. It is as if one were turning down the volume on sounds and thoughts, and working with thoughts and sounds not against them. Often by giving sounds and thoughts recognition and time, they leave of their own accord. The more one struggles to eliminate sounds and thoughts, the more obstinate they become. To aid in the gentle ridding of bothersome thoughts and sounds, the following imagery is helpful: (1) white fluffy clouds moving across the horizon and eventually out of sight, (2) a leaf floating down a stream, (3) fish in a fish tank swimming by, or (4) a helium-filled balloon floating up into the sky and eventually out of sight.

Focused Breathing

Focused breathing is the technique by which all attention is placed on the breath: observing the rise and fall of the chest, feeling the flow of air in and out; being aware of the rhythm and rate of breathing. The therapist suggests that patients say "relax" on the exhalation and picture at the same time sinking comfortably into the chair or mattress. Focused breathing can be used (1) to begin relaxation, (2) as the only technique to help relax, and (3) to quiet a busy mind. Broussard used relaxation (focused breathing and progressive muscle relaxation) with a patient with severe emphysema with resultant decreased heart and respiratory rate and increased sense of well-being (Broussard, 1979, pp. 1962–1963). It has been the author's experience that some patients' anxiety level increased when patients focused on their respiratory problem; they did better focusing only on muscle relaxation and imagery.

For cancer patients who are more imaginative and want to go further in working with breathing, the concepts of rhythm and love and light can be introduced.

As a person watches his or her breathing, he or she becomes aware of a rate and rhythm to the breath. As a matter of fact, most things in nature have a natural healthy rhythm and cycle that is easily observed, such as the flow of water at the seashore, branches of trees swaying in the breeze, and birds in flight. We are part of nature and thus have our own natural, healthy rhythm and balance. With quiet, gentle, full breaths, we become very aware of our individual rhythm. By beginning and ending each day with relaxation, we link the beginning to the end of the day. By relaxing each day, we link one day to the next. A flow of beginning to the end and one day to the next becomes apparent—a gentle yet steady rhythm to our life. Patients become aware of their own healthy rhythm, are quick to recognize a state of dysrhythmia, and can return to a state of equilibrium through the practice of relaxation. Eventually, they can think themselves into a quiet, peaceful state without going through the entire ritual of relaxation (see Donahue, 1987).

Regarding the second concept, many believe in the healing power of love and light. These images are frequently used in meditations and at spiritual workshops. Most patients would agree that love expressed by family and friends is healing for them. A positive thought and image to suggest to the patient is to pull in that love, to breathe it in, and allow it to flow as warmth to every part of the body. Fear of the unknown and discomfort can be perceived as darkness. Imagining light flowing in with each inhalation and filling the whole being may disperse the image of darkness and lessen the fear. With each exhalation, the clinician suggests sighing out tension, worry, and discomfort.

Scanning, Allowing Release, and Visualizing the Release

PPMRI has three components: (1) scanning a muscle or part of the body, (2) willing tension or discomfort to leave, and (3) picturing how tension or discomfort might leave the body. It is often not enough to will tension or discomfort to leave. It is more powerful to combine the thought with the image; it makes it more real.

Patients find it logical to clear the head first, and then work down the body with the flow of gravity. This, however, can be modified, and at times it may be more valuable to start with the feet and work up; the guide is always what seems to make sense to the patient and what works for the patient. Basically, muscles across the forehead, eyes, cheeks, lips, jaw, neck, shoulders, arms, chest, stomach, pelvis, buttocks, back, and legs are scanned. The patient is encouraged to (1) focus on one muscle at a time noting any tension, knots, discomfort; (2) allow release of tension; and (3) picture or sense tension leaving, for example, knots loosening, weight being lifted off shoulders, muscles going limp, tension flowing out of fingers and toes in the form of a liquid, and limbs becoming heavy. It is important to spend time exploring how the patient experiences tension leaving. Some patients cannot envision tension yet are still able to attain quiet and relaxation.

The following is an example of an approach for working with specific muscle groups.

> The eyes, even when closed, can continue to be on guard, to watch. Note whether you are watching yourself or watching what is going on in the toom. Allow yourself to stop watching and allow your eyes to come to total rest, supported in the socket. (A success can be measured when the watching stops even if for only a brief moment.) Your jaw is another common site for holding tension. Note clenched teeth, lips pressed tightly against each other. To let go of any remaining tension, separate the teeth and lips and put the tip of the tongue behind the upper two front teeth. The muscles of your legs work very well in walking and running. At this moment there is no need for your legs to work. Say to yourself, "Not now, save the energy for healing." The muscles of the legs may hold tension in locked joints, curled toes, tight thigh muscles.

After scanning, the clinician may suggest that patients (1) be aware of the weight of the legs and allow the bed to take even more weight, (2) allow the legs to become heavy by being filled with sand, (3) allow tension to flow down and out through the toes in the form of a liquid, or (4) picture legs floppy like a rag doll. Special attention can be given to muscles or parts that pose a particular problem. Sending in love and warmth, or coolness, or picturing an optimally functioning immune system are additional special approaches for problem areas. Props can be used to allow the patient to more easily visualize and work through letting go. Untying actual knots in a rope or manipulating floppy limbs of a rag doll have been useful. With the scanning of each muscle group, the caregiver encourages the patient to conserve energy for healing. Healing is carefully explained as balancing, not curing, oneself on all the levels—physical, emotional, intellectual, and spiritual.

Once the body has been scanned and relaxed, the practitioner asks that patient to take a few moments to experience the relaxed state and to commit it to memory. The author suggests that the patient thank himself or herself for this special quiet time and return to a full state of alertness.

Feedback

Feedback is one of the most important parts of the relaxation process. In order for PPMRI to become a personal technique that a patient can relate to and utilize, it is important to have a dialogue after PPMRI. What was the experience for him or her? Were there any words that were confusing? What images came to mind and what meaning did they hold for the patient? What was comfortable or uncomfortable? Each person is different in preferred pace, words, and images. Through evaluation with the patient, the clinician builds a bank of positive images and experiences. Together with the patient, the clinician creates a very personalized relaxation technique. This is one of the arguments against initially handing out prerecorded tapes, which are often too generalized to meet individualized needs and can become boring. Borkovec and Sides (1979) noted live instruction to be significantly better than taped instruction.

When working with patients there are no automatics, no assumptions, no pat ways. The process of teaching and expanding PPMRI is like a dance—listening and moving with the patients, swaying to their rhythms, teaching them some new steps, and altering the rhythm on occasion for variety and special emphasis.

Variations on Theme

The following techniques are variations or extensions of the PPMRI:

* Focused breathing
* Visualization prescribed by Simonton and Achterberg
* Secret room/Mind room
* Passive imagery
* Sensory awareness

Patients give clues and cues as to what might work best for them. Depending on (1) previous coping mechanisms, (2) preferred leisure activities and surroundings, (3) level of sophistication, (4) motivation, (5) amount of imagination and creativity, (6) feelings of safety and openness to the experience, and (7) amount of success with PPMRI, the nurse can offer the patient and family variation on the theme (Snyder, 1985).

For many, focused breathing alone is best. Simple, familiar, and basic to most people, it may be the only thing patients can hang on to in a crisis. The nurse teaches the patient to count or to repeat the word "relax" on each exhalation. In the author's experience with patients with reactive nausea and vomiting, focused breathing or counting breaths is successful in decreasing intensity and duration of episodes.

Relaxation/visualization as outlined by the Simontons works well with cancer patients who are highly motivated and want to actively participate and work on specific muscles or areas of the body. This technique was successful with a 50-year-old male with chronic myelogenous leukemia and thrombocytosis who wanted to lower his platelets. After a bone marrow aspiration, a photograph was taken of the patient's own megakaryocytes. In a relaxed state, he visualized his megakaryocytes and platelets decreasing in number but optimally functioning.

A second case was a 45-year-old female with breast cancer who suffered pain in the right arm postmastectomy. She found it difficult to describe her pain. In discussing it, she arrived at a clear and imaginable description of her pain: "a steel bear trap whose ragged jaws had a deathlike grip on her flesh." After fantasizing how the pain was caused she imagined how the pain could be relieved. She chose to become Superwoman and pull the jaws apart with her bare hands. Her right arm was immobilized so she was questioned about whether she could pull the jaws apart with one hand. Like Superwoman, she felt able to do anything; subsequently she controlled the pain and reduced her need for pain medication. Having a clear description of pain helps the patient gain a sense of control. By listening to and joining with the patient's own description and images, the nurse can facilitate plausible and meaningful solutions for the patient.

R/I approaches often borrow from standard hypnotic inductions. One induction guides the patient down ten steps to a "secret room" where special work can be done. Anderson and Savary present a similar exercise that they call the "mind room" (1972). A "mind room . . . is a place in which your mind, in its altered state of consciousness, can deal with a problem that might seem insurmountable in the reality state" (Anderson & Savary, 1972, p. 82). Patients who enter the secret room/mind room mobilize their inner resources, namely strength and wisdom.

There are two approaches when using imagery, (1) directive or (2) "free floating," unstructured and permissive. The guided, active and directive approach selects images that are aimed at a specific therapeutic end. The Simonton, Achterberg, and "escape imagery" techniques fall into this category. The other approach is passive and permissive, allowing the free flow of imagery to help the patient become aware of whatever material is most important (Crampton, 1984, p. 23). The patient is encouraged to assume a relaxed state and then to ask the inner self, "what do I need to get in touch with now?" The patient is asked to describe any feelings or visual images that surface, and the therapist explores that until the meaning is clear. M.I. was a 32-year-old mother with acute lymphoblastic leukemia referred for anxiety. She reported feelings of claustrophobia only while in the hospital. She was tearful and described several episodes of panic attacks accompanied by chest pain. After medical testing, it was concluded that the symptoms of heart attack were due to anxiety. M.I. responded well to relaxation sessions. It was mutually agreed to try passive imagery. The patient attained a relaxed state and then asked the inner self, "What do I need to get in touch with today?" Encouraged to allow anything to surface without judging it and then to describe it out loud, she described a jittery, agitated inner feeling. She wept; she was afraid to die, and feared for her 3-year-old daughter's future. She experienced release and relief, explaining that this was the first time she had looked head on at her fears.

Sensory awareness is a sensitizing of the individual to a momentary experience such as breeze on the arm, awareness of breathing, feeling feet flat on the floor, or sounds being heard (Keane, 1979). By returning attention to the experience of the moment, gradually one becomes absorbed, comes to quiet, and can listen to the teacher within. By getting in touch with inner wisdom, perhaps there is the possibility of experiencing life moment-to-moment without feeling hopeless or afraid.

Strengths and Problems with PPMRI

The strengths of PPMRI include the following:

1. It helps the cancer patients get back some control.
2. It helps the cancer patients get in touch with their inner resources.
3. It is applicable and helpful for the majority of problems experienced by cancer patients.

The problems of PPMRI and suggestions for dealing with these problems are listed below:

1. Relief is too short; as soon as the patient stops PPMRI, discomfort or anxiety returns. With continued practice, the patient may lengthen the duration of the relaxed state.
2. Patients with reactive or anticipatory nausea and vomiting can acquire a conditional nausea and vomiting to a relaxation tape or exercise. The clinician may suggest that the patient only do focused breathing or specific imagery when in the hospital during an actual infusion of chemotherapy and use muscle relaxation techniques only at home.
3. Patients have best results and feel most deeply relaxed when listening to the therapist. They become discouraged if they feel they cannot do it as well on their own. As a solution the health professional might make a tape with a specific focus and meaningful images to listen to intermittently. Similarly, the clinician should reinforce that this technique has a positive effect on all levels: physical, emotional, intellectual, and spiritual. Change may be subtle. They may as a result become aware of a physical change and yet unaware of a better balance emotionally, intellectually, or spiritually. By keeping a log, subtle progress may become more evident to the patient.
4. Outpatients do not like to practice on their own at home. It reminds them of

the hospital; specific techniques may be taught to use only at home while others are saved for clinic visits.

5. Some patients express feeling more out of control in a relaxed state. For example, not able to move an arm or not sure where they are. Encouragement of moving arms and legs and opening eyes may assure patients of their control. The therapist will allow for greater control on the patient's part by suggesting that he or she pick the time and place to do relaxation.

APPLICATION OF RELAXATION AND IMAGERY TO SPECIFIC PROBLEMS OF THE CANCER PATIENT

The following problems are associated with cancer and its treatment: helplessness/hopelessness/depression, pain, nausea, and vomiting, anxiety, fear of painful procedures, insomnia, shaking chills, and nutritional deterioration. Medications are never withheld but are used in combination with PPMRI, unless the patient's discomfort level is so low that the patient would like to try using PPMRI alone. Predicting who will master PPMRI and how much relief a patient will experience is difficult. PPMRI does not work for everyone. Clinically it is important to encourage the patient to adopt an open attitude expecting to reduce, not necessarily eliminate, the discomfort.

Helplessness, Hopelessness, Depression

M.S., a 50-year-old female dying of lung cancer, had been admitted for palliative radiotherapy for shortness of breath. The radiation had not given her relief and was stopped. She was referred for relaxation because she was noncompliant in daily care and with prescribed medications. The patient appeared restless, short of breath, disheveled, and had a strong body odor. She talked openly about feeling angry and hopeless because nothing else could be done; she wanted to go to sleep and never wake up. She blamed herself for failing treatment, for behaving badly, for her divorce, for letting her children down, and for deliberately being "nasty" to her mother and friends. She felt she was not worth their concern. She was depressed and hopeless but asking for help in her behavior and words.

M.S. was intrigued by PPMRI but doubted whether it would work. She felt uncomfortable with focused breathing so that PPMRI was emphasized. Surprisingly, the patient found imaging easy. She chose the woods of New Hampshire, where she had grown up and had revisited prior to this present admission. After three sessions over one week, the patient became more compliant with her personal care and medications and began to share what her final wishes were: (1) to get out the anger and tears; (2) to make peace with her children; and (3) to die in the home that she loved. During a PPMRI session M.S. was guided in a fantasy conversation to say good-bye to her 11-year-old son and 9-year-old daughter who now lived with their father on the West coast. She was able, through imagery, to cuddle and rock her babies and tell them how sad she was that she wouldn't be there for their special times. M.S. expressed some of the anger, but never did cry. PPMRI helped M.S. feel safe in expressing her feelings. It helped her as a mother with unfinished business with her two young children. By mastering PPMRI, M.S. felt better about herself and laughed with surprise that she was so adept at this self-help technique. She left the hospital with a smile of peace. Later she died at home in the care of her mother and aunt.

Pain

It is generally held that the best candidates for behavioral intervention are patients with moderate pain that is not completely controlled by analgesics (Cleeland & Tearnan, 1986, p. 195). These people are alert enough to comprehend and well-motivated to practice. Prior to intervention, it is imperative to assess the pain problem. Assessment includes the following: (1) descriptions of pain, i.e., color, sensation, images of objects or animals; (2) influence of persons, environment, time of day on the pain experience; (3) belief system concerning the illness and pain; and (4) techniques already used by the patient to cope with pain. A patient is guided through an imagery/relaxation procedure focusing on a pleasant scene that then sets the scene for going further and deeper with specific imagery to lessen pain. To illustrate, two patients with pain problems will be mentioned: a relapsed leukemic patient suffering from chronic urticaria subcutanea, and a bone marrow transplant patient with stomatitis. Both patients did well with a modified hypnotic induction/relaxation rather than standard PMR. Both chose a pleasant image. Patient 1 chose to see himself in a cool, quiet room in the cellar where he often went to be "far away from the busy world." Patient 2 chose to feel and see herself riding a horse in a wide open field. This patient lived on a farm and was a horsewoman in competitions.

Both patients used imagery to counteract the pain. When patient 1 felt the coolness of the room and visualized cold water running down his arms and legs where he felt pain, he obtained relief.

Patient 2, riding horseback, saw herself winning the competition. Interestingly, patient 2 also visualized coolness, specifically, ice coating her mouth to numb the open, raw nerves. Cleeland and Tearnan suggest additional imaging techniques: glove anesthesia, the transfer of analgesia to painful areas of the body, and the transformation of pain (manipulation of the components of the image of pain) (Cleeland & Tearnan, 1986, p. 210). While relaxed and imaging, one particular patient's pain appeared to be a separate entity. She questioned it directly as to why it was there, and then dismissed it (Griffin, 1986, p. 805).

Nausea and Vomiting

Often considered worse than the disease, nausea and vomiting can be the cause for many patients to stop chemotherapy treatment. PPMRI is an excellent adjunctive therapy to chemotherapy and adequate antiemetic medications. It can reduce the intensity as well as the duration of nausea and vomiting but, in the author's experience, usually does not eliminate it.

Scott, Donahue, Mastrovito, and Hakes compared the antiemetic effects of a program of patient education and relaxation exercises with guided imagery versus a combined regimen of Reglan, Decadron, and Benadryl (Bristol Myers Company, Hillside, NJ) in patients receiving highly emetic chemotherapy for treatment of gynecologic cancer. The patients responded positively to a prechemotherapy education and welcomed the opportunity for self-help. Both programs were helpful. The relaxation group had a 4-hour shorter emetic period. As a result, a combined treatment was recommended (Scott et al., 1986, p. 178–187).

Ideally, the nurse therapist would work several times with the patient before the next infusion of chemotherapy. If time permits, the therapist personally guides the patient through a relaxation early on the day of treatment, just prior to treatment, and then periodically reinforces it throughout the infusion. This one-on-one attention often results in a success that, as a first experience, will encourage the patient. If the therapist cannot be available, patients are encouraged to listen to the personalized tape or do the relaxation procedure on their own.

When using imagery for nausea and vomiting, the patient is asked to pick a place or an experience from the past that is remembered as beautiful and positive. Focusing on reexperiencing a pleasant time extends the relaxed state and has a healing effect by bringing a positive time to the present again. Beach scenes, wooded trails, favorite rooms, horseback riding, and a special dinner and dance with a spouse are a few of the chosen images. The therapist should caution the patient to beware of emotionally charged scenes that add to the stress and are therefore counterproductive. Focused breathing alone has been helpful for anxious, agitated patients anticipating nausea and vomiting. The therapist counts the breaths with the patient, suggesting slow deep inhalation and slow long exhalation.

Anticipatory nausea and vomiting are difficult to correct. Patients can suffer from nausea and vomiting in the absence of the stimulus, chemotherapy. Coming to the hospital, smelling hospital odors, or just thinking about the treatment can precipitate the conditioned nausea and vomiting response. Patients are instructed to practice PPMRI the night before, on the way to the clinic, and while waiting to be seen.

M.M., a 26-year-old male with Hodgkins disease, with a history of nausea and vomiting secondary to chemotherapy, stated, "I feel really bad today. I don't think relaxation will work." M.M. was led through the relaxation and a scene he chose in the woods. To his amazement, he had no nausea and vomiting in the clinic and only a few hours of mild vomiting at home, as opposed to 5 to 9 hours.

Music therapy and guided imagery have been used to decrease chemotherapy-induced nausea and vomiting. Frank's study (1985) investigated the effects of music therapy and guided visual imagery on anxiety and perceived nausea and vomiting secondary to chemotherapy. Fifteen study participants received the same chemotherapy agents and doses. Antiemetics were administered to all. The guided imagery plus music consisted of five posters of environmental scenes accompanied by cassette tapes with music suitable to the scene. Statistically, significant reductions of (1) anxiety state, (2) perception of degree of vomiting and length of vomiting, and (3) length of nausea occurred in postintervention. This might be used for other high anxiety situations for cancer patients such as bone marrow aspirations and pain. (pp. 47–52).

Anxiety

Relaxation gives the anxious patient some control and also helps emotions surface that can then be dealt with rather than suppressed. M.C., a 30-year-old male with the diagnosis of AIDS, came as an outpatient looking for a way to feel more in control. M.C. chose to imagine a mountaintop ledge where he could leave the ground and fly with a hawk. During the feedback time, M.C. reported that he had not wanted to come back. Crying, he explained that this was the first time he had expressed his feelings since his diagnosis. His family did not know of his illness and he reported he had little communication with others. M.C. released some sadness, fear, and guilt during the relaxation sessions that might not otherwise have been expressed. He felt relieved. R/I is also helpful in decreasing anxiety in children. Lamontagne, Mason, and Hepworth studied the effect of R/I on anxiety in second-grade children (1985, pp. 289–292). The relaxation training program consisted of 10 age-appropriate stories on tape that led the children in muscle relaxation and guided imagery. Anxiety decreased in the experimental group. These successful results indicate relaxation could be learned and utilized by children with cancer to help cope with their disease and treatments. In addition, hypnotherapy has been reported as a useful intervention for pain management in children with cancer (Hilgard & LeBaron, 1984). More recently, video game distraction is shown as a successful tool for reducing conditioned nausea and self-reported anxiety in pediatric cancer patients receiving chemotherapy (Redd et al., 1987, pp. 1–5).

Fear of Painful Procedures

Cancer patients often develop fear of procedures because of a previous bad experience. They may become noncompliant or require large amounts of sedative prior to a procedure. Bone marrow aspiration (BMA), spinal tap, and venipuncture are good examples of short, simple procedures that provoke anxiety and pain.

R/I techniques help with accessibility to veins. Diane Scott (1987) reported success with a female patient with difficult veins. The patient was asked to image herself in her upcoming vacation. Her vein came up, and the procedure was completed comfortably.

Ideally, the therapist would have several days to teach and reinforce relaxation prior to a BMA. Special emphasis is placed on relaxing buttock muscles because the posterior iliac crest is the site of choice for BMA. Some of the practice time should be performed with the patient in the prone position since this is the BMA position. If the therapist can be available to personally guide the patient through PPMRI, it is usually a successful first experience. With the patient in the prone position, the therapist guides the patient through the pre-BMA relaxation. Then the therapist talks the patient through the actual procedure, interjecting comments like "you'll feel the cold betadine, the doctor will now aspirate the marrow" to alleviate the anxiety of what is coming next. Focused breathing alone, progressive muscle relaxation, and PPMRI have all been successful.

One 74-year-old male with acute leukemia found BMA particularly uncomfortable. After PPMRI training, this man, an ardent football fan, chose to mentally run with the ball down the football field. His reply to the doctor was, "I didn't even know you did it."

Insomnia

Focused breathing, PMR, and PPMRI have been helpful for patients with alteration in sleep patterns. Patients have been able to both fall asleep and return to sleep once awakened.

Shaking Chills

PPMRI helps quiet shaking chills secondary to the infusion of amphotericin. After learning relaxation for anxiety, two patients decided to apply their techniques to these shaking chills. One patient used PMR alone, while the other used PPMRI with skiing down the slopes as his choice of image.

Nutritional Deterioration

R/I was studied as a nursing intervention to improve the nutritional status of the cancer patient nutritionally at risk. The five groups included: (1) a control group, (2) patients receiving nutritional supplements, (3) patients using relaxation and imagery, (4) patients using both relaxation and nutritional supplements, (5) visits only. The greatest weight gain was in the R/I group. This suggests that the use of R/I, a noninvasive nursing intervention, is successful for slowing or reversing nutritional deterioration in the cancer patient (Dixon, 1984, pp. 330–335).

PHYSICIAN, NURSE, AND FAMILY—VITAL MEMBERS OF THE RELAXATION TEAM

The nurse therapist not only works intensely with the patient, but is a liaison between patient and physician, patient and nurse, and patient and family. It is advantageous to the nurse therapist to educate and update these members about the procedure and to obtain their support for the work with the patient. Very often R/I has been viewed by health professionals as a waste of time, a bit of quackery, a last ditch, or of no value. Eventually, they can be won over if they are included in the whole process.

Whether teaching R/I to inpatients or outpatients, space, interruptions, and coordination of personnel are all problematic. Problems are less if one tries to work around other caregiver's schedules. The clinician can engage the patient's nurse and doctor as valued members of the R/I team by explaining the specific purpose of R/I, obtaining feedback from them as to the patient's progress, and asking for additional information about the patient that might be incorporated with imagery.

The therapist may ask to attend the BMA to coach the patient during the actual procedure. In the author's experience, doctors welcome the intervention. One physician stated: "I felt so relaxed myself, just listening to you. I think the BMA was easier for the patient because I was more relaxed." The author has accompanied anxious patients to the operating room, the computerized tomography scanning, and radiation therapy, coaching relaxation all along the way.

Being sensitive to staff needs and taking time to explain the procedure will usually engender cooperation and new converts of the benefits of R/I. The author often invites the doctor or nurse to join in the relaxation with the patient. If they are able to participate or observe, they are usually enthusiastic and supportive.

The family can often be more stressed than the patient, perhaps because they are able to do so little. With the permission of the patient, family members can be included in the relaxation session. They can use it for themselves, coach the patient in the hospital and at home, and reinforce the value of relaxation.

With the doctor, nurse, and family advocating and encouraging relaxation, the patient is certainly much more likely to value PPMRI and follow through on practice.

Two Complete Cases

CASE I

P.B., a 25-year-old mother with acute leukemia, had not responded to the first round of chemotherapy as an inpatient. Beginning her second round, the hospital staff reported she was noncompliant and referred her for relaxation. She had intense anxiety associated with BMA. She was also preoccupied and fearful about who would care for her 2-year-old daughter if she died.

During the assessment, P.B. revealed that the initial bone marrow aspiration had been a long and excruciatingly painful experience. This had left her terrified of having the procedure again.

Prior to her illness, P.B. had been a healthy, vibrant young wife and mother. She came from a large, close and supportive Catholic family. Her relationship with her family was good except with her mother who criticized her for being overdramatic, overreactive and too "dependent on pain and nerve medication." One of her three sisters was a match and was enthusiastically ready to donate her marrow for transplant as soon as P.B.'s marrow went into remission. P.B.'s husband, a 30-year-old construction worker, expressed his anger and frustration with frequent outbursts over the phone to the attending physician. P.B.'s daughter was a very "grown up" 2-year-old who often told her mother, "Don't cry, mommy. It's not good for you!" Prior to her marriage, P.B. had had an abortion for an unwanted pregnancy.

When asked about her previous methods of coping with stress, P.B. reported she did not know how she had dealt with problems because prior to her diagnosis, her life had been relatively problem-free. As a child, however, she had problems sleeping and her father had taught her how to relax her muscles, which she had found helpful. This mature young woman described herself as a "fighter" and was able to look realistically at her potential death and the meaning of separation from her young daughter.

The goal for P.B.'s treatment was to have the relaxation response replace her fear/anxiety response to BMA and to the future care of her daughter. The interventions employed focused on (1) teaching PPMRI prior to her next BMA, (2) guiding her through relaxation during the BMA, and (3) encouraging P.B. to talk about her fear and anxieties, particularly concerning her daughter.

P.B. participated in six sessions of PPMRI over a period of 3 weeks. At first she was reluctant to start because she had the mistaken impression that it was necessary to feel good and be able to concentrate fully to do the R/I exercise. It was clarified that with time she would be able to concentrate. Sitting in a chair she was guided through the relaxation. After her first session, much to her surprise, the tension and discomfort in her lower back (where she characteristically felt tension) disappeared and she felt relaxed and briefly out of her body.

At the third session, P.B. was waiting to report that she had talked with her daughter on the phone. She was very upset but had been able to calm herself with relaxation. During this session, the therapist commented on her success and recommended doing PPMRI while she was lying on her stomach in a supine position, like she would be in for the BMA. She reported being pleased with the results; she was able to relax herself and was feeling as through she had regained some self-control. She talked about being a fighter and expressed hopefulness. She continued to practice on her own.

After the fourth session, she told me she wanted to talk about something she had never told another person. Tearfully she explained she had an abortion prior to her marriage. The father was her present husband. Unknown to both their families, she had felt burdened by this for the past 6 years. Abortion was against her religion and she worried that the leukemia may have been God's way of punishing her. She stated she felt much better having talked about it.

The fifth session was during P.B.'s BMA procedure. It had been prearranged that the procedure would be done at the patient's bedside and that prior to the procedure she would be in a relaxed state. The physician and staff had all agreed and had been well oriented to PPMRI. The author coached her through the procedure, encouraging her to pay special attention to her breathing and to relaxing the buttock muscles. Throughout the procedure, P.B. was informed about what would happen next to alleviate her need to be on guard. P.B. remained relaxed and comfortable. When it was over she sobbed with relief.

At her last session, P.B. complained of a severe headache. She was nervous and shaky but as she progressed through the relaxation exercise, she felt calmer. That was the last session because the next day she unexpectedly died of an intracranial bleed.

In summary, P.B. was a frightened young woman who was considered noncompliant by the hospital staff and too dramatic and drug dependent by her mother. She saw herself at the start of treatment as helpless and out of control. She did very well using progressive relaxation but was never able, or willing, to add the imagery component. Relaxation helped her control her conditioned fear of the BMA and allowed her to experience the procedure with comfort. Being successful and calming herself, her self-esteem increased and she felt more hopeful. P.B. was also able to express problematic thoughts and feelings concerning the pain and anxiety of BMA. Later she unloaded feelings that had been "eating away at her for the last 6 years." She was more involved with her husband and daughter when they visited just prior to her death. While she unexpectedly died without "saying good-bye" and before she had resolved who would "fill her shoes" in mothering her daughter, she had, as a result of the relaxation therapy, many more quality moments than she might have had if the treatment had not been done.

CASE 2

R.R., a youngish, 65-year-old widow with lung cancer, 1 month postlobectomy, was self-referred for R/I treatment to "stop harming myself" and to "learn how to do the images right so I can fight my cancer." After reading Simontons' *Getting Well Again*, she felt responsible for causing her illness and wanted desperately to do something positive to stop the cancer. Her attempts to visualize were criticized by a friend, who said, "You are using the wrong images." Initially she appeared tearful and frightened, wondering how she had caused her cancer and anxious that if she did not use the "right" images it would come back.

Prior to her illness she had been in reasonably good health except for multiple addictions to alcohol, drugs, and food. A recovering alcoholic, she attended regular Alcoholics Anonymous and Overeaters Anonymous meetings. Her only child, a 33-year-old unemployed dentist, was also addicted to drugs and alcohol and had made one suicide attempt. The patient expressed guilt about her son. R.R. was involved with a man she described as possessive and domineering; she had only one other friend who lived in Florida. R.R. described herself as a loner, but since retiring from her job as a radiation technician, she spent her time ballroom dancing, attending opera, and experiencing the outdoors in boating, nature walks, and gardening. While not formally religious, R.R. recited affirmations every morning. She feared if she stopped this practice, her cancer would come back.

In the past, R.R. dealt with her problems through drug and alcohol abuse and through binge eating. Although actively involved in Alcoholics Anonymous, she continued to see evidence of destructive compulsive behaviors. For example, she had spilled milk on the rug and literally spent 2 hours cleaning it up with subsequent state of tearfulness and exhaustion. Her previous experience with relaxation occurred in a class on meditation where she learned breathing techniques and was given a mantra. She liked the meditation exercise and "was good at it" but discontinued its use after the class ended.

The long-term goal in working with R.R. was to have the relaxation response replace the anxiety, fear, and guilt. The following were short-term goals: (1) to clarify with R.R. that behavior and attitude alone do not cause cancer and that other contributing factors such as viruses and genetic predisposition are necessary; (2) to teach effective use of PPMRI; and (3) to encourage her to practice twice a day and when she was anxious.

R.R. did well learning PPMRI and faithfully practiced. In the beginning she was obsessed about doing it "right" and where to start the relaxation on her body. The therapist advised her to start where it made sense for her. She pictured tension leaving through the pores of her skin in the form of steam; she wanted a window open slightly so the steam could leave the room.

R.R. was often tearful after being guided through the exercise. She explained that the relaxation was more intense when she was guided and that she felt both a muscular and emotional "letting go." The clinician explained that often with the release of tension in a relaxed state that feelings and deep, well-protected thoughts might come to the surface. R.R. did some crying followed by a time of quiet talking.

After two sessions establishing basic muscle relaxation, R.R. reported she was practicing with success and was able to quiet herself both physically and mentally. She then decided on a form of guided imagery. R.R. picked fishing in a boat by herself on a lake in the mountains. She had often done this with her husband. During the exercise, she watched the fish swimming in the water. Over the weekend, she practiced the relaxation and imagery. During this time her son visited and they spent much of their time arguing. When practicing she could only picture herself outside the boat. After the visit she was able to picture herself again in the boat and later with her husband. The imagery became clear enough that she could see herself in the boat looking lovely in her favorite green dress. She then began reporting that she was becoming more assertive with her boyfriend and son. She started to plan her future and began visualizing moving to a better apartment.

She wanted to learn more visualization techniques. By session five, the "secret room" was used to deepen the relaxation and the "magic shawl" to help her let go of fear and guilt. She wrapped herself in this shawl as she sat in a comfortable recliner in her "secret room." The shawl had the power to give whatever she needed and to absorb what she did not want. R.R. stated she wanted continued peace and riddance of her fears.

By session seven, R.R. appeared physically more happy and relaxed. She was smiling, had bought some new clothes, and had started dancing again. She stated, "I thought I was going to die. Now it looks like I'm going to live so I had better start living." There were things she wanted to do in the remaining time of her life. She was asked to make a list before the next session. Her list included five items: (1) attend evening AA and OA meetings; (2) visit her friend in Florida; (3) move to a better apartment; (4) date other men; and (5) travel to London where her parents were born.

R.R. continued to practice PPMRI. Some of her obsessional thoughts continued, such as if she stopped practicing, her cancer would come back. She also did not think to apply the technique to other aspects of her life (anxiety over spilled coffee on her living room rug) until it was pointed out.

She began to use relaxation in other tense situations. She worried that at times she did not get "deep" enough and needed frequent reassurance and reminders that there was no one right or wrong way to use the technique and that it was important she was doing something for herself that made her feel good.

After eight sessions, the goals were reviewed and it was decided that they had been sufficiently accomplished, even though some personal problems remained that she wanted to continue to work on. She and the nurse mutually agreed to terminate and a psychotherapist was recommended. One year later she called to thank the nurse for her help and to explain that she had accomplished everything on her list except for the trip to London.

CONCLUDING REMARKS

A current nursing study suggests that there is a relationship between nursing interventions and quality of life in cancer patients, with the perceived caring attitude of the nurse and perceived self-care ability (i.e., personal control) as mediating cognitive variables (Padilla & Grant, 1985). Both caring activities and personal control act to affirm self-worth and for that reason impact on quality of life (Padilla & Grant, p. 54). Relaxation and imagery are nursing interventions that communicate caring on the part of the nurse therapist and train the cancer patient to master a self-help technique, which gives a sense of control and enhances self-worth. R/I can positively impact on the cancer patient's quality of life.

Approximately 3 years ago Lawrence LeShan spoke as a guest speaker at Memorial Sloan-Kettering Cancer Center. When discussing how he helped cancer patients fight for their lives, he spoke poetically about helping them to get back in touch with the "song in their heart" (LeShan, 1983). He was referring to that part of a person that connects very deeply and feels passionately. He suggested that when some cancer patients reconnect regularly with something that gives them great joy or pursue something that they always wanted to do, the experience may extend their life or improve the quality of their life. Through relaxation and imagery a cancer patient may get to quiet so as to hear the "song in the heart" and tap into those long forgotten strengths.

Quality of life is also of concern for the nurse. The oncology nurse works in a high stress environment. It is strongly recommended that nurses teaching R/I to cancer patients practice it themselves in order to reduce job and personal stress, to increase the credibility of this intervention as they see it working on them, and to better understand the patient's experience, its sensations and difficulties. (See Chapter 13.) A few well-known relaxation nurses were interviewed to ascertain whether they used R/I in their daily lives. They replied yes but not in a disciplined way. They all reported that they did R/I for personal, daily challenges and attained a relaxed state while teaching patients. Dorothy Donahue offered that she has been teaching relaxation for so long that now it is a mind set that she automatically slips into (personal communication, April 30, 1987). Diane Scott recounted personal success with reduction of pain and anxiety (personal communication, May 2, 1987). Pamela Minarik, responsible for nursing staff and patients on 14 medical units, uses R/I especially after a long day. She uses focused breathing with imagery and has a variety of spoken and music tapes suited to her particular mood. She teaches other oncology and cardiology nurses how to teach relaxation to their patients. These nurses report increased creativity, feeling good, even euphoric, and increased energy with R/I (Minarik, personal communication, May 5, 1987). The author attributes surviving her mother's very long painful death of this past year to R/I. Not only was she able to teach her mother R/I but she used it to maintain her own physical and mental well-being.

R/I has the potential to positively impact the quality of life of both patient and nurse and to keep them in touch with the song in their hearts. A favorite toast to friendship seems quite appropriate: "A friend is someone who hears the song in your heart, and when you have forgotten it, can sing it back to you." It is indeed a privilege to work with cancer patients and to help them remember their song.

REFERENCES

Achterberg, J. (1985). *Imagery in healing: Shamanism and modern medicine.* Boston: New Science Library.

Achterberg, J. S., & Lawlis, G. F. (1984). *Imagery and disease.* Champaign, IL: Institute for Personality and Ability Testing.

Anderson, M. S., & Savary, L. M. (1972). *Passages: A guide for pilgrims of the mind.* New York: Harper & Row.

Beck, A. (1976). *Cognitive therapy and the emotional disorders.* New York: International Universities Press.

Beck, A., Emery, G., & Greenberg, R. (1985). *Anxiety disorders and phobias.* New York: Basic Books.

Benson, H. (1975). *The relaxation response.* New York: Avon.

Broussard, R. (1979). Using relaxation for COPD. *American Journal of Nursing, 79,* 1962–1963.

Borkovec, T., & Sides, J. (1979). Critical procedural variables related to the physiological effects of progressive relaxation: A review. *Behavior Research and Therapy, 17,*119–125.

Cleeland, C. S., & Tearnan, B. H. (1986). Behavioral Control of Cancer Pain. In A. Holzman & D. Turk (Eds.), *Pain management: A handbook of psychological pretreatment approaches.* New York: Pergamon Press.

Coburn, J., & Manderino, M. A. (1986). *Stress inoculation: An illustration of coping skills training. Rehabilitation Nursing, 11,* 14–17.

Crampton, M. (1984). *An historical survey of mental imagery techniques in psychotherapy and description of the dialogic imaginal integration method.* Montreal: Montreal Psychosynthesis Center.

Dixon, J. (1984). Effect of nursing interventions on nutritional and performance status in cancer patients. *Nursing Research, 33,* 330–335.

Frank, J. (1985). The effects of music therapy and guided imagery on chemotherapy induced nausea and vomiting. *Oncology Nurse Forum, 12,* 47–52.

Frankl, V. (1959). *Man's search for meaning.* New York: Simon & Schuster.

Goleman, D. (1986, October 7). Feeling of control viewed as central in mental health. *New York Times*, Section C, 1, 11.

Griffin, M. (1986). In the mind's eye. *American Journal of Nursing, 86*, 804–806.

Hall, H. (1984). Imagery and Cancer. In A. A. Sheikh (Ed.), *Imagination and healing*. Farmingdale, NY: Baywood.

Hilgard, J. R., & Lebaron, S. (1984). *Hypnotherapy of pain in children with cancer*. Los Altos, CA: William Kaufman.

Jacobson, E. (1938). *Progressive relaxation*. Chicago: University of Chicago Press.

Keane, B. W. (1979). *Sensing: Letting yourself live*. San Francisco: Harper & Row.

Krieger, D. (1979). *The therapeutic touch*. New Jersey: Prentice-Hall.

Lamontagne, L. L., Rew Mason, K. D., & Hepworth, J. T. (1985). Effects of relaxation on anxiety in children: Implications for coping with stress. *Nursing Research, 34*, 289–292.

LeShan, L. (1983). You can fight for your life. Lecture given at Memorial Sloan-Kettering Cancer Center.

Massie, M. J., & Holland, J. C. (1984). Diagnosis and treatment of depression in the cancer patient. *Psychiatry, 45*, 25–28.

Padilla, G. V., & Grant, M. M. (1985). Quality of life as a cancer nursing outcome variable. *Advances in Nursing Science, 8*, 45–58.

Redd, W., Jacobson, P., Die-Trill, M., Dermatis, H., McEvoy, M., & Holland, J. (1987). Cognitive/attentional distraction in the control of conditioned nausea in pediatric cancer patients receiving chemotherapy. *Journal of Consulting and Clinical Psychology, 55*, 1–5.

Scott, D. W., Donahue, D. C., Mastrovito, R. C., & Hakes, T. B. (1986). Comparative trial of clinical relaxation and an antiemetic drug and vomiting. *Cancer Nursing, 9*, 178–187.

Seligman, M. E. (1972). Learned helplessness. *Annual Review of Medicine*, 407–412.

Simonton, O. C., Matthews-Simonton, S., & Creighton, J. L. (1978). *Getting well again*. New York: Bantam Books.

Snyder, M. (1985). *Independent nursing interventions*. New York: John Wiley & Sons.

Stuart, G. W., & Sundeen, S. J. (Eds.) (1983). Disturbances of mood. In *Principles and Practice of Psychiatric Nursing*. St. Louis: C.V. Mosby.

10

RELAXATION/WEIGHT LOSS

ROTHLYN P. ZAHOUREK

Fat is not fun, fancy, funny, or fruitful. Fat people do *not* have more fun or better sense of humor. Fat is not stylish and contributes to health problems, including heart disease and diabetes. It diminishes one's longevity, productivity, and quality of life. Self-esteem, self-assurance, and success in personal as well as professional lives are all compromised for the obese individual. Being fat means "it doesn't fit." Forty to eighty million Americans (two thirds of whom are female) struggle with not "fitting" because of obesity.

Fat-phobic Americans obsessively fear gaining weight and frown upon those who do. This particularly American obsession has resulted in many who are not significantly or dangerously overweight seeking help for weight loss and those with significant extra poundage feeling especially bad about themselves. Weight loss is big business and a problem preoccupying, and often confounding, the housewife, model, and salesman as well as the therapist, nurse, and scientist. All seek a safe, comfortable, and lasting method to become slim, trim, and healthy.

The term *obese* derives from the Latin and means to overeat or devour. While overeating is usually associated with obesity, many overweight people eat less than normal-weight others but expend much less energy. Generally, *obesity* is defined as exceeding ideal body weight by more than 20 percent (Wolman, 1982, p. 1). Obesity is also generally characterized by early or late onset. Early onset (developing in childhood) is thought to be more dependent on deep psychological issues or physiological and genetic determinants. Later onset is considered reactive and is usually correlated with stressful periods in an individual's life and the changes associated with events such as pregnancy and aging. This form of obesity is more successfully treated; weight loss is more rapid and more lasting.

This chapter will focus primarily on an adjunctive method of treating the person who wants to lose weight. Relaxation and imagery techniques (R/I) are incorporated into a comprehensive approach that is based on an assessment of the person and an understanding of the numerous theories of obesity. While many exist, those theories that seem most relevant are discussed. Similarly, a brief discussion of the research on treatment is included and the reader is referred to the references for a more comprehensive review.

RELEVANT THEORIES OF OBESITY

Fat Cell Theory

Fat is stored in adipose tissue either in larger or more adipocytes. Hypercellular and hypertrophic adipose tissue is associated with early-onset obesity, and hypertrophic tissue occurs in obesity developing later in life. During the first year of an infant's life, fat cells increase in size, their numbers increasing only slightly. A gradual increase in number and size occurs with growth. A sharp increase occurs in puberty, and adult levels are reached in late adolescence. It is believed that individuals with early-onset obesity never lose fat cells, they simply become smaller. Cell size is now being related to insulin resistance and the regulation of calories used in the obese. It is now also accepted that weight regain is dependent on physiological as well as psychological factors (Bjorntorp, 1986).

Internal Regulation

The appetite and recognition of satiety is located in the hypothalamus. In obesity several factors seem to go awry; new information is substantiated in animal studies on regulation of food ingestion, use and storage of calories, and energy expenditure (Wolman, 1982, p. 3). For currently unknown reasons obese individuals do not associate fullness of the stomach with satiety, which is experienced as relaxation and calmness.

Set Point Theory

The set point theory of obesity helps explain why some obese individuals seem to eat normal to small amounts of food but are unable to both lose weight and maintain the weight loss. A set point is a weight that the body tries to maintain as normal for that individual. Through animal studies and studies of starvation researchers are learning that even with varying amounts of food intake and energy expenditure, many individuals will come close to maintaining a weight that is normal for them. When individuals with a high set point try to lose weight and then try to maintain the weight lost they are in a state of starvation rather than health. Such individuals then will need to alter their set point in order to obtain and maintain a lower weight. It is speculated that exercise on a regular basis may be successful in altering the set point, but it must be maintained or the individual reverts back to the former point. According to Keesey (1986), "safe and effective means for accomplishing substantial reductions in set point do not currently exist. But the growing evidence that set points can be altered by various neuroanatomical, physiological, and pharmacological manipulations should serve to intensify the search for procedures capable of reducing an obese individual's regulation level of body weight . . ." (p. 84). The set point theory has altered the perception of many treating the chronically obese client. Many question the value of chronic dieting for minimal weight loss because of corresponding metabolic and psychological depression as well as the disordered lifestyle and eating patterns that develop.

Theories of Eating Patterns

Stunkard and Mendelson (1976) describe three major eating patterns leading to obesity: satiety failure, night eating, and binge eating. Those who experience *satiety failure* do not feel full and satisfied no matter how much they eat. They are constantly nibbling and report eating large quantities of food during a day. After gorging they feel nauseated but not satisfied. The *night eaters* eat little all day but begin to eat excessively and constantly in late afternoon or early evening. Eating seems to relieve boredom. Some awaken during the night out of a sound sleep feeling ravenous. Feeling lonely and unable to sleep, these people experience comfort from eating. *Binge eaters* control their eating much of the time but on occasion, like an alcoholic, lose control and do nothing but eat large quantities of food. Often done secretly or away from home, these individuals feel totally out of control, ashamed, and guilty. A dissociative state seems to occur during the binge and may be associated with partial amnesia.

Categories of Psychological Obesity

In 1958 Hilde Bruch described two categories of obesity: reactive and developmental. *Developmental obesity* originates in infancy and results from a mother's rejection of her infant. To compensate for these feelings the mother overprotects and overfeeds. Food is love, and, as a result, all the infant's needs are met through food. The infant then does not learn to distinguish between bodily urges and sensations. The child develops a distorted body image and a poor sense of owning his or her own body.

Reactive obesity, on the other hand, occurs later in life and results from traumatic or stressful events. Bruch believes that both types of obesity must be treated by resolving the underlying causes, or deterioration of function will occur. Foreyt (1977) enlarged these categories: maturity-onset obesity, reactive, and early-onset neurotic obesity. Maturity-onset obesity develops in adult life and is usually associated with aging and a decrease in activity but maintenance of usual caloric intake. Major psychological disturbance is not generally associated with this type of weight gain. Reactive obesity resembles Bruch's description in that it occurs in reaction to stress, loss, or decreased biological or social roles. The personality structure remains intact while the coping mechanism is maladaptive. Early-onset neurotic obesity again resembles Bruch's description: food is associated with reduction of tension, eating and hunger are dissociated, and body image is distorted. While eating relieves anxiety it promotes guilt and more anxiety. This type develops in families where food is consistently used as both a reward and a punishment.

Psychodynamic Theories

Research on the psychology of obesity yields contradictory and controversial "facts." Richard Hagan (1976) reviewed the literature and concluded the following: (1) people *do* and *do not* overeat for psychological reasons; (2) eating *does* and *does not* reduce anxiety; (3) individuals losing weight *do* and *do not* risk symptom substitution; (4) the obese *are* and *are not* more responsive to inner cues; (5) the obese *do* and *do not* have greater responsiveness to the taste and palpability of food; and (6) the obese *do* and *do not* need and defend their large size.

Most agree that overeating serves some emotional purpose, usually relieving stress and anxiety and soothing other strong negative and positive feeling states. Overeating also seems to be either directly associated with or a delayed reaction to a myriad of emotions: excitement, joy, fear, anger, loneliness, boredom, and loss. Depression is commonly associated with obesity, but the question continues to be which comes first, the depressive personality or the obesity. The answer must be determined by a careful individual history evaluating whether a recent loss has occurred or threatens to occur and whether an early history of deprivation or abuse was experienced.

The symbolic value of fat as a protective covering has been speculated as an important meaning of excessive weight. According to this theory, fat prevents sexuality (and sexual acting out) and having to do things that are physically hard because of physical inability, and it prevents general feelings of vulnerability. Being fat also allows the individual to project an image of bigness, power, and invincibility. Losing weight for individuals whose fat has these meanings precipitates a disturbed sense of self, depression, and intense feelings of vulnerability.

Bychowski (1973) studied "neurotic obese" women. He speculated that the roots of the problem were difficulties arising from symbiosis, separation, or the Oedipal phase. He claimed that food means strength to a weakened ego and overeating eases separation anxiety.

Suzy Orbach's book, *Fat Is a Feminist Issue*, describes in detail how some of these theories are manifest for women (1979). She focuses on the meaning of food to the overweight woman. Food has magical qualities associated with both fatness and thinness. Food becomes a drug, both a painkiller and a tranquilizer; it keeps you alive but it should never be genuinely enjoyed. It must be eaten quickly and secretly to resolve a crisis; it causes guilt, providing only momentary pleasure and little satisfaction. Food is used not only as love but also for prevention of future hunger, celebration of a success, soothing a hurt, filling of time, and prevention of boredom.

Fat has other psychological and sociological meaning: the overweight woman doesn't measure up to cultural body standards, she is outgoing and jovial, she refuses invitations to swimming and dancing parties, and she envies others who are thin. Fat also means avoidance of shopping trips for clothes, phobias of mirrors, and preoccupation with future thinnes, as well as current appearance and the kind of food being eaten. For the overweight woman, being fat also comes to mean that she always takes care of others and never herself, she never says no, she has an excuse for failure, her mother failed somehow, she is protected and powerful, and she is a little different. She is earth mother looking for a man who will see through the layers of fat to the wonderful person she is underneath, and she is never a sex object.

Thinness to Orbach also has special meaning for the overweight woman: "Everything in life will be better"; "I will be more competent, sexy, active, and in control." But there is a *but*: "I may not be taken seriously and may be seen as vain, a sex object, selfish and narcissistic, and other women won't like me."

The application of Orbach's work is especially relevant to the psychological understanding of and intervention with the obese client. Her books are often recommended to clients. The meaning of fat and thinness, as she describes it, is easily understood and can then be assessed with the client in a collaborative manner. Where applicable, the dynamics are used in a tailormade imagery intervention. In addition, she believes the goals of treatment need to include helping the obese person to (1) express feelings through means other than eating, (2) alter the self and world image, and (3) learn to eat normally rather than being on a perpetual diet and the seesaw of weight gain and loss.

Meyer (1976) summarized the possible psychological meanings of obesity as follows: (1) an overidentification with the mother; (2) an oral sadistic attack at mother, her breast and her hypothetical pregnant uterus and future siblings; (3) a defense against being devoured by being big and powerful; (4) a defense against depression and psychotic disorganization.

These psychological theories are controversial in the literature. They are, however, useful in understanding the possible psychodynamics of the client and subsequently implementing an intervention that is sensitive to client needs as well as countering resistance if treatment becomes stalemated.

Externality Theory

Schacter and Rodin (1974) demonstrated that often the obese person's eating behavior is determined by external cues rather than by internal cues of hunger. This characteristic applies to many aspects of the individual's life in addition to a hypersensitivity to smell, taste, and other food cues. Their research results have not been replicated but in planning treatment the individual's responsiveness to cues is important for both behavioral and imagery approaches.

Learning Theory

This theory purports that overeating is an overlearned behavior that has generalized to both cues from the environment and inner emotional states. Overeating is observed at home and the child mimics the pattern that is then positively reinforced in the family. Cleaning one's plate and being rewarded for eating *all* of one's dinner in order to not deprive poor starving children somewhere in the world has become a cultural norm that certainly reinforces eating beyond the point of feeling full.

Body Image Disturbance

Stunkard and Mendelson (1976) described several forms of body image disturbance with the obese individual. Disturbances range from mild misperceptions to severe delusional ideas about one's body. For the overweight person a predominant factor is constant preoccupation with one's size to the exclusion of all else. Individuals see the world through glasses that compare them to others based on size. Envying those who are thin and having little or no respect for those who are fat, they begin to disregard most people. The body image distortion may be overevaluation or under-evaluation of size. Early-onset obesity generally is characterized by more severe body image problems and is most severe when the obesity develops in adolescence. For the obese adolescent the negative body image is serious since it colors a total self-concept (Wolman, 1982, p. 20). For both obese adolescents and adults, when weight is lost a negative body image can continue and intense anxiety can be experienced when a pound or two is gained.

These are a few of the many theories that will guide the process of assessment and intervention.

INTERVENTION

Assessment

Before before beginning treatment a comprehensive assessment is important. First, medical and major psychiatric problems should be ruled out. Next, the development of the problem and the meaning of fat, food, and thinness to the individual should be explored; this information provides the basis for the treatment plan. Recognizing the individual's style of processing information (auditory, visual, kinesthetic, etc.) and listening for metaphors for the meaning of the weight all provide insights not gathered on routine histories (see Appendix IV).

Treatment

Treatment methods range from self-help groups to major surgical procedures, including Overeaters Anonymous (OA), Weight Watchers, psychotherapy, drugs, bypass surgery, stomach stapling, group therapy, diets, exercise programs, hospital controlled starvation, behavioral approaches, and hypnosis. The self-help groups and the behavioral approaches have been most successful, but all programs report a low rate of individuals, particularly those with early-onset obesity, being able to maintain weight loss over an extended period of time. Research throughout the years has been problematic and often inconclusive. Lack of adequate follow-up, the presence of many uncontrolled variables, failure to report attrition, inadequate short-term follow-up, and lack of consistent standards for reporting data have plagued the evaluation of studies of obesity (Foreyt, 1977). The programs that seem to have the most reliably consistent success utilize behavioral approaches.

The author feels a combined and modified behavioral, multimodal, and supportive psychotherapeutic approach is most successful in trying to meet the individualized needs of clients with weight problems. This approach includes health and diet education, imagery, and suggestive and relaxation techniques. These techniques can also be applied in groups; participation in self-help groups as Overeater's Anonymous and Weight Watchers is encouraged. Similarly, a reasonable diet and exercise program is essential for reducing caloric intake, burning calories, and hence losing weight.

Because weight loss is different from other habit disorders and addictions—the individual has to continue eating to survive—the approach cannot eliminate the unwanted behavior. Changing old habits, recognizing new ways to meet needs, and working toward normal eating patterns are essentials in treatment. These goals, clearly stated early in treatment, reassure the clients that they will not have to be on diets the rest of their lives, which reduces some of the feelings of deprivation in anticipating a long period of dieting.

Appreciating the psychological aspects of obesity and weight loss frames an individualized approach. Particularly important issues include coping with intense feelings of deprivation while on a diet; learning to find pleasure other than with food; dealing with the meaning of the eating behavior, food, fat, and leanness; and learning to cope with feelings in various new ways. Developing assertive behaviors and a positive self and body image similarly are psychological goals in treatment.

R/I techniques provide several benefits in this combined treatment approach. First, relaxation techniques provide pleasure and relief of tension that both reduce the stress of weight loss and provide a new avenue for pleasurable experiences. The patient also feels nurtured and as if something special has been given. Imagery techniques often speed the process of change and provide an opportunity for behavioral rehearsal, modification of self and body image, increased enjoyment of low calorie foods, expanding avenues for pleasure, and building self-control.

Several imagery exercises are described in the literature on weight loss. In *Fat Is a Feminist Issue, II* (1982), many of the exercises utilize imagery; for example, the ideal kitchen, breaking into a binge, increasing food awareness, fat/thin part of the body, the family meal, the Chinese meal, and the supermarket fantasies. Kroger and Fezler (1976) describe several standard imagery exercises for weight loss, and Citrenbaum, King, and Cohen (1985) illustrate numerous indirect suggestive techniques and metaphors for working with the obese client. Kline (1982) and O'Connell (1985) illustrate hypnotic and R/I techniques in groups for weight loss.

Treatment Phases

Treatment is divided into three phases. The first conjointly establishes the goals and plans the process. Contracts and timetables may be set. The second works on the processes of actually changing eating and activity behaviors, losing weight, and dealing with plateaus and slips back into old behaviors as well as possible weight regain. The third establishes a method for maintenance and works toward termination.

In phase one the therapist tells the client to first observe his or her own eating behavior, usually by keeping a food record. The food record is set up in columns on which the client records the time of day, the kind of food, and the individual's feeling state, and it is recorded *before* he or she eats. The individual is encouraged to not focus on losing weight but on learning about his or her eating patterns. The client is then encouraged to eat enough to maintain his or her usual weight. This is particularly important since many clients are very knowledgeable and experienced in how to gain and lose but not in how to maintain, which is the ultimate goal. This also reduces pressure that they must lose weight immediately because they have entered treatment. In some cases where a great deal of negativism or discouragement exists about losing weight a paradoxical directive might even be given for the individual to eat enough to gain 5 pounds.

This initial approach also reframes the situation of losing weight for the client. Many have entered treatment after trying numerous diets and methods of treatment. They are accustomed to being told from the start that they must lose weight by decreasing food intake and exercising more. The above approach focuses on learning to eat and being satisfied in a different way; the emphasis on the number of pounds lost is not as great.

In the second phase of treatment, the focus is on the process of weight loss. How is life different with new eating behaviors and habits? How are people responding to the clients? How are they feeling about themselves as they are losing weight? Imagery exercises about self-image and developing new behaviors in various situations are incorporated. Plateaus are potential problems as are periods of discouragement because of episodes of weight gain. Imagery exercises promoting increased self-confidence and self-control as well as becoming more physically active all help the successful completion of this phase.

In the final phase reinforcement is given and methods of maintaining through behavioral, R/I methods are given. Frequency of sessions may be reduced and termination is planned (see Appendix V).

CASE EXAMPLES

"Threatened"

A 33-year-old married mother of three entered treatment to lose 25 pounds. She worked full time and described herself as successful and happily married. She had been overweight since the birth of her first child and had not been able to return to her normal weight. She wanted to lose weight to feel better about herself and because she worried about the health consequences. She was generally a night eater and described coming home from work tired and tense having to cook for her family. She nibbled the entire time she cooked and continued eating throughout the evening. Her food record indicated no breakfast, diet food for lunch, and then numerous snacks in the evening after a moderate dinner. She was most tense and bored in the evening. Relaxation techniques were taught and she was encouraged to tell her family that when she came home from work she was going to spend 15 minutes by herself relaxing before she started to cook. She also imagined seeing herself in a mirror as thinner; she saw herself in a bathing suit. In her mind's eye she looked better than she had in years. She began to lose weight and was feeling increasingly good about herself.

Suddenly she reached a plateau and was feeling both anxious and discouraged. During the imagery exercise again she stood in front of the mirror. She imagined herself at her present weight but when she was instructed to reduce it she became more anxious. In asking her to become more aware of what was causing the anxiety, she reported that her marriage was not as good as she had reported on the initial history. She had become bored and was aware of looking at men she worked with and finding them attractive. She could fantasize an affair when she was overweight but now it was threatening because once thin, she would be more available and attractive. She then decided that the weight she had lost was good and that while she wanted to lose more she was not ready at this point. She decided to terminate after several more sessions where she focused more on her marital relationship than on the weight loss.

"Pregnant"

A 25-year-old social worker came to lose 100 pounds in order to become pregnant and begin a family of her own. Her husband had never complained about her excessive weight but was encouraging her to lose for the sake of a successful pregnancy. Overweight since childhood, she was not optimistic. She had tried numerous diets, doctors, drugs, and Weight Watchers. She had always been able to lose but could not keep it off. She overate at meal time and realized she was not satisfied unless she had stuffed herself. This woman was told that losing the amount she wanted would take some time and she agreed. She was also told that she had become expert in gaining and losing and that for the first month she would work on simply eating enough to maintain her weight. We would do R/I exercises to help her reach her eventual goal. Since obesity may unconsciously be associated for women with rejection of sexuality there was concern about this woman's potential success since the motivation for weight loss was to become pregnant.

This woman was resistant to discussing psychological issues but motivated to control her eating. She responded well to relaxation and imagery exercises related to food, putting smaller amounts of food on her plate and noticing more rapidly when she was full and then associating the full feeling with satisfaction. She also liked the "Food Fairy Story" (see Appendix VI) and metaphors of losing to gain something one wants very much. She lost weight steadily and became pregnant when she had lost 55 pounds.

"Helper"

Another woman, also in the helping professions, came to treatment wanting to lose 60 pounds. She responded well to a discussion of the importance of losing weight by learning to eat normally. She did not want to have to give up some of her favorite foods and was feeling deprived even before she entered the office for her first appointment. She agreed she needed more exercise and had begun a regular program of swimming. This 30-year-old woman, married to a man who liked her at her present weight, was highly accomplished, attractive, very busy, and seldom caring of herself and her own needs. She had been overweight as a child and had numerous unresolved issues with a very rejecting mother. She had been the responsible caretaker in the family. She thoroughly enjoyed the relaxation exercises, was enthusiastic about the process, and responded well to images that helped her develop pleasure from other sources (see Appendix VI). She also responded well to images of self- control and to behavioral rehearsal. She could imagine herself in her favorite restaurant eating her favorite foods.

She was guided by the therapist to notice as much as she could about the food—how it looked and smelled before she actually tasted it. She then tasted it in her imagination. She held the food in her mouth savoring its flavor and allowing the taste to be "ever so satisfying" and "fulfilling." She was to eat only enough to be satisfied and could realize that smaller amounts were satisfying. She knew she could always return another time and eat the same food again. While this woman swam she often replayed the R/I exercises in her mind. She lost weight slowly and learned through a self-image exercise that she was comfortable at a weight above what she had set as her goal.

"Mother Food"

This next example describes how psychological issues can be uncovered through imagery and how that process can give useful cues to what is happening when treatment is stalemated. This 50-year-old female secretary came for treatment to lose 35 pounds. She too had been overweight as a child. A few years earlier she had managed to lose a great deal of weight through a diet doctor who prescribed diet pills. Her Russian Jewish family had been distressed with her weight loss and worried she was seriously ill and at death's door. Her family had spent time in concentration camps during World War II and could not imagine why she wanted to be so thin.

She had been able to keep the weight off until a romantic relationship broke up and her mother died. After that she began to steadily gain weight. When she came for treatment she was slightly depressed but very motivated to pursue another love relationship. She responded well to self-image exercises as well as to relaxation for stress management. She chose a sensible diet and joined a health club. Losing about 2 pounds per week, she felt good. One Sunday she found herself on New York's Lower East Side in a Jewish delicatessen. She gorged on cabbage soup and fattening knishes. When she left she could not figure out how she had gotten there and was feeling both physically ill and disgusted with herself. In doing relaxation and imagery she was asked to relive that Sunday afternoon and to have a better understanding now of how that happened. After the exercise she explained that her mother always made those foods for her. Her life now was quite lonely and she missed her mother very much. She decided she could not lose any more weight at this point. In discussing her unresolved grief, she was encouraged to stay in treatment to deal with the depression. She was unwilling but agreed it was needed. In a follow-up call she stated she was feeling better but was not losing weight. However, she was maintaining rather than gaining and was eating, in moderation, knishes and cabbage soup.

SUMMARY

All of these cases demonstrate the combined approach to the overweight client. Clearly, an understanding of the theories of obesity are important in mapping a treatment plan and providing intervention. Because the process of losing weight is time-consuming and plateaus and slips back into old patterns or weight gain occur, the ability to deal with a long-term relationship and with discouragement and outright depression is important. A detailed description of the exercises can be found in the appendices.

REFERENCES

Bjorntorp, P. (1986). Fat cells and obesity. In K. D. Brownwell & J. P. Foreyt, *Handbook of Eating Disorders*. New York: Basic Books.

Bruch, H. (1958). Developmental obesity and schizophrenia. *Psychiatry, 21*, 65–70.

Bruch, H. (1973). *Eating disorders: Obesity, anorexia nervosa; The person within.* New York: Basic Books.

Bychowski, G. (1973). Neurotic obesity. In N. Kiell, *The 1976 psychology of obesity.* Springfield, MA: Charles C. Thomas.

Citrenbaum, C. M., Cohen, W. I., King, M. E. (1985). *Modern clinical hypnosis for habit control.* New York: W. W. Norton.

Foreyt, J. P. (1977). *Behavioral treatment of obesity.* New York: Pergamon.

Hagan, R. L. (1976). Theories of obesity: Is there any hope for order? In M. Williams & I. Foreyt, *Obesity: Behavioral approaches to dietary management.* New York: Brunner Mazel.

Meyer, B. C. (1976). Psychological and physiological aspects of obesity. In N. Kiell, *The psychology of obesity.* Springfield, MA: Charles C. Thomas.

O'Connell, E. (1985). Hypnosis for Weight loss and smoking. In R.P. Zahourek (ed.). *Clinical hypnosis and therapeutic suggestion in nursing.* Orlando, Grune & Stratton.

Orbach, S. (1979). *Fat is a feminist issue: The anti-diet guide to permanent weight loss.* New York: Paddington.

Orbach, S. (1982). *Fat is a feminist issue II.* New York: Berkley Books.

Schacter, S., & Rodin, J. (1974). *Obese humans and rats.* Washington, DC: Eirbaum/Wiley.

Stunkard, A. (1976). *The pain of obesity.* CA: Bell.

Stunkard, A., & Mendelson, M. (1973). Obesity and body image. In N. Kiell, *Psychology of obesity.* Springfield, MA: Charles C. Thomas.

Wolman, B. B. (1982). *Psychological aspects of obesity.* New York: Van Nostrand Reinhold.

BIBLIOGRAPHY

Abramson, E. (1977). *Behavioral approaches to weight control.* New York: Springer.

Brownell, K. D., & Foreyt, J. P (1986). *Handbook of eating disorders.* New York, Basic Books.

Lazarus, A. (1977). *In the mind's eye.* New York: Rawson Associates.

Miller, W. R. (Ed.) (1980). *The addictive behaviors.* New York: Pergamon.

Pescatore, E. (1973). A personal reaction to weight loss. *American Journal of Nursing, 73,* 227.

Stuart, R. B., & Davis, B. (1972). *Slim chance in a fat world: Behavioral control of obesity.* Champaign, lL: Research Press.

White, J. H. (1982). An overview of obesity: Its significance in nursing. *Nursing Clinics of North America, 17,* 191–198.

Williams, M., and Foreyt, J. (1976). *Obesity: Behavioral approaches to dietary management.* New York: Brunner Mazel.

When your client has a weight problem. (1981). *American Journal of Nursing, 81,* 550–527.

Zahourek, R. P. (Ed.) (1985). *Clinical hypnosis and therapeutic suggestion in nursing.* Orlando, FL: Grune & Stratton.

11

RELAXATION/IMAGERY WITH ALCOHOLICS IN GROUP TREATMENT

GLORIA KUTNER
ROTHLYN P. ZAHOUREK

INTRODUCTION

Alcoholism is a devastating and costly disease. The loss to business and industry alone in the United States is at least $10 billion yearly. This does not include alcohol-related illnesses, estimated at 30 to 50 percent of all hospital admissions. But the real losses due to alcoholism can be measured only in human terms: devastated families, illness, and death.

There are an estimated 10 million alcoholics in the U.S. Another 10 million are considered "problem drinkers," meaning that alcohol in some way interferes with normal social functioning. Contrary to one of the myths about alcoholics, only 3 percent of alcoholics are on skid row. The remaining 97 percent are found in all walks of life: housewives, students, clergy, policemen, doctors, and nurses. Each alcoholic impacts on the lives of three or four other persons intimately; that's 40 or 50 million persons nationwide whose lives are seriously affected by the pain of alcoholism. Of the 10 million alcoholics, only 10 percent ever receive treatment.

Alcoholism treatment involves helping people not to drink. Recovering alcoholics must make changes in major areas of functioning. To maintain sobriety, the physiological, psychological, social, and vocational aspects of life must be evaluated and modified where needed. The individual must first be detoxified from chemicals, then engaged in a new social network, and helped to find new experiences that will aid in the development of self-esteem.

A relationship seems to exist between stress and alcoholism. While stress is not seen as a causative factor in the development of alcoholism, the management of anxiety and stress can influence recovery. Initially the potential alcoholic may drink to feel relaxed. At first drinking is usually moderate and controlled and consistently produces a pleasant experience. Over time tolerance develops: to get the same effect, the individual must drink more, and relief drinking becomes excessive drinking. Mood swings into euphoria now are more often followed by a backward slide into emotional pain. The person has lost control of his or her drinking and crossed the imaginary line into alcoholism. A vicious cycle is set in motion (Johnson, 1980). The drinking that once provided stress relief now creates its own stress in the form of poor job performance, mental distress, financial problems, unpredictable mood swings, family discord, and a lowered self-esteem.

RELAXATION/IMAGERY IN ALCOHOLISM TREATMENT

A useful adjunct within a broad spectrum treatment program, relaxation/imagery (R/I) training accomplishes several goals. First, R/I training is an active treatment tool that engages the patient in nonverbal exercises. The exercises are pleasant and produce stress reduction, comfort, and pleasure. The process also emphasizes the patient's control and helps develop a psychophysiological skill that promotes a sense of mastery over self and environment.

Several theories support using R/I techniques in the treatment of alcoholism and substance abuse. One theory considers the use of alcohol or substances as a method to reduce tension and anxiety. This has been further refined in the exploration of specific stressors and the importance of the individual's perceived sense of self-control. Drugs and alcohol increase that sense of self-control, particularly in social and interpersonal situations. If the individual becomes intoxicated, however, drinking becomes a self-handicapping behavior, providing an external justification for failure (Jones & Berglas, 1978). Still another theory is concerned with alcohol's production of positive affective state, or an altered state of consciousness, rather than the relief of tension as the motivator for continued and compulsive substance abuse (Sher & Levinson, 1982). In addition, alcohol also reduces sensitivity to all affective states as well as the cognizance of potential sources of tension. R/I training can be a useful treatment modality in both reducing tension and producing a positive affective state. This augments a sense of coping and control and induces a nonchemical pleasurable response.

Achterberg and Lawlis (1980) include relaxation techniques in their discussion of behavioral approaches to the treatment of alcoholism. Their three-phase program using relaxation has been successful with compliant and motivated patients. In phase one, the client is taught muscle relaxation with breathing exercises to facilitate relaxation. The therapist focuses on the client's successful participation with statements like "you are doing very well" and encourages recognition of physical responses that indicate the client is doing it right. The second phase emphasizes the cleansing of the body. Patients are told that relaxation helps the body's organs more efficiently rid themselves of poisons. Individuals have the power to rid themselves of both chemical poisons and psychological problems such as guilt. In the third phase the individual learns relaxation, a method of stress management that can be applied in everyday life. This program is incorporated into treatment that includes other behavioral interventions, including didactic factual information, experiential exercises, contracts, development of problem-solving skills, and Alcoholics Anonymous (AA).

Since stress relief drinking appears to be one of several factors contributing to increased alcohol use, therapeutic approaches in alcoholism treatment are designed to help the individual reduce or cope more effectively with stress and tension and the need for drinking. Behavioral techniques in addition to relaxation include social and self-management skills, assertiveness training, meditation, and biofeedback. All the techniques encourage self-regulation of physiological processes to combat anxiety, and many utilize visualization for increasing relaxation and for behavior rehearsal. With these the alcoholic can learn a new sense of power, control, and self-mastery.

In the authors' experience, patients have reported that regular use of relaxation has helped them deal more comfortably with generalized anxiety, insomnia, and tensions related to specific situations, and has promoted an increased feeling of well-being. Visualization techniques have been helpful in anticipating problematic situations in which the individual feels at risk for drinking, such as funerals, weddings, Christmas, job promotions, and others. Many principles in AA relate to relaxation and imagery. "One day at a time" and "Easy does it" are common AA slogans that encourage the individual to experience life in a more relaxed manner; doing so will promote sobriety. Similarly, AA recommends that individuals "act as if." This approach implies that the individual's ability to imagine more healthy behaviors is the first step toward implementing them. "Keeping the memory green," another slogan, encourages the recovering alcoholic to keep in mind a clear image of the past consequences of drinking. A strong element of AA is the sharing of experiences through the stories (qualifications) told at each meeting. These stories stimulate vivid imagery through which the recovering alcoholic identifies with others and begins to feel part of a group rather than isolated and alone.

RESEARCH ON R/I WITH ALCOHOLICS

The data on the usefulness of relaxation training with alcoholics are equivocal. In his book, *The Addictive Behaviors*, Miller (1980) reviews the literature and criticizes most studies for poor methodology or reporting insignificant positive outcomes. The majority of studies rely on physiological measures of relaxation (e.g., measuring alpha waves, muscle potential, blood pressure) and not on treatment outcome. One study reports its findings in terms of numbers of alcoholics who remain abstinent after treatment, but it lacked controls. Based on the studies reviewed, Miller concludes that relaxation techniques contribute only slightly to successful alcoholism treatment.

A more recently published review of the research on relaxation and meditation training for substance abusers also emphasizes that the results have been equivocal and suggests additional and better-controlled research (Klajner, Hartman, & Sobell, 1984). These authors conclude that the choice of technique should be tailored to the individual and related to needs served by drinking such as positive affect, euphoria, or reduction of stress in interpersonal situations. Success often depends on the technique being utilized, the amount of time spent with the patient, motivation and compliance, and therapist's availability to provide booster sessions when needed. In summarizing the research, they emphasize that the supportive evidence comes from methodologically weak investigations and the negative findings relate to discontinuation of treatment after brief training. Their recommendations for further research address the following methodologic issues:

1. The need for appropriate control groups in order to rule out the placebo effect that may in and of itself be valuable;
2. Adequate follow-up and assessment at over 18 months;
3. Proper assessment with reliable and valid instruments that measure anxiety, perceived sense of control, expectation of positive affect, and substance abuse; and
4. Measures to rule out variables of motivation and treatment expectation compared to the use of relaxation techniques.

No research was found on the use of imagery and relaxation techniques combined. In the authors' experience the combination of these techniques provides relaxation, pleasure, and an opportunity for behavioral rehearsal of enhanced coping behaviors in difficult situations. By mentally rehearsing a potentially stressful encounter in a relaxed state the individual can explore various affective reactions as well as behavioral responses. In strict behavioral terms, the substance abuser can then more easily cue positive responses to stimuli that previously prompted drug or alcohol use.

Estes, Smith-Dijulio, and Heineman, in their book, *The Nursing Diagnosis of the Alcoholic Person* (1980), describe relaxation techniques as behavioral tools to treat alcoholism. The position of this school of thought evolves from the tension reduction hypothesis (TRH) formulated in the 1940s and 1950s, which states that alcoholism develops as a learned coping behavior. According to the TRH, tension-relief drinking is an important etiologic factor in the development of alcoholism. In recent years, however, the TRH has been challenged.

Instead of TRH, Powers and Kutsch (1985) have proposed a stress reduction hypothesis (SRH). Historically, experimental studies testing TRH have narrowly focused on the relationship between alcohol use and tension or anxiety. Stress may be manifest by symptoms other than tension or anxiety, however. Other stress responses include anger, depression, lowered self-esteem, and feelings of rejection. The SRH views these responses in the context of the person's life as they occur over a period of time rather than as single events. Stress, therefore, is not only a broader concept than tension, it is also an interactive and ongoing process between a multitude of stressors and stress responses.

CLINICAL APPLICATIONS

The following sections describe group treatment utilizing R/I but these techniques are applicable in individual counseling sessions as well. In a group both general and more individualized needs can be met with the various exercises.

Inpatient Relaxation Group

The Alcoholism Service at St. Vincent's Hospital Department of Psychiatry is made up of a 25-bed Inpatient Unit and an Outpatient Department. As a department in the division of psychiatry in a New York City medical center, the treatment goal is abstinence.

The inpatient population consists primarily of chronic alcoholics, with a small percentage of mixed substance abusers. Many have had previous treatments at either this or other treatment facilities. Most patients have had major losses (e.g., spouse, children, jobs, money, self-respect) due to their drinking. Approximately 10 to 25 percent are from "skid row," either living on the street or in flop houses, with negligible family or social ties.

The treatment is based on the medical model, utilizing an interdisciplinary team (physician, nurses, social workers, mental health technicians, recreational and occupational therapists). This team provides a broad spectrum treatment plan that incorporates AA and Al-Anon principles, family and milieu therapy, education, individual and group counseling, and referrals for aftercare. The average length of inpatient treatment is three weeks.

Patients may be detoxified on the unit or transferred from other facilities for further alcoholism treatment. The regular "detox" at this facility is a 5-day Librium (Roche Laboratories, Nutley, NJ) detox, which, however, may be shortened or extended according to patient needs (see Meyers, 1985, for more information).

All patients receive a medical work-up on admission and most physical ailments are evaluated and treated concomitantly with treatment for alcoholism. For medical or surgical emergencies patients are transferred to the general hospital.

Patients with dual psychiatric diagnoses (e.g., alcoholism and major affective disorders; alcoholism and paranoid schizophrenia) are also admitted for evaluation and treatment and may receive neuroleptic and antidepressant medications.

The nursing staff is responsible for maintaining the therapeutic milieu, monitoring detoxification, administering medications and treatments, and individual and group counseling.

This patient population, therefore, is varied; not all are appropriate candidates for the relaxation group. Generally, those who are acutely psychotic, actively suicidal, or who, for any other reasons, might be disruptive are not candidates for the group.

The inpatient group meets twice weekly but patients are encouraged to borrow and use a relaxation tape available on the unit between group sessions. They are also urged to practice daily rather than waiting until they feel anxious. All appropriate patients participate in at least two relaxation sessions during the course of their alcoholism treatment. Attendance in the group is not mandatory, but participation in all unit groups is weighed by the treatment team in evaluating each patient's motivation and progress in treatment.

The relaxation group on the inpatient unit consists of 7–10 patients and the leader. There is no suitable space to do the relaxation lying down, but comfortable chairs that provide good support for the back are available. This is important, since it is otherwise difficult to relax.

An opening discussion of about 15 minutes provides: (1) education about stress and the relationship of stressors to drinking, and (2) an opportunity for patients to share verbally.

The group opens with a discussion about why relaxation techniques might be helpful to recovering alcoholics. Most patients agree they often used alcohol as a relaxant, as a means of coping with anxiety in stressful situations.

Newly sober alcoholics need support and recognition that this period in their lives is particularly difficult. They have gone through detoxification and are now trying to live, perhaps for the first time in many years, free of chemicals. They are not only isolated from their usual drinking environment, but are also trying to cope with 25 other newly sober patients and various staff members. Additional contributing stressors include: introduction to treatment modalities such as groups, AA, lectures and family meetings, fears about discharge planning, guilt and remorse over physical deterioration, and social and financial losses due to drinking.

In addition to all of these particular stressors is the pervading anxiety around the loss of alcohol, the one relaxant which consistently, albeit with disastrous results, offered relief. It is important to acknowledge this loss because often, in the same way patients deny their alcoholism, they may deny the reality of the difficulty of trying to live sober (Carruth & Pugh, 1982). Frequently there is an almost palpable sense of relief in the group when the stressors and anxiety of early recovery are recognized by a treating person. It is as if patients were waiting for "permission" to acknowledge their own anxiety and fears. Of course, discussion of these pressures should be balanced with support and encouragement.

Next in the preliminary discussion, group members are asked to share with each other how or where they physically experience anxiety. What body cues let us know we are anxious? The signs most frequently given by group members include tension in the pit of the stomach, headaches, muscle tightness in the shoulders and neck, and insomnia. Somatic and behavioral indicators of anxiety other than those mentioned by the group are enumerated by the leader, as are stress-related illnesses. Through group participation patients recognize additional and previously unrecognized signs of stress.

Most people are unaware of habitual patterns of muscular tension and tightness, but alcoholics are particularly out of touch with their bodies since they have been, in effect, anesthetizing themselves with alcohol. The group leader emphasizes the interconnection between the body and mind and between feelings and thoughts, and how feelings are manifested by physiological changes in the body.

As a sharing experience, participation in the relaxation group is valuable for alcoholics. Chronic alcoholics are frequently socially isolated and very self-involved. Many do now know how to socialize without alcohol. A structured group with a specific task-oriented goal is, for most, a relatively nonthreatening experience. Although patients are asked to share experiences with the group, verbal participation is not mandatory. Given the choice, patients who at first are reluctant to speak often join in. For patients with minimal social skills, the ability to stay with the group and share by listening and doing the relaxation exercise is itself significant.

Breathing is an important component of any relaxation technique. Often persons restrict their breathing when under stress. This compounds the discomfort by increasing tension, and it decreases oxygen intake and excretion of metabolic wastes (Lowen, 1975). Before beginning the actual relaxation experience a simple explanation about the importance of breathing is given. A brief breathing exercise is demonstrated to facilitate more relaxed diaphragmatic breathing. Group members are asked to place their hands on their abdomens and, while breathing through the nose, to think of pushing the hands away with the belly. If anyone has trouble getting air down into the belly, pretending to yawn usually helps. Patients are given the task of becoming more aware of their breathing and noticing how breathing changes with their emotions, especially anxiety. They are instructed that deep slow breathing can be used by itself as a relaxation technique.

In the authors' opinion, Jacobson's progressive relaxation (1938) technique (see Chapter 2) is best suited for use with alcoholics in early treatment because, with tensing and releasing of specific muscle groups, a patient develops an awareness of the difference between tension and relaxation. Patients are asked to notice the difference between how their muscles feel when they are tight and tense, and how they feel when the muscles let go and relax.

Control is an important issue in alcoholism treatment. The alcoholic may be either openly defiant, trying to run his or her own treatment, or may be compliant but secretly (usually unconsciously) clinging to the belief that he or she can still manage his or her own life and can still drink. In either case the patient's infantile ego translates into "Nobody's going to tell me I can't drink." Unless patients wholeheartedly accept the reality of their alcoholism, they will keep fighting treatment and reject help (Tiebout, 1954). The AA saying "let go and let God" recognizes this struggle for control and the inability of the alcoholic to let things evolve. Because the relaxation experience is a physical letting go, it can be a small but significant step in that acceptance process. Patients are encouraged to be in the moment, or present-oriented, to accept that the body is different every day, and to listen to the body without judging.

Newly sober alcoholics do not tolerate high levels of anxiety (Wallace, 1977). While the group should be structured and members encouraged to actively share, a nonpressured, nonthreatening atmosphere, in which patients feel they have options, is more conducive to learning to relax. The emphasis should be on feeling good rather than exploring painful issues.

Once the group has been guided through the progressive relaxation, suggestions are made to help deal with mind wandering or obsessive thoughts. Group members are given the choice of focusing on the breath and counting each inhalation and exhalation repeatedly from one to four, or focusing on the breath and repeating a phrase such as "I am relaxed." They may choose instead to create a pleasant and relaxing image by visualizing themselves some place they'd like to be, filling in all the details in the mind's eye. If the mind wanders, they are instructed to simply notice that it has wandered and to gently bring it back to the chosen focus. Patients are allowed to choose their focus because although many choose to imagine, not all have that ability.

During this first session, the leader has also used guided imagery after inducing a state of deep muscle relaxation. Scenes that involve water (e.g., the beach) seem almost universally the most relaxing. (It is important to first ascertain if anyone in the group is water phobic.) Regardless of whether the imaging is guided or not, there is a short interval of 4 or 5 minutes in which the leader does not speak. This period of silence gives each participant a chance to be with himself or herself.

Before ending the relaxation experience, the leader gives positive suggestions to the group. The following is an example.

> You feel relaxed and good about yourself. And remember that this relaxed feeling is a part of you. It comes from deep within you and you may have it back again whenever you choose. Think of it as a gift you can give yourself, something loving you can do for yourself.

Alcoholics have relied for years on alcohol, on a substance outside themselves, to feel good. The positive suggestions attempt to give back the power to relax to each individual.

The relaxation exercise is ended gradually with a request that group members slowly wiggle their hands, then their feet, and in their own time when each feels ready, to open their eyes. The group concludes with another 15-minute discussion of patient reaction. Patients are asked to make comments, discuss any problems, and share something about their experience.

For the second relaxation session the group follows the same basic format: opening discussion, relaxation experience, and closing discussion. Those who have practiced individually since the last group session share their experience or any problems in the opening discussion. After a brief review the progressive relaxation experience is repeated. Not surprisingly many patients report it is easier to relax during the second session. When there is a group of particularly interested and motivated patients the leader might introduce an autogenic technique for the second session. The idea is to give these patients, within the imposed time limitations, exposure to more than one relaxation method and let each choose his or her preferred method for individual practice.

The use of soft relaxing music is not a necessity for successful relaxation therapy, but patients often prefer it. Patients are able to relax without music, but on trials with several groups in which music was played for the first session, but not for the second, patients almost unanimously found the music enhanced their ability to relax.

Most patients find relaxation pleasurable. There is a deep sense of calm and quiet by the end of the session. Comments such as "This is the most relaxed I've felt in years" are not uncommon. A small percentage experience a "high." On the other extreme are those few patients who cannot sit quietly for 20 minutes. They become restless, squirm in their seats, and may want to leave the group. The most common problem patients report is difficulty keeping their concentration. It is the rare patient who can clear the mind of extraneous thoughts. Information and encouragement are dovetailed by the leader into the discussion of reactions. For example, the "high" that some people experience is probably attributable to the brain's own chemicals, the endorphins. This type of "high" is reinforced by the leader as a positive "natural" high and as further evidence that the capacity to relax lies within each of us. Patients who have trouble focusing are advised that this is the most difficult aspect of relaxation and to gently bring themselves back to their "focus" should it wander. Encouragement is given through reassurance that relaxation is a learned skill that becomes easier with practice. Patients are encouraged to practice daily, even if sometimes it is very difficult to relax. The ability to relax may vary with the vicissitudes of life, or for that matter, for no discernible reason. That we are all subject to changing feelings, moods, and circumstances often goes unrecognized by the alcoholic. If life is not smooth sailing, the alcoholic concludes something is wrong (Tiebout, 1954).

Some problems in running the inpatient relaxation group have been noted. Some are related to the technique per se, while others are specific to the setting and treatment program.

Occasionally one of the group members experiences relaxation as a threatened loss of control or of physical or ego boundaries. This concern might also be voiced in questions about the relationship of relaxation to hypnosis. To allay this anxiety, the leader explains that relaxation and hypnosis are similar and reiterates that the goal is to experience relaxation and not a trance state, although a deep pleasant state might be the result.

If the experience makes them uncomfortable, patients are told to simply open their eyes and sit quietly; or, if they prefer, they may do the relaxation with eyes open. Expressions that denote choice, such as, "If you would like to relax a little more . . ." are used often to emphasize that it is up to the individual how much he or she wishes to relax. Over the course of 3 years, an uncomfortable reaction occurred only twice. In both cases the patients opened their eyes and stopped participating. In the concluding discussion the leader recognized that, yes, this type of relaxation technique could make some people feel "weird" instead of relaxed. This body-oriented technique, then, is not suitable for these persons, but they might respond well to other forms of relaxation such as guided imagery.

On occasion patients threatened to disrupt the group with nervous laughter. This self-consciousness seems more prevalent among men than women. One particularly contentious patient, who grudgingly attended the group and was negative and contradictory during the opening discussion, started laughing self-consciously once the relaxation exercise was begun. He attempted to deal with his discomfort by disrupting the group and soon his giddiness spread to two patients seated nearby. The group leader ignored the laughing and continued with conviction. Gradually the laughter subsided and the patient settled down. In the discussion after the exercise, the leader acknowledged that initially some people might feel self-conscious doing the relaxation exercise. In the next session, this patient seemed more comfortable and was able to participate without laughing. Although in this case ignoring the laughter extinguished the behavior, it could prove necessary to ask the patient to leave the group if that patient could not control himself.

The patient who walks out during the relaxation exercise is another possible source of disruption. Before beginning the relaxation the leader asks all group members, out of consideration for each other, to remain until the exercise is finished. Unfortunately, some patients do not heed this request and, in that case, it is generally better to let the individual leave, rather than disturb the whole group.

Staff members have had to occasionally interrupt the group to get a patient called for medical procedures. To deal with this sudden intrusion and help the patients get back into the relaxation, the leader tells the group members to bring their focus to the breath, to take a deep inspiration, and then to slowly exhale. They then proceed with the exercise. Once patients are very relaxed, however, they often seem to be able to ignore these untimely interruptions.

The biggest problem in running the group is patient motivation. Ideally, the group should meet every day to reinforce the technique. Most patients do not practice regularly if left to themselves. Ths relaxation tape available on the unit is an attempt to bridge the gap between sessions.

Most patients who borrow the tape use it on a daily basis as well as for specific problems. Such problems might include headaches, insomnia, or anxiety before going on an interview for a half-way house or outpatient program.

Outpatient Group

The focus of the relaxation group in the outpatient clinic was somewhat different. Now outside the protective environment of the hospital, patients were confronted with stressors they had previously dealt with by drinking. Despite the fact most patients have had a period of sobriety the association between drinking and relaxation persisted. Many wished to recreate this comfort through "normal social drinking" and required follow-up individual and group alcoholism treatment in addition to the relaxation group.

In various stages of recovery, most patients in the relaxation group had at least 3 months of sobriety. Some had experienced minor slips (periods of drinking) during these 3 months. Others had been dually addicted or carried dual diagnoses of alcoholism and another major psychiatric illness. None of the patients was acutely psychotic during the course of the group. All had been referred to the group by their counselors for severe stress and anxiety that had not been managed through the normal course of counseling. Cotherapists, a psychiatric nurse clinical specialist and a psychologist, conducted the groups, which met weekly for 10 one-and-a-half-hour sessions. Some but not all had experienced the relaxation group in the inpatient unit. The groups consisted of all men except for one cotherapist.

The group sessions focused on the stresses of early sobriety and learning to live sober in a drinking society. Although now sober, many patients realized that problems in their lives continued. The problems of disrupted families, unemployment, and finding new social networks had to be faced.

Attendance at AA was encouraged. According to their principles "people, places, and things" that normally are associated with drinking should be avoided in early sobriety. Some situations and people understandably could not be avoided and in the initial group sessions patients were asked to identify those instances. Some mentioned walking by a favorite bar or liquor store provoked both anxiety and "drink signals." For others, running into old "drinking buddies" was stressful and produced a desire to try drinking again. Being alone, looking for a job, enduring holidays, going to welfare, interacting with friends, roommates, and family members, and speaking at AA meetings were additional difficult situations identified. A few patients also commented on phobic symptoms (e.g., heights, subways, being alone) and one member of the group had suffered from agoraphobia for many years.

During the early sessions the therapist asked each patient to describe his or her individual stressors. Likewise, each was asked to note where in the body he or she felt anxiety and tension. Each member was encouraged to be specific and to become aware of how these symptoms lessened or were exacerbated.

During every session the therapist provided time to discuss relevant events of the previous week. The discussion was focused on stressful situations—how patients experienced the stress and coped. Group members were asked to give each other suggestions about alternative ways to handle stressful encounters. Successes, support, and new ideas for interesting ways to relax were also shared. At each group session cotherapists used relaxation or imagery exercises. Progressive relaxation with muscular tightening and letting go was done during the first and second sessions of the group in order to help patients contrast sensations of tightness and softness in their bodies. Attention to rhythmic breathing augmented the progressive relaxation.

In subsequent sessions imagery was employed. Standard images described elsewhere in the book were utilized in addition to some scenes chosen by the group. One such scene was attendance at an AA meeting. During this scene the patients were encouraged, in fantasy, to leave home with the intent of going to a meeting.

> As you are leaving your home to attend an AA meeting, you are feeling confident and relaxed. You're sure of yourself and looking forward to what you will be able to get out of the meeting. As you walk toward the building, your relaxation and comfort continue. If you have any tension, take a nice deep breath and relax. Enter the building and find the room for the meeting. While you are doing this again focus on being relaxed and comfortable. You are looking forward to what you will be able to learn from the meeting. When you enter the room, find a comfortable seat toward the front. Sit comfortably and relax waiting for the meeting to start. Again, if you have any tension, breathe evenly and relax as much as possible. During the meeting listen carefully to the speaker and learn what you can, still feeling relaxed and comfortable. You would like to say something at this meeting. You might want to make a comment or just say your name. You raise your hand and continue breathing easily and comfortably. The meeting is over now and if you wish to talk with others present, you may do so. When you're ready, come back to the present relaxed, alert, and comfortable.

Attendance at and engagement in AA is a treatment goal in the clinic. Active use of this support group and utilizing the step program, while important for recovery, are often difficult for the newly sober alcoholic. Frequently he or she is uncomfortable in groups and the focus on alcoholism and the admission of need for help promotes anxiety. Because of this discomfort many newcomers sit in the back at AA meetings, trying to be invisible. Sometimes months go by before they are able to say even their name. Likewise, many newly sober patients go to meetings but talk to no one else; they go directly home after the meeting. Anxiety tends to breed more anxiety until the patient is nearly phobic. This does not ensure their finding a sponsor or utilizing the program to its fullest. The imagery relaxation exercise, conducted almost like a desensitization process, promotes more rapid, comfortable engagement and enables the patient to utilize this invaluable support.

Another helpful imagery exercise for the early recovering alcoholic deals with experiencing a "drink signal" (a desire to drink) when passing a liquor store or bar.

The exercise is as follows and might vary in content depending on what group members have been discussing.

> Imagine yourself walking down a street. It's a pleasant day and as you walk you notice your surroundings and how you are feeling. From a distance you notice your favorite bar or liquor store. If it has a neon sign, be aware of how the sign looks. Notice also how you are feeling. As you approach the bar or liquor store, what are you thinking to yourself? If you are feeling a desire to go in or a desire to drink take a deep breath and relax. Encourage yourself to think about the day and what the weather is like. Approach the bar or liquor store. Notice the front of the building. If it's a liquor store be aware of the window decorations and the bottles displayed. If it's a bar what does it look like? What is attractive about it? Are your old friends inside? In either case, if you want to go in or if you want to drink take a deep breath and relax as you have been learning. Decide consciously that you will not go in and that you will not drink *now*. Cross the street and feel yourself lighter, more comfortable and more relaxed. Pleased with yourself and confident about your decision, continue walking away feeling confident and comfortable. The next time you have to walk down this same street, you might choose to walk down the side without the bar or liquor store. You feel more comfortable away from the stimulus of drinking.

Following the exercise, experiences are shared and discussed. The leaders reinforce feelings of control and awareness of the possibility of choice. This exercise can be modified for patients who only drink at home alone or who have difficulty in social situations. The exercise can also be done with individual patients in one-to-one sessions. A small percentage of patients incorporate relaxation into their lives, even after discharge. Some are self-motivated and practice individually and others get support and reinforcement from the outpatient relaxation group.

Local yoga institutes provide inexpensive classes in meditation and relaxation for patients who do not have outpatient relaxation therapy available but wish to continue their practice. For home use there are several relaxation tapes and records ("new age" music, environmental sounds, as well as guided relaxation) available by mail through *Psychology Today* and at local book and record shops. Suggested readings for those who wish to learn more about relaxation include: *The Relaxation Response*, by D. H. Benson and *You Must Relax*, by Edmund Jacobson, both available in paperback.

CONCLUSION

Living sober means more than not drinking. Sorbriety implies a calm, relatively satisfied, and more mature outlook on life. Recovering alcoholics must make major changes in lifestyle and attitudes if they are to maintain sobriety. Although the primary goal in group relaxation training with alcoholics is teaching a more adaptive method for dealing with stress, there are other therapeutic benefits as well. Sharing in a group setting promotes new relationships. Recovering alcoholics become more aware of their bodies, which were once anesthetized with alcohol. Relaxation also aids in the alcoholic "letting go" of external worries and developing a sense of inner control. Furthermore, relaxation training educates the recovering person about stress and stressors and provides an alternative nonchemical means of coping. All of these therapeutic benefits can contribute to the process of learning to live sober.

REFERENCES

A guide to drug information: Do you know the facts about drugs? Hollywood, FL: Health Communication.

Achterberg, J., & Lawlis, F. (1980). *Bridges of the body mind: Behavioral approaches to health care.* Champaign, IL: Institute for Personality and Ability Testing.

Benson, D. H. (1975). *The relaxation response.* New York: Avon Books.

Carruth, G., & Pugh, J. (1982). Grieving the loss of alcohol: A crisis in recovery. *Journal of Psychosocial Nursing and Mental Health Services, 20,* 18–21.

Estes, N. J., Smith-Dijulio, K., & Heinemann, M. E. (1980). *The nursing diagnosis of the alcoholic person.* St. Louis: C. V. Mosby.

Jacobson, E. (1938). *Progressive relaxation* (2nd ed.). Chicago: University Of Chicago Press.

Johnson, V. E. (1980). *I'll quit tomorrow.* San Francisco: Harper & Row.

Jones, E. E., & Berglas, S. (1978). Control of attributes about the self through self handicapping strategies: The appeal of alcohol and the role of underachievement. *Personality and Social Psychology Bulletin, 4,* 200–206.

Klanjer, F., Hartman, L. M., & Sobell, M. B. (1984). Treatment of substance abuse by relaxation training: A review of its rationale, efficiency and mechanisms. *Addictive Behaviors, 9,* 41–55.

Lowen, A. (1975). *Pleasure: A creative approach to life.* New York: Penguin.

Miller, W. R. (Ed.) (1980). *The addictive behaviors.* New York: Pergamon.

Powers, R. J., & Kutash, I. L. (1985). Stress and alcohol. *International Journal of Addictions, 20,* 461–482.

Sher, K. J., & Levenson, R. W. (1982). Risk for alcoholism and individual differences in the stress response—dampening effect of alcohol. *Journal of Abnormal Psychology, 91,* 350–367.

Tiebout, H. M. (1954). The ego factors in surrender in alcoholism. *Quarterly Journal of Studies on Alcohol, 15,* 610–612.

Wallace, J. (1978). Critical issues in alcoholism treatment. In S. Zimberg, J. Wallace, S. Blume (Eds.), *Practical approaches to alcoholism psychotherapy.* New York: Plenum.

BIBLIOGRAPHY

Brodsley, L. (1982). Avoiding a crisis: The assessment. *American Journal of Nursing, 82,* 1865–1871.

Cohn, L. (1982). Alcoholism: The hidden diagnosis. *American Journal of Nursing, 82,* 1862–1864.

Kurose, K., Anderson, T. N., Bull, W. N., Gibson, H. M., Grubb, P., Krefetz, N., Naqui, A. S., & Smith, M. (1981). A standard care plan for alcoholism. *American Journal of Nursing, 81,* 1001–1006.

Meyers, S. (1985). Metaphor and indirect suggestions in the treatment of recovering alcoholics. In R. Zahourek (Ed.), *Clinical hypnosis and therapeutic suggestion in nursing.* Orlando, FL: Grune &Stratton.

Ramseir, McFarland, G. K., & Wasli, E. L. (1982). Nursing diagnosis in caring for the adult psychiatric patient. In L. Shottis Brunner & D. Smith Suddartk (Eds.), *The Lippincott manual of nursing practice* (3rd Ed.). Philadelphia: J. B. Lippincott.

Stockwell, T., Hodgson, R., & Rankin, H. (1982). Tension reduction and the effects of prolonged alcohol consumption. *British Journal of Addiction, 77,* 65–73.

Tiebout, H. M. (1953). Surrender versus compliance in therapy. *Quarterly Journal of Studies on Alcohol, 14,* 58–68.

12

STRESS MANAGEMENT, RELAXATION TRAINING, AND IMAGERY WITH PRISON INMATES

PAUL SLOAN

Their work in prisons has seldom been explored in nursing literature, but the expanding role of nurses in correctional settings offers many opportunities (Bernier, 1986). This recent article emphasized that, with the growing number of prisoners, a great need exists for competent nurses to work with inmates on a preventive as well as a therapeutic basis.

Such therapeutic activities might include work with acute and chronic illnesses as well as addictions. Stress management is seen as valuable in prevention and treatment. The implications, however, reach beyond prison inmates in the exploration of relaxation and imagery (R/I) with problematic populations who have complex health-related issues.

This chapter focuses on the use of R/I techniques with an unusual population, prison inmates. These individuals have a high level of stress and are not generally taught imagery techniques, although relaxation training has been used widely. In 1975 Norris reported using biofeedback training to teach inmates to relax, control stress, and experience physiological control. Self-control training for inmates (Cheek & Baker, 1977) utilized behavior modification techniques of relaxation, self-image improvement, and assertiveness. Relaxation and stimulus control instructions were effective in reducing insomnia (Toler, 1978). Vasillos and Hughes (1979) measured relaxation by increases in skin temperature and found relaxation training and autogenic suggestion groups had greater anxiety-tension reduction than male inmates in direct instruction groups and skin temperature feedback groups.

Nurses employed in prison infirmaries, as well as nurses working with similar populations who are difficult but "captive audiences," could consider this approach. This population has the potential for being motivated to achieve a relaxed waking state (Bandler & Grinder, 1979). This naturally occurring altered state of consciousness in which the subject is more responsive to suggestion is associated with a R/I response (LaBaw, 1969). With any population these techniques provide not only reduction of stress and anxiety but also enhancement of problem-solving skills and practice of alternative feeling states as well as behaviors. With a problematic population such as prison inmates, particular issues need to be considered and allowed for when planning any therapeutic strategy. Resistance, manipulation, lack of control, and suspicion, as well as a high potential for antisocial behavior, must be understood and anticipated when working toward therapeutic goals or rehabilitation.

Colorado State Prison, located in Canon City, Colorado, housed 2836 inmates at five different locations in 1982. A total of 29 inmates were involved in a dual stress management and group therapy orientation program. These inmates were referred because of insomnia and hypertension. Four open-ended groups were conducted over a period of 6 months. Two groups took place concurrently, one at the medium security facility, the other at the minimum security facility. The length of each group was about 3 months; then it was terminated or continued as a psychotherapy group. A cotherapist was present in the medium security groups but not at the minimum security groups.

When inmates asked if the techniques were hypnotic, clear explanations of relaxation and stress management were given because a well-known issue in prison life is one of control and dominance of the stronger over the weaker. While R/I techniques are similar to hypnosis, to offer hypnosis in this setting could attract curiosity-seekers or people who would use it to exploit others for their own gain. Using the techniques for stress management was emphasized.

Stress management, while currently hailed as a major coping method for the general population (Wallis, 1983), can also serve a number of functions for correctional institutions and their inmate populations. Here it provided the following: (1) treatment of insomnia and hypertension; (2) screening for group therapy subjects; and (3) orientation for pregroup therapy training.

Overall, it offered treatment for the frequent requests for tranquilizer and sleeping medications. In a population where drug- and alcohol-related crimes ranged between 65 and 80 percent, motivation for requesting sleeping medication was certainly suspect. Complaints of insomnia and tension were evaluated by mental health workers. Unless the insomnia was a symptom of a major depression and the inmate was acutely suicidal, relaxation training was offered as the first step in dealing with the problem.

Besides meeting the need for treatment of insomnia, the secondary benefits of relaxation impacted the daily stressful situations a prison inmate faces. The group served as a nonthreatening didactic method of orientation for group psychotherapy. This was useful since mental health treatment in this setting holds the same initial stigma and resistance common to the general population outside the prison walls. Of the 2836 inmates in the Colorado State Corrections system, 10 percent were involved in psychotherapy groups; in addition, 23 Alcoholics Anonymous group meetings were held per week. A limited number of mental health staff in an overcrowded institution can best serve the need for treatment through group psychotherapy, although individual treatment is not totally ruled out.

STRESSES OF PRISON LIFE

Prison living is, in itself, stressful, especially during the adjustment period. Movement from one facility to another, for example, from maximum security to medium security, can demand continued vigilance on the part of the prisoner until he becomes familiar with the new inmates and guards. Inmates commonly complain about interpersonal conflicts with other inmates or guards. A frequent source of frustration was the inmate or guard who achieved a sense of control over others by actions that were perceived as constant harassment. Each change of facility for the inmate makes him "the new kid on the block," to be tested and tried by the others.

Experienced prisoners define the term *inmate* as new to the system—scared, and often presenting a macho image to protect himself. An inmate usually has to prove himself by not backing down to bullying. Then he gains enough respect to garner the support of others. Once a prisoner is adjusted and knows the ropes, he is considered a *convict,* or a more seasoned prisoner capable of coping with the prison environment. In one group discussion, heads nodded knowingly as an inmate described his relief after night lock-up when, in the relative safety of his cell, he could finally breathe a sigh of relief that he had made it through another day. Prisoners commonly reported feelings of vulnerability to being stabbed, having personal items stolen, or contraband being found or planted in their cells. Even at night some experienced surprise searches by guards looking for contraband. To be suspected as a party in contraband, usually drugs, alcohol, or knives, meant knowing you were always being watched.

The physical structure of the prison itself produced a feeling of being trapped, cornered, at the mercy of the system. Some swore they would not be so stupid as to escape, but others indicated that the oppressive sense of being locked up tempted the fantasy of freedom if the opportunity arose.

Depression and fear were seen more prominently in those inmates who had not developed an adequate interpersonal support system within the prison walls. Each change of facility recreated uncertainty and disorganization.

Gibbs (1982) described a similar disruption in the experience of jail for drug abusers. These inmates can be shattered psychologically by abrupt entry into an unfamiliar and chaotic situation where all control over one's life is lost.

Another source of frequent complaint by inmates was the inequity of the prison system's conduct rules and arbitrary interpretation of these rules by the staff. The prisoners felt that disruptive behavior moved an inmate through the system just as rapidly as good behavior because no unit manager wanted a troublemaker around for very long. All of these viewpoints, whether valid or not, produced a level of frustration that was reinforced by the system rather than alleviated. Mental health treatment was an available service and although many inmates were not prepared to accept it as a viable way of dealing with stress, the following group approach offered them a reasonable option.

DIDACTIC APPROACH: RELAXATION TRAINING

Prisoners complaining of insomnia or hypertension were screened by one of the mental health staff and offered the stress management class. At their first session the dual purpose of relaxation training and pre-group therapy instruction was explained. The group was to be structured and didactic and not psychotherapeutic. They were told psychotherapy involved a more personal commitment to growth and change. Relaxation training could, if individuals applied themselves, be very effective in decreasing the toll of physical stress on the body and in effecting better sleep. Members were cautioned, however, that no guarantee could be made to "relax" one's mind, and they were reminded that an internal conflict that persistently arose was the province of psychotherapy—group or individual.

At the beginning of each session a specific method of relaxation training was explained, demonstrated with the group experientially, and discussed afterward. The second part of the session focused on an explanation of the pre-group therapy orientation. Sometimes, on request, the same relaxation exercise was repeated at the next meeting. Prisoners were encouraged to practice the exercise as much as three times a day to train and sensitize their bodies to the pleasurable feeling of relaxation.

Each relaxation exercise was prefaced with an explanation of its benefits to the body, in terms of either preventing stress-related illnesses or providing rest, and easier concentration when studying. The five different methods used in the group are explained in the following sections.

Jacobson's Progressive Relaxation Exercise

Jacobson's Progressive Relaxation exercise was adapted to a 15-minute period in which all the main muscle groups were tensed and relaxed systematically, from toes to head (Jacobson, 1938). In this way the exercises were found to be easier to remember. The suggestion of progressively relaxing the whole body from feet, legs, back, arms to facial muscles seemed more effective when the move was from large muscles to smaller muscles in the head. This experience was reported as effective by all the inmates who participated in the classes. This technique was described as basic to good relaxation methods because it put the inmates in touch with their bodies and helped them identify areas of the body that tensed up unconsciously, such as shoulder, neck, and facial muscles. As they tensed and relaxed each muscle, they were told repeatedly to notice the different sensations in the muscles when tense as opposed to being relaxed. They were encouraged to do the exercise while sitting in a chair so as to avoid falling asleep before covering the main muscle groups of the whole body.

"Sunshine" Exercise

The "Sunshine" exercise, usually covered at the second sessions, was essentially a sensory awareness and visualization experience walked through by the instructor, who was careful to explain each time that the inmates were free to close their eyes or keep them open. Feedback from convicts verified the importance of this, especially at the first meeting, when a group of men were largely strangers to each other. The element of distrust was always strong at first. Closing your eyes in a group of unknown convicts was tantamount to soaping your face and hair in the shower without a friend to keep an eye out for homosexual rapists behind you. Usually after the first session with the adapted Jacobson exercises, they were familiar enough with each other to be able to close their eyes for the entire session with occasional brief glimpses to reassure themselves that everyone else's eyes were closed too. The basic method in the Sunshine exercise was guided imagery and suggestion. First, they were told to visualize a pleasant nature scene and imagine themselves in it with the sunlight slowly coming out over their feet, feeling the warm rays of sun gently penetrating every fiber of their toes and ankles, calming every muscle and nerve as it gradually rose up to the lower legs. The pleasant feeling of warmth was suggested to gradually extend over the entire body. The use of descriptive and tranquilizing words as well as the tone of the instructor's voice was important in producing the desired effect of complete body relaxation and peace of mind.

"Stairstep" Exercise

The "Stairstep" exercise was usually done around the third session. The therapist explained that these exercises could be somewhat hypnotic, and that practicing them was an exercise in which the inmates maintained complete control. The therapist instructed them to close their eyes and visualize themselves at the top of a beautiful staircase with 20 steps. As they progressed down the stairs they were to let themselves feel more completely relaxed until they reached the bottom step when they would be deeply relaxed but awake and free to open their eyes at any time if they so chose. Keeping the eyes closed screened out distractions and helped them concentrate on the visual images. Frequently they were told to stop on the twelfth or tenth step and to notice how their breathing was becoming more relaxed and to let themselves feel the steady, slowed rhythm of their abdomen rising and falling. At the bottom they were to picture in their mind's eye a beautiful verdant indoor garden and to go through the five senses (sight, hearing, smell, touch, taste); for example, colors of favorite flowers and plants, the scent of fresh spring water, the touch of leaves or the railing of the staircase, the sound of a bubbling fountain or favorite background music that is relaxing, and the taste of a favorite food. This form of imagery allowed the individual to provide his own specific affective components from pleasurable memories and to reexperience them. The sensation of taste was usually saved until last. They were told to picture a comfortable chair in the middle of the garden and to see themselves settling down in it only to find a plant or tree of their favorite vegetable or fruit within arm's reach. Picking the ripe produce from the vine, they were told to recall how fresh and delectable it was to taste and to imagine this fruit of the earth nourishing their body, restoring vitality and energy as they calmly rested. They were reminded that their own bodies were composed of vitamins and minerals derived from the earth through this plant and that this plant from the world of nature had a purpose in nourishing their bodies. As a child of nature, each of them had a purpose for living and they each possessed the mind and the will to search out their own individual purpose in life. No feedback was solicited or offered on this very personal existential part of the group experience, allowing for a maximum sense of privacy. This existential element was used here as a potential impetus to later discussion in therapy groups and simply to stimulate thinking about purpose in life as an exercise of meaning and benefit to everyone. The importance of this theme cannot be overemphasized when we speak of rehabilitating offenders. One phenomenon that supports this belief is the use of transcendental meditation (TM) programs in prison settings. Ferguson (1977) found TM to be highly effective in eliminating drug abuse among inmates as well as producing all the positive effects reported by Abrams and Seigal (1978), who found it reduced anxiety, neuroticism, hostility, insomnia, and disciplinary infractions. Ellis (1979) concluded that TM programs could well be the most self-sufficient, potent rehabilitation program available and should be a model for use in prison settings. Orme-Johnson (1982) reported TM reduced anxiety, recidivism, and crime where 1 percent of the population engaged in TM. It is reasonable to assume that the regular practice of meditation exercises would produce a reflective attitude toward a purpose in life, in addition to relaxation. This would enhance one's own personal belief system and could integrate one's daily routine into a world view, involving the whole person and his potential for a higher consciousness.

Autogenic Training

The simple repetitive practice of "autogenic training" was offered at the fourth session. It was presented as an alternate method likely to work if the previous ones did not when practiced alone. A handout described this exercise, giving a brief history of autogenic training and its use in reducing stress by astronauts, athletes, and creative artists. The instructor followed the process of the handout, which went as follows:

With each breath, say to yourself, eight times each:

* My arms and legs are heavy.
* My arms and legs are warm.
* My heartbeat is calm and regular.
* My breathing is relaxed and comfortable.
* My abdomen is warm.

*   My forehead is cool.

*   My mind is quiet and still.

In repeating these phrases the instructor naturally fell into a rhythmical and even sing-song delivery. Tapping a foot lightly as if keeping time to music or lyrics was helpful in setting a pace.

Breathing and Visualization

A simple breathing exercise and the visualization of a uniquely relaxing scene were used together, or as an adjunct to Jacobson's deep muscle exercises. The breathing exercise was adapted from the writings of Tarthang Talku (1978). The inmates were told to concentrate on their breathing, noticing the natural rhythm in the rise and fall of the abdominal wall and chest. They were told to be aware of the brief pause that occurs just after exhaling and again after inhaling and before breathing out. In monitoring this simple action they could feel their whole body gradually relax more with each breath, imagining a sinking deeper into relaxation, releasing more pent-up tension with each exhalation. An important footnote in the induction of a relaxed waking state is the tone of voice. A monotone voice would not be considered an asset in most forms of communication. Yet, repeatedly, subjects of group hypnosis have commented on this. "Your voice would put anyone to sleep," an inmate said as he stretched and yawned. "I wouldn't advise you to take up public speaking." The more low-pitched and droning the voice, the more powerful the suggestion of the relaxed response. On the other hand, a more dramatic or entertaining voice could raise the expectation of something imminent. An eerie or ghostly voice could be equally distracting from the task at hand.

PRE-GROUP THERAPY ORIENTATION

Pre-therapy training followed naturally on the heels of the relaxation experience. After a half hour of relaxation and discussion about the experience, the benefits of relaxation training were enumerated, including how relaxation reduced stress, maintained health, prevented stress-related illnesses, and could nurse one back to health. The limits of relaxation training were pointed out to draw the discussion to group therapy as a method of resolving psychological conflicts.

By this time the inmates were more comfortable with each other and had shared their feelings about the relaxation exercise. It was a positive experience. A printed handout was passed out as a means of stimulating discussion about group therapy. The handout was taken from a list of 12 curative factors in group therapy, from *Group Therapy* by Irvin Yalom (1975). Three of the factors were given in one session as an aid to group discussion, and this led to more personal sharing and continued growth of interpersonal trust. It also taught clearly what could be accomplished in group endeavors. It was believable because the inmates were already experiencing some of the therapeutic benefits of groups, such as catharsis. "That must be what happened last week," a Vietnam veteran remarked. "I just got it all off my chest and I felt good afterwards."

RESULTS AND EVALUATION

Attendance and follow-up in groups were primary issues in evaluation. The nature of the prison setting made it difficult to do a time-limited group. One might assume a "captive audience" in a prison would be part of the package. Not so. Education programs, work schedules, parole board hearings, reconsideration hearings in court, and even recreation schedules interfered with attendance, not to mention that inmates would simply not hear their names called over the speakers in their units. Forgetting what day it was and oversleeping were frequent reports for even well-intentioned inmates. Taking less responsibility for use of time seemed to be a byproduct of prison living. Time schedules were decided for them by the structure of the system. Among the many losses experienced with imprisonment, a most significant one is the loss of control over one's own life (Sease, 1978).

The poor attendance record was obviously a major factor in the turnover. It is estimated that about half of the turnover was caused by the prison setting itself and about half by the immaturity and lack of motivation of the inmates themselves. Inmates earned their parole or went to honor camps from minimum security and abruptly left the group. Others who simply did not continue to attend may have screened themselves out of the group when it became obvious that they could not obtain drugs by complaints of insomnia. These were the same convicts who rarely practiced the exercises on their own. They also sung the praises of marijuana and alcohol as their favorite methods of relaxation.

The turnover also disrupted the group by escalating the level of distrust that was actually quite strong from the outset. "Group therapy will never work here," one inmate asserted. "Convicts can't even trust themselves; how can they trust each other?" In one sense this was true of the younger inmates in particular. They had not established disciplined habits. They distrusted their own capacity to control their impulses and relied more on the immediate effects of chemical agents for tension reduction.

One of the two groups conducted at the minimum security facility showed promise of becoming an ongoing psychotherapy group. This group contained mostly older convicts who were more consistent in attendance. They were also less inclined to externalize the causes of their problems, and they gave feedback about practicing the exercises on their own.

The outcome of the medium security groups was more successful. Longer sentences and lower turnover were factors. The two ongoing therapy groups formed in this setting were stable for respective reasons. One group benefited by the addition of an older convict at the point it became a therapy group. He testified to the meaningful and growing relationships he had experienced in other prison therapy groups. Another who had been in the stress management groups persistently reached out to an untrusting member, pleading with him to give the group a chance to work. These two men shared highly sensitive information about their crimes, family relationships, rage, and the wrongs done to themselves and others by their incarceration.

The other ongoing therapy group progressed from the didactic stress management group to a therapy group according to plan. Although there were disruptions due to the institutional system itself, the stability of attendance and the growing trust among members was obvious. In addition, the medium security groups also had a cotherapist who served that facility. All of these stabilizing influences contributed to the effective functioning of the group as it progressed from structured and didactic to open and therapeutic processes.

EVALUATION SUMMARY

One indicator of behavioral change in prisoners can be measured by the number of disciplinary infractions and the resultant loss of "good time," days awarded for good behavior and taken off one's sentence. In comparing the good time lost in 1982 and 1983 (roughly before, during, and after the stress management groups), there was a distinct decrease in the days lost. In 1982, the group of 29 inmates lost a total of 245 days good time. As of October 1983, they lost 119 days good time. During this period seven inmates were granted parole, which could account for some of the decrease. It could also be argued that when inmates prepare for parole board hearings they tend to conform to the system to show the board they are cooperating by using mental health services. This could also indicate that a change in attitude accompanies a readiness to attend groups. Attending a stress management group may be one incremental step in a series of small gains that are necessary to effect real behavioral change.

The reduction of sleep disturbance and hypertension was informally reported by all inmates who participated as beneficial. No doubt the group phenomenon had a positive effect on this. Listening to others extol the benefits and pleasures of simply relaxing without alcohol or drugs influenced one not to be the oddball who would get nothing from it. Many did not practice the exercises during the week, and some not at all, but there were no more complaints of insomnia or requests for sleeping pills.

The increased confidence in the ability to control anger emerges as another benefit. The phrase, "I'm afraid I'll go off on him," was heard often as an inmate described his anger at a guard who watched his every move or shook down his cell in an effort to catch him, unawares, with contraband. Harassment and intimidation by other inmates caused intense stress; to back down from the power quest of such people was to concede to their dominance. To stand up to a bullying inmate could mean significant risk. Inmates who exploded into violence when wronged could generate enough fear to be left alone. For some, this was the only option in the face of a life-threatening environment. A prison therapist described people who lose their tempers easily as "having little self-respect." Easy loss of temper, and the violence often associated with it, represents an effort to gain respect from others, particularly among men who grow up learning that their survival depends on constant assertion of their toughness (Cholst, 1978). For many inmates, as Norris (1975) pointed out, it was a revelation "as they experienced psychophysiological control and realized that their responses are not mediated totally externally." It amounted to the experiential learning of control from within. Unlike prison norms, it was not imposed by outside forces. It was a choice that increased one's confidence in self-control. One convict who had returned to prison over three times said, "I never really believed I could control my temper until now." It gave them a sense of control or empowerment versus the fear of being powerless.

Group discussion was guided to reinforce the idea that to be easily provoked by others was to be under their control, not your own. Control is a precursor to self-discipline. The group was utilized to crystallize this concept of self-discipline with talk of meditation, the power of the Far Eastern mystics, the use of relaxation by athletes, and the benefits of a relaxed waking state for learning and thinking clearly. The instructor took ample opportunity to sum up the group process in terms of control as an aid to assertiveness, a de-escalation of aggressiveness. For example, in a calm state, one can think more clearly and see more alternatives to violence. Being able to relax, stop, and reflect gives one time to choose between more or less desirable results of actions.

While the early states of group cohesiveness enhanced the teaching process and had a positive effect on stress management, the chemical means, mainly alcohol and marijuana, still maintained their place as quick and easy tension reducers. The use of the five senses in the exercises on visual imagery added a hypnotic effect, and hopefully an effective link to a self-generated way of relaxing. But in the context of a prison where alcohol and marijuana are still somehow easily available, a method that requires practice is hard-pressed to compete with the immediacy of chemical ingestion.

In summary, the combination of stress management and pre-group therapy training served several purposes. Sleep disturbances and hypertension were treated. Drug requests decreased. Convicts had the opportunity of experiencing self-training methods of relaxation that worked in the group and individually with practice. One inmate said, "This is the first time I've felt relaxed since I first came to this place." The common type of resistance to mental health treatment was countered in a positive way. Above all, the inmates learned through experience that they could achieve, by their own efforts, a pleasurable feeling of the relaxed waking state. Working with difficult clients in problematic settings is common for nurses. The intent of this chapter was to, again, demonstrate that relaxation/imagery techniques have numerous implications and serve numerous purposes both for groups and individual treatment.

REFERENCES

Abrams, A., & Seigal, L. M. (1978). Transcendental meditation program and rehabilitation at Folsom State Prison—A cross-validation study. *Criminal Justice and Behavior, 5*, 3-20.

Bandler, R., & Grinder, J. (1979). Frogs into princes. Moab, UT: Real People Press.

Bernier, S. L. (1986). Corrections and mental health. *Journal of Psychosocial Nursing, 24*, 20-25.

Cheek, F. E., & Baker, J. C. (1977). Self-control training for inmates. *Psychological Reports, 41*, 559-568.

Cholst, S. (1978). Therapy of loss of temper and crimes of violence. *International Journal of Offender Therapy and Comparative Criminology, 22*, 124-254.

Ellis, G. A. (1979). *Inside Folsom Prison transcendental meditation and TM-SIDHI program.* Palm Springs, CA: ETC Publication.

Ferguson, R. E. (1977). *Transcendental meditation program of MCI (Massachusetts Correctional Institu-*

tion) Walpole—An evaluation report. Pacific Palisades, CA: Massachusetts Department of Mental Health, World Plan Executive Council.

Gibbs, J. J. (1982). Disruption and distress: Going from street to jail. In N. Parisi (Ed.), *Coping with imprisonment* (pp. 29-41). Beverly Hills, CA: Sage Publications.

Jacobson, E. (1938). *Progressive relaxation* (2nd ed.). Chicago: University of Chicago Press.

La Baw, W. (1969). Assisting adults and children with remedial uses of their trance capability. *Behavioral Neuropsychiatry, 1,* 24-30.

Norris, P. A. (1975). Biofeedback applications in a consciousness training program. Paper presented at the American Correctional Association Annual Congress of Corrections Proceedings. Houston, August 18–22.

Orme-Johnson, D. (1982). Prison rehabilitation and crime prevention through the transcendental meditation and TM-SIDHI program. In L. V. Hippechen (Ed.), *Holistic approaches to offender rehabilitation.* Springfield, IL: Charles C. Thomas.

Sease, S. (1982). Grief associated with a prison experience: Counseling the client. *Journal of Psychological Nursing and Mental Health Services, 20,* 25-27.

Toler, H. C. (1978). Treatment of insomnia with relaxation and stimulus-control instructions among incarcerated males. *Criminal Justice and Behavior, 5,* 117-130.

Tulku, T. (1978). *Skillful means.* Berkeley, CA: Dharma Publishing.

Vasillos, J. G., & Hughes, H. (1979). Skin temperature control—A comparison of direct instruction, autogenic suggestion, relaxation, and bio-feedback training in male prisoners. *Corrective and Social Psychiatry & Journal of Behavior Technology Methods and Therapy, 25,* 119-124.

Wallis, C. (1983). Stress: Can we cope? *Time,* June 6, pp. 48-54.

Yalom, I. D. (1975). *Theory and practice of group psychotherapy* (2nd ed.). New York: Basic Books.

13

STRESS MANAGEMENT WITH STAFF GROUPS

ESTHER SIEGEL

It is axiomatic that hospital-based nursing practice creates some vulnerability to the negative effects of stress. The pace is hectic. Medical technology is awesome, which at some level translates to mean that patients are sicker. In significant ways, medical centers represent a microcosm in bold relief of sociocultural issues, dilemmas, and the triumphs inherent in advanced technology.

Nurses in their role as caregivers must traverse a precarious course between high level technical competence and maintaining concern for the components that represent the heart of nursing—the human and humanizing elements. An environment with its parts structured in this way provides ample situations for both gratification and stress simultaneously. Seldom is the atmosphere a neutral one.

Nurses must acknowledge that states of both stress and gratification can and do exist; one need not negate the other since they are not mutually exclusive terms. Rather, it is necessary for nurses first to become attuned to subjectively experienced symptoms of stress, and second, to become skilled at channeling the energy thus generated toward neutralization of the negative effects of stress.

This chapter will describe a stress management group project started 6 years ago at a large urban university medical center. The use of relaxation and imagery (R/I) techniques has been central to the format of the groups. Over time, the groups have evolved and assumed varied forms but the underlying premises remain the same, that is, the ability to control elements of "dis-stress" (Selye, 1974) resides within each of us. The discovery of how to establish the locus of control within oneself becomes the foremost task in stress management.

STRESS AS CONCEPT: STRESS AS PROCESS

As a word, *stress* has assumed lexical significance. It depicts concept, experience, and response. It is frequently overused and misunderstood. Hans Selye, whose name has become synonomous with stress-related research, defined it in both simple and abstract terms. Simply defined, stress can be seen as the rate of wear and tear on the body and as a nonspecific response of the body to any demand made upon it (Selye, 1956, 1974). In the latter publication Selye talks about stress in a way that he had not done in his earlier work, that is, he examines it holistically from psychological, philosophical, and physiological perspectives.

One way to examine stress is to look at what it is not. According to Selye, it is *not* merely nervous tension. While emotional stimuli rank high in activating a stress response, it should be conversely noted that low animal forms and even plants without nervous systems reflect the effects of stress (Selye, 1974, p. 18). Stress is *not* always a nonspecific result of or cause of damage. This becomes apparent when you look at the wide array of activities that can serve as stressors without necessarily causing or resulting from damage. One has merely to be present at any celebratory event that marks a rite of passage to note the increased stress and tension levels and the adaptive capacities that are invoked responsively. Finally, stress is *not* something to be avoided. While this last statement may seem self-evident, it is an important one on which to reflect. Since a total absence of stress is equivalent to death, it follows that goal-setting regarding stress levels should aim at reduction and titration rather than elimination. The determination of what constitutes acceptable, manageable, while at the same time productive, stress levels is important and can be arrived at by individual exploration, reflection, and decision. In the basic language of stress, the flight-or-fight mechanisms coupled with adaptive and defensive reactions can be applied to all areas of response. Since neither fleeing or fighting provide practical solutions for most stressful situations, it is necessary to sort out which events require yet another approach—one of adaptation rather than defense. One may argue that any gradation or alternate response on the flight/fight continuum represents a form of adaptation that becomes, in effect, the sine qua non in a complex social structure. Obviously, a nurse who is reprimanded by a supervisor has learned alternatives to either leaving the floor or engaging in heated battle on the spot. What he or she will most likely do is control against the wish to engage in battle or flee from it.

While self-control is not to be eschewed—quite the contrary, it is necessary and desirable—nevertheless, it should be recognized that symptoms of chronic stress are frequently associated with stimuli (stressor)-response (defense)-control (internal response).

The author is not advocating a lessening of self-control, but rather a reduction in kind and number of issues that are perceived as stressors. Selye describes an alternative mechanism that he terms a *syntoxic response*. Implied by this is a passive tolerance toward stimuli—a tolerance that permits a kind of peaceful coexistence with specific stressors. This implication will be discussed further in relationship to the literature on mind/body response.

The literature on stress frequently points to burnout as an end product of unmanageable or unmanaged stress. Rather than defined, burnout is usually described as a dynamic process with gradual insidious onset and predictable outcome, uniformly agreed on as stages of disillusionment (Edelwich, 1980). Maslach (1976, 1978) has studied and written about burnout as it pertains to and affects people in the helping professions. She describes the first stage as emotional exhaustion accompanied by physical exhaustion. The second stage is characterized by negative, cynical, dehumanized attitudes about the work being done and the people being cared for. The final stage is one of total disgust, a kind of terminal burnout. Welch, Medeiros, and Tate (1982) include feelings of helplessness, low status, the intensity of the work setting, and issues of funding in addition to disillusionment as factors that make nurses vulnerable to burnout.

Since burnout is conceived of as unrelieved stress, it follows that measures for its prevention or management, if it develops, are the same as those for recognizing and combating stress.

Rather than focus further on stress burnout as concepts—the reader is no doubt sufficiently well steeped in the variety of form and manifestation of stress in symptom formation—this chapter will provide a cursory examination of nurses for whom stress has reached unmanageable levels and who would be more accurately designated as being in "dis-stress."

Each nursing specialty describes its own particular kind of stressors. Critical care nurses talk of the day-to-day ongoing intensity of caring for patients who, by definition, are critically ill. They readily admit the alertness and vigilance required provide the challenge and attraction to their area of specialization. The part that wears them down, however, and serves to produce a prevalent gallows humor is related to the difficulty they experience in providing care to those patients whose lives are being maintained by medical technology—by life support systems that maintain a nether world somewhere between life and death. Nurses describe the frustration they experience with the needs of patients' families, often interpreted as demands that cannot be satisfied. When questioned further about these feelings, the comments reflect a sense of hopelessness within themselves that reverberates in response to the "demands."

Pediatric nurses describe the sadness associated with caring for young children who are terminally ill and, again, the attendant strain of supplying comfort to the families of acutely ill or dying youngsters.

Nurses in medical units describe similar difficulty from another vantage point of the life cycle. The lyrics change but the melody remains the same, that is, the experience of helplessness and frustration in response to particular inevitability, the pain of attachment and loss, and the stress of being empathically connected to others while maintaining the prescribed detachment.

The variety of form represented by the specialties in nursing is superimposed on a structural constance. The hospitalized sick person, at whatever age, represents a continual reminder to the caregiver of need—need to be cared for, attended, and ministered to with the recognition that recovery is not the sole measure of success in the care of patients.

Following are brief profiles representing two composite categories of actual nurses: (1) stressors encountered by new inexperienced practitioners and (2) those more likely described by the seasoned clinician. Included are extrapolated themes most frequently expressed.

Themes in Opposition: The New Nurse

Competence/incompetence: "I feel so disorganized—can't seem to get everything done—there's so much to know—will I ever get it in order?"

Idealism/disillusionment: "I came into nursing because I wanted to help people—to make a difference—it's not the way I thought it would be—some patients treat me like a maid."

Self-expectation/guilt: "I feel bad when I become impatient—some people are so demanding and get on my nerves—I know they're sick but they make me mad—then I feel guilty."

Fantasy/reality: "I know people have to die—sometimes it's a relief when they do—but it's hard especially when they're young—it's even hard to talk about it."

The Experienced Clinician

Humanism/objectivity: "Sometimes the law and the fear of lawsuits makes caring for patients in a humane way very hard to do. I try to be objective about the way things are—what we can and can't do—but I feel really conflicted about it."

Status needs/getting the job done: "I know all that stuff about the whole person—but bedpans and cleaning up after people all the time—I don't even mind it so much, it's the way others think about it—we don't get much respect."

Scheduling problems/needs for self: "I knew nursing would not be a 9–5 job but after a while rotation to other shifts and working weekends really puts a crimp in your outside life."

Need to grow/need to serve: "I enjoy bedside nursing—I'd hate to give it up—I'd miss direct patient care but it's hard to keep growing professionally at the bedside."

MIND/BODY RESPONSE: SELECTED LITERATURE

Stress, like pain, is subjectively perceived and experienced. Selye (1974) and Lazarus (1971) emphasize the importance of perception as a key determinant in the stress phenomenon. Perception is defined as a component of cognition. Viewed from this perspective the emphasis for mind/body relatedness is a cognitive one (Claus, 1980) and therefore amenable to educational modification. The dictum becomes: alter perception and the response is altered. The latter comment is congruent with the Selye concept of syntoxic mechanism as antidote to excessive or unnecessary stress. By this

I mean making a conscious decision to be unresponsive to particular stressors. The key words are *conscious* and *decision*, both implying that the locus of control resides within the individual. Thus far we are primarily in the realm of cognition and behavior.

An additional and important dimension in the approach to stress management falls in the domain of what Epstein refers to as the "so-called minor hemisphere" (1981, p. 50) or right-brain function. Relaxation, visualization, and imagery are techniques integrally related to hypnosis but, as pointed out by Zahourek (1985), are ones that can be used with less formal knowledge than specified by hypnosis proper, which implies "formal induction of an altered state with specific suggestions accompanying the induction" (Zahourek, 1985, p. 225). The use of relaxation and imagery falls under the rubric of hypnotic techniques and can be used within a variety of contexts so long as the methods are appropriately adapted to the frame—that is, the goals are clear and the visualization techniques tailored to those goals.

Relaxation* and its benefits have been described in full detail by Luthe (1969) and later by Benson (1975), who termed it the "relaxation response." Benson states that relaxation activates an innate mechanism available to all, which can serve as an antidote to the flight/fight response activated by the sympathetic nervous system—a method for using "one innate mechanism to counteract the effects of another" (Benson, 1975, p. 178).

The use of guided imagery and visualization has been documented in the psychiatric literature as an effective means for learning, experiencing, and increasing affective response for self-exploration and as a means to expand imagination (Kosbab, 1974). Epstein (1981) characterizes guided imagery and its associative expansion of right-brain activity as a method for holistic processing of information as compared to left-brain capacity for interpretative function. The latter is described as linear thought linked with cause and effect, rational and evaluative in nature. Combining both functions is posited by Epstein as basis for providing synthesis or as means for achieving a balance of hemispheric function.

Simonton and associates (1978), who are oncology specialists, demonstrated a relationship between the ways in which individuals cope with stress and the incidence of illness. In response to these findings, the Simontons developed a treatment program that included learning a positive attitude toward life (cognition) in combination with relaxation and visualization techniques (imagination).

LeShan (1974) goes a step further in prescribing meditation on a regular basis as an enabling mechanism for the individual to summon his or her inner resources to counter stress. Meditation when practiced regularly produces a physiological state of deep relaxation coupled with an increase of alertness. Tension indicators are reduced and the metabolic rate and heartbeat slow down. This physiological state appears to be the opposite of the state brought about by stress.

In a study by Donovan (1981), the researcher found that relaxation with guided imagery represented a useful adjunctive tool for coping with stress. Taught in groups, it was found to be efficient and practical for use with oncology nurses.

---

*See Chapter 2 by Hope Titlebaum.

More recently Randolph, Price, and Collins (1986) reported validation of the positive effects of a 2-day burnout prevention workshop that included cognitive and experiential components for the reduction of stress. The content was specifically designed for nurses and the stressors they experience. Self-regulation techniques, imagery, meditation, and conceptual information on stress and burnout were included. The study concluded that a significant reduction of stress-related symptoms resulted from those who participated as compared with a control group who did not.

STARTING THE STRESS MANAGEMENT GROUP PROJECT

The stress management group project was started on a trial basis. Six months elapsed between the planning phase and its implementation. Although the concept was welcomed with enthusiasm by nursing leadership, its actuality was met with reluctance. As an outsider to the institution, I proposed my role be a consultant, which would preserve my neutrality within the departmental hierarchy. I suggested the groups consist exclusively of staff; leadership presence was viewed as an inhibiting one.

The idea was first presented to the head nurses, realizing that without their support and interest it would not be a viable plan. Those interested presented it to their staff. Participation was and continues to be voluntary. The proposal suggested a series of eight weekly sessions for 45 minutes to 1 hour in duration.

An underlying premise and one clearly stated at the outset to the nurse participants was this group would not concern itself with the care of patients but rather with the care of nurses. We would not be involved with examining expertise or quality of practice. The assumption was that staff members were offering the best care possible. This group would not chastise, exhort, or demonstrate better methods for delivery of care—this task would be left with clinical supervisors and inservice educators. Rather, the groups would provide a safe retreat from the pressure of patient care where group members would be encouraged to pay attention to self—the whole of oneself with a view toward some introspection as a means for preventing symptoms of "dis-stress."

Ideally, this kind of group should be able to meet in a quiet setting, one that would promote a sense of relaxation. Since large medical centers invariably have space problems, our groups have generally met in whatever room can be made available. On some units this could mean an all-purpose staff room not necessarily safe from intrusion by nonparticipants. The range of meeting places has run the gamut from unoccupied patient rooms to the head nurse's small office. On some level, not having an ideal setting can be pointed out as having an advantage; that is, one need not have ideal circumstances in order to use relaxation techniques.

While this chapter's focus is on relaxation and imagery as tools for management of stress, cognitive methods and discussion of pertinent topics were also an important part of the process, although not mentioned here.

One such factor emphasized during the groups was the educative aspect that serves to accomplish what Maslow (1959) called the malady of deficient knowledge—

of literally not knowing what is good for oneself. The discussion that followed the relaxation and imagery focused on examining those elements which emerge individually as stress reducing and therefore deemed "good."

THE STRUCTURED EXERCISES

The following exercises were adapted from several sources that emphasize mind/body unity (Benson, 1975; LeShan, 1974; Pelletier, 1977; Simonton, 1978). Extrapolation was made from a chapter that described a group project designed for stress prevention with an elderly population at a senior citizens center (Siegel, 1983). The exercises are framed to elicit connection with an inner core of strength. The order of presentation is purposeful, with sequencing designed to move in the direction of the general to specific; impersonal to personal; and fantasy to reality. Framed in this way, the use of imagination is encouraged toward an end goal of a practical action plan.

Although this kind of progression is recommended, it is not imperative. Much of what is gleaned and applied from the exercises is a function of the climate within the group itself, that is, the context within which the learning takes place.

Prior to the presentation of the structured exercises, the leader will need to talk with group members about confidentiality, the importance of a safe climate within the group, and the value of the use of imagination in reducing stress. Some groups require more preliminary discussion and information regarding stress reduction. The variation in knowledge, acceptance, and responsiveness to the use of relaxation and imagery is assessed at the outset. A resistant group tends to have difficulty with the exercises.

The exercises are offered in succession, usually one each meeting. Since there are variations in groups, the rules for presentation of the exercises cannot be hard and fast ones. For example, Exercise 1 may require more than one meeting. It will depend on what precedes what follows by way of discussion within the group.

Preceding each of the exercises, the following relaxation technique was used:

Relaxation

Get into a comfortable position and take a deep breath; relax. Then count: (1) — Roll your eyes up. Keep your eyeballs up and close your eyelids. (2) —Inhale deeply and hold your breath. (3) —Let your breath out slowly. Roll your eyeballs down, keeping your eyelids closed. Imagine yourself floating down.

Now take three deep breaths and exhale slowly. Continue to imagine yourself floating in a comfortable position, feeling light and buoyant. Now start to relax all of your body. Relax the muscles of your head and neck, then your arms, chest, abdomen and legs. Take a deep breath and as you let it out feel your whole body relax. Remain relaxed for 30 seconds. Be conscious only of your breathing—inhale—exhale fully.

Visualization

Exercise 1—Fantasy Trip to a Meadow.

The leader directs the group as follows: In this relaxed state with eyes closed transport yourself to a meadow—it may be remembered from childhood or from imagination. Find a tree in the meadow. Go to the tree and lean against it.

As you lean against the tree, imagine the sun shining on leaves and warming you. Imagine your feet firmly planted on the ground. Imagine yourself being able to sway with the wind as a tree is able to without falling because your feet are firmly planted.

Remain so for a few minutes. Take in all the smells around you; feel the sun; feel the coolness of the earth.

Remember the feelings; remember the tree in the meadow; you can return to it at other times.

Inhale fully, exhale slowly. Return to the room and open your eyes.

The imagery of the meadow and a tree are sufficiently neutral, pleasant and accessible to most people. The suggestions are both concrete and symbolic of a "return to nature" as restorative. The tree as identificatory object represents both strength and flexibility.

Following the exercise, the group is encouraged to process the experience. Each member is given ample time and encouraged to describe individual visualizations in detail with the emphasis on the sensory components.

Exercise 2—Fantasy Trip to Inner Guide.

With eyes closed imagine yourself traveling along a path. It could be real or imagined. Travel the path slowly and take time to notice everything along the way. Notice the colors, smells, and sounds. As you travel along the path, try to imagine coming to a place—a safe, comfortable, accepting place, real or imagined, a place where you feel thoroughly at home.

Upon arriving there, look around you. Make note of what you see, hear, smell. It is a familiar place or one that you imagine you would like to visit. In this place try to find a guide—someone you either know or perhaps knew at another time in your life or someone you would like to have as your guide.

Now talk to your guide. Ask him or her a question of importance to yourself. If your guide is impatient or unresponsive to you, ask him to be more patient and responsive to you.

Remain so for several minutes.

Look around you once more—at the guide—at the place so you can remember it. You will be returning there again.

Come back to the room and open your eyes.

When processing this exercise it is important for each group participant to be encouraged to set the frame in which the imagining took place. Ample time should be allowed for elaboration and in-depth description. The leader must also be alert to individuals for whom imagery and visualization present a problem and assist them in the finding of a safe, comfortable place. The process, however, must be accomplished in a way that does not diminish self-esteem. Inevitably, there is at least one person in the group who will express having difficulty with imagination by saying, "I'm just not good at this kind of thing." My response to this type of comment is both neutral and educative. Rather than provide a more typical reassuring response, I find the neutrality of further explanation about the use of imagination to be, in fact, reassuring.

Before proceeding with the next exercise, "Best Decision," the leader assists each individual in establishing the scenes from memory of the previous journeys. Participants are encouraged to elaborate the details. Doing this is both practical and salutary. Details from preceding exercises provide necessary context for successive ones. It has been my experience that unless encouraged otherwise, there is a tendency to abridge rather than elaborate. The leader's encouragement is helpful on two levels—it validates importance to the experience and indulges each participant with equal time and attention. This kind of active leadership also protects members from revealing too much about themselves.

Exercise 3—Best Decision.

With eyes closed, return to the safe place. From the vantage point of feeling safe, return to a particular good time in the past. Try to remember the happy quality of that episode—the people who shared it with you, everything that made it a happy time for you. Stay in that time. Focus on the different aspects of the memory—on as many details as you can remember.

Now try to remember a decision you made at that time, bearing in mind that this was the best decision possible at that time.

Stay with the memory for a few minutes.

Return to the present and open your eyes.

Following this exercise, each participant is asked to describe his or her experience. In processing the material, the leader needs to tease out real or symbolic aspects of the best decision. One's best decision as it emerges in this context can be both illuminating and reassuring to the individual. It can serve to validate choices made in a variety of areas—vocational, interpersonal, and so on. Frequently participants express surprise at the kinds of images that present themselves—"almost out of nowhere" said one nurse as she related the context and experience of deciding to transfer from an unrelated field of study to pursue a career in nursing.

The goal of the next exercise, "Pleasurable Activity," is to provide a bridge between past and present. It can serve to tie the threads of the preceding two into an activity that can offer pleasure and reduce stress.

Exercise 4—Pleasurable Activity.

With eyes closed return again to the safe place. Again return to that happy time when you made the best decision possible. Let your thoughts wander around in that time and in that decision.

Now identify an activity you have loved in the past but have perhaps stopped doing. Try to imagine yourself doing it again. Try to picture what keeps you from doing it and what steps you could take to change that. Or maybe there is something you have always wanted to try but have put off. Imagine yourself doing it now.

Stay with the thought for a few minutes.

Return to the present and open your eyes.

Each participant is encouraged to explore at least one activity that would provide an offset to current activities of daily living. The leader must persist in providing guidance, encouragement, and educative explanations regarding the importance of assuming control over oneself in terms of developing inner resources as a bulwark against the negative aspects of stress. Others in the group are often an additional source of encouragement to the participant who expresses an interest in a specific activity but negates its possibility.

Some Notes on the Exercises: Questions and Answers

On the preceding pages I have described visualization exercises, provided in sequential order and designed to evoke internal response specific to the individual's needs. Since they are presented in a progressive order the reader may well have formulated a number of questions related to group attendance. This is a particularly valid issue based on the irregularity of nurses' schedules because of time off from work, rotation to other shifts, or an especially demanding assignment that cannot be left to another for completion. A few of these questions might be (1) How effective can sequential exercises be when offered to an open-ended group? (2) Can sufficient safety be established in an open-ended group to permit the sharing of experiences? and (3) Is continuity necessary or even important for the participant to obtain some benefit?

At the outset I asked the same questions of myself, knowing that group process provides an important dimension to the outcome. Obviously, if given a choice, it would have been stipulated that consistent attendance would be expected. Under the circumstances, however, this kind of demand would have been unreasonable and impractical. Consequently, it increased the demands on the leader for repetitive explanations albeit with attempts made to avoid sounding repetitive, inventing inclusive techniques for new participants, and, paradoxically, establishing the seeming disadvantage as an advantage, that is, the importance of flexibility in formulating a stress management regimen. In short, the style of the group was thus used as a model for demonstrating how flexible attitude could enhance and facilitate rather than inhibit or impede effectiveness.

In general this kind of group requires active leadership. The leader must be prepared to encourage, coax, persuade, and persist, preferably with the use of humor as adjunctive method. This is particularly so with members who make it known at the outset that they lack imagination. Since it is truly my belief that the potential for imagination is an inherent one, it is not difficult for me to express this with sincerity and conviction—both of which serve as persuasive tools.

The issue of sequence, while desirable and recommended if at all possible, need not be slavishly adhered to if other factors within the group meetings prevent such adherence. A most important aspect that should be remembered and responded to is the recognition that the point of the group is to provide participants with methods for coping with and relieving stress. The group process therefore should at all costs be geared toward a comfortable, safe, and accepting atmosphere, one in which participants can feel free to leave if need be and equally free not to return if it does not suit.

Example: A Brief Vignette

This example highlights some of the points made in the discussions of the preceding exercises. Recently while walking toward the cafeteria in the medical center, I was hailed from behind by a nurse who said she had been looking for me and wondered if I had a few minutes to talk with her. Although I could not exactly place her in the context of a specific unit, she did look familiar to me. She reintroduced herself to me and laughingly reminded me of "the hard time" she gave me in the group a few years ago. With that comment, I remembered her in an instant.

Mary J. had participated in one of the groups on the medical service. At that time she was an inexperienced practitioner with less than 1 year of experience. Although she attended group sessions with regularity, she invariably made negative comments about the format, particularly the use of imagery and visualization. She described herself as someone "who could never do that kind of stuff—it's not active enough for me."

Since it was common knowledge that group attendance was voluntary, her regular attendance was interpreted by me to mean that at some level she was gaining something from the experience despite the criticism and protest. My response to her was consistently nondefensive. I focused on the process rather than the content of her remarks, that is, the regularity of her attendance and, with encouragement, her actual ability to do the exercises. Her presence, in fact, added stimulation to the group. Meeting in the corridor, she quickly came to the point of what she wanted to say to me. She explained how almost in spite of herself, she started to use parts of the exercises, "and in the funniest places," i.e., in the subway, as a problem-solving device, as a stimuli-reduction method. In short, she wanted me to know how helpful this particular approach had been in terms of stress management.

SUMMARY

On the preceding pages I have focused on the use of specific relaxation and visualization techniques as one method for coping with stress. A stress management program includes additional pieces geared toward self-assessment, a kind of stress inventory, as prerequisite. Interventions should aim specifically toward alleviation based on the individual self-assessment. In this context relaxation and imagery techniques become important weapons in the armamentarium of stress management.

REFERENCES

Benson, H. (1976). *Relaxation response*. New York: Avon.

Cherniss, C. (1980). *Staff burnout*. Beverly Hills, CA: Sage.

Claus, K. E., & Bailey, J. T. (1980). *Living with stress and promoting well being: A handbook for nurses*. St. Louis: C. V. Mosby.

Donovan, M. I. (1981). Study of the impact of relaxation with guided imagery on stress among cancer nurses. *Cancer Nursing, 4*, 121–126.

Edelwich, J., & Brodsky, A. (1980). *Burnout*. New York: Human Sciences.

Epstein, G. (1981). *Waking dream therapy*. New York: Human Sciences.

Keane, A. Ducette, J., & Adler, D. C. (1985). Stress in ICU and non-ICU nurses, *Nursing Research, 34*, 231–236.

Kosbab, F. F. (1974). Imagery techniques in psychiatry. *Archives of General Psychiatry, 31*, 283–290.

Lazarus, R. S. (1971). The concepts of stress and disease. In L. Levi (Ed.), *Society, stress and disease* (Vol. 1). London: Oxford University Press.

LeShan, L. (1974). *How to meditate*. Boston: Little, Brown.

Luthe, E. (1970). *Autogenic therapy research and theory*. New York: Grune & Stratton.

Maslach, C. (1976). Burned-out. *Human Behavior, 5*, 17–21.

Maslach, C. (1978). The client role in staff burn-out. *Journal of Social Issues, 34*, 111–124.

Maslow, A. (1959). The need to know and the fear of knowing. *Journal of General Psychology, 66*, 297–333.

Pelletier, K. R. (1977). *Mind as healer, mind as slayer*. New York: Delta.

Randolph, G. L., Price, L. L., & Collins, J. K. (1986). The effects of burnout prevention training on burnout symptoms in nurses. *Journal of Continuing Education in Nursing, 17*, 43–49.

Siegel, E., & Liefer, A. (1983). A staying well group. In M. Rosenbaum (Ed.), *Handbook of short term therapy groups*. New York: McGraw-Hill.

Selye, H. (1974). *Stress without distress*. New York: Signet.

Simonton, O. C., Matthews-Simonton, S., & Creighton, J. (1978). *Getting well again.* New York: St. Martins.
Welch, I. D., Medeiros, D. C., & Tate, G. A. (1982). *Beyond burn-out.* Englewood Cliffs, NJ: Prentice-Hall.
Zahourek, R. P. (1978). Overview—The context of clinical hypnosis in nursing practice. In R. P. Zahourek (Ed.), *Clinical hypnosis and therapeutic suggestion in nursing.* Orlando, FL: Grune & Stratton.

BIBLIOGRAPHY

Albrecht, T. L. (1982). What job stress means for the staff nurse. *Nursing Administration Quarterly, 7,* 1–11.
Braillier, L. (1982). *Successfully managing stress.* Palo Alto, CA: National Nursing Review.
Cameron, M. (1986). The moral and ethical components of nurse burnout, *Nursing Management, 17,* 42b–42e.
Davis, A. J. (1984). Stress. *American Journal of Nursing, 84,* 365-366.
Jacobson, S. F., & McGrath, H. M. (Eds.) (1983). *Nurses under stress.* New York: John Wiley.
Lachman, V. S. (1983). *Stress management: A manual for nurses.* New York: Grune & Stratton.
Oberst, M. T., (1973). The crisis prone staff nurse. *American Journal of Nursing, 73,* 1917–1921.
Smythe, E. E. M. (1984). *Surviving nursing.* Menlo Park, CA: Addison-Wesley.
Snyder, M. (1984). Progressive relaxation as a nursing intervention: An analysis. *Advances in Nursing Science, 6,* 47–58.

APPENDIX I

As described in *Nursing: A Social Policy Statement* (1980), the scope of nursing practice encompasses intervention with:

1. Self-care limitations.
2. Impaired functioning in areas such as rest, sleep, ventilation, circulation, activity, nutrition, elimination, skin, or sexuality.
3. Pain and discomfort.
4. Emotional problems related to illness and treatment, life-threatening events, or daily experiences such as anxiety, loss, loneliness, or grief.
5. Distortion of symbolic functions, reflected in interpersonal and intellectual processes such as hallucinations.
6. Deficiencies in decision-making and ability to make personal choices.
7. Self-image changes required by health status.
8. Dysfunctional perceptual orientations to health.
9. Strains related to life processes such as birth, growth and development, and death.
10. Problematic affiliative relationships (p. 10).

APPENDIX II
Guidelines for Relaxation and Imagery Intervention Techniques

A. Principles of Basic Progressive Relaxation
1.   Have client get into relaxed position in a reasonably quiet environment.
2.   Have client take a pleasant relaxing breath
3.   Direct client to relax muscles in a logical progression; start at toes and work toward the head or work from the top of the head to the toes
4.   Don't worry if you forget a muscle gropu as you are helping the client to relax
5.   As the person begins to relax muscles, comment on potential changes in sensation, e.g., "you may feel warmth, coolness, heaviness, lightness, or softness as you relax."
6.   Extremities (feet and hands) will most likely produce noticeable changes in temperature and sensation
7.   Keep voice soft, rhythmical, soothing, and monotonous
8.   Encourage and reassure client that he or she is doing well
9.   Comment on signs of relaxation as you observe them
10. Have client take deep and/or relaxing breaths and/or focus on rhythmic breathing
11. Couple relaxing experience with increased comfort or the desired change in the client's state, e.g., "As you become more relaxed you will feel more comfortable."
12. Encourage client to practice the technique
13. Reinforce that it is the client who is doing the relaxation and that as the therapist you are enabling the implementation of the technique

B. Principles of Imagery Intervention
1.   Use same basic principles for relaxation
2.   Plan with the client whether imagery will be guided by therapist or more free floating and directed more by the client and less by the therapist
3.   Encourage client to visualize or imagine a pleasant scene, sensation, color, experience, set of sounds, etc.
4.   Utilize as many of the senses as possible: touch, kinesthetic, hearing, sight, smell, and taste
5.   Allow sufficient freedom for client to elaborate on and/or develop his or her own images
6.   For most purposes, except desentization, make sure imagery scene is relaxing and comfortable rather than threatening
7.   Emphasize the client's control over what is imagined or visualized

C. Techniques for Ending the Procedure
1. Prepare client for the end of the procedure and count from one to five or ten. This can be coupled with suggestions for comfort, full orientation, and relaxation following the procedure.
2. Ask client to open eyes slowly, take a nice breath, and become fully oriented to place, time, etc.
3. Ask client for feedback about experience.
4. Emphasize successes, i.e., "you look more relaxed," or "your breathing became easier during the procedure," or "you have a vivid visual imagination."
5. Outline with client future goals and plan for modifying procedure if necessary.
6. Encourage clients to practice on their own.

APPENDIX III
Guidelines for Clients' Practicing on Their Own

1. Find a comfortable quiet place and a time that is likely to be uninterrupted
2. Use the relaxation techniques that you have been taught
3. Focus on easy relaxed breathing and letting your body become comfortable
4. If you are using a visualization or imagery excercise do so, remembering to allow as many of your senses as possible to be activated
5. Enjoy the experience
6. If you are modifying a symptom, sensation, or behavior, focus on accomplishing the change in small steps and easy to manage ways
7. Imagine the outcome you want to accomplish
8. If you are uncomfortable, stop and try again later
9. At the end allow yourself some comfortable time to reorient and to feel relaxed and comfortable. Give yourself a few minutes before returning to your daily tasks
10. Contact your therapist with any questions or concerns.

APPENDIX IV: OUTLINE FOR ASSESSMENT OF OBESITY

I. Presenting Problem
   A. Why does the patient come for treatment now?
   B. Is the patient self- or other-referred?
   C. What is the motivation for treatment—medical, cosmetic, general sense of well-being?
   D. How much weight does the client want to lose?
   E. How fast do they want to lose the weight?
   F. What are the client's current eating habits: favorite foods, when do they overeat, how often, what do they overeat, what feelings occur when they overeat?

II. Weight Gain and Loss History
   A. How long have they been overweight?
   B. What have they done in the past to lose weight?
   C. How long have they been able to keep weight off?
   D. What seems to precipitate weight regain?

III. Family History
   A. Is there obesity in other members of the family? Who?
   B. What is the meaning of food in the family?
   C. What is the meaning of fat in the family?
   D. What does being thin mean to both the individual and the family?

IV. Self and Body Image
   A. How does the person describe himself or herself as an overweight person?
   B. What are adjectives and metaphors used to describe the self and body?
   C. What adjectives and metaphors are used to describe the body and the self at their ideal weight?
   D. What do they anticipate will happen to them and their lives when they reach their ideal weight? What will be good and not so good?

APPENDIX V: OUTLINE OF TREATMENT APPROACHES FOR WEIGHT LOSS

Treatment is multimodal, holistic, and individually planned. It must be tailored to the individual client's specific behavioral style of eating, the meaning of both the overeating behavior and being overweight, and the individual's personality and methods of processing information and coping with stress.

I. Physical
   A. Any physical reasons for the weight problem?
   B. Any contraindications for dieting and losing weight?
   C. Choose a diet that is nutritionally adequate.
   D. Reinforce with the client that the ultimate goal is eating normally rather than being on a perpetual diet.

II. Cognitive
   A. What is the individual's understanding of the weight problem?
   B. What is the individual's understanding of the meaning of losing weight?
   C. Reinforce the intellectual reasons for losing weight.
   D. Provide information on the process of loosing weight, i.e., plateaus, the value of exercise, the value of relaxation and imagery as adjunctive tools.

III. Affective
   A. Management of affective changes: "pink cloud," "black despair," "grey discouragement"; anticipate these and educate patient regarding these changes in feeling states.
   B. Encourage enlargement of affective pleasures from additional sources, not only food.
   C. Encourage recognition of affective changes and the recognition of the difference between hunger and other feeling states.

IV. Behavioral/Educational
   A. Food record.
   B. Reward system; money to one's self after a certain amount of weight is lost.
   C. Instructions on eating on a smaller plate, smaller portions, eating more slowly.
   D Always sitting to eat and doing nothing else while eating.
   E. Picture on refrigerator or on closet door of oneself as overweight or at ideal weight.
   F. Eating three meals a day.

V. Imagery
   A. Self image excercise: strong and in control; happy, successful.
   B. Visualization of strengths.
   C. Body image: slowly see self losing weight; feelings as begin to lose weight.

D.   Imagery of pleasant experiences; paint vivid pictures and sensations.
E.   Images of enjoyment of smaller amounts of food and feeling full.
F.   Build images of self soothing; seeing self as relaxed.
G.   "Food Fairy Story."
H.   Stories of other peoples experiences with successful weight loss.
I.   Use images of lightness, energy, and grace in various settings.
J.   Healthy food images.

APPENDIX VI: EXERCISES TO AID IN WEIGHT LOSS

Food Imagery

Choose a vegetable or fruit that the client likes and then thoroughly describe it while the client is relaxed and comfortable.

Examples

Picture a head of broccoli. Notice what a beautiful dark green it is. The top of the broccoli is actually the flowers of the plant. It is so green it's almost blue. The stalk is strong and sturdy and blue-green leaves grow off this stalk. The broccoli is crunchy and crisp. You can eat it raw or cooked. However you want to eat it fully enjoying its flavor, particularly now that you have learned so much about its beauty.

Picture a round red apple. Its color is a beautiful red. Its skin is smooth and shiny. Hold this shiny smooth apple in your hand and feel its smooth cool weight. Cut the apple in half and notice how the fruit is constructed. Its core is geometric and designed perfectly, the seeds displayed in an orderly fashion. The meat of the apple is pure white. It is moist and juicy. Taste the apple. When you bite it is crisp and crunchy—its flavor a wonderful mix of tartness and sweetness. Hold the apple in your mouth and experience its flavor fully.

Hunger Differentiation Images

You are walking down the street. The odor of fresh baking bread and pastries smells very good to you. You take a deep breath and note that it smells good. As you continue walking you come upon the bakery where the bread and pastries are being baked. Look in the window and notice all the baked goods. They have overbaked that day so the window is crowded with cakes and pies and cookies and breads. Because it's so crowded the picture is jumbled and messy. The frosting from the cake has dripped onto the pies and breads. Allow your vision of all this to be saturated. Take a nice deep breath and as you do find that you are relaxing and ready to walk on down the street. Allow a sense of satisfaction to fill you as you continue walking. If you experience any sense of hunger, differentiate between whether that sensation is mouth hunger or stomach hunger. Tune into your body as you walk and make a conscious decision about any sense of hunger. If you are really hungry or needy for something realize that soon you will be able to have something that will both be satisfying and help you reach your goal.

Pleasure/Satisfaction Images

(This can be done in real life as well as with the imagination.) You are in a restaurant and have ordered your favorite dinner. When it comes, become aware of how it looks on the plate. Smell the aroma and take a moment to enjoy the visual picture of how the food is arranged on the plate. Enjoy the aroma. Next, taste your favorite food. Hold the food in your mouth and fully enjoy the flavors and the taste. Eat slowly allowing yourself to completely enjoy the experience. Notice how you are becoming more and more satisfied; because you are eating slowly you are recognizing that you are getting both full and satisfied. The portion they have given you is quite large. As you eat you realize that you *can* leave some because you have become full and satisfied. You *can* decide to leave what is left realizing and feeling comfortable in the knowledge that you *can* return at another time to enjoy the same dinner or you *can* decide to ask to have a doggy bag and take what is left home for another time.

Pleasure Images

These exercises can incorporate all of the senses; the goal is to enhance pleasure through means other than eating and food. These are done following, or as a part of, a relaxation exercise.

A New York City Street

(This can be altered to other living environments. The purpose is to help the individual appreciate more fully and sensually what is around him or her every day.) Picture yourself on a pleasant street in New York. It is a lovely day and you are walking with a leisurely pace noticing and enjoying what is around you. On many New York streets are vegetable and flower vendor shops. These are well known for their lovely arrangement of fruits, vegetables, and flowers. Notice the stacks of bright orange oranges, lemons, and limes. The apples are bright red and stacked in orderly pyramids. Vegetables have been arranged in a similar orderly and attractive manner. The colors seem even more intense since you have let your eyes feast on their beauty. There are also beautiful bunches of flowers. Every variety of tulip seems to be there. It's amazing how many different colors of tulips there are. Bright orange, red, violet, white, pink, and yellow—even tulips that are mixed colors. Bright crystals of dew drops rest on all of these wonderful things. Choose a color that you want for today from these wonderful bunches of tulips. Now choose some vegetables and fruits. Think about their freshness and how satisfying they will be when eaten. Make your purchases and continue on down the street feeling relaxed and comfortable. You are lighthearted as you quicken your pace and your step, pleased with yourself that you have taken a few moments to thoroughly enjoy the world around you. (This can be modified to be a beach, a garden, a field, or a meadow or even one's own living room. The important goal is to enhance relaxation and pleasure.)

Self-Image Exercises

These are ego-building and enhancing self-control exercises based on situations presented by the client where problems exist for maintaining self-control or moderating eating behaviors.

Pleasure Images

Picture yourself home alone in the evening after a busy day at work. You want to relax and may feel a bit bored and restless. Think about all the possible things you could do. Picture these possibilities and see how they feel to you. You pick a book you've been wanting to read. (Pause) Find a comfortable spot and read. (Pause) You decide to watch TV. (Pause) You decide to take a brisk walk. (Pause) Think about other possibilities. (Pause) Imagine now that you decide you would like to eat something. Approach the refrigerator or cabinet. Pick out something that is good for you and you know fits well into your weight loss plan. Find that what you eat satisfies you quickly and leaves you feeling comfortable.

Food Fairy Story

This is a true story I am about to tell you that can help you in achieving your goal of a more healthy weight. One night I was out to dinner with several colleagues. We were at a favorite Chinese restaurant and we were talking about maintaining a healthy weight and preventing weight gain. Most of us agreed that we had been raised to always clean our plates and that if we did not we were depriving other children who had less than we did. This had caused a great deal of guilt in us; it was a strong message that if we did not eat everything put before us we were doing damage to others.

One person in the group mentioned that she and the members of her family had never had a problem being overweight. She did not belong to the "clean plate club." She explained that in her family a tradition existed about food that had been very influential. A "food fairy" existed. To have good luck everyone left a little bit of each food on their plates for the food fairy. When the fairy was happy you had good luck. If *you* had a food fairy to bring *you* good luck what would that fairy look like? Take a few moments to develop a picture of that fairy. You might even want to give the fairy a name.

Weight Loss Exercises

Body Image

Imagine that you are standing in front of a mirror. You are at your present weight and can see yourself either dressed or nude. Take time to notice how you look. What do you like about your present shape? What do you want to change? Note that even though you wish to change your weight there are many things about you that are pleasant and attractive about your present appearance. Now begin to see the image of yourself change.

You have lost five pounds. (Pause) Notice how you look and how you feel about how you look. (Continue reducing the amount of weight until the goal is obtained. Ask at each change for the clients to notice how they look to themselves and how they feel at the new weight. Encourage the clients to be aware of the weight at which they feel most comfortable, explaining that it might be a weight that is not their previous goal.)

New Weight Self-Image Exercise

Imagine yourself at a comfortable new weight. Take a good look at yourself. How do you feel at this new weight? What kind of things are you doing now? Observe yourself in some pleasant activity. How do you move? How are others reacting to you now? How do close friends react? Business associates? Family members? Strangers? How do you feel with their reactions to you? If any reaction is not what you want take a moment to alter your picture and make it more what you want. Take another few moments to experience a new weight.

Helpful Suggestions to Integrate into Weight Loss Exercises

1. Metaphors of lightness, energy, and health.
2. Suggestions of self-control and patience, i.e., "Many good things that we want to accomplish take time. You didn't graduate from high school overnight or learn a new skill all at once." "There are many ways to feel good and well cared for. Sometimes just relaxing and doing something you have wanted to do for a long time can be a treat."
3. Suggestions for learning body sensations: "There are many forms of sensations that can be interpreted as hunger. Sometimes we are not hungry but

want something to suck on or to munch and crunch. Sometimes our stomachs really are empty and our body needs nurturance and sometimes we are full before we have really realized it. It can be helpful then to learn about these different sensations and to learn new and more healthy ways to be full of good food when our stomachs and bodies need to be fed and to learn when our mouths need something. Our mouths can be satisfied in lots of ways and the sensation we're looking for can be satisfied with things we know won't produce weight gain.

AFTERWORD

The tradition of nursing is to provide comfort and relief from suffering. With the many technological and pharmacologic advances over the years it has seemed less necessary for nurses and health care givers to be inventive and creative in meeting these needs. Consumers have often told us that our practice has become invasive, mechanical, and cold. As modern medical care has saved more lives with drugs and machines, the "caring" aspect of health care has become less apparent.

Nursing has probably been most responsive to the criticism. Movements to explore alternative methods have been enthusiastically adopted by individuals and groups of nurses and have been institutionalized in some schools of nursing. Necessity may have spurred this rather quiet revolution. Nurses spend long hours with those who are dying and those who are in intense pain. The "easy" means of relief are not always indicated, acceptable to, or successful with patients. As a result, many nurses have explored alternatives and have discovered relaxation and imagery techniques. By integrating these with other approaches, many have found them to be successful and satisfying.

The purpose of this book has been to provide a theoretical base and a resource of numerous clinical case examples. This material provides a base from which practitioners with various amounts of experience and levels of educational preparation can begin to integrate these approaches meaningfully and effectively into their practices. Hands-on clinical training and supervision are recommended.

Now, like Lucy, experiment with your stick and resolve to tell the others.

Index

AA, (Alcoholics Anonymous) 205, 212, 213
Achterberg, J.
  alcoholism and, 204
  foreword, vii
  Image-Ca technique and, 172-173
  imagery and, 55, 77
    ANS and, 62
Acquired immune deficiency syndrome (AIDS), 184
ACTH, 32
Adrenocorticotrophic hormone (ACTH), 32
Adverse reactions, imagery and, 22-23
Ahsen's system of imagery, 55-56
AIDS, 184
Alcoholics Anonymous (AA), 205, 212, 213
Alcoholism, R/I techniques and
  general considerations for, 203-205
  inpatient group for, 207-212
  outpatient group for, 212-214
  research on, 205-206
  sobriety and, 212-215
  stress and, 204-205
Alpha waves, 31
Altered state of consciousness, 7, 8-10, 22, 123 (f).
    See also Trance state
Amphotericin, shaking chills from, 185
Analogy, Erickson's use of, 105
Anesthesia, recovery from, 96
ANS, 62
Anxiety
  cancer patient and, 169-170
  meditation and, 44
  PPMRI and, 184-185
  relaxation-induced, 23
  relaxation training and, 34-35
Armstrong, M., 61
Array theory, 64
Artistry, imagery and, 8

Assertiveness training, 78
Assessment process for R/I technique, 19-20, 124-125, 240-241
Asthma, 93
Atmosphere for staff group, 232, 236
Attentional component in relaxation, 32
Audiotape. See Taped instruction
Autogenic training, 46-47
  stress management and, 221-222
Autonomic nervous system (ANS), 62
Autonomy, fairy tales and, 109
Awareness meditation, 45, See also Meditation

Beck, A., 170
Behavioral rehearsal
  for anxiety, 79
  for dying, 80
Behavioral relaxation training (BRT), 48-49
Benson, H., 7, 30, 44-45
  technique developed by, 44-45
Bernstein, D.A., 41
Bettleheim, B., 11, 116
Binge eater, 194. See also Obesity
Biofeedback, 35, 66. See also Systematic desensitization
  pain and, 36-37
  technique for, 47
Bioinformational theory, 64-65
Bladder catheterization, 95
BMA. See Bone marrow aspiration
Body image
  imagery and, 57
  problems with, 197. See also Obesity
Bone marrow aspiration (BMA), 184-187. See also
    Cancer patients
Borkovec, T.D., 41
Brain, structural theories of, 60-63

Brain hemispheres, 32-33. *See also* Right brain
    function
Breast feeding, 14-15
Breathing exercise, 46, 209
    focused breathing technique as, 176-177
    PPMRI and, 176-177
    stress management and, 221-222
BRT, 48-49
Burnout, 15, 229
Burnout prevention workshop, 232
Burn patient, 15

Cancer patient
    general considerations for, 168-169, 189-190
    Image-Ca technique for, 172-173
    nausea and vomiting in, 16-17
    nutritional status and, 17
    preferred approach for. *See* Passive progressive
        muscle relaxation plus imagery
    relaxation training and, 37-38
    Simonton approach for. *See* Simonton approach
    stress and, 15
    theoretical framework for, 169-170
Carbon dioxide production, meditation and, 31
Cartisian dualism, 4-5
Chemotherapy. *See* Cancer patient
Child
    as candidate for R/I techniques, 17
    death imagery and 163-167
    object constancy and, 58-60
    stress management techniques and, 39
    suggestion and, 96-97
Chills from amphotericin, 185
Chronic anxiety, 29. *See also* Anxiety; Stress
        response
Chronic distress, 3. *See also* Anxiety; Depression
Chronic pain, 20. *See also* Pain
    precautions for, 23
    secondary pain and, 21
Chronic stress, 122, 228. *See also* Stress
Cognition
    Horowitz's theory of, 62-63
    v somatic relaxation, 33, 36
Concentrated attention, law of, 86
Concentration, difficulty with, 21
Concepts, basic. *See* Definition; Theoretical
        framework
Conjunctive suggestion, 89. *See also* Suggestion
Contemplation, 46. *See also* Meditation
Contingent suggestion. *See also* Suggestion
Control issue in illness, 169, 176, 180, 184
Conversational postulates, 89
Coping mechanisms
    relaxation responses as, 6

stress management procedure and, 128-129. *See
        also* Stress management   procedure
Coue, E., 85-86
Cousins, N., 5
Creativity
    comparison of relaxation, imagery and hypnosis
        for, 12 *(t)*
    imagery and, 8
Crisis situation, 18
Critical care nurse, stress and, 229
Cystic fibrosis, 39
Davidson, R.J., 32-33

Death. *See also* Dying patient
    imagery of, 79-80
    nurse's fear of, 156-167
Definition
    of hypnosis, 9
    of imagery, 7-8, 53-54
    of relaxation, 7-8
    of suggestion, 85
    of trance state, 8-10
Depression, 18
    cancer patient and, 169-170
    PPMRI and 181-182
Descartes, dualism and, 4-54-5
Developmental obesity, 194, *See also* Obesity
Diagnosis and assessment for R/I technique, 19-20
Diagnostic guided imagery, 131-133
Differential relaxation, 43-44. *See also* Progressive
        relaxation
Difficult patient, 140-142
Direct *v* indirect suggestion, 88-89. *See also* Sug-
        gestion
Dissociation, 57
Dissociative suggestion, 90
Dominant effect, law of, 86
Dream work, 78-79
Dualism *v* holism. *See* Mind-body connection
Dying patient
    child as, 163-167
    death imagery and, 157-159
    general considerations for, 155-157
    preparation for death and, 159-167

Eating patterns, obesity and, 194. *See also* Obesity
ECT, 62
Ego building, imagery for, 77-78
Eidetic image, 54, 55
Electroconvulsive shock therapy (ECT), 62
Electromyogram (EMG), 47
Electroneuromyometry, 29
Ellis, A., 130
Emergency room patient, 18

EMG, 47
Enactive mode of cognition, 62-63
Endorphines, 64
Enkephalines, 64
Epstein, G., 65, 77
Erickson, M., 9, 91, 104-105
Exercise, stress reduction and, 48
Expectation, positive, 19
Experienced clinician, attitudes of, 230
Externality theory of obsity, 196. *See also* Obesity
Extraverbal suggestion, 9. *See also* Suggestion
Eye movement, 18-19

Fairy tales. *See also* Storytelling
    developmental characteristics of, 107
    developmental themes in, 109-111
    general considerations for, 105-107
    internal absorption and, 108
    internal conflicts and, 107
    as learning vehicles, 11-112
    levels of meaning in, 108-109
    psychotherapy and, 113-117
    unconscious processes and, 107-108
Family members, cooperation of, 185-186
Fat, *See* Obsity
Fat cell theory of obesity, 193. *See also* Obesity
Fear of painful procedures, 184-185
Feedback to patient, 19
Fight-or-flight resonse, 30, 31, 64, 122
Flint, M.B., 6
Focused breathing technique, 176-177
Folklore, 102-103. *See also* Storytelling
Functional theories of brain. *See* Theoretical
    framework, for imagery

Gardner, Dr. R., 111
General adaptation syndrome, 32
Generalized referential index, 90
Goleman, D., 6
Grounding technique, 48
Guilt feelings, Simonton approach and, 171-172,
    187
Gynecologic patient, 14-15

Healing
    comparison of techniques for, 12 *(t)*
    imagery for, 77, 133-134. *See also* Cancer patient
    nursing framework for, 11, 14
Helplessness
    cancer patient and, 169-170
    PPMRI and, 181-182
Hemispheric specialization, 32-33. *See also* Right
    brain function
Historical perspective, 4-7

Holistic movement, 5. *See also* Mind-body connection
    tion
Holmes "Schedule of Recent Experience", 123
Holographic model of brain, 63
Hopefulness, 19
Hopelessness, 16. *See also* Depression
    PPMRI and, 181-182
Horney, K., 56
Horowitz, M., 54-55
Horowitz, M.J., 62-63
Humanistic movement, 5
Hypertension
    imagery and, 77
    relaxation training and, 35, 38-39
    stress management and, 225
    stress response and, 31
Hypnogogic image, 54-55
Hypnopompic image, 54-55
Hypnosis
    definition of, 9
    storytelling and, 115
Hypotensive state, 23
Hypothalamus, 32

Image-Ca technique for cancer patient, 172-173
Imagery, 124. *See also* Passive progressive muscle
    relaxation plus imagery
    Achterberg's system of, 55
    Ahsen's system of, 55-56
    alcoholism and. *See* Alcoholism, R/I techniques
        and
    applications for, 76-80
    breathing and, 222
    classificatin of, 55 *(t)*
    clinical application of, 67-68
    definition of, 7-8, 53-54
    directive, 179
    for dying patient. *See* Dying patient
    exercise, 233-235
    fairy tales and, 116
    free floating, 179-180
    historical perspectives on, 68-71
    Horowitz's system of, 54-55
    hypnosis v, 10-11, 12-13 *(t)*
    hypnotizability and, 9
    music therapy and, 183
    for problem-solving, 16, 134-135
    "stairstep" exercise and, 220-221
    stress and, 231
    stress management procedure and
        healing, 133-134
        problem-solving, 134-135
        receptive, 131-133
    "sunshine" exercise and, 220

(Imagery continued.)
techniques, 71-76
theoretical framework for. *See* Theoretical framework, for imagery
weight loss and, 198, 199. *See also* Obesity
Imagery mode of cognition, 62-63
Imagination
in child, 59-60
hypnotizability and, 9
physiology and, 66
power of, 6
terminology and, 11
Immune response, 39
Implied directive, 89-90
Incest, storytelling and, 117
Indirect *v* direct suggestion, 88-89. *See also* Suggestion
Information retention, imagery and, 8
Inner advisor, stress management procedure and, 135-139
Inner processes, imagery and, 78-79
Inpatient relaxation group for alcoholics, 207-212
Insomnia. *See also* Prison inmates, stress management for
in cancer patient, 38
PPMRI and, 185
relaxation training and, 35-36
Institute for the Advancement of Health, mind-body controversy and, 6-7
Internal regulation theory of obesity, 193. *See also* Obestiy
Interpersonal dynamics, nursing framework and, 11,14
Interspersed suggestion, 90. *See also* Suggestion
Intervention process
guidelines for, 20-21
precautions for, 22-23
problems encountered in , 21
research questions and, 23-24
scope of, 24-25
self-techniques and, 21-22
Intravenous line, problems with, 94-95, 98
Intraverbal suggestion, 9. *See also* Suggestion
Invention, imagery and, 8
Irrational ideas, refutation of, 129-130

Jacobsen, S.F., 7
Jacobson, E., 29-30, 43

Krieger, D., 11,14
Kroger, W.S., 85-87

Lactate, anxiety and, 31
Lamaze method

for childbirth, 5
for difficult patient, 139-140
Lancet, mind-body controversy and, 6
Lang, P.J., 64-65
Laterality, 61-62. *See also* Hemispheric specialization
Lawlis, G.F.
alcoholism and, 204
Image-Ca technique and, 172-173
Laws of Suggestion, 85-87. *See also* Suggestion
Laying on of hands, 11, 14
Learned helplessness, 169-170
Learning, imagery and, 8
Learning theory of obesity, 196-197. *See also* Obesity
LeShan, L., 189
Leukemia, case history of, 186-187. *See also* Cancer patient
Lexical mode of cognition, 62-63
Life change, stress and, 123
Live *v* taped instruction, 40-41, 178
Lung cancer, case history of, 187-189. *See also* Cancer patient

Mahler, M., 58
Mantra meditation, 46. *See also* Meditation
Marital relationship, fairy tales and, 110
Marks, D., 65-66
Medication, suggestion and, 92
Meditation, 188
pain and, 37
stress and, 231
stress management procedure and, 21
technique, 44-46
v progressive relaxation, 33
Memory
enhancement in elderly, 39
imagery and, 8
physiological response and, 65
Mental processes, comparison of techniques to enhance, 12 *(t)*
Metabolic changes during meditation, 31, 44
Metaphor, 102-103. *See also* Storytelling
imagery and, 80
problem resolution and, 112-113
suggestion and, 91
Mind and Immunity, 6
Mind-body connection
controversy over, 4-7
Rogers' theories of, 11
stress and, 230-231
Mindfulness meditation, 45. *See also* Meditation
"Mind room", 179
Motivation, 17, 18, 19

alcoholism and, 212
  suggestion and, 9
Motor functioning, trance state and, 8
Muscle-sense, 30
Muscular response
  to relaxation, 7, 10, 12 *(t)*, 33
  to tension, 29-30
Music therapy, 16, 183
Mutual storytelling technique, 111

Nausea and vomiting, 16-17
  PPMRI and, 182-183
Negative thought, 86
Neurolinguistic programming (NLP), 18-19
Neurotransmitters, 63-64
New England Journal of Medicine, mind-body controversy and, 6
New York Times, mind-body controversy and, 6
Nightingale, F., 4
Nontherapeutic suggestion, 97-98
Nonverbal communication, storytelling and, 115
Nonverbal suggestion, 9. *See also* Suggestion
Notes on Nursing, 4
Nursing: A Social Policy Statement, 14, 24-25
Nursing framework, holistic approach to, 11, 14
Nursing process, R/I techniques and
  assessment and diagnosis for, 19-20
  intervention for, 20-21
  motivation and expectation in, 19
  patient selection for, 17-18
  precautions for, 23
  problems in, 21
  research questions for, 23-24
  self techniques and, 21-22
  trust and rapport and, 18-19
Nutritional deterioration, PPMRI and, 185

Obesity, 192-193
  assessment of, 197
  case examples of, 199-201
  theories of
    body image disturbance, 196-197
    eating patterns, 194
    externality theory, 196
    fat cell theory, 193
    internal regulation, 193
    learning theory, 196-107
    psychodynamic, 195-196
    psychological categories, 194-195
    set point theory, 193-194
  treatment for, 197-199
Object constancy, 58-59
Obstetric patient, 14-15. *See also* Lamaze method
Oncology nurse, stress management for, 15-16

Open-heart surgery patient, 37
Optimism, fairy tales and, 110
Orbach, S., 195-196

Out-of-body experience, 23, 57
Outpatient group for alcoholics, 212-214
Outpatient setting, 15
Oxygen consumption, stress and, 31

Pacing, 94
Pain, 15, 20. *See also* Chronic pain
  imagery for, 78, 179
  PPMRI and, 182
  relaxation training and, 36-37
  visualization for, 21
Painful procedures, fear of, 184-185
Parasympathetic activity, 31
Parenting, suggestion and, 96-97. *See also* Suggestion
Passive progressive muscle relaxation plus imagery (PPMRI), 173
  anxiety and, 184-185
  approach to, 174
  assessment for, 174, 175 *(t)*
  breathing exercise for, 176-177
  case examples of, 186-189
  depression and, 181-182
  feedback for, 178
  goals for, 175
  insomnia and, 185
  nausea and vomiting and 182-183
  nutritional deterioration and, 185
  pain and, 182
  preliminaries for, 175-176
  problems with, 180-181
  shaking chills and, 185
  strengths of, 180
  teamwork for, 185-186
  tension release with, 177-178
  variations of, 178-180
Patient populations, 14-15
Pediatric nurse, stress and, 229
Pediatric patient. *See* Child
Peer support, 19
Phantom limb, 57
Phobias, 34
Physician, cooperation of, 185-186
Physiological response. *See also* specific response; Theoretical framework
  imagery and, 8, 77
  to relaxation, 10, 12-13 *(t)*, 1
  tension and, 29-30
Play, 59-60
Poppen, R., 48

Posthypnotic suggestion, 91-92. *See also* Suggestion
Postoperative voiding, 95-96
Practitioner, 5-6
  attitude of, 189-190
  relaxation for, 12, 174
  stress and, 227-232. *See also* Stress management
    procedure, with staff groups
Pre-Cartesian philosophy, 4
Precautions for R/I techniques, 22-23
Presupposition suggestion, 89. *See also* Suggestion
Pre-therapy training for stress management proce-
    dures, 222-223
Preverbal imagery, 55
Prison inmates, stress management for
  autogneic training and, 221-222
  breathing and visualizatin and, 221-222
  general considerations for, 216-218
  pre-therapy training and, 222-223
  progressive relaxation and, 219-220
  results and evaluation and, 223-224
  "stairstep" excercise and, 220-221
  stressors and, 218-219
  summary of, 224-225
  "sunshine" excercise and, 220
  TM and, 221
Problems patient, definition of, 140-142
Problems, potential, 21
Problem-solving guided imagery, 16, 134-135
Progressive muscle relaxation. *See also* Passive
    progressive muscle relaxation plus im-
    agery
Progressive relaxation, 22, 29, 35, 123-124. *See also*
    Systematic desensitization
  alcoholism and, 209
  as relaxation technique, 7
  stress management and, 219-220
  technique for, 41-44
  theoretical model for, 29-30
  v meditation, 33
Pseudohallucinatory images, 57
Psychiatric patient, 17-18
  chronic, 34
Psychobiology, theoretical model for, 32-33
Psychodiagnostic storytelling, 112
Psychodynamic theories of obesity, 194-195. *See
    also* Obesity
Psychoimmunology, 6
*Psychological and Behavioral Treatments for Disor-
    ders of the Heart and Blood Vessels*, 6-7
Psychological issues in obesity, 194-196, 201. *See
    also* Obesity
Psychological rapport, 105
Psychotherapy
  fairy tales and, 113-117

imagery and, 78-79
  storytelling and, 103-104
Psychotic patient, 17-18

Quality of life for cancer patient, 189

Rapport-building techniques, 18-19
Reactive obesity, 194-195. *See also* Obesity
Recall, 44
Receptive guided imagery, 131-133
Reframing, 88
Relaxation, definition of, 7-8, 28
Relaxation response
  as relaxation technique, 7
  theoretical model for, 30-31
Relaxation techniques
  applications for
    alcoholism. *See* Alcoholism, R/I techniques
      and
    anxiety, 34-35. *See also* Anxiety
    assessment, 124-125
    cancer, 37-38. *See also* Cancer patient
    hypertension, 35. *See also* Hypertension
    insomnia, 35-36. *See also* Insomnia
    miscellaneous disorders, 38-39
    pain, 36-37. *See also* Pain
    stress, 231. *See also* Stress
    stress management procedure, 123-125. *See
      also* Stress management procedure
    weight loss, 198-199. *See also* Obesity
  example of, 233-235
  hypnosis v, 10-11, 12-13 *(t)*
  imagery for, 76. *See also* specific techniques
  relaxation response and, 7. *See also* Relaxation
    response
  theoretical framework for. *See* Theoretical
    framework
Renaissance, dualism and, 4-5
Repetition, 88
Representational system, 18
Research. *See also* Theoretical framework
  on alcoholism, 205-206
  on mind-body controversy, 6-7
  on nursing intervention, 14-17
  questions for, 23-24
Resistance to storytelling, 115-116
Respiratory rate, 31
Responsiveness, imagination and, 9
Restless patient, 21
Rhythmic breathing, pain and, 36-37
Right-brain functin, 61-62. *See also* Hemispheric
    specialization
  stress and, 231
Risks, personal growth and, 110-111

Rogers, M., 11

Schilling, D., 48
Schwartz, G., 66
Schwartz, G.E., 32-33
"Secret room", 179, 188
Seigel, B., 5
Selection of technique, 41
Self development, theoretical foundation of imagery phenomena and, 58-60
Self image, theoretical foundation of imagery phenomena and, 56-57
Self-talk, stress management procedure and, 129-130
Self techniques, teaching of, 21-22
Selye, H., 32, 228-229, 230
Sensory awareness, 180
Sensory information and relaxation, 15
Sensory quality of imagery, 8
Set point theory of obesity, 193-194. *See also* Obesity
Setting for staff group, 232, 236
Shaking chills, PPMRI and 185
Shulik, A., 87
Significant others, precautions for, 22
Simonton approach, 5, 77, 170-171, 187
    for cancer patient, 77, 170-173
    guilt feelings and, 171-172, 187
    problems with, 171-173
    stress and, 231
Skin temperature, 47, 217
Smoking, 39
Sobriety, 214-215
Somatic relaxation, 33
    v cognitive relaxation, 33, 36
SRH, alcoholism and, 206
"Stairstep" excercise, 220-221
Storytelling. *See also* Fairy tales
    as diagnostic strategy, 112
    Ericksonian approaches to, 104-105
    general considerations for, 101-102, 117
    imagery and, 80
    psychotherapy and, 102-104
    techniques for, 111-117
    theoretical foundations for, 102-103
Stress, 39-40
    alcoholism and, 204-206
    chronic, 122, 228
    discussion of, 228-230
    mind/body response and, 230-231
    necessity for, 228
Stress Awareness Diary, 121
Stress management procedure, 11, 15-16. *See also* Prison inmates, stress management for

assessment prior to, 124-125
coping skills procedures and, 128-129
framework for, 121-122
hierarchy for, 126-128
imagery and. *See* Imagery, stress management procedure and
inner advisor and, 135-139
irrational ideas and, 129-131
relaxation methods for, 123-125
self-talk and, 129-130
with staff groups, 232-233
    exercises, 233-237
    setting, 232-236
suggestion and, 125-126
thought stopping method for, 129
Stressors, 123
    prison inmates and, 218-219
Stress reduction hierarchy, 126-128
Stress reduction hypothesis (SRH), alcoholism and, 206
Stress response, 30-31
Structural theories. *See* Theoretical framework
Suggestibility, 87-88
Suggestion, 8-9
    applications for
        bleeding, 93-94
        children, 96-97
        emergency room, 92-93

    perioperative, 95-96
    assessment for, 125
    definition of, 85
    design for, 126
    formulation of, 88-89
    general considerations for, 84-85
    nontherapeutic, 97-98
    stress management procedure and, 125-126
    techniques, 9-10, 89-92
    terminology and, 10-11
    theoretical foundations for, 85-88
Suicidal patient, 18
"Sunshine" excercise, 220
Sweeney, S.S., 7
Symbolism, 103. *See also* Storytelling
Sympathetic nervous system activity, 31
Syntoxic response, 228-229, 230
Systematic desensitization, 34

Taped instruction, 124
    v live instruction, 40-41, 178
Taste sensation, imagery and, 221
Techniques. *See* specific techniques
Tension, release of with PPMRI, 177-178
Tension reduction hypothesis (TRH), 206

Terminal illness. *See* Cancer patient; Dying patient
Theoretical framework
  alcoholism and, 204-205
  for cancer patient, 169-170
  for general adaptation syndrome, 32
  for imagery, 60-61
    array theory, 64
    biochemistry, 63-64
    bioinformational theory, 64-65
    body image, 57
    Epstein's theory, 65
    holographic model, 63
    Horowitz's modes of cognition, 62-63
    laterality, 61-62
    self development, 58-60
    self image, 56-57
    summary of, 65-67
    triune brain, 61
  for progressive relaxation, 29-30
  psychobiology and, 32-33
  relaxation response and, 30-31
  for storytelling and metaphor, 102-103
  for stress management procedure, 121-122
  for suggestion, 85-88
Therapeutic storytelling. *See* Storytelling
Therapeutic touch, 11, 14
Thermograph, 47
Thought stopping for stress management procedure,
    129
TM. *See* Meditation

Tower, R.B., 59-60
Trance state. *See also* Altered state of consciousness
    ness
  comparison of relaxation imagery and, 10-11,
    12-13 *(t)*
  definition of, 8-10
  in hospital patient, 88
  reorientation from, 92
Transcendental meditation. *See* Meditation
Transference, 104
Transpersonal imagery, 55
Traumatic incidents, fairy tales and, 109
TRH, 206
Triune brain, 61
Truism, 89

Unconscious processes in psychotherapy, 104

Verbal suggestion, 9. *See also* Suggestion
Video game distraction, 184
Visualization. *See* Imagery
Vomiting, 16-17
  PPMRI and, 182-183

Waking suggestibility, 87-88
Weight gain, 17, 38
Weight loss, 198, 199
Wellness continuum, 122
Wolpe's systematic desensitization, 34
Workmen's compensation, 20